INDONESIA AND NEIGHBOURING COUNTRIES

anila

PHILIPPINE
ISLANDS

SULU
SEA

PACIFIC   OCEAN

SULAWESI
SEA

Menado

Ternate

Biak

SULAWESI
(CELEBES)

Buru

Ambon

Jayapura

IRIAN JAYA
(W. NEW GUINEA)

ung
ndang
(Makasar)

BANDA   SEA

Merauke

Flores

ARAFURA SEA

Timor

TIMOR SEA

Darwin

AUSTRALIA

The Indonesian Tragedy

The Indonesian Tragedy

Brian May

ROUTLEDGE & KEGAN PAUL
London, Henley and Boston

First published in 1978
by Routledge & Kegan Paul Ltd
39 Store Street,
London WC1E 7DD,
Broadway House,
Newtown Road,
Henley-on-Thames,
Oxon RG9 1EN and
9 Park Street,
Boston, Mass., 02108, USA
Set in 11 on 12 pt Imprint by
Kelly and Wright, Bradford-on-Avon, Wiltshire
and printed in Great Britain by
Redwood Burn Ltd,
Trowbridge and Esher

British Library Cataloguing in Publication Data

May Brian
    The Indonesian tragedy.
    1.   Indonesia – History – 1966–
    2.   Indonesia – Politics and government – 1966–
    I.   Title
    958.8'03   DS644.4   78–40050
    ISBN 0 7100 8834 5

To the memory of
my father, Sydney Herman May,
and my mother, née Rosalie Marion Clark

Contents

Contents

Contents

Illustrations

Preface

This book is based on observations made during four years of reporting when I was Bureau Manager of Agence France-Presse in Jakarta from November 1968 to January 1973. While it contains a more comprehensive account of events since the 1965 *putsch* than has been published previously, it is not a history, but an exposition of the theme expressed in the title. Much of the book is a tale of Western-aided despotism. But the present suffering of the people, although it is extensively described, does not constitute the tragedy. This lies deeper, and it has been necessary to refer to the history and culture of Indonesia in an attempt to elucidate it. An opinion on the causes of a society's predicament cannot be proved. I have tried to bring the reader to see the problem as I see it, largely by depicting Indonesia as I experienced it.

There is remarkable misapprehension of what is happening in the Third World, particularly those parts of it ruled by governments that would perish if Western aid were withdrawn. For instance, Ralf Dahrendorf, Director of the London School of Economics, former Science and Research Commissioner of the European Communities, and brief visitor to Jakarta, said during the BBC's 1974 Reith lectures that Indonesia was one of the 'threshold countries', which he described as 'those which are about to reach, or have reached, a threshold of development which enables them to make headway without outside support'.[1] In fact, if Indonesia is near any threshold at all, it is that of a

xiii

Malthusian cemetery. At the end of 1975 the *Sunday Times*, London, proposed that the richer countries set up an agricultural fund to help the poorer parts of the world. But centuries of experience in Indonesia have shown that increases in food production are cancelled by population rises; and the trend of research findings in various poor countries is that modernization of farming benefits the slightly better off at the expense of those most in need.

Talk of transferring wealth from the richer nations to the poorer is so impracticable that its sincerity is questionable. It is my view that Western aid to Indonesia, which rarely amounts to more than a subsidy of exports, is against the interests of both the Indonesians themselves and the so-called donor countries. Aid is linked with domestic policies that are robbing desperately poor people of work; this acceleration of the socio-economic catastrophe for which Indonesia is heading could help the Soviet Union to do another Angola, a possibility that is discussed in the final chapter.

Brian May
Zierikzee

Acknowledgments

I should like to record my thanks to those who helped at various stages of the work. Dr Michael Leifer supplied information, which improved the perspective of certain passages dealing with the early independence period. Dr Ingrid Palmer read the chapter on the economy and made a comment that I have attributed to her. Dr D. H. Penny and Dr Harold Crouch replied to questions by post, although I had not met them; and my colleague, Mr Errol Hodge, answered numerous requests for material. Mrs Franca M. Pont-Peer, assistant librarian at the Koninklijk Instituut voor Taal, Land-en Volkenkunde, Leiden, speedily tracked down borrowed books and posted them to me. Four academics who helped have asked me not to thank them publicly, for fear that if they were linked with the book the junta would impede their work on Indonesia or that of others associated with them. While preserving their anonymity, I express my gratitude to them; two, in particular, devoted immense time to careful scrutiny of the manuscript and saved me from several howlers. Similarly, I cannot openly thank Indonesians who helped, because to do so would expose them to harassment. But I am deeply grateful to them, and I ask their forgiveness if I have caused offence by presenting what they may feel is too gloomy a view of their country's prospects. My wife pointed out certain passages that were not clear. Although burdened with heavy domestic and professional tasks, she found time to type the draft and to make numerous amendments to the manuscript. Without her help it would have taken considerably longer to produce the book.

Note on spelling

Indonesian spelling was changed in 1972 under an agreement
with Malaysia to adopt a common orthography. I have followed
the current practice of using the old spelling for twentieth-
century persons, since those living usually retain it, and certain
defunct organizations (e.g. Pemuda Rakjat), whose names should
be allowed to remain as they were conceived. The new spelling
has been used for other words, including transliterated names
from early history. The important differences between the two
orthographies are: in the old *j* is pronounced like *y* in *yacht* and in
the new as in *jam*; *tj* is pronounced rather like *ch* in *chew*, in the old
spelling, but with a suggestion of *t* as in *tube*, while in the new
spelling the same sound is represented by *c* (the town of Tjirebon
is now Cirebon). To avoid complicating the text the full Indonesian
names of some organizations have been confined to the glossary.

Introduction
Roots

The tragedy of what are called developing countries takes various forms. The most obvious is almost total economic inertia, with its pitiful consequences, as in Bangla Desh. Less recognized, but more pernicious, is the wasteful pursuit of Western-type economic goals that lie beyond impenetrable cultural barriers; the depletion of already damaged traditional structures, from which a better life might be evolved; the persistent erosion of the irreplaceable for the sake of the impossible. The inertia is still there, but is concealed by spurious economic activity. This is the tragedy of Indonesia and, with modifications, of certain other countries. In smaller nations the barriers may yet be demolished by cultural change, although this is not necessarily desirable. But in the larger ones, possibly including China, which has yet to face the issues of industrialization, the transformation would require an education programme that is financially out of reach: the total annual Indonesian gross domestic product per head for example, is only one-third of the amount per head spent on education alone in the United States. And even if funds were available, the change in outlook would probably not be radical enough; nor would there be sufficient capital to create suitable employment for the newly educated.

Since the sixteenth century the countries that were colonized have been subjected to a series of Western cultural shocks, against which political independence affords no protection. Western ideas, including those of parliamentary democracy and Marxism, continue to drift in and are ill-digested; Western techniques have lengthened lives, and populations soar disastrously because peasants persist in believing that large families are essential to ensure that enough children will survive to take care of the old. In the isolated, mestizo cultures of the towns people have acquired appetites they cannot satisfy and aspirations they cannot attain; and Western development concepts are imposed upon masses that are culturally unfitted to exploit them. The problem is not mainly one of technical inexperience, but of a state of mind. The failure of development plans to overcome economic inertia aggravates the tragedy; for by confusing the issue it reduces the likelihood of finding more appropriate methods.

Of those countries that are under direct Western influence, Indonesia has probably suffered most. Since the Suharto junta overthrew President Sukarno in the mid-1960s, the people have been driven along an illusory economic path with exceptional ruthlessness. As if to clear the way for development, along lines conceived in the West, the junta instigated the massacre of hundreds of thousands of innocent and ignorant peasants, who were considered to be Communist Party supporters; of the large numbers of people who were cast into makeshift gaols, nearly 100,000, including some of Indonesia's best writers and thinkers, are said to languish under detention.[1] Every spontaneous social and political force has been crushed; the people have been deprived of such little initiative as they possessed, even in village co-operatives. Yet after ten years of sacrifice enforced in the name of development, it is still arguable whether most Indonesians are slightly better or worse off than when the junta seized power. Despite Indonesia's revenues as the world's ninth largest oil producer, and thousands of millions of dollars of foreign aid, the World Bank said in May 1975 that increased help would be needed if the poverty suffered by the majority were to be alleviated substantially in the next decade.[2]

Before the Second World War the indigenous populations of colonized countries were usually called 'backward'. The image was of people insufficiently rational to lift themselves from poverty or to escape the bondage of crippling superstition and barbarous custom. There was admiration of Afro-Asian arts, and interest in the philosophy of some of the subject peoples; Eastern religion

2

Introduction

commanded the respect of those who had studied it, and the adherence of coteries of the type that seek salvation by exotic means. But generally the attitude had not changed much since Marx wrote of India in 1853:[3]

> We must not forget that these idyllic village-communities, inoffensive though they may appear, had always been the solid foundation of Oriental despotism, that they restrained the human mind within the smallest possible compass, making it the unresisting tool of superstition, enslaving it beneath traditional rules, depriving it of all grandeur and historical energies. We must not forget the barbarian egotism which, concentrating on some miserable patch of land, had quietly witnessed the ruin of empires, the perpetration of unspeakable cruelties, the massacre of the population of large towns, with no other consideration bestowed upon them than on natural events, itself the helpless prey of any aggressor who deigned to notice it at all. We must not forget that this undignified, stagnatory, and vegetative life, that this passive sort of existence evoked on the other part, in contradistinction, wild, aimless, unbounded forces of destruction and rendered murder itself a religious rite in Hindostan. We must not forget that these little communities were contaminated by distinctions of caste and by slavery, that they subjugated man to external circumstances instead of elevating man into the sovereign of circumstances, that they transformed a self-developing social state into never-changing natural destiny, and thus brought about a brutalising worship of nature, exhibiting its degradation in the fact that man, the sovereign of nature, fell down on his knees in adoration of Hanuman, the monkey, and Sabbala, the cow.

After the war the word 'underdeveloped' was substituted for 'backward', but 'developing' soon displaced it. The changes were promoted to some extent by postwar goodwill and by recognition that the old, popular conception needed qualification. But possibly the greatest factor was that the new term served the interests of neo-colonialism. 'Developing country' was a cruelly misleading euphemism; it helped to create the illusion that the former colonies would eventually achieve living standards comparable to those of the West if they followed Western models and accepted·

3

Western capital. Not only politicians, financiers and exporters, but economists and academics, developed a vested interest in this deception. A new development jargon was invented, in which a favoured phrase was 'economic take-off'. About the beginning of this decade an American economist, whose name I have forgotten, arrived in Jakarta with the news that Indonesia's 'take-off' was about to begin. His announcement, which was greeted as a magic utterance, was published under big headlines. But Indonesia has not taken off yet; nor has any other former colony of sizeable population.

The development vogue among academics also serves those whose purpose is to detract from Western culture. In 1919 the Dutch economist, G. L. Gonggrijp, wrote in a footnote to one of his articles[4] that he had used the phrase 'semi-civilized nations such as the Javanese' with hesitation, because 'there are a large number of people for whom the height of wisdom consists in a derisive attitude towards Western civilization, often accompanied by a glorification of some or other Utopia or of a vaguely defined East.' Since Gonggrijp's time assaults launched against Western culture by minimizing its achievements and exaggerating the virtues of others have increased; the useful word, 'primitive', has consequently almost passed out of the language, except when applied to societies long dead. Sometimes the detractors are motived by a commendable reaction to colonialist attitudes, but the distortion is still there. J. C. van Leur, for instance, some of whose valuable work was published posthumously in 1955 and reprinted in 1967,[5] may have been right when he criticized a scholar who wrote Indonesian history 'from the deck of the ship, the ramparts of the fortress, the high gallery of the trading house'; but he himself might be accused at times of writing from the *kraton*.

Van Leur's writings are detailed and his arguments are often bolstered with quotations from Max Weber and other masters of sociology. One would expect, therefore, that when comparing what he calls the 'might' of the Javanese with the 'power' of the colonizers in the seventeenth century he would point to the fundamental causes of European domination. But whatever his intention he fails to do this. Van Leur explains the Dutch domination of the Javanese very simply: 'the progress of Dutch power must be attributed . . . to the sturdier rigging and greater speed of the

4

ships, the more powerful cannon-royal, the greater mobility of armed troops.' He may be right in arguing that European political hegemony in Asia was not 'based on the preponderance of a more highly developed economic system', which, it is true, was left at home. But in considering the remarkable seizure of the Indies by a handful of Dutchmen, one must look at Holland's culture, not merely its military superiority in the archipelago. Van Leur says that apart from war techniques, the Dutch colonizers brought nothing new to Indonesia. What they carried with them, in fact, was the most devastating weapon of all, European dynamism, which has until now been approached in the East only by the Japanese.

The most obvious significant fact is that while the Portuguese and Dutch had landed in Java, there was no sign of Javanese in Portugal or Holland. Europe was then expanding; Asia was stagnant. The Javanese mind showed not the slightest indication of reaching beyond mysticism and the pursuit of occult power, whereas Europe was already engaged in scientific and philosophic exploration that was to change the world. Copernicus was dead before the Dutch set sail for Java; the self-taught Italian mathematician, Tartaglia, had solved cubic equations and written what is regarded as the first mathematical treatise on ballistics (1537). While the Dutch were establishing themselves in the Indies, the first English-language newspaper was being printed in Amsterdam (1620); Huygens was improving the telescope, making astronomical discoveries and inventing the pendulum clock. Bacon, Galileo, Kepler and Descartes all died in the seventeenth century, and Newton and Leibnitz had done their best work before the end of it. William Harvey discovered the circulation of the blood before 1616. Two hundred years later Sir Thomas Stamford Raffles,[6] Lieutenant-Governor of Java during the British interregnum, described native rulers as 'semi-barbarous'; printing techniques, physiology and pure mathematics were then unknown to them. This is the comparison that should be made if we are to understand why Indonesians were so easily controlled by the Dutch and why most of them barely subsist today. The need to emphasize such a platitude reflects the extent to which political expediency and cultural masochism have degraded discussion of the world's greatest social problem, the condition of the Afro-Asian peoples.

These days Raffles would probably be accused of racism. However, he was not a racist, but was merely putting a convenient label on a society which, with its primitive agricultural implements and lack of modern knowledge, was on a different cultural level from that of Europe, which had just been refreshed by the Enlightenment. He went out of his way to insert footnotes containing exceptions to what he called 'the general standard'.[7] One was the Panambahan of Sumenep, Nata Kasama, who liberated his slaves, was well read in Javanese ancient history, had a general knowledge of Arabic literature, geography and Arabic treatises on astronomy,[8] and whose curiosity in mechanics delighted those with an opportunity to converse with him. Another was the young nobleman, Raden Saleh, who was sent to Bengal to be educated under the eye of Lord Minto, Governor-General of India. Before he was sixteen Raden Saleh had won a prize in a public mathematics examination in Calcutta, and knew the history of Europe, particularly that of Greece and Rome. He was (like all the Javanese élite) graceful and polite; Englishmen who met him felt that he would be 'conspicuous among those of the same age in first societies in Europe, as an accomplished gentleman'.

Raffles said that since this was the first instance of the 'capacity of the Javan character to improve under a European education', it might 'enable the reader to form some estimate of what that character was formerly in more propitious times, and of what it may attain to hereafter under a more beneficent government.' There is no evidence that more propitious times ever existed in the sense implied by Raffles, whose object in conjuring them up was to make his much reiterated point that the Javanese would be better off under the English than under the 'ungenerous' Dutch. Raffles did a service by being perhaps the first to point out that an individual Javanese could excel in following and applying the complex rules of a Western deductive system. But it does not follow from this that an entire society, or even a significant number of those who rule it, will acquire, or will ever wish to acquire, a truly Western-type motive.

Nor is it to be inferred that Europeans have an innate superiority that guarantees their supremacy in the ups and downs of civilizations. After having been conquered by the barbarian Crusaders, the cultivated Arabs, with Byzantium, handed back to Europe the remains of Greek science and philosophy, with Indian numerals as a bonus; but it took a long time for Europe to develop commerce and social organization, including guilds, of Arab standards, and to comprehend Moslem algebra and its Indian foundations. Yet once the intellectual advance was under way, it rapidly accelerated. And in 1973, when the government of Pakistan was embroiled in heated controversy about whether the moon had been sighted with sufficient certainty to permit the end of Ramadan, American astronauts had landed on it; this anecdote does not mean that Moslems are ignorant of almanacs or that their astronomers cannot excel in the twentieth century, but it exemplifies the basic divergence of the cultures.

When the needier countries are understood better, doubtless words more appropriate than either 'backward' or 'developing' will be found to designate them. A term suitable for some peoples would be 'spiritually oriented', as opposed to the rational and material orientation of the West; this phrase has the advantage of describing their most important characteristic while suggesting the cause of their poverty. The meaning of spiritual relevant to Indonesia's problems is 'concerned with mysticism, spirits, and supernatural beings'; it has little to do with moral qualities, although these are present. To say that Indonesia is spiritually oriented is thus not inconsistent with the fact that its religious leaders frequently pocket the *zakat*.

Java's economic stagnation is not new, but has been the subject of controversy for the greater part of two centuries. In 1827 the Governor-General of the Netherlands Indies, Viscount Du Bus de Gisignies, held an inquiry and reported to the Dutch government:[9]

When after a long period of time all ground on Java has been opened up, it will have over its whole surface a population quite the same as that which now inhabits and cultivates a part of that surface; namely a population which, huddled together everywhere, will consist of countless millions of tenants on whole, half, and quarter acres of land, each farming to obtain his food, each growing rice and nothing else, each farming for an income like that of the meanest day labourer, each using what his small plot of land yields him and his land rent leaves him to gratify the essential needs of life.

7

At that time it was estimated that while the peasants clung to their miserable rice plots four-fifths of Java lay waste; Raffles's figure was six-sevenths. Du Bus's forecast was extraordinarily accurate. As the population rose the peasants put just enough new land under cultivation to fulfil their unchanging meagre needs. The huddling continued down the years until landless people flooded into towns, while many peasants subsisted on plots that could only grow cassava and maize. Twelve years ago the condition of Central Java was so pitiful that Clifford Geertz described it as a 'post-traditional rural slum'.

There are some who believe that the Dutch caused the persistent stagnation. This argument was developed in the 1950s, when certain American academics recreated Indonesia in their own image and assumed that, but for the wicked Europeans, the Javanese would now be driving tractors by day and watching television by night. It is true that the Dutch plundered a vast amount of wealth from the Indies; but this does not mean that, had they not done so, the Javanese would have still produced it. Nor did the Dutch rule the Indies for as long as is often implied. At first they were concerned with trading posts, not territory; their administration did not cover the whole of Java until early in the nineteenth century, and they did not extend their government to the entire archipelago until the twentieth century. The theory of colonial obstruction, to give it a name, will be examined in chapter 11; meanwhile some glimpses of Indonesian history will be sufficient to show that it is at least highly dubious.

Excluding the Papuans and certain minor ethnic elements, the Indonesians are Malays, who are thought to have migrated to the archipelago from about 3000 BC to 300–200 BC, probably in substantial waves. The Javanese, with whom we are most concerned, since they are by far the largest group, have long been predominant. Pure Malay, identical with the language spoken in Malaysia, is confined to Sumatra, where other languages, including Batak and Achenese are also spoken. But Malay was the *lingua franca* of the whole archipelago, and upon independence was adopted as the national language. Now containing numerous Javanese words, it is called *bahasa Indonesia* (Indonesian language); Sumatrans say that few Javanese write it grammatically. The sacrificing of their language by the Javanese dates from the independence struggle, when young revolutionaries saw in

8

Malay an instrument for uniting the people against the Dutch. But because education is sparse, it is questionable whether most Javanese speak Indonesian in their homes, despite the exclusive use of the language in newspapers and on the wireless.

Small kingdoms, that is to say, clearings inhabited by tribes subservient to petty rulers who filched the common land, appear to have existed in the first century AD. These kingdoms had their own ethnic and tribal religions. One of the puzzles of Indonesian history is how they were penetrated by Hinduism. Large-scale immigration from India has been ruled out, and the conversion of the rulers by unlearned Indian pedlars is considered to have been impossible. The pedlars brought Tamil, the language of trade, essential words of which were adopted by the indigenous people; but it required Brahmans to bring Sanskrit, the language of religion and philosophy. Some Brahmans might have followed the traders as missionaries; others might have been invited by Indonesian rulers. But, however they came, van Leur[10] was convinced that they were welcomed and encouraged because they could legitimize the ruling dynasties, as they had done in India, by providing 'mythological sanction to genealogy and tradition'. To this has been added the irresistible speculation that the Indonesian rulers sought occult power from the Brahmans:[11] 'If they wanted the superior status of the kings of India, they had to acquire the sacred knowledge from which these princes drew their magic strength.' Certainly their conversion was superficial; for they continued their previous religious practices.

A mythological and mystical view of history has persisted since the beginning of recorded Indonesian civilization. Kings and usurpers alike used court writers, much as a modern dictator uses public relations men, to establish divine right and to invent high-sounding titles such as 'the lord, the killer of his enemies' and 'he who gives form to the world'. In the Hindu period, the kings were seen as incarnations of Vishnu; after the nominal victory of Islam over Hinduism, dynasties traced their lineage on the one side via Mohammed and the prophets to Adam and on the other to the heroes of the *wayang* world and gods that true Moslems considered pagan; a Sumatran dynasty claimed descent from Alexander the Great; as late as the second half of the nineteenth century rulers of Surakarta were still boasting a special alliance with Ratu Kidul, the goddess of the South Sea, and Suann Lawu, the ruler of the spirits on Mount Lawu.[12] Today some Indonesians say that General Suharto sees himself as fulfilling some mystical purpose in Javanese destiny, but the precise rationalization is not known, as far as I am aware. Sukarno, unlike Suharto, was too widely read in Western literature to involve himself in mythological legitimizing, although in many respects he ruled like a traditional Javanese king.

Coinciding with most of the Hindu period was the Sumatran Buddhist kingdom of Srivijaya, the early trade of which has been investigated by O. W. Wolters[13] in as much detail as the sparse and fragmentary records permit. The kingdom's power, which has been absurdly romanticized, rose in the seventh century; it suffered a severe jolt in the eleventh, when an Indian king sailed in, captured the ruler and looted his treasure; it faded in the thirteenth. Wolters has put together a picture of trade in the seventh and eighth centuries, after much hard work on bits and pieces of lost Chinese encyclopaedias and materia medica, from which he has deduced the nature of some of the exports to China, mainly pine resin, benzoin and camphor; only a few traces of the kingdom are left in Sumatra. Wolters produces no evidence that would disprove a hypothesis that Chinese and, at times, Tamils, were the brains behind the trade and that the kings were mostly concerned to raid competing transit ports and to protect their own, from which they collected stapling dues.

There was also a Buddhist kingdom in Central Java, but the only relic of it is the huge monument of Borobodur, about forty-four metres high at the apex of the stupa, situated on a hill near Yogyakarta. Four hundred statues and 1,400 exquisite reliefs chiselled in the circular terrace walls illustrate the life of Buddha; it is considered certain that they were copied from models shipped from India. The monument is believed to have been built in the late eighth or early ninth century over a period of about ten years. There is speculation about the name of the ruler who ordered it, but nothing is established. The Dutch sociologist, B. Schrieke,[14] thought the monument explained the vacuum that appears to have existed in Central Java for a considerable period from about the time of its erection. After estimating the amount of labour required for construction, which included transporting and lifting 42,000 cubic metres of stone, he concluded that the economy of the region must have been ruined by neglect of rice cultivation and that a famine caused the entire peasantry to flee from their ruler and open up new fields elsewhere.

The last important kingdom to remain Hindu until its extinction was Majapahit, which was founded in East Java in 1293 and lost its influence at the end of the fourteenth century. The kingdom broke up during the reign of the second king and the regency of the third, but was consolidated and extended by the rigorous action of its Prime Minister, Gajah Mada, whose illustrious name has been given to the university at Yogyakarta. The story of Gajah Mada comes from the *Pararaton* or *Book of Kings*, which in its extant form was written in the sixteenth century. The narrative is doubtless adorned with the usual rationalizations and inventions, but scholars accept the general drift of it. Gajah Mada was an officer of the royal guard, who restored the king after he had been overthrown, and finally brought parts of Java and other areas under subjection. Javanese acceptance of legend, and belief in self-congratulatory panegyrics is so strong that even to the educated mind Majapahit is scarcely on a lower level than Rome; but the Dutch scholar, C. C. Berg, believes that its rule was confined to Java, Bali and Madura. To whatever extent Gajah Mada controlled the other islands, he did not govern them as the Romans governed barbarian Europe or as the Dutch governed Indonesia. He established no colonial governments, but merely sent out forces from time to time to collect tribute, often from so-called princes, who had legitimized their rule with myths after conquering primitive communities with the aid of bandits. The little raja on Buru Island, whom the Suharto government paid $7,500 for land used as a political prisoners' settlement, would have been a potentate among them.

Islam, like Hinduism, came to Indonesia from India. It was adopted in parts of Sumatra in the thirteenth century, but did not begin to spread throughout the archipelago until the fifteenth. It was then superimposed on the mixture of Hinduism and Javanese ethnic religion, thus completing the basis of the syncretism that was to evolve and predominate in Java until the present, when only a minority perform the duties prescribed by the Islamic law (the Shari'ah). Superficial though the conversion was in spirit, the form was made the pretext for battle in the incessant conflict between the princes. The Gujerat traders who brought Islamic ideas to the coast were not missionaries; nor were they received at courts with the respect that had been accorded the mystical Brahmans, but were looked down upon and apparently obliged to live in compounds. At the same time the Javanese port princes are assumed to have thought, as their forbears did of Hinduism, that the new religion was associated with an occult power that was giving its adherents increasing influence in the region; they therefore accepted as much of it as they understood or felt they needed, while for the most part continuing their Hindu and, above all, their indestructible Javanese customs. They gave themselves Islamic names, but were hardly Moslems. This typically Javanese contradiction between inner experience and outward forms is apparent today in the smallest details of private and public life and was manifest in politics, such as they were, while they lasted; in economic affairs, with the government applying Western formulae while the society remains devoid of Western-type motive, the contradiction is the essence of the Indonesian tragedy.

The flourishing of Moslem traders from India provided a motive for a Portuguese crusade in the Indies, which was as unsavoury as those that had been launched from Europe against Arabs in earlier centuries. To the Portuguese all Moslems were Moors, the same people whom they had ejected from Portugal after a long struggle. Having failed to vanquish them in North Africa, the Portuguese sought to hound them in Asia. Their principal aim was conquest of the valuable spice trade, but religious fanaticism intensified the zest with which they mercilessly looted Moslem ships and plundered the indigenous people. For all their espousal of Christ, they were exceptionally rapacious; St Francis Xavier, who visited Ambon, in the Moluccas, said the only word they understood was 'rapio'. In 1511 they captured Malacca and fortified it with the tombstones of their Moslem enemies, made of material that the Moslems had seized when desecrating Hindu temples in Gujerat. The rival princes of Ternate and Tidore, impressed with the apparent invincibility of the Portuguese, each sought to win Portugal's patronage in return for a cloves monopoly. The Portuguese accepted a Ternate proposal to establish a base on the island, but after years of quarrelling with its formidable Moslem ruler they tried to cheat him of his share of the cloves profits. War was averted when an oath of friendship was sworn in 1570 by the sultan, on the Koran, and by the Portuguese governor, on the Gospel. The next day the sultan was murdered when he visited the Portuguese fort. His son swore to avenge him, and in 1574 the Ternate fort fell after a siege lasting nearly five years. The new sultan became powerful in the region; he cordially received Sir Francis Drake, doubtless regarding him as a useful potential ally against the Portuguese and the Spanish, who by this time were established in nearby Manila (1571). After their defeat by Ternate the Portuguese formed an alliance with Tidore. But their volatile energy was spent, and they were weak and virtually isolated when the Dutch came on the scene.

A badly led expedition of four Dutch ships arrived at Bantam, north-west Java, in 1596, after more than half of the 249 members of its crews had died during a voyage of fourteen months. The Dutch were merely joining in the traditional peddling trade; but this first, brief contact with Java was to lead to the welding of a collection of unstable, warring states into a unified Netherlands East Indies. The Dutch made a bad impression on the Javanese when they lost their nerve and killed an inoffensive prince and many of his retainers. But they managed to conclude a meaning-less treaty of friendship with the Bantam ruler; and after losing one of their ships when Javanese attacked them north of Surabaya they returned to Holland with goods that yielded a small profit for their backers.

Other independent expeditions followed; some lost heavily when ships were captured by the Spanish and Portuguese, but others did well. The behaviour of the Dutch was uneven. Rough men were often recruited as crew, because the average sailor found the high death rate on the voyages too risky. Drunken bullies robbed the Indonesians when they dared; some sailors joined Indonesian pirates. But on the whole it seems that the traders were well received, particularly in the Moluccas, despite their refusal to form an alliance against the Portuguese. A Balinese king gave an admiral a beautiful girl, who insisted on remaining with him when he tried to refuse the present. On the other hand, a rash admiral sank Achenese boats when he thought that traders from Aceh, in the north of Sumatra, were plotting with the Portuguese to seize his ship; but on the order of an Amsterdam court his company paid 50,000 guilders in compensation to Achenese merchants.

After the arrival of the Dutch the Portuguese, based on Goa, tried to seize control of trading posts, but their attempt failed. On Christmas Day, 1601, five Dutch ships drove off a Portuguese fleet of thirty when it appeared in the Bantam roadstead. By this time a political event in Europe had given the Dutch government an interest in the Indies: Spain, the traditional enemy of the Netherlands, had formed a union with Portugal under Philip II in 1580. According to van Leur[15] it was this, and not a desire to promote trade, that prompted the Dutch government to intervene and amalgamate the independent companies into the United East India Company. A merger was not necessary financially, for by this time expeditions were on the whole profitable. The government, van Leur said, 'strove for the establishment of a political and military instrument able to bring force to bear against the Spanish monarchy.' The Dutch government's decision transformed the picture at sea. Trading ships that were equipped only to defend themselves were replaced by powerful, heavily armed fleets, backed by the Dutch government and sailing under instructions to attack Portuguese bases. By 1605 the Dutch had defeated the Portuguese at Tidore and at Ambon, which became the first Dutch territory in the Indies. But it took thirty-five more years to capture Malacca.

The founder of the Dutch empire in the Indies was Jan Pieterszoon Coen, a ruthless, imaginative man, who was twice the company's Governor-General. Coen claimed that between 1613 and 1623 the company's revenues totalled only 9,388,000 guilders compared with an expenditure of 9,396,000 guilders. He sought to enrich Holland with a grandiose plan to make his capital in Java the centre of intra-Asian trade from Japan to Persia and to develop spice gardens with Dutch-led colonies of Madagascarese, Burmese and, above all, Chinese, whom he considered industrious and peaceable. His plans were rejected, partly on the ground that they would further impoverish and embitter the native peoples. But within the permitted limits, which included instructions to grab a spice monopoly, he acted vigorously, punctuating his reports with abuse of his directors.

The English East India Company, which had only one-eighth of the capital of its Netherlands rival, had a habit of following in the wake of the Dutch when they opened up trading posts. One result of this practice was that British competition, combined with that of the Chinese, forced up pepper prices. Coen stopped buying pepper at Bantam, the main trading centre, and prepared to move his factory to Jakarta, where he secretly converted a minor post into a fortress. After an inconclusive naval battle with a superior English force, he sailed to the Moluccas for reinforcements. English and Javanese from the port of Bantam besieged the Dutch fortress in 1619, but withdrew in confusion after quarrelling about who was to occupy it. Coen returned, burned the town of Jakarta, and founded a new town, Batavia, with Dutch-style canals and bridges, which was to become the capital of the Netherlands East Indies. At the same time he blockaded Bantam and drove the English from the Java Sea, capturing seven ships. He then secured the nutmeg monopoly by killing almost the entire population of the Banda Islands, a republican people who fought valiantly and competently against superior weapons.

When the Dutch installed themselves at Batavia the dominant kingdom in Java was Mataram, founded in 1582 with the usual mystical rationalization. Its ruler, Agung, was styled Susuhunan, which means 'he to whose feet people must look up', a title that he did his best to make literally true. In 1618 he began a series of unsuccessful attacks on Batavia, during which he cut off its water supply by blocking a river. He mobilized thousands of men for the final assault in 1629; but because his ox-drawn wagons became bogged in long, primitive roads, despite ingenious attempts to traverse them, his force was stranded without supplies. When Dutch warships destroyed 200 rice-laden vessels that were heading for Batavia, starving Javanese soldiers retreated and were left dying on the roads. Only twelve Dutch and a smaller number of Japanese mercenaries and Chinese were killed in the fighting in 1629, while town life was scarcely disturbed. The total Javanese casualties are unknown, but after one of the earlier attacks the Mataram commander executed nearly 800 of his men for having been defeated. The Javanese possessed cannon, but were armed mainly with spears.

The defeat was easily explained away by Mataram's court poets in the *Babad Tanah Jawi*. Agung, they wrote, could have quickly destroyed Batavia by occult power, but chose not to do so. He sent two commanders – Purbaya who was loyal, and Madureja, whom he knew to be a traitor. Madureja was given command of the troops; but Purbaya flew through the air and destroyed part of the citadel wall with a thaumaturgical utterance. Having thus demon-strated Mataram's power, Purbaya withdrew. But traitorous Madureja, unaware of the king's true purpose, fought on and was slain. This denouement suited everyone. The grateful Dutch, the poets said, later sent envoys to Mataram with presents, which constituted tribute and showed that Batavia realized it was a Mataram vassal. Further warfare was therefore unnecessary.

The company's policy at that stage was to keep to its trading posts and avoid expensive territorial conquest. Agung, whose prestige among his real vassals was undiminished by his setback, was thus free to pursue his ambition to extend his influence. His adventures ended in a humiliating defeat when he invaded Bali in 1639, having failed to persuade the Dutch to join him. Probably in the hope of winning Turkey's support, Agung declared Islam to be the official state religion; he followed the Bantam ruler in sending envoys to Mecca, and assumed the title of the Great Sultan Muhammad. Agung's son and heir, Amangkurat I, was less interested in fighting the Dutch than in slaughtering princes, including close relatives, whom he feared as potential rivals. The Dutch took advantage of this situation and shrewdly sent a dele-gation, which, under the guise of offering the company's services, persuaded Amangkurat to agree that only ships with a company pass could trade with Ambon, Banda, Ternate and in the west beyond them. As a sign of vasselage the company agreed to supply the sultan with annual presents, which he regarded as tribute, estimated to have cost no more than 60,000 guilders in the most expensive year. The sultan reciprocated by forcing people on the coast to deliver wood and rice to the Dutch, at no cost to himself. In the words of a company official, the Dutch Governor-General did not concern himself about the sultan more than 'an elephant about a fly', but merely indulged his haughtiness. 'Compared with the Directors in Amsterdam', Vlekke[16] points out, 'the sultan of Mataram was a poor man.' For a time the company had to borrow heavily and manipulate the books to pay dividends; but during 1613–54 it made a profit of 25 million guilders, of which 9.7 million were remitted to Europe and the balance retained as working capital.

After capturing Malacca from the Portuguese in 1641, the Dutch were masters of the seas in the region. They had a good hold on the Indian cloth trade and Japanese copper exports. To keep up the price of cloves and nutmeg, they destroyed spice gardens on all islands except Ambon and the Banda Islands, and obliged the impoverished inhabitants to buy rice, for which their soil was unsuitable, at prices they could not afford. By the middle of the century, fulfilling Coen's dream, they had made Batavia the centre of trade on a route from Japan to Persia via Ceylon, where they occupied most of the maritime provinces, and India. They easily defeated Makasar in 1667, and secured a monopoly of its trade. Various stratagems brought the Sumatran ports under their influence. Before the end of the seventeenth century they had the entire archipelago at their mercy.

While the Dutch were cruel to the foreign victims of their imperialism, Amangkurat's savagery was inflicted on his own people. His entire court lived in fear of their lives, which they frequently lost because of his whims. He rid the court of Moslem theologians, probably because they favoured one of his brothers in the succession, and rejected the title of Sultan in favour of the traditional Javanese Susuhunan; upon his orders Moslem teachers and their families totalling about 6,000 people were all killed on the spot when he summoned them to a meeting. Such was the awe of royal blood that when one of his brothers tried to murder him the court aristocrats merely blocked the way, allowing themselves to be slain rather than molest a prince. Not until the monarch withdrew from the sight of sacrilege was his brother seized and put to death.

In 1677 Prince Trunajaya of Madura led a revolt against him. He burned down the *kraton* and seized the crown jewels, the royal elephants and the harem, but was forced to withdraw to Kediri, where he claimed to be King. Amangkurat tried to reach the Dutch, but died on the way after advising his son to ally himself with the company. In 1678 Dutch troops marched into the interior for the first time, suffering a severe ordeal in the jungle. They supported Amangkurat's son, Amangkurat II, in a battle against Trunajaya, who was subsequently lured from a mountain hideout and murdered on the new ruler's orders. The new king, a weak man, became the company's vassal. When he died the Dutch ejected his son, who was hostile to them, and put the heir's uncle on the throne with the title of Pakubuwana, 'the pivot of the world'. Under a treaty signed with Mataram in October 1705 the Dutch obtained trade and territorial concessions that were to last until the Second World War. They had already put Bantam under their control by helping the ruler's ambitious and unscrupulous son to overthrow his father, despite strong resistance from the people. The British, forced to leave Bantam, built a fort, the remains of which may still be seen, at Bengkulu, on the west coast of Sumatra.

The Dutch put an end to destructive wars among the ruling Mataram family by enforcing division of the kingdom into two parts, Yogyakarta and Surakarta, in 1755. From that time the company governed most of the inhabitants of Java, who were then roughly estimated at 3–5 million. The two new states were only nominally sovereign, as were five other small states, and were bound to accept the advice of Dutch Residents. The Dutch brought peace to the peasants when they forbade fighting among the princes and stopped the invasions of East Java by the Balinese, who used to plunder the land and drag off prisoners as slaves. After its centuries of war-ravaged history the realm of Java could at last be said to be unified. What the native kings had failed to do was achieved by a foreign trading company with an army that totalled only 1,000 Europeans and 2,000 Asians towards the end of the eighteenth century.[17] This seems to indicate that the 'might' of Mataram, as van Leur called it, was inversely proportional, both economically and militarily, to the grandiloquence of the titles affected by its rulers.

But there was still plenty of fighting ahead, not only against Javanese, but people in other parts of the archipelago, and the British. When the Dutch supported Russia's attempt in 1780 to stop Britain from interfering with shipping, the British blockaded their home ports. Batavia wanted to sell its accumulating goods to foreign traders, but the Amsterdam directors insisted in keeping to the old monopoly. This mistake was disastrous for the company, the fortunes of which declined further when the Treaty of Paris (1784) gave the British freedom to sail in all the archipelago seas, with the result that they had no difficulty in smuggling the coveted spices from the Moluccas. Americans and Danes also began to appear in the Indies. All this was too much for the company, and on 1 March 1796 the Dutch government bought the colony for the price of its debts, 134 million guilders.

When the Netherlands followed France in the Revolution, European ideas of administration were thrust upon the Javanese.

Introduction

The Dutch Governor-General, Herman Willem Daendels, tried to make civil servants of the Indonesian rulers, as Napoleon had done with the European feudal kings. But Napoleon, who had annexed Holland, considered that Daendels was too immoderate, and recalled him. The British government, at war with France, decided to expel the Dutch for strategic reasons and leave the Javanese to their own rulers. Batavia surrendered six weeks after Lord Minto, Governor-General of India, had arrived with 12,000 men on 3 August 1811. Minto's view that the British should remain prevailed, and the English East India Company took over, with Thomas Stamford Raffles as Lieutenant-Governor. With the help of Dutch advisers, Raffles radically changed the entire machinery of government. He also took the first steps to end slave trading and improved the crude judicature, marring this reform with an attempt to introduce the jury system, which was unknown to the Dutch and hopelessly unsuited to the Javanese and Chinese. For all his genuine concern for the Javanese, his liberal utterances were contradicted by some of his actions. His troops took the sultan of Yogyakarta prisoner and were allowed to divide the royal treasure among themselves, according to rank. When the sultan of Palembang, in Sumatra, refused to sell Bangka tin production to the British, Raffles sent a force to punish him for the massacre of the Dutch, which followed his own inciting of a Palembang rebellion; the sultan fled. Raffles's most important reform was to abolish the forced cultivation of export crops. He believed that if peasants were free to cultivate what they liked both they and his company would benefit. To this end all land was considered to be vested in the Batavia government and was leased to peasants for a rent paid in produce. The system was difficult to administer, but in the first year, with village head men obliged to collect the produce, it worked well. When Raffles tried to encourage initiative by making leases with individual peasants, revenue fell. The Dutch, who retrieved the Indies in 1816 under a treaty agreed upon with Britain in 1814, adopted the land rent system, which required only more time in which to organize it.

With the British out of Java, the next to trouble the Dutch were the Javanese themselves, led by Prince Diponegoro, perhaps the most respected figure in Javanese history and certainly the nation's greatest war hero outside legend. The Dutch, who feared him, had robbed Diponegoro of the Yogyakarta sultanate, to which he was heir. He vanished from the court, spent a period meditating in caves to increase his spiritual power, and launched a guerrilla war in 1825. News spread among the people that Diponegoro was the long-prophesied Ratu Adil, the delivering prince; a magic sword was said to have fallen from the heavens at his feet. Most of the aristocracy, without whose nod few people would fight, supported the rebellion for one reason or another. By this time the Dutch had increased their forces in Java, to repel European rivals. But it took five years to vanquish Diponegoro who, using tactical skill rather than magic, waged battles in which the Dutch army lost 15,000 dead, including 8,000 Europeans. It is estimated that 200,000 Javanese died in the war, about nine-tenths of them from famine and disease. The rebellion ended when the Dutch shabbily tricked the prince into going to their headquarters to negotiate, arrested him and exiled him to Celebes. The entire archipelago was unified in the late nineteenth and early twentieth centuries. A costly war against Aceh, fought largely to stop piracy, lasted from 1873 to 1904. The Dutch controlled Bali from 1849, when they intervened to stop fighting between feuding kings. More than 250 petty rulers throughout Indonesia, many of them heads of small, primitive communities, such as Dyak headhunters, were forced to accept Batavia's tutelage.

After the first quarter of the nineteenth century, Dutch economic policy in the Indies falls into three periods, with the usual overlapping: the culture system, the liberal policy and the ethical policy. By 1830 the Indies government was heavily in debt, following the war with Diponegoro; and the Dutch exchequer had been drained by the cost of fighting in Europe. The only hope of solvency seemed to lie in more efficient exploitation of the Indies; Johannes van den Bosch, who had ideas on the subject, was sent out as Governor-General to organize it. Van den Bosch followed Du Bus, whose astonishing prediction of continued peasant stagnation has already been mentioned. He did not share the view of Raffles and some Dutch that the Javanese, if left to themselves, would fan out from their minimal plots and produce an abundance that would enrich both themselves and their exploiters. He considered that the peasants were too ignorant, if not too lazy, to earn more than subsistence. They must therefore be forced to cultivate commercial crops; then they would learn how to work and would come to appreciate the rewards of overcoming their inertia.

Forced labour was not new in Java: the peasants had been obliged for centuries to deliver all except their means of subsistence to their rulers; the company had merely extended an existing system when it forced the people to produce crops, including coffee, which it introduced. The company squeezed coffee out of the peasants as tribute through the hereditary rulers, whom it appointed as regents. The regents, who profited from this operation, co-operated in driving the people to the limit. Sometimes they farmed out the management to Chinese, whose exactions were so cruel that in 1768 peasants in one area vainly begged the Dutch to oust their rulers and take over the territory. Van den Bosch went farther than the company, and organized the entire production of commercial crops. The peasant had to pay land rent, officially one-fifth of his crop, but often more, or grow designated produce, mostly sugar, on one-fifth of his rice land; when the harvest was worth more than the land rent the surplus was paid to the villagers. Since the culture system, as it was called, was only applied to the best land, most of the people were unaffected; but those whom it embraced suffered fearful hardship. The only escape from land bondage was exhausting work in the ever increasing sugar mills; in some regions people starved because their regents and their Chinese agents forced them to use almost the whole of their rice fields for sugar; villagers sometimes had to walk long distances to places where they were obliged to work, and occasionally had to remain away from home for considerable periods; those who tried to escape were flogged, as were labourers who broke unendurable contracts in the twenties. But the system was a boon to the government and provided the Javanese aristocracy with more money to fritter away. Between 1831 and 1877, when forced culture was being tapered off, the Dutch treasury received 823 million guilders from its vast Javanese plantation, or about 30 per cent of its national budgets during that period.

Satisfactory though it was financially, the culture system clashed with the economic liberalism that gripped Europe in the second half of the nineteenth century. Open up the country to private enterprise, it was said, free the peasants from compulsion and everyone would be swept to prosperity by the forces of a free economy. This new thinking, like today's development vogue, was a mixture of *naiveté* and unscrupulousness; the Javanese masses were bound to be kept poor by the superior commercial skill and industriousness of the Europeans and Chinese. In a back-handed recognition of peasant helplessness, the government forbade Chinese and other non-indigenous inhabitants to buy land. This was one of the provisions of the Agrarian Law of 1870, which inaugurated the liberal policy. The peasants leased their land to plantation companies for rents so small that they were obliged to work on it for a pittance; wage slavery thus replaced forced cultivation. Sugar production in Java more than doubled in 1870–85. New, lucrative crops, including tea and cinchona, flourished; and a start was made with rubber, which later became the most valuable export. But the government had lost most of the forced cultivation revenue, and failed to tax the companies properly; by 1898 the Indies debt totalled 100 million guilders.

At the same time the condition of the people worsened. The Dutch conscience eventually awakened, and gave birth to the ethical policy. In 1901 the government accepted the 'moral duty of the Netherlands towards the people of the Indies'. A committee, the first of several, was appointed in 1902 to inquire into the 'causes of diminishing welfare in Java'. These searchings were no mere exercises in hypocrisy; there was genuine and legitimate surprise, even despair, that no Javanese, unlike so many Chinese, had responded to the new economic climate. The ethical policy consisted in extended irrigation, education, emigration from overcrowded parts of Java, public health measures, agricultural extension and vast rural credit – in 1917 alone more than 10,000 institutions helped more than 1,300,000 farmers. The government allocated 40 million guilders in 1905 to 'ameliorate economic conditions in Java and Madura'.

From 1900–25 the Dutch spent 158 million guilders, not including wages and the value of compulsory labour, on irrigating 2.5 million acres and on drainage and flood control. But at no stage was there any sign of improvement in production; in fact, rice yields per hectare in the main farm areas of Java were 6 per cent lower in 1914–23 than in 1878–87. At the end of 1925 Indonesians had a debit of more than 100 million guilders in credit institutions, but it was highly questionable whether they had been better off at any time since a quarter of a century earlier, when little government credit was available. More money often meant less production. The futility of trying to help the peasants by direct welfare methods was spotted as early as 1903 by an Indies official, Controleur J. van Alst. He said capable men with affection for the Javanese and understanding of them had tried irrigation, better farming methods, rural credit and emigration to less populated areas, but Java's welfare was diminishing. The real question, he said, was how to improve the Javanese spirit of enterprise; without that everything else would prove futile. But the government continued its policy until by 1939 it had spent about 250 million guilders on irrigation, drainage and flood control since 1880, without increasing per capita consumption of cereal crops.

Meanwhile the Dutch had done well for themselves; it was estimated that in 1928 12–15 per cent of Holland's national income came directly or indirectly from the Indies. But it would have been hard to persuade the government to provide more welfare, since its considerable expense and effort were rendered futile by a continuing increase in the population, which had risen in Java from 6 million in 1825, 9.5 million in 1850, 18 million in 1875 and 28.4 million in 1900 to 35.7 million in 1925. In the 1971 census the population of Java and the small island of Madura was found to be 76,099,579, while the total for Indonesia was 119,182,542. The spectre of Malthus has already appeared; at the estimated growth rate the population would be 280 million by the year 2000, and would obviously be unable to feed itself long before then. The problem of Javanese economic impotence is thus of great importance to the world. If it cannot be resolved, it should at least be understood well enough to prevent false remedies. If this is to be done many academics will have to abandon their hobby horses and politicians will need to step down from their platforms. The urgent need for completely fresh inquiry will be more apparent when the following account of the present débacle in Indonesia has been read.

PART ONE

The end of the Old Order

CHAPTER ONE

The prisoners

At first sight the political prisoners' settlement on Buru Island, looming up beyond the distant swamp, looked like a Nazi concentration camp in a tropical setting. A barbed-wire fence dwarfed the shoulder-high *alang* grass; and watch-towers, spaced along it, blotched the sickly blue of the sky. But the closer we approached, walking along the track from our landing place on the muddy Wayapu River, the clearer it became that there were differences between a Nazi camp and this grim creature of the Indonesian Army. The watch-towers, made of crudely split logs, were perilously lop-sided; sentries drooped listlessly on their benches in the small cabins at the top, overcome by boredom and the steamy heat; there were no searchlights and no packs of savage dogs. And the night after our arrival – an almost endearing, typically Indonesian touch – the main gate fell from its hinges when a soldier tried to swing it open.

We were a small party of Indonesian and foreign journalists, who had been allowed to accompany the Attorney-General, Lieutenant-General Soegih Arto, on an 'observation trip', just before Christmas 1969. Security men had opposed our visit, but were over-ruled on the ground that reports from the scene, however unfavourable, would dim the horrific Devil's Island image created in some newspapers. About 10,000 of the Indonesian Army's political prisoners would spend the rest of their lives there, as far as anyone could tell, although none had been convicted of any offence and none would be brought to trial. The young men would never know women, and few of the married were to see their wives and children again. At that time only 2,500 had arrived from their prisons to pioneer the settlement. Baperu, the authority in charge of the operation, said that only healthy men aged no more than forty-five were being transported. This statement proved to be false; there were men much older than that, and some were so weakened by their earlier imprisonment that they died on the voyage from Java. The army chose Buru Island, three degrees south of the equator, in the Moluccas, because it was remote and could not be used for any other purpose in the foreseeable future. The island is nearly as large as Bali; but its vast areas of jungle and of swamps infested with malaria-carrying mosquitoes make it so forbidding that down the centuries it has attracted a population of only 30,000, who manage to subsist along the coast.

Indonesia's political prisoners were then officially stated to total 69,000, with 47,000 others who had been freed being obliged to report regularly to authorities; but figures that were announced from time to time varied so greatly that it was impossible to accept any of them. A mixture of muddle and fabrication was partly responsible for the inconsistencies; another factor was that while some prisoners were being released others were being arrested, usually at the whim of local military commanders, who were incapable of distinguishing between suspicion, or even personal dislike, and evidence of crime. As Soegih Arto said in September 1971: 'It is a floating rate, like the Japanese yen *vis-à-vis* the dollar.' In September 1969 Amnesty International estimated the number of prisoners, including rebels in ethnic groups, at 117,000.

Most of the prisoners were arrested after the general's coup that followed a *putsch* carried out by junior army officers on 1 October 1965, when Sukarno was President. Scholars are still debating to what extent, if any, the Communist Party (PKI – Partai Komunis Indonesia) was behind the *putsch*, in which six generals and a junior officer were murdered. But the generals seized the opportunity to wipe out the PKI, which was the world's third largest Communist Party, provoke the killing of hundreds of thousands of peasants and overthrow Sukarno. If there had been a Communist conspiracy few could have taken part in it, but the scores of thousands who were arrested were supposed to have been involved. At a press conference in October 1969 Soegih Arto said the 69,000 were classified as follows: class A, 5,000 'hard-core Communists' against whom evidence was complete – a few had been convicted and the rest would be tried later; class B, 11,000 'hard-core Communist leaders' against whom there was not sufficient evidence to try them, although they were known to be guilty; class C, 26,000 mild Communists and fellow travellers, who were to be released; status undetermined, 27,000.

Those on Buru Island were the vanguard of class B, 10,000 of whom were to be shipped there. They were put in three widely separated camps set up on the Wayapu River in an area of 100,000 hectares bought from a local raja for $7,500, and told to get on with planting rice and other crops. The army would support them for eight months; after that they must feed themselves. There were 700 in the one camp that we were allowed to visit; to give them a start the army had cleared a small area, felling the tall trees and setting them ablaze with the undergrowth. Each day the prisoners left the rectangular barbed-wire enclosure under escort to work in the blackened landscape from dawn until dusk. The army provided seed, tools, cooking utensils and a ration of rice and salted fish.

Our 'observation' was extremely brief; the overnight stay at the camp and the return trip from Jakarta by plane, jeep, boat and on foot took eighty-seven hours, of which only ninety minutes were spent with the prisoners. We were forbidden to speak to any except a few whom officers selected; but we defeated the restriction when we shook off intelligence men by darting individually among prisoners working in the fields, calling out that we wanted to take just one more photograph, and asking questions while we focused our cameras. We had heard much in Jakarta about the 'hard-core Communist leaders' in class B; we were given an impression of calculating, disciplined men, steeped in the diabolical tactics of Marxism-Leninism, who had been posted at vantage points to launch revolution, with the support of Peking. To our astonishment the few hundred that we saw turned out to be mostly peasants of such limited education that it was questionable whether they would even have been able to understand Mao Tse-tung's little red primer. More astonishing still, a good proportion were mere youths who had been as young as sixteen, even twelve, at the time of their arrest. I asked Soegih Arto how these lads, some of whom spoke Indonesian badly, could have been Communist cadres. He said that youth and innocent looks did not mean that a prisoner was not a hard-core Communist. 'The face does not always reflect the heart,' he explained. 'These have something in their hearts – and in their heads. They are good actors, too. They could certainly have been cadres at sixteen. We had people of twelve fighting against the Dutch.' Most Indonesians are good actors, in the sense implied by Soegih Arto, and the prisoners were probably no exception. But it was impossible to see how these boys could have been leaders of a revolutionary conspiracy in 1965.

The settlers worked in the khaki clothes they had been wearing for years; none possessed shoes, and some had scabies on their feet, which they had picked up when wading among parasites in the swamps; a few had plaited themselves the broad, conical hat that is common in South East Asia. They were, on the whole, a resilient looking band; some gave a humorous, open smile, even when lifting their feet from the mud to show us the swollen rash. It seemed that many were not Communists, nor even fellow travellers. One, the father of four children, whom he had not seen since 1966, said he had no political interests whatever. He used to perform in a theatrical act, as one of two traditional Javanese clowns. His partner was a member of Lekra, a cultural organization, which the army branded as Communist; this was enough to get them both arrested. Another prisoner said he had belonged to a student body organized by Communists, but that he was also a Catholic. To prove his story he began to sing 'Ave Maria'. Our enjoyment of his performance was interrupted by a security man, who shouted that we must go back to our base. But the singer continued to make his point, and his well-produced tenor followed us plaintively as we walked through the burned grass to our quarters. That night a Western correspondent, known for his admiration of General Suharto, said: 'No society which had anything positive to offer, not even, in the extreme case, a fascist society, would be unable to absorb these lads.'

The prisoners slept and ate in large bamboo huts. A communal bed of bamboo matting ran the length of the hut on each side, leaving a wide corridor in the middle for eating; every prisoner had a mosquito net. We found this arrangement comfortable enough when we spent the night in one of the larger huts, about 34 by 6.5 metres, with security men lying at intervals between us. The settlers had already planted 134.5 hectares, we were informed, and had sold turnips to river sailors to obtain money for tobacco. Soegih Arto, who had won a reputation for skill in unorthodox commerce when he was Consul-General in Singapore, suggested that they should also sell 500 kilograms of beans, already harvested and stored for an emergency; this, he said, would enable them to buy soap, which the army did not feel obliged to supply.

The peasants, the entertainer, and the student were not a complete cross-section of the settlement. One of the three camps contained 800 prisoners with higher education, high school certificates or artistic achievement. Soegih Arto said they had been segregated because they would make more trouble than the others. Asked how these isolated men could ever be included in the politically rehabilitated community that the government proposed to set up on the island in the remote future, he said: 'We shall try to brain-wash them.' We were not allowed to visit this camp, although it was only eight kilometres upstream; but three of those to be brain-washed were paraded for us outside a hut, to which they had been brought for the occasion. They were Pramoedya Ananta Toer, who has been described as the best writer of Indonesia's independence generation, the Angkatan '45; Professor Dr Suprapto, former chairman of the National Law Association; and Slamet Muljono, a former Deputy Mining Minister and a member of the Indonesian Scientists' Association, which had links with the PKI. Pramoedya had been reported dead by a Dutch newspaper; apparently the army wanted to show that he was still alive. The three men looked fit enough, but security men stopped us when our questions were of consequence.

It is unlikely that any of these three prisoners could describe his thinking in words that would fit into the army's crude index of political categories. Obviously none of them was involved directly or remotely in the murders of 1 October 1965. Their only offence was that they thought differently from the generals; and had Sukarno not been overthrown they would have remained free men. Pramoedya had visited Moscow and Peking, but so had others who were not arrested; and that did not make him a Communist. He was a leftist – a term he would want to qualify – but he stopped short of the PKI, and went no farther than Lekra, many of whose members did not consider themselves to be Communists. Had he felt like joining the PKI, it may be assumed that he would have done so openly; for he was outspoken to a fault. Pramoedya's works are still being translated into English and doubtless other languages; one critic has described him as 'the kind of writer who appears only once in a generation, or once in a century'.[1] As far as I know his writing is unblemished by political propaganda. He is aware that no political group has a monopoly of either virtue or cruelty; the two main characters in one of his best stories *Bukan Pasar Malam* (*Not an All-night Fair*) are represented as having been victims of Communist imprisonment. Many of his best-known works were written in colonial gaols, where he spent two and a half years after having been captured when fighting the Dutch in 1947. While the Dutch had no objection to his writing, his Indonesian captors took a different view. I asked Soegih Arto whether Pramoedya was allowed to write on Buru Island. The general smiled and his eyes twinkled impishly. 'He is allowed to write', he said. 'But he has no pencil and paper.' This became one of Soegih Arto's favourite jokes; he was still repeating it with relish two years later, in December 1971, when another group of journalists went to the settlement.

By various stratagems, including the imposition of a $400 fee for the trip and an unnecessarily early deadline for applications, the army managed to limit the second batch of journalists and TV men to half a dozen. One of the party, Peter Schumacher, a Dutch correspondent resident in Jakarta, was expelled after the publication of his report; another, Dom Moraes, of the *Asia Magazine*, and Frank Fischbeck, the photographer who accompanied him, were forbidden to enter Indonesia again. All of the 10,000 class B prisoners had now arrived. The three settlements had grown to eighteen, of which the journalists saw four; houses had been built in some, each accommodating fourteen men. Individual beds, covered with a thin mat, were an improvement on the communal system, but holes had developed in some of the mosquito nets. The fields were well-irrigated; an officer explained that this was because many irrigation workers belonged to Sobsi, the Communist trade union. Places of worship had been built; for the army insists that prisoners should embrace some religion to show that they adhere to 'Belief in God', the first article of the national creed, *Pancasila*. About 40 per cent had become Christians, most of them Catholics.

Life on Buru Island was obviously better than it had been in the gaols, halls and sheds that had housed most of the prisoners before their transportation. But even in the barest essentials it left much to be desired. There was a shortage of tablets to treat the numerous malaria victims; several prisoners, whose ages were put at more than sixty, were said to be suffering from TB and asthma; and some of the few who dared to speak up said they were not getting enough to eat. A German priest, who was allowed to visit the camp regularly, was moved by the care with which the fit and the young looked after the sick and the old. Prisoners complained that there was a shortage of faeming implements and a surplus of tools for making furniturr; the export of furniture and handicrafts was increasing, but only a small part of the proceeds was devoted to the settlement, they said. The implication was that officers were exploiting the prisoners' labour for personal profit. This accusation is consistent with an Amnesty International report that some prisoners in Java and West Kalimantan (formerly Borneo) were forced to work as virtual slaves on public works and as officers' personal servants.

Pramoedya Ananta Toer and Suprapto were again paraded, but without Slamet Muljono, who might well have been ill or dead. This time the journalists saw them at a military post, where prisoners were dancing frantically to the wild ringing and clashing of *gamelan* music, for which they had made their own instruments. Here, at last, was a true Nazi touch. The men had been ordered to put on a joyous welcome for the new head of Baperu, Brigadier-General Wadli; it had been the same at Auschwitz, where prisoners were made to sing to show they were happy. The two men from the intellectuals' camp, as it was called, had deteriorated in the two years since they had first been put on view. When I saw Frank Fischbeck's photograph of Pramoedya in the *Daily Telegraph Magazine*, published in London, it was so unlike the face I had seen in 1969 that I thought a mistake had been made; it was not until I found the same photograph in an Amnesty International publication that I was convinced that the caption was right; the smiling, well-composed man had been pitifully shrunk by moral and physical privation. In his report Dom Moraes wrote that the men looked frail when they entered the post 'awkwardly and shyly, like small boys caught at an adult party . . . Suprapto had a beautiful, wrinkled face, but though he is fifty-six, he seemed somehow less old than Pramoedya, who is forty-six.' They had a 'strange defeated humble look: not so much as if they were broken, but as if their hearts were. They shook hands with an unaccustomed air and sat down on the bench.'

Pramoedya answered questions in a soft, slightly hoarse voice, hesitating and looking at military officers, while the journalists kept their tape-recorders running. 'It's very hard to say', he said, when asked whether he had anything to tell the press. He gave a 'tiny, apologetic laugh'. It was also 'very hard to say' whether he was able to write on Buru Island, but after a short reflection he added: 'No.' He said he wanted to write, but was 'too tired, always too tired'. Asked whether he had writing materials, he again said: 'It is very hard to say.' After looking at the officers he went on: 'Yes, I am allowed. I have materials. But I am too tired. We have to dig the fields. We report at 6 a.m. and work until 1.30 p.m. Then from 2.30 p.m. to 5 p.m.'

Moraes continues: 'Suprapto said in a husky, rather weak voice: "We are not accustomed to agriculture. We can do it, but –" with the same apologetic laugh as Pramoedya "we are not very productive". Had they enough food? "It is very hard to say", said Pramoedya softly.'

Suprapto said he had never been a Communist, and did not know why he was arrested. He had taught law at Bandung University and had his own practice. He had defended many peasants and liberals in court. Perhaps some of his clients were Communists: he did not know. Pramoedya gave a different kind of answer when asked if he were a Communist. As an artist and a thinker, he had spent all his adult years in passionate examination of the individual and social problems of mankind; he might well have marvelled at the simplicity of those who only thought in terms of labels. 'I am what I am', he said. 'I have no clear political ideas. I have no political education. I am a humanist. I was a member of Lekra, but that is not a communist organization . . . If I could write I would write my memoirs. But I cannot write. I am too tired. Professor Suprapto and I are in the same camp. So are several writers I know, but we do not meet in the same field, and when we meet we are too tired to talk. So I do not write

and I do not talk . . . I am a writer. That's all. That's all. I want
to write. One day I will write. That is my work and my dedication.'
Moraes wrote that Pramoedya 'paused, and looked down at his
hands, which were locked in his lap. Suprapto looked at him with
a sort of understanding pity.' The officers felt that the interview
had already gone too far. One of them barked: 'Time's up.' Errol
Hodge, of the Australian Broadcasting Commission, thrust two
notebooks and a pen into Pramoedya's hand. Moraes asked him
whether he could deliver any messages for him. 'Clothes', he
replied. 'We need clothes.' Moraes gave Pramoedya his pen, and
the journalists left, wondering what would happen to the pens and
paper.

A 67-year-old Catholic nun, who had been in Indonesia for
thirty-four years, told Peter Schumacher that many of the prisoners
were illiterate and could not be considered Communists in any
sense of the word; large numbers had joined Sobsi simply in the
hope of obtaining better working conditions. She confirmed that a
considerable proportion of the younger prisoners were only fifteen
and sixteen when arrested; most of them had belonged to the
Communist youth organization, Pemuda Rakjat.

The discovery on the island of so many ignorant peasants, some
of whom were young, illiterate, or both, raises the question of why
they should be kept there as class B prisoners, under the trans-
parent pretext that they were 'hard-core cadres'. On the face of it
the detention seems pointless, particularly when it is realized that
more Communists remain free than are under detention. In
January 1969 an army officer told Jakarta newspaper editors that
200,000 Communists were still active in Indonesia; he said they
had been among 300,000 listed as cadres in the PKI register of
3 million members. These figures were put out for the propaganda
purposes of the moment, and the estimate of 200,000 was probably
no more than one of those wild assumptions that the army treats
as if they were precise statistics. But they underline the contradiction that while scores of thousands of militants lurk in the revolutionary breeding ground of overcrowded Java and other areas,
where millions of peasants barely subsist, a mere 10,000 are
condemned to exile on Buru Island. Arbitrary arrest by local
military commanders is a partial explanation. The haphazardness
of the whole affair is shown in the system of classifying prisoners.
No rational basis is possible except that some were PKI members,

some suspected members and some members of affiliated organizations. But this would not get round the fact that it was not illegal to be a member of the PKI until the army pounced on it, and that only a few members could have been involved in the 1965 conspiracy, assuming that the party was seriously implicated at all. Nobody has ever explained by what criteria the 27,000 who remained undivided in 1969, more than three years after the *putsch*, were eventually classified.

Yet, excluding its irrational element, the paradox of detaining relatively few on Buru Island for life while large numbers of more dangerous men are free may be partly resolved. A key to the solution is the detention of totally innocent writers and academics. The generals regard almost any intellectual activity as a threat to their power and to the political stability that they feel is essential to the nation's economic development. They foresaw that most thinkers, even the very conservative, would create trouble enough as the army tightened its political grip; and they were determined that this latent opposition should not be strengthened. That is why, in my view, Pramoedya and the others were not released when the frenzy that swept the nation after the *putsch* had died down. With the more disobliging thinkers out of the way, the army's enforcement of harsh economic measures and its cynical replies to protests against corruption caused only quickly suppressed demonstrations in the streets and whispers in the universities. Apart from a few striking exceptions, newspaper criticism was pathetically oblique; and most of the editors, though not lacking in courage, were eventually tamed by the arrest of some and threats to the newsprint supplies of all. But the spirit of the creative mind is harder to extinguish; and one can imagine the biting comments made by men like Pramoedya on the numerous, senseless official exhortations, which would have been widely ridiculed except in a country where mysticism prevails over other kinds of thought. The combined influences of radical artists and academics would have strengthened those who dared to criticize the army's policies and, what was more dangerous, to smile at declarations that were evidently absurd.

It now becomes possible to advance a hypothesis to explain why the illiterate young peasants were detained; they were needed to help feed the writers, academics and others unused to farming. While the men who were accustomed to sedentary work were able to use their hands, they had neither the strength nor the skill to pioneer the plantations or the irrigation that was essential to the survival of the crops. Apart from that, they were not, as Suprapto wryly put it, very productive. Experienced farmers and young men were needed to get the settlement under way and to feed those who became too weak or too old to work. When those who were now middle-aged could no longer grow their own food, there would be others, at present in their thirties, to look after them. These in their turn could be fed by those now in their twenties. Eventually the settlement would dwindle to a few old people, rendered harmless and perhaps imbecilic by being cut off from normal human relationships for the greater part of their lives. In the end there would be only the dead. Then one of the last paragraphs of Pramoedya's *Bukan Pasar Malam* would read like a prophecy: 'And perhaps one day my body would be buried beside them . . . It remained only to sweep up what was left.'

Such a vision of the settlement's future would be consistent with the intellectual, aesthetic and spiritual qualities that are rarely absent from Javanese actions, whether or not the participants are fully aware of them: the culture permeates even those practices that are copied from the West. The Javanese delight in classification for its own sake, and attribute an almost ontological significance to classes that they have arbitrarily defined. The elaborate division of prisoners into categories, partly in accordance with what was considered to be their degree of indoctrination, is an example. It would have been expedient to lump together all those in classes A and B, few of whom would be tried and almost none released; but such a simplification would offend the Javanese mind. Similarly, the slow extinction of the settlement in predictable stages would resolve the discords created by the *putsch*, and fulfil the Javanese quest for harmony – a proposition supported by a contributor to an Amnesty International report. Aesthetically it would resemble the mystical unfolding of the all-night shadow play, the *wayang kulit*, in which good battles with evil; in fact, a painting of Hanuman, the righteous white monkey of the *Rāmāyaṇa*, vanquishing the demon, Ravaṇa, hangs behind President Suharto in his office. There are few generals, however corrupt or cruel, who do not have a genuinely spiritual side; they believe – although it would be hard to say precisely in what. 'These have something in their hearts – and in their heads',

Soegih Arto said of the prisoners. The emphasis was on the heart; for while the brain might be washed, the heart, once evil had infected it, was probably beyond redemption.

General Suharto, the President, is a mystic who is known to listen to his *dukuns* before making important decisions; it is scarcely conceivable that he would have failed to consult them before approving the Buru Island settlement. One can imagine a *dukun* advising him: 'There has been great violence, but this was an exceptional event, like an earthquake or the eruption of a volcano. Now it is time to restore harmony. The evil must be put away, but humanely, in accordance with the second principle of *Pancasila*. On the island they can do no harm; and the settlement will be a warning to others.' Thus there would be no floggings or chain gangs, as in the British penal settlements in Australia. It would be more civilized than that; and sadder, for the Indonesian prisoners have been deprived of hope.

For a long time the army tried to keep up the fiction that while there was not enough evidence to convict class B prisoners, all were involved in the coup. During an interview in November 1972 I asked Suharto if he really thought that Pramoedya knew of the conspiracy. 'No', he said with a smile; but Pramoedya, he went on, was a member of Lekra, which the PKI had established as part of its plan to 'consolidate its forces and overthrow the government'. If the coup had succeeded, people like Pramoedya would have ratified it, he said. Suharto made no further comment; apparently he considered he had said enough to justify the destruction of artists and academics on Buru Island.

Most of the married men on the island are doomed to spend the rest of their lives without their families, wondering how their wives and children are faring in a world that becomes increasingly remote. The army emphasized to the women that once they landed they could never return; it pointed out that six primary schools were to be the sole source of education. Soegih Arto announced, not without satisfaction, that on thinking it over 75 per cent of the wives had decided not to join their husbands and half were seeking divorce. Men interviewed by journalists on the second visit said the island was not a fit place for their families, and they did not want them there. But in August 1972 271 wives and children arrived; they were the first of a handful that were to brave the almost total isolation of the settlement. In theory prisoners may send their closest relatives one card a month. But Mrs Pramoedya said in Jakarta that she had not heard from her husband for three years, although she had written to him every week; Pramoedya said he had only received two letters from his wife. The army confiscated all Pramoedya's assets when it arrested him; his wife sells cakes to keep herself and their eight children and is helped by friends.

Forbidding though it is, the future of men deprived forever of their wives and children is not as desperate as that of the young, who are condemned never to know a woman at all. Doubtless sex will find its outlet: Soegih Arto told a press conference in Jakarta that prisoners played female roles in drama with such success that visitors took them for girls. I asked him whether there was any prospect of some of the men marrying the eighty class B women who, it was said, were to be shipped to the island. 'The women will be too old by that time', he said cheerfully. The picture of women grown into hags, and men turned effeminate, seemed to gratify him.

By July 1972 fifty-seven of the Buru Island prisoners were officially stated to have died. But Soegih Arto said that conditions had improved, and boasted that the settlement looked so much like a holiday resort that the island's indigenous people, backward and poverty stricken, were asking if they could live there. In August 1972 the Moluccas Military Command announced that it had asked Security Headquarters for permission to sell, on behalf of the prisoners, vegetables, fish, 500 tons of rice and 5,000 tons of dried cassava, which were surplus. If the sefigures were correct the communes, for that is what they were, had developed a model economy that might well be copied by Indonesia's under-nourished majority. Later it was reported that officers were selling rice for their own profit, while the prisoners were being kept alive with cassava. The army continued to issue inexplicably contradictory figures about the number of political prisoners. In February 1972 General Sumitro, then Deputy-Commander of the security body, Kopkamtib, said the total detained for involvement in the *putsch* had been reduced to 18,570, including those on Buru Island, plus a very small number yet to be classified. Since the *putsch* 125,473 had been released, he said – with a precision that is unattainable in the haphazard state of records in remote regions. Of these still detained there were 2,494 class A, who would be tried when enough judges could be found, and 16,076 class B. Apparently about 2,500 had been demoted to class B since Soegih Arto's press conference in October 1969, while others had been either promoted to class B, originally 11,000, or arrested only recently. The figure took a leap when Adam Malik, the Foreign Minister, said on 30 June 1976 that the total held in connexion with the *putsch* was 40,000. In 1975 Amnesty International issued an estimate of 55,000 political prisoners of all kinds, based on information about prisoners scattered throughout the Republic. Indonesian sources put the total in 1976 at nearer 100,000. They said there was not a medium sized town that did not have from a few to about twenty political prisoners; Surakarta, a large town in Central Java, had 700–800. Whatever the exact number may be, there are certainly scores of thousands of men and women who are suffering greater misery than those on Buru Island; for in their small gaols and sheds they have not even the consolation of open air, the sun and the stars.

Most Indonesians are unconcerned about the prisoners. It is probable that the majority of the better educated, the only group whose views on such an issue could have the slightest effect, prefer them to remain in detention, even if only to be on the safe side. As Ruth McVey has pointed out,[2] the élite tacitly or actively encouraged the anti-Communist onslaught. This is not surprising, since bitterness intensified by fear had gripped both right and left in 1964 and 1965. While the left was convinced that the CIA was organizing a generals' coup against Sukarno, rumours spread that the Communists possessed lists of people they intended to kill in a rebellion. No lists appear to have been produced. But the fears, on both sides, were real.

A few liberal-minded journalists managed for a time to ask questions about Buru Island; and the Catholic Church issued a plea for 'just and humane treatment', pointing out that prisoners were only being held 'on indications'. A move was made to hold a university discussion of the whole question of prisoners, but Kopkamtib forbade it on the ground that it was 'improper interference in a matter of government policy'. The typical leaders who rouse the people when the left is oppressed were necessarily silent; they were either prisoners themselves or dead.

CHAPTER TWO

Sukarno's burden

The struggle for unity

The most important political prisoner taken by the junta was the founder of the nation, President Sukarno, although he remained free until after he had been deposed in March 1968. It is perhaps not too much to say that no leader in this century has been so misrepresented as Sukarno, sometimes wickedly, sometimes wantonly, and sometimes through sheer ignorance. A world familiar with his flamboyance knows little of the studious leader who read voluminously while formulating an ideology to unite the diverse people of the archipelago in a struggle for independence. There was self-righteous indignation when Indonesia walked out of the United Nations in January 1965 after Malaysia had been admitted to the Security Council; but Sukarno's statement that the UN was in any case obsolete, because the threatening issue was no longer the Cold War, where a balance was preserved, but the mounting conflict between the Third World and the imperialist powers, would hardly be as scorned today as it was when he made it. Few who have read what are said to be his errors of judgment know that he predicted, years before it broke out, that a Pacific war would lead to Indonesia's independence. His private life also needs to be seen in a more just perspective, in which his undisciplined acts would not be allowed to obscure the more creditable side of his nature. But no attempt will be made here to provide even a sketch for a new portrait, a task that must be left until private correspondence and documents yet to be unearthed have been studied.[1] The main purpose of this chapter is to support the theme of the book by representing Sukarno's policies in the light of the immense cultural burden that he shouldered. If the image of Sukarno that emerges is more favourable than those previously depicted, this is because many of his critics have misunderstood the fundamental problems that confronted him, and have consequently found fault in his unwillingness to adopt solutions that were impracticable.

Sukarno was born on 6 June 1901. His father, Raden Sukemi Sosrodihardjo, was a Javanese school teacher in the service of the Dutch. The absence of a link between Sukarno's name and his father's is explained by the fact that Javanese do not think in terms of surnames. 'Raden' indicates that Sukemi belonged to the *priyayi* class, consisting originally of aristocrats by breeding or assimilation, whose various, traditional administrative roles under the old kings were debased and exploited by the Dutch. The fact that Sukemi was obliged to live on the poor salary paid to native teachers shows that his was a withered branch of whatever family tree it belonged to. Sukarno said that his mother, who was married to Sukemi when he was working in Bali, came from a Brahman family.

When Sukarno was fifteen his father sent him to Surabaya to attend a high school (Hogere Burger School), where twenty native children were admitted with 300 Dutch. He boarded frugally at the house of a family friend, the celebrated Raden Oemar Said Tjokroaminoto, who was paid a pittance as full-time leader of Sarekat Islam, an early national party. After completing the school course he went to the Bandung Technical Institute, where he graduated in May 1926 with the degree of Engineer, the highest Dutch qualification in architecture, building construction, town planning and related subjects. By this time he had acquired perfect Dutch, which was a considerable achievement, since he had begun his education in his mother tongue, Javanese. In common with educated Dutchmen of the period he had a good knowledge of English, in which he was to write much of his private correspondence in later years, and could read and speak German and French at a moderate standard. He also spoke and wrote Malay, which was to become the language of Indonesia. On patriotic grounds Sukarno rejected attractive opportunities to join the Dutch civil service, for which he was well qualified. After a short and unremunerative period working with a partner as a consulting architect and engineer, he devoted all his time to the independence struggle, living from hand to mouth. The revolutionary passion that was to inflame Sukarno began in his adolescence, when he lived with the Tjokroaminoto family in Surabaya. A combination of conditions made it almost inevitable that a lonely, rather introverted boy with the necessary ability and character would develop into an independence fighter. At school Sukarno was occasionally humiliated and knocked about by some of the Dutch boys, while the house seethed with the ideas of reformists and revolutionaries who frequently passed through. Tjokroaminoto himself believed the best results could be achieved by co-operating with the Dutch and pressing for reforms. Sukarno, though he was to reject this view, learned much from his host; not the least was Tjokroaminoto's art of oratory, which he studied while watching him at meetings.

Conversations with his stimulating elders and observation of Indonesian poverty gave him an appetite for wider understanding. Though still a mere boy, he sat up at night reading a wide range of books, which fired his romantic spirit with an urge to lead his people to independence. He says in his autobiography:[2]

> Mentally I talked with Thomas Jefferson, with whom I feel friendly and close because he told me all about the Declaration of Independence he wrote in 1776. I discussed George Washington's problems with him. I relived Paul Revere's ride. I deliberately looked for mistakes in the life of Abraham Lincoln so I could argue the points [sic] with him . . .
> I will always feel friendly toward America. Yes, friendly. I say that publicly. I put myself down on record. I state it in print. A grounding such as mine could not leave me unfriendly to the United States of America.
> In the world of my mind, I also communed with Prime Minister Gladstone as well as Sidney and Beatrice Webb; I came face to face with Mazzini, Cavour, and Garibaldi of Italy; Austria's Otto Bauer and Adler; Karl Marx, Friedrich Engels, and Lenin, and I chatted with Jean-Jacques Rousseau, Aristide Briand and Jean Jaurès, the grandest orator in French history. I drank in these stories. I lived

their lives. I actually was Voltaire. I was the great fighter
of the French Revolution, Danton. A thousand times I,
myself, in my black room saved France singlehanded. I
became emotionally involved with these statesmen.

But the masses of the Netherlands East Indies were vastly
different from those on whose backs the great names of history
had risen to power. They were diverse in language and culture,
separated by islands and enslaved by superstition of unfathomable
psychic depth. The peasantry, consisting mostly of smallholders,
were not land hungry; they lived on plots not much more diminu-
tive than those with which they had been content when the
archipelago, including Java, was sparsely settled and there was
plenty of room to expand. Free for the most part of forced cultivation, their main grievance in Sukarno's time was Dutch taxes.
But the village was their horizon, and revolts without exception
were local.[3] They had little idea of Javanese, let alone Indonesian,
nationhood. All they wanted was to be free to pursue their
village life without undue exploitation. They produced no Wat
Tyler to rouse the countryside and lead a multitude to confront
the rulers in the capital; at one stage some of them even begged
the Dutch to drive out their rapacious princes. The leader they
awaited was no plain man of the people, but the mystical Ratu
Adil, the righteous prince, whom God would send to deliver
them from oppression.

Faith in the Ratu Adil was nourished by belief in prophecies,
which, although improvised from time to time as an expression of
princely aspiration or popular despair, were assimilated by the
people and attributed to Jayabaya, a twelfth-century king of
Kediri. The Ratu Adil, they believed, would bring them houses
built of stone and freedom from taxes. From time to time, as late
as the 1920s, mystics arose in small isolated regions, each convinced
that he was the Ratu Adil. Pathetic stories are told of these
deluded men; sometimes they and their tiny bands of followers
were mown down by Dutch bullets and slashed with swords
while wearing charms (*jimats*) that were supposed to ensure their
invulnerability. Such was the bulk of the material from which
Sukarno was to try to forge the basis of an independence movement; the proletariat, although much was made of it by some
Indonesian Communist leaders, was negligible.

Organized nationalism is generally considered, perhaps superficially, to have begun with the founding of the Budi Utomo
(noble endeavour) by medical students in 1908. Limited to Java,
it sought better educational and trading opportunities, agricultural
improvement and the propagation of humanism; but it attracted
no mass following. The Indische Partij, founded in 1912, aimed
at full independence. The Dutch easily crippled it by exiling its
strongest leaders; but its domination by Eurasians would, in any
case, have limited its popularity. About the same time another
movement sprang up; deeply rooted in the Javanese culture, it
spread with a frenzy that unnerved the Dutch far more than the
agitations of those whose ideas were imported from the West.
This was the Sarekat Islam, which developed into a cult that
was more dangerous because it became almost totally irrational.
The movement began reasonably as the Sarekat Dagang Islam
(Islamic Traders' Union), which was set up to fight Chinese
middlemen. A successful boycott of Chinese merchants in the
Solo batik market gave Islamic petty traders and their followers a
sense of power that they had never experienced before. Tens of
thousands of people of all kinds rushed to join the organization,
which, more broadly based now than at its origin, changed its
name to Sarekat Islam and adopted a four point programme:
promotion of indigenous trade, support of all who innocently
got into difficulty, development of the natives, and promotion of
Islam. These goals, which were kept modest and sober for fear of
Dutch repression, were soon lost in a welter of mass hysteria
when the mythical Ratu Adil, who was always a greater threat to
the Dutch than any mortal leader, took charge of popular imagination. In the spring of 1913 a rumour spread across Java that a
child of Mohammed had come from heaven to liberate the people.
Many thought that this deliverer must be Tjokroaminoto, and
rushed to hear him speak and touch his clothes. Oaths were sworn
and holy water was drunk at secret meetings. By 1918 the SI had
rallied nearly half a million members.[4] But when Tjokroaminoto
said three years later that the Ratu Adil would not come as a
human being, but would take the form of socialism, the movement
lost its magic and the Dutch were able to relax for a while.

By this time some branches of the SI were dominated by
Marxists of varying hue. Marxism, like other Western exports,
had been introduced into Java by Dutchmen, who formed the

45

Indische Sociaal-Democratische Vereeniging (ISDV) in May 1914. After the exiling of two important Dutch leaders and the withdrawal of a disillusioned third, proselytized Indonesians proved themselves at least as capable as their teachers. The ISDV altered its name in May 1920 to Partai Komunis di Hindia (Communist Party in the Indies), which was changed to Partai Komunis Indonesia in June 1924. A series of wrangles in the SI between Communist-led revolutionaries and Tjokroaminoto's moderates split the movement irrevocably in 1921. The Communists went on alone to wage the only real struggle against the Dutch until they were totally suppressed after immature attempts at revolution in 1926 and 1927. The Dutch, who were determined to wipe out the party's mass following, made 13,000 arrests and hanged some Indonesians for involvement in killings; 1,308, who could not be convicted under the law, were sent to a malaria-infected settlement at Boven Digul, New Guinea, where they were allowed to take their families if they wished. The party was then inert until the end of the Japanese occupation.

Although the party was as bizarre as would be expected in such an environment, some of its leaders possessed ability that matched their considerable courage. But the mass membership with whom they had to work was poor. Party organizers disappeared if they were not paid and most often stole funds entrusted to them. Adolf Baars, one of the founders of the ISDV, lamented that the native Communists demanded protection money from the peasants and were mere bandits who hoped to be kings. He wrote:[5] 'when we Western revolutionaries become involved in the movement here we are often brought to the brink of despair by this absolute lack of a sense of solidarity, which means that nearly every native who gets a few pennies belonging to the movement in his hands uses the money for his own benefit. And the universality of this is terrifying.'

This was the dismal situation that faced Sukarno in 1927 when he cast aside his scarcely used drawing boards and became a full-time independence fighter. The people, cruelly reminded that the white man was invincible, remained cowed in their villages, where they awaited the arrival of the true Ratu Adil; the remnants of their established militant leaders, almost to a man, were driven into believing that the only possibility was to co-operate with the

Dutch in the hope of winning concessions. But Sukarno, brimming with energy and optimism, was not discouraged. No sooner had the sun set on the Communist Party than he rose, with his entirely fresh concepts, like a new star. At school and at the Technical Institute he had been no merely bookish rebel; he had been active in youth clubs and study clubs, which have so often been the germs of revolutionary movements, and was already known within a limited circle as a magnetic speaker and challenging writer. His essay, *Nationalism, Islam and Marxism*, published in 1926, passionately argued the ideological common ground on which secular nationalists, Moslems and Communists could unite against the Dutch. In this work he drew on Marx, Engels, Kautsky, Radek, the Koran, Mohammed Abdu, Sun Yat-sen, Gandhi, T. L. Vaswami, Gustav Klemm, Dietrich Schafter, Ernest Renan, H. G. Wells and others. The result might have surprised some of the authors he quoted; but in the intellectual hotchpotch of the prevailing political climate, in which Islam itself was mostly mixed with Hinduism and ethnic religion, while Marxism was little more than a set of slogans, Sukarno's synthesis came as a shaft of clarity. Right from the beginning Sukarno was convinced that unless what he saw as the three main socio-political streams joined forces, independence could never be won. He found it futile to dispute the form the state should take, although he had ideas about this at an early stage; for the argument would be interminable and the Dutch would exploit the friction in order to divide and 'go on ruling.

To those brought up amid some semblance of national coherence, the need for unity to achieve so precious a goal as independence may seem so obvious that it would hardly have been a major issue. But the small Indonesian movement was split into groups that were perpetually engaged in controversy. Today's fratricidal strife in the Arab world and the destructive civil war that ravaged Angola even before independence had been secured illustrate the kind of blindness with which Sukarno was confronted. There was no physical violence, because the rivals were all too weak, but the spirit was violent to the extent that unity was almost impossible. It took a man of exceptional stature and vision to remain aloof from factions and rise above the wrangling. Sukarno was at all times a conciliator in those days; not merely, as some seem to think, because he was obsessed either with a lust for power, a longing for the traditional mirage of Javanese harmony or both, but because, like Tjokroaminoto, he knew that unity was vital in order to achieve independence. Again and again he made concessions; and, although there was a core to his own beliefs that he would not yield, he practised as well as preached his doctrine that different schools of thought must give as well as receive in the national cause.

In December 1927 Sukarno achieved a federation of the seven Indonesian parties of any account. These included his own organization, the Perserikatan Nasional Indonesia (Indonesian National Association), which he had formed on 4 July 1927, a date that expressed his avowed emotional involvement with the American Revolution. The federation's unity was in fact shallow and depended on Sukarno's insistence that discordant issues be avoided; but it helped to spread the idea of an Indonesian entity among the educated. The rousing of the masses was left largely to Sukarno's association, which aimed openly at *merdeka* (freedom) and was renamed the Partai Nasional Indonesia (Indonesian National Party – PNI) in 1928.

Sukarno had been steeped since boyhood in the myths of the *wayang*, the all-night Javanese puppet play, performed either with leather figures (*wayang kulit*), whose shadows are projected on an illuminated screen, or wooden dolls (*wayang golek*). The puppeteer (*dalang*) describes the action, speaks the dialogue, and delivers the harangues of the heroes. The plots and characters are from the Hindu epics, the *Mahābhārata* and *Rāmayāna*; but the Javanese have adapted them down the centuries to reflect their own view of the world. The main plot in the *Mahābhārata* consists of the struggle between two princely families, the Pāndavas and the Kauravas, over a kingdom that the Kauravas had usurped. It is thought that for a long time the conflict was toned down in Java, because it was inconsistent with the Javanese belief that 'all is one' and that good and evil must co-exist; since nothing could be said to be totally right or wrong, there could be no final victory of virtue. But the harmony that the Javanese sought to maintain was purely Javanese; for what they saw as the world was merely Java and all that it might embrace. It was, therefore, not precluded that a struggle would take place against any order with values alien to their own. When the Dutch intervened there was, it is true, an attempt to rationalize their presence in Javanese terms by pretending that they were vassals of the Mataram king;[6] but there was also a growing recognition that the Dutch had disrupted Javanese harmony, and that a battle must be waged to restore the traditional order, which was seen as reflecting that of the cosmos. The Javanese eventually came to identify themselves with the Pāndavas, while branding the usurpers, the Dutch, as the Kauravas; and in *wayang* performances the antagonism between the families as depicted in the *Mahābhārata* was fully restored. Spectators could exult in the triumph of the Pāndavas as if it were their own victory over the white oppressor.

For a leader as romantic as Sukarno the story of the Pāndavas and Kauravas was an ideal instrument for rousing the masses. He invoked the myth in an oracular style at the beginning of his essay, *Nationalism, Islam and Marxism*: 'Like the son of Bhīma, who was born in an age of struggle, Young Indonesia now sees the light of day, at a time when the people of Asia are dissatisfied with their lot – dissatisfied with their economic lot, dissatisfied with their political lot and dissatisfied with their lot in every other respect!' His readers required no footnote to tell them that Bhīma was one of the Pāndavas and that the son referred to was Raden Gatutkaca, a popular *wayang* hero. But mythology was only one of Sukarno's weapons. His reading of Western writers had given him a feeling for historical processes and a knowledge that today's ruling nations are tomorrow's mendicants. His charisma, his oratorical gift, his appeal to myth and his energetically argued analyses stirred alike the educated, partly educated and illiterate when he addressed meeting after meeting in Javanese towns.

The Dutch became increasingly uneasy. As early as 1927, the year after Sukarno published his essay, M.W.F. Treub, political adviser to Dutch business concerns, had written that there was 'ferment in the Indies'.[7] The 'native movement', he said, was a 'mélange of three tendencies' – nationalism, Communism and Islam, which must be separated and repressed. Before long the Dutch had had enough of Sukarno. In the early hours of 29 December 1929 they arrested him at Yogyakarta in a round-up of PNI leaders, most of whom were subsequently released. He was sentenced to four years' imprisonment at a trial in Bandung that lasted from 18 August until 22 December 1930; but his sentence was commuted and he was freed on 31 December 1931 after having spent two years of acute discomfort in a small cell.

Sukarno's trial defence speech was published in Indonesian in 1931 under the title *Indonesia Accuses*. Its vitality is such that an English edition published in 1975 was soon out of print.[8] The speech contains an analysis of imperialism, and provides keys to Sukarno's future thinking. He asserted that the PNI was a revolutionary party, but said 'we are not people who go about making revolts'. He denied that the PNI had initiated or exploited a prophecy that something unusual would happen in 1930; on the contrary, the party had gone out of its way to save the people from being provoked by such an empty belief. The PNI's task was to promote nationalism so that the people would be ready for independence when future events made it possible:[9]

> We don't know, for instance, but that the Dutch might in the last instance come to the realization that it would be better if their colonial rule were brought to an end peaceably. We don't even know, but that by then Western capitalism might already have collapsed . . . In short, for ourselves, for any human being, the future is a kind of closed book – closed to the question of *how* that final step of the Indonesian people will be taken, closed to the question of *when* that final step will take place.

This statement was no mere tactical ploy to avoid a conviction on a charge of inciting to revolt. Sukarno was, in fact, doing what he said: trying to inculcate nationalism into a people who, on the whole, had no conception of what it meant; historical circumstance would determine the moment of independence. It is important to see this clearly; for in the guided democracy period Sukarno was acting in the same way, rallying the people to Nasakom with a goal to be achieved in a manner and at a time that could not be predicted. In each period the awareness had to be created first; given the backwardness of the masses and the impossibility of educating so vast a number, revolutionary exhortation was the only feasible course.

Immediately upon his release Sukarno resumed the struggle; but the situation that had developed after his arrest showed the pathetic weakness of the independence movement. It seemed that once Sukarno was removed from the scene all faith was lost.

There was scarcely a protest at his detention. On 25 April 1931 the PNI's four remaining leaders dissolved the party on the dubious ground that the court's judgment at Sukarno's trial automatically made it illegal, although there was no official statement that this was so. They formed a new party, Partai Indonesia (Partindo); and in December 1931 a rival group began a club, as they called it, which became known as the New PNI.[10] Sukarno set about trying to repair the split in the unity that he had tried so hard to establish. His incarceration had put him in a strong moral position; for withdrawal and isolation were traditionally seen in Java as a source of renewed spiritual power. At a meeting in Surabaya at the beginning of 1932 he was hailed as if he were some holy man who had emerged from a remote cave after years of refreshing meditation. With his usual mixture of poetic feeling and political shrewdness, he likened himself to the *wayang* character, Kokrosono, whose joy at winning the magic weapon, *nanggala*, during a period of reclusion was dampened by the plight of his two children. Sukarno was acclaimed when, referring to the split, he declared: 'Brothers, be sure that as long as Bung [brother, comrade] Karno has life within him, for as long as he feels power in himself, he will stake all his energy on reuniting the two wings with their body.' When he ended his speech all stood while he led in the singing of 'Indonesia Raya', which is now the national anthem. But the emotions he aroused that day and the following day and the efforts that he made afterwards were insufficient to mend the breach; and in April 1933 he became Chairman of Partindo, while still emphàsizing the need for a single, unified independence movement. The Dutch kept a good watch on him; after rearresting him in Batavia on 1 August 1933 they exiled him early in 1934 to the island of Flores, Eastern Indonesia, this time without a trial. He lived there with his wife, Inggit, until he was transferred to a house in Bengkulu, West Sumatra, early in 1938. His exile continued until soon after the Japanese landed in the Indies in January 1942.

The two men most conspicuous in splitting the movement were Mohammad Hatta and Sutan Sjahrir. About the end of 1931, at the age of twenty-two, Sjahrir returned from Leiden, where he read law, to become Chairman of the New PNI;[11] Hatta, who had read economics at Rotterdam, took over the chairmanship when he followed Sjahrir from Holland in August 1932. Both engaged in polemics against Sukarno, whose attempt to awaken the masses by emotional rather than rational means offended the sense of intellectual discipline they had acquired in Holland. Neither had the capacity to make contact with the masses; nor, being Sumatrans, could they understand that Javanese mysticism made their policies impracticable. But because of their Western way of thinking, they have been falsely represented in the West as sensible men battling against the half-baked ideas of a demagogue who was intellectually their inferior; many Asians have no such illusions. Hatta and Sjahrir both emphasized the need for efficient organization rather than what they believed to be Sukarno's mere rabble-rousing; Sukarno, on the other hand, felt that the Javanese people had to be inspired with the ideas of nationhood before they could be organized. Hatta said that little could be achieved until the masses were educated in a suitable programme; but Sukarno saw that peasants waiting for the Ratu Adil would be as numerous at Hatta's classes as Londoners at a Fabian Society meeting on a hot evening.

Sjahrir was a tortured person, one of the casualties of so-called acculturation, whose education in Leiden made it difficult to reconcile himself with his own people. He said he 'felt at home' in Holland, and seemed bent on proving to himself and others that he had an intellect that compared with those in the West; indeed, his analyses of tactical requirements in Indonesia, with their apt quotations from Western writers, were probably as good as could have been written by anyone in his radical school. But they were largely irrelevant, because they took no practical account of the crippling superstition of the Javanese, by far the largest ethnic group, without whom independence could never be achieved. It would have been astonishing if Sjahrir, a Minangkabau looking at Java through European spectacles, had been able to see the road to independence with Sukarno's clarity. Ridiculing Sukarno's widely loved evocation of the image of *Ibu* (Mother) Indonesia, with its beautiful landscape and fertile soil, he said: 'Mother Indonesia as a mystical experience is outside the realm of practical politics.' This gibe might have won an approving smile among dons; but it disqualified him as a leader of the Javanese, who, in addition to being mystical, were well described by Sukarno as an *artiestenvolk*. Sukarno did not appeal to the people's emotions simply because he was himself emotional but, above all, for practical reasons. 'I know the job', he was to say in earthy English at a later stage, when he was President. It was the same during the independence struggle: he knew what had to be done and that his talents suited him for the task.

Sukarno approached Sjahrir and his associates with tact, carefully avoiding dispute, and pleading with them to join forces with him against the Dutch; but they never went to him. That he should have made all the advances was a measure of his stature; their failure to respond was a measure of theirs. In spite of their zeal for organization, Hatta and Sjahrir 'were content with a mere thousand members or so' in the New PNI;[12] on the other hand within less than a year after Sukarno had become Chairman of Partindo, the party's membership nearly trebled, with branches increasing from about two dozen to seventy-one and members from about 7,000 to 20,000.[13] When the Japanese arrived, after Sukarno had been out of the picture for more than eight years of exile, they found that he was the man to whom the people looked as leader. A Japanese inquiry into public feeling at the beginning of 1943 found:[14] 'His name is on the lips of all, whether they know him or not; Indonesians of all groups are concerned about him ... They speak of rumours such as that "Sukarno will be king of the archipelago" and that "the Japanese will appoint him Governor-General". But they have not the faintest notion of politics.' Hatta and Sjahrir's club might have educated a few people along more elevated lines; but it was Sukarno who created the only wave on which Indonesia was capable of rising to independence.

The yellow men

The Japanese bombing of Pearl Harbor on 7 December 1941 was joyfully welcomed in Java. For years faith had been growing in a prophecy that little yellow men from the north would free the land from the white man. The prophecy, although attributed to Jayabaya, appears to have originated in the first quarter of this century, when it replaced an earlier one that a delivering force would arrive from India; it evolved and took various forms. Possibly the Japanese initiated it themselves; for when they launched the Pacific War they were quick to exploit it. They told the Javanese in leaflets dropped from the air:

53

We announce to you the arrival of the Japanese army. The Japanese army will land in Indonesia in order to fulfill the prophecy of His Majesty Jayabaya . . . Remember: His Majesty Jayabaya said yellow men from the north would come to liberate the Indonesian people from the slavery of the Dutch. Look for the yellow skins.

The Dutch retaliated in broadcasts from America by quoting a version which predicted that the yellow men would depart after 'a year of corn'. Neither the Japanese nor the Dutch mentioned that Jayabaya had also prophesied that after the yellow interregnum the Javanese would rule themselves, free of all foreign oppression. But it was this prospect that excited the Javanese most; and many saw Sukarno, now freed from a further period of reclusion, as the Ratu Adil who was to bring it about.

While Sukarno recognized the value of his charisma, he had never made use of the Ratu Adil and Jayabaya myths, with their danger of provoking uncontrollable, suicidal escapades. Nor did he need Jayabaya to foretell the arrival of the yellow men. His observation of events brewing in the Pacific had long convinced him that Indonesia's deliverance would be the outcome of a clash between Japan and the West; as astonishingly early as 1928 he predicted the Pacific War of 1941. In a passage that typifies his blend of Javanese poetic declamation and the historical insight derived from his Western studies, he wrote:[15]

The time will shortly call upon us to become the witnesses of a great struggle in the Pacific, among the imperialist giants, America, Japan, and England, who will engage in a struggle for plunder and domination; time may soon hurl us into the midst of the typhoon that will overwhelm the Pacific. The first rumblings of the thunder can already be heard. Like a lion that has unsheathed its claws, ready to destroy Japan at whatever moment it may choose, like the demon Dasamuka, who has opened wide his many mouths, ready to devour his enemy, so America has encircled Japan with heavy and powerful naval bases, in Dutch Harbor, Hawaii, Tutuila, Guam, and Manila. And likewise Japan is adding to its arsenal, while England builds a naval fortress at Singapore.

When the Japanese arrived Sukarno had no hesitation in supporting them, while making it clear that ultimate independence was his aim. While he disliked Fascism and knew the aspirations of Japanese imperialism, it was of no concern to him that he might be contributing to the overthrow of Western democracy; the main enemies were the imperialist powers, who had been squatting in Asia for centuries. In his 1926 essay he had rejected the argument that Asia's Western rulers were 'guardians' who would 'one day relinquish their "guardianship" '. The 'prime cause' of colonialism was 'the search for gain'; he did not believe that the 'elder brothers' would leave when the colonies had 'come of age'. Notwithstanding the vices of the Berlin-Tokyo Axis, Sukarno saw no greater political and social evil than the endless suppression and exploitation of his own people; he felt that nothing was to be lost by co-operating with the Japanese and that in the turmoil of the war he could use his political skill to Indonesia's advantage. As it turned out, he was right. What would have happened if the Axis had won the war is unknown; but it is certain that the Indonesian people would have fared no worse economically, not because the Japanese would have been more generous than the Dutch, but for fundamental reasons that are discussed in later chapters.

Sukarno was first approached by the Japanese in Padang, West Sumatra; the Dutch had taken him there, but left him when they fled. After a stormy trip to Jakarta lasting four days and nights in an eight-metre motor-boat, he met Hatta, Sjahrir and other leaders to discuss tactics. According to his biography, he told Hatta: 'The Japanese will not stay here long. They will lose the war and we will destroy them.' The Japanese, he said, were cruel; but it was necessary to appear to collaborate with them.

In fact, the collaboration was more than a mere appearance, and Sukarno's services to the Japanese strained the loyalty of some of his Indonesian supporters. His most loathed act was the help he gave to the conscription of labourers for Japanese construction and maintenance work in Indonesia and other parts of South East Asia; according to one estimate only about 70,000 of more than a quarter of a million *romushas*, as they were called, ever returned to Indonesia. It may be said in Sukarno's defence that the Japanese would have conscripted workers whether he, Hatta, and other nationalists had supported them or not. If moral judgment is to

55

be passed his motive should be taken into account. Was he seeking self-aggrandizement, or was his sole aim to achieve Indonesian independence? The answer to this question appears to be in his favour. Lieutenant-General Imamura, the first Japanese Commander-in-Chief in Java, said:[16] 'I gained the impression that he was a man of iron resolve. All his thinking was centred on independence, and his passion for it would never desert him.' And Dahm, who is at times critical of Sukarno, finds:[17]

> Never, during the period under consideration here, did Sukarno attempt to misuse this [the people's] trust for the increase of personal power . . . His constant exertions for unity in the movement were, for example, in striking contrast with the actions of Hitler, who in and after Landsberg wilfully sowed disunity in the party in order to strengthen his own position . . . Sukarno was never intentionally ruthless but always conceived of himself as a spokesman of the people. It is interesting to note a remark in the spring of 1943 by a high-level Japanese employee flatly denying that Sukarno had the qualities of a 'great leader' because he had never once kept a dossier on the sins of his co-workers, and permitted subordinates to associate with him without any particular show of respect.

During his early negotiations with the Japanese Sukarno toured Java, where the joy with which the people greeted him impressed upon the military command that if they wanted a relatively easy time he was the man they must deal with. The essence of his tactics was to take the Japanese at their word when they publicly proclaimed themselves as liberators, and to manoeuvre them into positions that obliged them to make concessions; he made it clear that Indonesians could not be expected to support Nippon whole-heartedly unless they felt they were working for their own freedom. In official talks with Sukarno the Japanese military government could obviously not commit Tokyo to granting independence after the war, and a good deal of political double-talk ensued. But Sukarno's arguments were so convincing that the Japanese allowed him to organize rallies, ostensibly in the Greater East Asia cause, at which he cleverly chose words that united factions and raised national feeling to a pitch never before attained. Speech after speech implied that the

Indonesians looked upon the Japanese as the guarantors of their coming freedom. The Japanese were trapped by their own propaganda. If they had stopped Sukarno, the hollowness of their claim to be liberators of Asia would have been exposed, and they would have had a large, rebellious population on their hands without adequate forces to control it; by allowing him to continue his harangues, they risked being faced with a powerful independence movement in the event of their victory. To appease the nationalist and Moslem élite the Japanese initiated the appointment of Indonesians to civilian posts that they could never have acquired under the Dutch. Sukarno's tactics obliged them to go farther in that direction; by this means the Indonesians gained civil service experience that prepared them to govern when the chance came.

The Allied counter-offensive gave the Indonesians a further opportunity. In the autumn of 1943 Gatot Mangkupradja, one of three who had been tried with Sukarno in 1930, successfully proposed that the Japanese train an Indonesian defence force. Sukarno declaimed that the Indonesians were 'pouring out . . . blood in the war for Greater East Asia'. At the same time he made it clear that their ultimate aim was not the glorification of the Rising Sun, but the independence of Indonesia, when he added: 'Every enemy who later attempts to infringe on the position of the people will be liquidated, if only the entire Indonesian people are filled with the military spirit and the spirit of heroism.' This was typical of his tactics throughout the period. The defence force was later deployed, first against the Japanese, then against the Dutch; it was a major factor in the winning of independence. With Suharto and Nasution among its leading officers, it formed the foundation of the Indonesian Army.

In November 1943 Sukarno, Hatta and Ki Bagus Hadikusumo, a Moslem leader, were received and decorated by Hirohito. Sukarno, according to Japanese sources, tried in vain to wring a promise of independence from the Prime Minister, Tojo. Despite his disappointment, Sukarno, who was on his first visit abroad, was immensely impressed by the array of both religious shrines and efficient armament factories and found a 'holy spirit, inhabited by a will of steel'. He was obviously delighted to see Western technology achieved by a nation that had not lost its Asian values; and while he knew of the Japanese streak of cold-blooded cruelty, he saw also a pronounced national idealism. He noted what he called the 'activity' and 'self-discipline', which, he must have seen, made such a contrast with the relative lethargy and blind emotionalism of the people he led. But superior to the Japanese though the Japanese were in all effective respects, Sukarno did not lose his resolve that Indonesia's relations with Japan, as with all nations, should be one of equality and mutual respect; while he sought a partnership with Japan, the condition was always that Indonesia must never be a subject. In what Dahm describes as a 'truly heroic period' Sukarno doggedly wheedled concessions from the Japanese that led to the formation in August 1944 of a mass organization, Barisan Pelopor (Pioneer Corps), which gave the Indonesian leaders uncontrolled contact with all classes in both town and country.[18] For the Japanese the organization was a means of winning further co-operation in their attempt to stave off defeat; but Sukarno, while still attacking Western imperialism as the main enemy, used it to help prepare the people for whatever independence struggle the fortunes of war might necessitate.

On 7 September 1944 Sukarno received the news he had fought for. The Japanese military command called him from a labour camp where he was working as a volunteer and read a firm announcement by the government in Tokyo that Indonesia was to be granted independence in the future. This unexpected decision was too much for him. At first he was speechless. For years the Japanese had not only refused to commit themselves to independence; they had denied Indonesia's existence and had even spoken officially of the 'natives of Java'; Tojo had refused Sukarno's request that Indonesians should fly their flag and sing the national anthem. Now Japan not only recognized the whole of the Dutch East Indies as a nation in its own right, but guaranteed its independence; the red and white flag could be flown and the anthem sung at last. The next day, when Indonesian leaders called to thank the Commander-in-Chief at a ceremony, Sukarno broke down. Dahm records:[19]

> He stood there sobbing helplessly, the man who was hated by the Dutch and feared by the Japanese because with an unerring instinct he had noted their weaknesses . . . and despite all his 'egregious errors' had again and again proved right in the end. As one who fought passionately, he likewise reacted with emotion.

An Indonesian declaration sponsored by Sukarno emphasized that the people were laying the foundation of an Indonesian state, while being engaged in a 'life-and-death struggle together with Dai Nippon'. Nobody will ever know to what extent Sukarno meant this and similar declarations of fraternity and loyalty; he had a complex, Asian mind, and was capable of experiencing simultaneously thoughts and feelings that a Westerner would find conflicting. It could not have escaped him that the Japanese had become more generous only because the war had turned against them, and he might have suspected that an Allied victory would nullify his rhetorical pledges. He might even have felt that, with nationalism at last roused and armed, the greatest hope of freedom lay in Japan's defeat; for it must have occurred to him that a political change in Tokyo could lead to a harder policy and that, in the end, a victorious Europe could be less ruthless than a Rising Sun intoxicated with power. At the same time his preference for the Japanese culture could have made him hope that Japan would be both triumphant and honourable; there was obviously more than simulation in the vehemence with which he declared that Indonesians would fight alongside the Japanese if the Allies landed on their soil. In any event his scorn of Western individualism and materialism and his admiration of what he saw as traditional Eastern social co-operation and spirituality could have fired him to make such pronouncements without cynicism in the heat of the time.

Sukarno's joy at Japan's promise of independence was soon dampened by the slowness of the army in carrying it out. The military commanders not only delayed Tokyo's proposals to prepare the people for self-government; they tried without success to foment rivalry between the Moslems and secular nationalists by allowing the Islamic organization, Masjumi, which they had sponsored a year previously, to build up its own military force. Sukarno then began to speak more and more openly. In a speech he made it clear, without directly saying so, that the reason for the reluctance to free Indonesia was that it was 'the greatest booty of Asia, as the Americans once called it'. In this context he urged Indonesians to prepare to fight with anything they could lay their hands on, 'though it be spears or sharpened bamboo'; he said pointedly that independence was not a 'piece of paper' but depended on 'survival of the fittest'. The

Japanese eventually allowed what amounted to a constitutional congress which began on 28 May 1945. They hoped that it would become bogged down with interminable arguments; but in July Sukarno surprised them by rallying all factions, except four Chinese, when after meeting strong Moslem opposition he tearfully begged for agreement at such a critical hour. The Moslems, who had adamantly insisted on an Islamic state, accepted a compromise, known as the Jakarta Charter, which provided that Islamic law was only binding on those professing the faith. The constitution born at that congress, with minor amendments, is the one nominally in force today; its main ideas were those developed by Sukarno when a young man. It provides for a system of government that is predominantly presidential.

Although the Indonesians now had a constitution, they still lacked independence. Sukarno, while pressing the Japanese, was himself under pressure from Indonesians whose impatience for nationhood outran their common sense. He could already foresee a successful conclusion to the game he was playing more and more overtly against the Japanese; his main problem was to hold down the nationalist fervour, which, while cleverly arousing it, he had been careful not to unleash prematurely. Unnecessary and probably abortive rebellion would have dissipated energies that would be needed to fight the Dutch, who were already preparing a return from bases in New Guinea; and if nationalist feeling had been allowed to degenerate into chaotic bursts of immature, revolutionary frenzy, large-scale Allied intervention would have been almost certain. Sukarno's aim was clearly to show that Indonesia was a legitimate nation led by responsible men. Nevertheless he found it tactically correct to declare publicly that he was 'impatient'. On 7 August the Japanese set up a Committee for the Preparation of Independence. Sukarno, with perfect timing, then showed that he had finished with them by declaring that Jayabaya's 'year of corn' was over, thus implying that the Japanese could now be expected to return home. But his careful tactics were condemned by his opponents, who wanted to establish the new nation in outright defiance of the Japanese. Sjahrir tried to persuade Hatta to declare independence, but Hatta declined on the ground that only a declaration by Sukarno would win the trust of the people. According to a statement that Sukarno made later, he had accepted 24 August as Independence Day when he and Hatta conferred with the Japanese near Saigon earlier in the month. But after their surrender on 15 August the Japanese were under Allied orders to maintain the status quo. In the early hours of 16 August youths, including Adam Malik, the future Foreign Minister, who had been threatening to launch their own revolution, embarked on an escapade that remains a blot on the first page of the republic's history: they kidnapped Sukarno and Hatta to force their hand. Sukarno ridiculed his captors, who released him on the evening of the same day. But although he denied it in his autobiography, the kidnapping seems to have increased the pace against his will; for that night, at a hastily arranged meeting in the house of a sympathetic and influential Japanese naval officer, Admiral Maeda, he, Hatta and others drew up a proclamation. It took hours of wrangling until 7 a.m. to prepare this brief document, which read: 'We, the people of Indonesia, hereby declare Indonesia's independence. Matters concerning the transfer of power and so forth will be executed in an orderly manner and in the shortest possible time.' Some of the Indonesians wanted more defiance in the proclamation; but Sukarno did not want to risk provoking the Japanese, who, although they were obliged under the surrender terms to maintain the status quo, had given an informal assurance that they would not obstruct a declaration of independence provided they were not identified with it and that it did not cause disorder.

After a short sleep Sukarno read the proclamation to a small gathering outside his house at 10 a.m. on 17 August. The Indonesian flag was run up and the anthem sung. What might have been a jubilant, ceremonial rally had it been properly prepared could have seemed to a passer-by to be no more than some ill-attended revivalist meeting. Sukarno appears to have shown none of the emotion that might have been expected from him. He was exhausted by this time; and perhaps he was a little saddened that the nation's birth could have been precipitated by so grotesque an event as the kidnapping of its founder by his own compatriots. But that afternoon joy began to sweep the country when youths commandeered a Japanese radio transmitter to which they had access and broadcast the news. Spontaneous revolts broke out in the big towns of Java, and popular organizations took over administrative buildings, not without casualties in their own ranks.

At war with the Dutch

The day after the proclamation the Preparatory Committee elected Sukarno President of the Republic of Indonesia with unlimited powers for six months and Hatta Vice-President; but the Republic had to suffer four years of bloody struggle before the Dutch conceded independence. The first big battle was with British troops, who began landing in Java in September.[20] Fighting broke out in Surabaya late in October, after the 49 Indian Infantry Brigade had been sent there to evacuate prisoners of war. There were elements of bungle in the British operation. When he ordered a force to go to Java, Vice-Admiral Lord Mountbatten, Supreme Commander South East Asia, had no information that a revolution was under way. Confused by what they found, the British dropped leaflets in Surabaya from a plane on 27 October, ordering Indonesian guerrillas to surrender their arms. This convinced the Indonesians that the British were softening them up for the Dutch. The next day well-organized guerrillas launched attacks on British positions and individuals. British headquarters in Jakarta detained Sukarno and obtained his agreement to stop the fighting. According to a British report (the origin of which I cannot disclose), Sukarno at once flew to Surabaya and went into the battle with a national flag 'at great personal risk', saving both the Brigade and the Allied prisoners of war. The fighting stopped, but the British made the mistake of assuming that Sukarno could control every angry band that sprang up in and around the town. In a confused situation the 49 Brigade Commander, Brigadier A. W. S. Mallaby, was shot dead. The British then resolved to capture the town, supporting their soldiers with murderous air attacks and naval shelling. The ill-armed civilians of Surabaya, led by the legendary Bung Tomo, put up a strong and courageous resistance, which independent observers still remember with admiration. The British, despite their superior weapons and forces, including crack Punjabi troops, took three weeks to subdue them. Subsequently the British facilitated the return of the Dutch.[21]

It has been said that the resistance at Surabaya convinced the British that the Indonesians were a people to be reckoned with; doubtless they were no less impressed by Sukarno's responsible handling of the affair. But the Dutch government saw nothing except its interests in the Indies, which it strove to maintain with a curious mixture of paternalism, double-dealing and brutality; the Indonesians claimed that in Celebes alone the notorious Dutch officer, 'Turk' Westerling, massacred thousands of people, including women and children. Failure of negotiations led to two military operations against the Republic, which the Dutch euphemistically named 'police actions'. The first began in July 1947 and ended when the United Nations Security Council called for a ceasefire at the request of Australia and India. A conference sponsored by the Council on board the US naval transport, *Renville*, in Batavia confirmed on 19 January 1948 the basis of an agreement that had been made at Linggajati, near Cirebon, in November 1946. This provided for a United States of Indonesia, including the Republic, which was considered to consist of territory then remaining under its control, and separate puppet and semi-puppet states set up by the Dutch, who by this time had occupied not only the smaller islands but parts of Java and Sumatra.

During further discussion on interpretation of the agreement the Dutch held bogus plebiscites, without the stipulated UN supervision, to determine whether the small states would merge with the Republic or remain autonomous within the federation. The collapse of the talks led to the second 'police action', a bloody affair, which was aimed at crushing the Republic altogether. It began on 19 December 1948, when the Dutch launched a surprise bomb and paratroop attack on Yogyakarta, to which the republican government had moved from Batavia to escape NICA (Netherlands Indies Civil Administration) troops in January 1946; the Dutch quickly arrested Sukarno, Hatta, Sjahrir and half of the Indonesian cabinet. Strong pressure by the United States, which threatened economic measures against the Netherlands, led to the freeing of the prisoners and to a settlement reached at the Round Table Conference, which began at The Hague on 23 August 1949. Sovereignty was transferred unconditionally on 27 December to the United States of Indonesia, consisting of the Republic and the fifteen Dutch-sponsored States. The Indonesians continued to regard the States as a network of Dutch enclaves. All were rapidly absorbed into the Republic, with the spilling of blood here and there; and on 15 August 1950 a constitutional amendment replaced the United States of Indonesia with the

Republic of Indonesia. The only territory left in abeyance was the Dutch slice of New Guinea, the fate of which was to be negotiated within a year. As the price of sovereignty the Indonesians were saddled with the Netherlands Indies public debt, much of which had been incurred in the war against themselves, but Indonesia repudiated what was left of it in 1956. It has been written that British and American sympathy with the Republic showed that Sukarno was wrong when he warned during the war that Allied imperialism was a menace to be feared.[22] But in principle he was right; for the 'search for gain', which, he said, was the motive of colonialism, persisted with undiminished virulence in neo-colonialism, which he was to name Nekolim, a force that contributed to his overthrow in the sixties.

The parliamentary interregnum

It is often implied in newspaper articles that Sukarno governed Indonesia from 1945 until just after the *putsch* of 1 October 1965. In fact, the Indonesian political élite, whose rule he had made possible, abandoned his presidential constitution and whittled down his powers within a few weeks of the independence proclamation; by 1949 he had been reduced to a mere figurehead.[23] It was not until anarchy threatened in April 1957 that he took the lead again by appointing a cabinet of his own choice after the previous government had resigned in the face of regional rebellion. His authority was not assured until 5 July 1959, when in partnership with the army he decreed the restoration of the 1945 constitution; even then it was qualified by the army's abuse of martial law. His power thus lasted only a few years, during which he had to reconcile ethnic, military and other elements that threatened to tear Indonesia apart. Yet in the West he is accused of having ruined, in this brief period, a nation which, in fact, he just managed to save from crumbling.

The leading figures in the rapid moves that brought about Sukarno's eclipse at that time were Sjahrir and Hatta, the two who had done most to split the independence movement when he was in prison. Both rejected Sukarno's presidential system and wanted an immediate start in preparing for parliamentary democracy; they were strongly supported by the largely *priyayi* élite, many of whom were probably anxious to develop the limited authority they had enjoyed under the Japanese. In dubious circumstances Hatta, who was Vice-President, issued a decree after a meeting on 16 October 1945 that the KNIP (Komite Nasional Indonesia Pusat – Central Indonesian National Committee), which was merely to have helped the President, should have legislative powers. Sjahrir was quickly made Chairman of a KNIP Working Committee. With Sukarno absent from Jakarta, further tactical manoeuvres led to Sjahrir's declaration on 11 November that ministers would be responsible to parliament, which was yet to be formed. Three days later Sjahrir, assuming the title of Prime Minister, announced the formation of his own cabinet. Sukarno, who for twenty years had fought the Dutch and held out against the Japanese, was thus brought down in less than four weeks by the intrigues of his own countrymen. When he returned to Jakarta he endorsed the *fait accompli*.

There have been various attempts to explain why Sukarno accepted his defeat so resignedly, and some writers have gone so far as to attribute motives and even feelings to him without evidence. A probable reason was that he had no choice. He commanded little unqualified support among the élite, who were in a position to engineer the decisions. His support among the people was overwhelming, as Sjahrir recognized, but any attempt to rally them would have split the nation at a critical time while exposing him to the risk of arrest by the Allies. He recalls in his autobiography that Sir Philip Christison, British Commander in Java, declared that the government would be fascist if Sukarno were head of state, Prime Minister and Commander-in-Chief of the Army; and he doubtless noted that while the Dutch refused to deal with him at all, they were prepared to talk with Sjahrir. Nevertheless, the abandonment of an idea that he had nurtured since early manhood was probably a great disappointment to him. His belief that in Indonesia the chief of state should be like a father, taking decisions on behalf of the family when they could not agree among themselves, was rooted in the culture and had nothing to do with Fascism. He scorned the Western parliamentary system as '50 per cent plus one democracy', and preferred the traditional village *musyawarah* and *mufakat* (consultation and consensus), in which ideas are pooled and synthesized, rather than mutilated in the cut and thrust of partisan debate.

Long before independence Sukarno asserted that political and economic ideas imported from the West were inapplicable in Indonesia. In an article entitled 'Political and Economic Democracy', published in 1932, he echoed Communists when he declared that political rights would not ensure economic justice for the masses; on the other hand, he implied in other writings that Indonesia, because of its rural conditions and the smallness of its proletariat, lacked the ingredients of a significant class struggle. With poetic and social insight he developed the idea of Marhaenism, based, he said, on an encounter he had when he was twenty with a Sundanese peasant named Marhaen. Like most Indonesians, Marhaen was neither a proletarian nor a landless farm worker dependent largely on labouring for others; he was a tax-ridden subsistence farmer. He and his kind were the 'end products of the [former] feudal system'.[24] Sukarno saw the *sate* pedlars and other petty traders in the same light. 'Our tens of millions of impoverished souls work for no person and no person works for them. There is no exploitation of one man by another.'

Although Sukarno had spoken of the class struggle as early as 1921 and remained under Marx's influence in varying degrees until the end, his social thinking was dominated by his conception of Marhaen. Doubtless he thought that once the main exploiters, the Dutch, were ousted, the Marhaens would be uplifted by their own creative energies. But, as in many other former colonies, independence exposed cultural factors that were even more of an obstacle to change than the new forms of colonialism. If Sukarno's concept of Marhaenism seemed vague, this was because he knew that Indonesian society was too complex, too different, to fit the politico-economic formulae developed in the West. He required no Western academics to tell him that his thinking was not tidy by their criteria. Writing of Marhaenism in his autobiography, he said:

These concepts which I put forward in the '20's and from which I have never deviated don't fall neatly into a box according to the Western mind but, then, you must remember I do not have a Western mind. Altering our people so that they fall into neat, orderly Western pigeon holes can't be done. Leaders who have tried failed. I always think in terms of the Indonesian [by which he meant 'Javanese'] mentality.

While Sukarno said he had an Asian mind, this does not mean that he was unfamiliar with the routines of Western thought. He was psychologically a Javanese, but his wide reading enabled him to adopt a Western reference frame when he felt it appropriate. One of the mistakes made by Western scholars is to assume that his thinking was solely or largely the outcome of his Javanese origin. Sukarno was not the unconscious instrument of a culture. There is abundant evidence that he knew the Western intellectual drill better than most Western politicians do, and understood its arbitrariness better than many academics; his views on what had to be done, and his mystical way of expressing them at certain times, arose not so much from his being Javanese as from his judgment of what he felt was suitable for the Javanese. A Javanese leader who had been brought up in the West from birth might well have adopted the same policies if he had understood the people as well as Sukarno did.

J. W. M. Martinot, who was Editor-in-Chief of the Dutch-managed Aneta News Agency in Indonesia from 1947 until 1955 and correspondent of Agence France-Presse from late in 1955 until the end of 1958 has made a useful comment (to the author). Martinot knew Sukarno well; he estimates that he travelled with him on more than 100 days, during which he usually had meals with him two or three times a day. He says:

> It is wrong to conclude from Sukarno's speeches that his
> reasoning was purely Javanese. In private he discussed and
> analysed Indonesia's problems in a Western fashion. He had a
> Western sense of humour – a sure indication that his mind
> was not simply Eastern. Sometimes he made jokes about his
> speeches and himself. This does not mean he was insincere;
> he deliberately used Javanese ways of thinking and
> speaking – in public – to win the hearts of the people for
> purposes that he believed in. Of course, Javanese legends and
> symbols appealed to his poetic side. But I think he saw
> them for what they were. His way of speaking to us at
> meals was that of a sophisticated Westerner. His style at
> breakfast was very different from that of his oratory the
> night before.

Sukarno admired Western efficiency and sometimes despaired of Indonesian haphazardness. On one occasion, when Indonesian photographers failed to arrive on time to travel with him by plane, he said bitterly to Martinot: 'I have worked all my life trying to make Indonesians of them; but they [people like the photographers] are still natives.' Dahm quotes him as expressing doubts about the ability of the Indonesian people:[25] 'Where then are our great Buddha statues, our *Mahābhāratas*, our Homers, our Dantes, our cathedrals, our temple of Peking? We can do nothing but copy, we are not capable of originals, not capable yet.' Both of these remarks show that Sukarno not only saw the culture from the outside, but that he sometimes did so with dismay. Western writers who extract labels from Javanese culture and triumphantly pin them to Sukarno need to be wary. Statements from his speeches, such as 'I am Nasakom', may indicate an uninhibited touch of paranoia rather than an identification with Javanese concepts of psychic and occult power; I knew a young poet who called himself 'the spirit of the working class' – and he was not Javanese.

Western sneers at Sukarno's thinking are mostly a legacy of ignorance; virtually nothing was known of the evolution of his thought until Dahm published the results of 'several years research in the Netherlands' in 1966, in German, and 1969, in English.[26] So vicious was the climate of neo-colonialism at the time that Dahm's invaluable scholarship was condemned as an attempt to 'whitewash Sukarno'.[27] No such attacks on Dahm are made today, but views that were possible before the facts of Sukarno's career were better known still linger in certain works. Dahm's own, indulgent smiles as Sukarno are of a different order, and may be regarded as a pedantic aberration. He dismissed Sukarno's thinking, for instance, by invoking Aristotle's ruling that 'synthesis is the source of all error'.[28] Nobody seriously interested in philosophy would bother to raise such an objection in such a context; the test of Sukarno's attempt to unite three Indonesian revolutionary streams was simply whether it worked. Dahm says that in espousing historical materialism Sukarno was merely switching from Jayabaya to Marx. This kind of joke is legitimate when made at the expense of Western thinkers, for whom the dialectic has replaced God. But applied to Sukarno it is below the belt; for it falsely implies that Sukarno was an ignorant Javanese whose adoption of historical materialism was less rational than that of its Western exponents. Sukarno wrote in his 1926 essay:[29]

Moslems must not forget that the Marxist materialist view
of history has often served to guide them in confronting the
difficult and complicated economic and political problems of
the world. They must also not forget that the Historical-
Materialist method for explaining events which have
already occurred here on this earth is also a method for
predicting events that are to come – and thus may be very
useful to their group.

Made by a young man who was trying to weld an independence
movement, this was a sensible statement; the use of historical
materialism as a handy, methodological tool should trouble no
philosopher since Wittgenstein. Sukarno's synthesis should be
seen in relation to the general background of syncretism, in which
it was possible for the revolutionary journal *Utusan Hindia* (*Indies
Messenger*) to publish in 1921 what Dahm describes as a Hinduized
Communist Manifesto:[30] 'Socialism, communism, incarnations of
Vishnu Murti, awaken everywhere! Abolish capitalism, propped
up by the imperialism that is its slave! God grant Islam the
strength that it may succeed.' Agus Salim, a *haji* and conservative
member of the Sarekat Islam, found himself able to say that
everything stated by Marx, including dialectical materialism, was
in the Koran.[31] On a more practical plane, Salim and Semaun,
the Communist leader, drew up a joint programme that was
adopted by the SI in March 1921. Tjokroaminoto and Salim said
that the programme, which unreservedly condemned capitalism,
was based on the Koran. A good deal of attention has been paid
to the subsequent split between the Moslems and the Communists. More significant is that their close co-operation was
ideologically possible in the first place. Sukarno's synthesis was,
in fact, ready made. Nothing illustrates more clearly his statement
that he was merely the 'mouthpiece of the people'.

Despite their rejection of his leadership, the parliamentarians,
who had elected themselves, frequently called on Sukarno to keep
dissident movements under control. The help he gave is described
by Feith as 'enormous'.[32] His outstanding rescue operation was
in 1948, when pro-Communist troops launched an uprising at
Madiun on 18 September, while the Republic was still struggling
with the Dutch. The Communists later claimed they were
provoked in this characteristically bizarre affair, but the revolt

was certainly the outcome of their attempt to rally the people
against the government on the ground that it was capitulating to
the Netherlands. Colonel (later General) Nasution put down the
armed rebels within several weeks, while Sukarno pacified the
people by once again appealing for unity and promising 'independence for Indonesia and freedom from all oppression'.

 The parliamentary interregnum was a catastrophic example of
attempts to plant Western political and economic roots in unsuitable ground. Most members of the eight cabinets that ruled
from the beginning of independence until guided democracy
were products of a mestizo culture. While their Eastern psychology
clouded their Western ideas, the education they had received
from the Dutch divorced them from the people. Politics was little
more than a game, imported with other luxuries from the West
and only played by a few hundred men. Numerous minute
parties sprang up, representing a motley of often overlapping
Western political and Eastern religious hues. But in a land of
Marhaens none could be related to any class that would provide
a social basis for action in the imitation Western political system.
In place of the class struggle that has occurred intermittently in
more developed societies, there was only the incessant wrangling
of economically classless cliques. While arguments raged over
foreign and domestic policy, the constant theme in the shifting
alliances and coalitions was the battle for sources of patronage,
by means of which a comfortable living could be assured and
loyalties bought. Politicians lived almost solely on the perquisites
of government, which they regarded as a right. The ruling parties
were thus devoid of the socio-economic substance that sustains
their Western prototypes, and their subsequent dissolution in the
inexorable stream of Javanese tradition was certain when the
army seized power after the *putsch* and put patronage on an
authoritarian footing. Academic analyses of the forces that were
supposed to be operating in the parliamentary days are interesting
as attempts to justify the name of political science by ingenious
classification along lines that are more appropriate in the physical
sciences;[33] but some of them now seem little more relevant to
the course of Javanese history than a catalogue of postage stamps
issued in the same period.

The absence of significant economic links between the politicians and society is explained by the fact that there was practically

no indigenous economic middle class. Too much has been made of small batik manufacturers and petty or minuscule traders, who are sometimes represented as constituting a small but vital current. This error was probably initiated by Wertheim, who, with Marx in one hand and Weber in the other, saw the Sarekat Islam as 'mainly concerned about the interests of the rising middle class'. Dahm has shown that this was not so.[34] But the question arises to what extent the term 'middle class' was justifiable at all. The Sarekat Islam's programme included a demand for Dutch training of indigenous traders; this suggests more a dream of improved status and living conditions than the birth of competitive enterprise as practised in Indonesia by robust Chinese. When Indonesia became independent it inherited an economy still run by the Dutch, with the Chinese fulfilling a subsidiary role, as shopkeepers and as middlemen between foreign exporters and subsistence farmers. Outside this there was little economic activity worthy of the name. The Dutch had tried in vain to stimulate indigenous enterprise. The reasons for their failure are discussed in later chapters. Meanwhile evidence of the situation that prevailed in the period under discussion is immediately relevant; for it shows the absurdity of blaming either Sukarno or this or that cabinet for an economic malady that is cultural.

The backward state of the indigenous economy in the 1950s is exemplified in a study by Clifford Geertz of two towns, one in East Java and one in Bali.[35] Admittedly, nobody would guess that such useful information lay between the covers of his book on the subject, with its catchy, magazine-like title, *Peddlers and Princes*. Nor would the sub-title, *Social Change and Economic Modernization in Two Indonesian Towns* lead a reader to suspect that it masked a picture of hopeless stagnation; yet if the word 'inertia' had been substituted for 'modernization', only some of Geertz's opening comments, not the facts that he records, would make it seem that the typographers had made a mistake. Geertz's trouble is that he is committed to the fashionable American, academic view that all or most countries sooner or later undergo an 'economic take-off'. Indonesia, he writes, 'by all the signs and portents' was 'in the midst of . . . a pretake-off period'. On the same page he avoids the ridicule of posterity by warning that, of course, development could 'misfire at any stage'. This hedging of intellectual bets, which is typical of his style, is applied again when he says of Modjokuto (a pseudonym for the East Javanese town): 'Bustling, fluid, "forward-looking", and yet for all that basically undynamic, the town seems stranded, at least for the time being, between the heritage of yesterday and the possibilities of tomorrow.'

Of the words that Geertz flings down with such gusto, the pertinent one is 'undynamic'. Modjokuto, which was created by the Dutch for their own purposes, would have become no less run down than other Javanese towns in the post-colonial period, and any bustling had nothing to do with economic vitality. In a town of 24,000 people Geertz finds only a few tiny, rudimentary factories and seven 'modern' stores that were run by indigenous Indonesians. Chinese establishments, as usual, dominated all trade and industry, but Geertz fails to provide perspective by saying how many there were – doubtless a very large number; nor does he give any comparison of turnover. He describes a row of shops on the front edge of the market place that the Dutch had leased to Javanese at nominal rents, to help them compete against the Chinese and strengthen the nucleus of a native shop-keeper class. But although he writes thousands of words about very little, he finds no space to discuss the overwhelmingly significant fact that long before he arrived most of the shops had fallen into Chinese hands; half a dozen case histories here would have emphasized the insignificance of the flicker of indigenous business initiative, which he associates with Islamic reform.

✓ But there are valuable observations in *Peddlers and Princes*. Of fundamental importance is that the bazaar mentality continued to dominate indigenous trade, which consisted almost entirely of peddling, and that even this lowly activity was alien to most Javanese, who did not care for trade at all. The bazaar, he points out, was 'at once an institution and a way of life, a general mode of commercial activity reaching into all aspects of Modjokuto society, and a sociocultural world nearly complete in itself.' The haggling of bazaar traders (which begins with a seemingly absurd margin between buying and selling offers) resulted from the absence of book-keeping; for nobody knew the true cost of anything and prices were established on the basis of bluff. In this crude, economic jungle, every pedlar was for himself; nobody trusted anybody; and the total lack of mutual confidence was a psychological barrier to the formation of even the smallest firm. The bazaar mind had an attitude to debt that partly explains Indonesia's chronic insolvency. Geertz finds that a pedlar would never spend his small capital if he could borrow. The rule recorded by Ju-Kang T'ien among Chinese in Sarawak, 'buy for ten, sell for seven, pay back three, and keep four', was also applied in Java; this meant that a man bought for $10 on credit, sold at a real loss of $3, made an artificial profit of $4 and went on owing $7.

In the bazaar this practice is more workable than it may seem. Creditors welcome debt accumulation because it binds the debtor to them; in the end their profits from high interest rates exceed their loss of capital. But when the bazaar mentality lingers in the centre, as it does in Indonesia, attempts to build a modern economy are sure to founder.

In spite of his sub-title, Geertz experiences in the end an 'uneasy feeling . . . that there is about Modjokuto's "shopkeeper revolution" an air of quaint irrelevancy' to the requirements of modern industrialization. But he adds that nevertheless: 'Whatever their shortcomings, Modjokuto's shopkeepers are what the Indonesian Government has to work with.' The government, it should be added, also had to contend with itself. And it is not surprising that ministers and bureaucrats, with both the anti-commercial and bazaar traditions behind them, began to mangle what was left of the Dutch economy. Import control was seized upon as an opportunity to put permits in the hands of the inexperienced élite and their parasites; so-called Indonesianization of business had the same effect. But almost invariably indigenous Indonesians, while fancying themselves to be business men, farmed back their privileges to Chinese, and exerted no more effort themselves than to collect their share of the profits. Shady banks were set up to take advantage of a black market in interest rates. And when wobbling enterprises collapsed, as they often did, the Dutch and Chinese were still there to blame for the general economic failure. While politicians sometimes took turns in ministerial office to enable themselves to establish perquisites, efforts were also made to put the economy in order by short-lived doses of orthodox fiscal action; but no Western economic measures could have withstood the manifold strains imposed by the pervading Javanese culture.

The economic and social dislocation caused by the Japanese occupation and the wars with the Dutch would in themselves have presented an enormous problem even for a government supported by a united and suitably trained people. In the fight for independence the Indonesians had ravaged plantations and destroyed valuable infrastructure. This scorched earth policy helped to bring the Dutch to reason by forcing them to finance their military operations from their own pockets, instead of bleeding the Indies to pay for them; but it left the new nation with a barren legacy. Indonesia was born with chronic inflation. The first Republic at one stage issued currency unbacked by any receipts at all; and note-printing presses ran on uncontrolled when the unitary Republic was formed in August 1950. The smuggling of primary products to foreign ports cost the exchequer badly needed foreign currency; and the dollar rose on the black market to 600 per cent of its official value in the first half of 1950 alone. Strikes broke out on the docks and what was left of the plantations. The largely illiterate nation was divided into 366 ethnic groups, according to one arbitrary attempt to classify them, ten of them with populations of more than one million at that time. Cutting through some of these were religious sects, secular nationalists of various kinds, Communists of every kind, bandits and petty war-lords with military rank, who, after fighting the Dutch, established enclaves in which they alone were the law. There was only a tiny nucleus of trained civil servants to help cope with all these problems; in 1940 the Dutch employed 221 Indonesians among 3,039 of higher rank. Poor though it was in quality, the Civil Service leaped in size from 420,000 (for the States and Republic combined) in February 1950 to 571,243 in 1952, as relatives, friends and supporters of those in power claimed the benefits of patronage.

By the mid-1950s it was clear that parliamentary democracy was not suited to Indonesia. Had the people been a valid electoral force, they would have insisted on the holding of elections in the early years of independence. When the poll finally took place on 29 September 1955 it was more an attempt to resolve political problems at the top and appease disruptive elements than to give voice to the bewildered, inarticulate masses. The elections showed the hopelessness of trying to impose an evolved Western system on feudal-minded Asians. The small 'political public', estimated by Feith at 1–1.5 million in 1950,[36] doubtless had as much idea of what they were about as most Western voters; but they constituted only a fraction of the 37,785,299 who cast valid votes. The huge turn-out of about 91.5 per cent reflected not enthusiasm for the elections but fear of punishment. Local political leaders spread rumours that voting was compulsory; and village heads, tied to parties under the system of patronage, often hinted that people who did not vote the right way would be penalized. In parts of Java there were tales of white men preparing to descend from the mountains and of imminent attacks by ghosts in yellow uniforms; *dukuns* sold potions to make people invulnerable; it was like the Ratu Adil cult in reverse. It has been said that while a sizeable minority were intimidated, most who followed their superiors did so from a feeling of social obligation.[37] But in Indonesia it is always difficult to tell where deference ends and fear begins, and one is rarely present without the other. Knowing this, many educated Indonesians regarded the elections as a farce, and were easily persuaded that a more authoritarian political system was desirable.[38]

Indonesia in the fifties provides an exceptional example of the truism that the fabric of history is damaged by the first line written about it. The events of that time were complex, with so many fluid, overlapping and intermingled factors, that it is questionable whether scholars will ever succeed in arriving at a common perspective. What is certain is that authority at the centre was destroyed by a confused mixture of ethnic discontent, military rebellion, sheer war-lordism and intrigue. Only a few of the highlights can be given here, but they will be enough to show that Indonesia was threatened with nothing less than disintegration until Sukarno re-established himself as a leader.

The Darul Islam movement's attempts to create the nucleus of an Islamic State in West Java in 1949 and in South Sulawesi and Aceh in 1953 caused prolonged fighting in which thousands were killed and plantations damaged. Typically, these battles were not solely ideological; in Sulawesi, for instance, a commander deserted to the rebels because his own force was to be cut in an abortive rationalization scheme. Leading officers of the divided army set themselves up as rulers in Sulawesi and North Sumatra, where they used troops and government equipment to smuggle vital primary and other commodities to and from Singapore on a large scale. In December 1956 rivalry inside the army and other factors led officers to seize power in West and North Sumatra. The East Indonesia commander at Makasar, South Sulawesi, declared a state of emergency throughout his area on 2 March 1957 and replaced the civilian governors with military men. One of his aides proclaimed a *Piagam Perjuangan Semesta* (Charter of Common Struggle), which, abbreviated to *Permesta* after the Indonesian fashion, was applied to the entire insurgence. This document aimed at a veritable carve up by war-lords of some of the nation's most valuable resources. It declared that each province must be allowed to form its own five year plan and that 'surplus areas' keep 70 per cent of revenues and 'minus areas' 100 per cent plus subsidies; it also made political demands.

With other officers threatening to take over the government, central authority collapsed; and on 14 March the Republic's seventh cabinet in little more than seven years resigned. Parliamentary government – Feith calls it constitutional democracy, despite the fact that the constitution in force had been framed provisionally in 1950 by a self-appointed élite – was now coming to an end. It had been a period not without conventional achievements, notably in diplomacy. Ali Sastroamidjojo, for instance, although his second cabinet was noted for exceptional corruption, achieved an important diplomatic feat by bringing India and China together at the Afro-Asian Conference held in Bandung, West Java, in April 1955, when Indonesia's turmoil provided an ironic background for a semblance of Third World unity. On the whole, however, the parliamentary interregnum was true to the stream of Javanese history in that it produced a small civilian and military élite who wrangled among themselves, feathered their nests, built up their prestige, jeopardized the nation's existence, and paid no heed whatever to what Sukarno later called the sufferings of the people.

Guided democracy

The cabinet's fall amid threatening chaos was Sukarno's opportunity to reassume leadership, but he moved cautiously. After he had been cast aside in the early days of independence, his political function was limited to choosing cabinet *formateurs*. Feith classifies politicians of the parliamentary interregnum into 'administrators', who were working for the immediate future, and 'solidarity makers', who 'tended to be concerned with images of a distant utopia'. If the idea behind these terms has any value, it would seem better applied to periods than to persons, although some politicians were more suited to one role than the other, as in all societies. 'Solidarity making' became essential when the administration inevitably broke down, and even the most dedicated 'administrator' would have had to try his hand at it to hold the nation together. At the beginning Sukarno, though described by Feith as the prototype of the 'solidarity makers', was certainly a strong supporter of the 'administrators', if this classification has to be used. He patiently sent for one *formateur* after another when politicians could not agree on which parties and which party members should govern the country. Feith recalls that Sukarno gave his full support to most of the actions of the Hatta cabinet, the first to be formed after the Round Table Conference; his speeches of that period 'placed considerable emphasis on the need for order, austerity, and hard work'.[39] According to Feith the first four cabinets (up to June 1953), all named by Sukarno's *formateurs*, were predominantly 'administrators'. Had they succeeded, that is to say, had they been able to triumph over themselves and the other formidable obstacles created by the culture, Sukarno would have been obliged to hold his peace. As it was, the conditions, rather than any desire Sukarno may have had, ensured that a man of his particular gifts would return to head the people he understood better than any of his rivals.

While Sukarno's influence gradually increased, his authority among politicians was so weak in 1951 that a government committee declared that he 'should not make a practice of intervening in the conduct of state affairs'. Sukarno had found means of trying to rally a divided nation and increase his own importance on what could be called non-partisan issues of state. The refusal of the Dutch to yield West Irian gave him an obvious opportunity; all political groups were committed, with varying degrees of enthusiasm, to the early acquisition of this territory as an integral part of Indonesia. In an inflammatory Independence Day speech on 17 August 1950, Sukarno vowed that Indonesia would go on fighting until West Irian had been 'returned to our fold'. After having been curbed by the Mohammad Natsir cabinet, he said in January 1951 that he was obliged to confine his remarks to what was proper for the head of state in a parliamentary system. But he ominously added that the constitution, to which he had sworn allegiance, defined Indonesia as consisting of all the former Netherlands Indies, which included West Irian. Although Sukarno was temporarily silenced, West Irian had already become one of a series of springboards from which he would leap to ultimate power. Another was the Bandung conference in April 1955, when his anti-imperialist speech, 'Let a New Asia and Africa Be Born', delivered in the presence of Chou En-lai, Nehru and Nasser, inspired the Third World and antagonized the West.

Whatever may be said of the 1955 elections, nothing approaching Western democracy existed in Indonesia before them. Assaults that were made on the political structure thus threatened not freedom but a floundering, pseudo-democratic élite. The most spectacular attack was what looked like an attempted coup on 17 October 1952 when army officers organized a mass demonstration, lined up tanks outside the President's palace, and tried to force Sukarno to dissolve parliament. Sukarno replied that he could not act without consulting cabinet. To the extent that it was inextricably complex and bizarre, this affair was a prototype of the bewildering *putsch* of 1 October 1965; but Sukarno handled the officers coolly, and it soon petered out. Sukarno shared the officers' disgust at wasteful political strife and other consequences of the ill-adapted parliamentary system; acting within the limits then possible, he had urged Natsir to form a *zaken* (business) cabinet, cutting across party lines. But he was too experienced to be caught up in a half-baked military plot, and sufficiently a Leninist to know that conditions had to be ripe for the radical change that he desired, the introduction of guided democracy.

Sukarno's idea of guided democracy had evolved from his democratic centralism, obviously borrowed from Lenin, which he outlined in the 1930s. In 1950, before the Natsir cabinet dampened his utterances, he spoke of the need for such a system; he urged it more strongly in October 1956 when he called on the political parties to hold a *musyawarah* and 'bury themselves' in the interests of unity. What he proposed, he said, was 'something which is guided but is still democracy'. Sukarno expounded his views with greater precision when he outlined what he called his *konsepsi* to a large meeting of politicians and others in February 1957. He did not ask for the abolition of parties, but proposed instead a cabinet representing all of importance, including the Indonesian Communist Party (PKI), which in provincial elections a few months later was to emerge as the strongest in Java. Sukarno asked the party leaders to give him their views within a week; replies varied predictably.

While Sukarno was considering his next move, the regional military rebellions broke out. After the government's resignation on 14 March 1957, Sukarno appointed Surjo, Chairman of the Indonesian National Party (PNI), as *formateur*. Surjo failed to win support. Sukarno, as President, then appointed Sukarno, as citizen, to perform the task. The political cliques were dumbfounded at this device; although the nation was crumbling, they had expected to continue their accustomed haggling at will. But Sukarno went ahead and in April 1957 formed a cabinet with Djuanda, a widely respected non-party man, as Prime Minister. Sukarno found it tactical to exclude the PKI at that stage; and the Masjumi, one of the two big Moslem parties, forbade its members to participate, expelling two who did. But although his success was qualified, Sukarno had at last formed a cabinet whose ministers agreed to accept office only as individuals, although most were party members.

The army was also a very important political pace-maker at that time. Its Chief of Staff, General Nasution, who had been reinstated after having been a leader of the 17 October *putsch*, had long urged restoration of the 1945 constitution. It appears that it was on his insistence, and it was certainly with his strong support, that Sukarno decreed a state of war and siege, in other words, martial law, when the government resigned on 14 March. When Sukarno whipped up a campaign to win West Irian, it was army officers, not rampaging mobs, who seized Dutch plantations and factories on their own initiative in December 1957 and began to run them partly for private profit. Their plundering followed a limited, differently motived occupation of enterprises by leftist union leaders.

Nasution, however, was not bent on plunder, and did his best to curb violation of the army's honour. The *Permesta* leadership, which continued to defy the centre, repeatedly demanded his dismissal; under the influence of the American CIA, it also called on the government to ban the Communist Party. In February 1958, while Sukarno was on holiday in Japan, rebels in Sumatra proclaimed a Revolutionary Government of the Republic of Indonesia (PRRI), at Padang; its Ministers included Dr Sumitro Djojohadikusumo, later Suharto's Trade Minister, who was to maintain close contact with American officials for many years. Encouraged by arms from the Western hemisphere and an approving statement by John Foster Dulles, the US Secretary of State, the rebels became more challenging. But Nasution acted with resolution. Despite the evils of civil war, he decided that the rebellion must be put down by force. Fighting began in March, and reinforced government troops were virtually in control by the end of June.

The American intervention was a gift to Sukarno. In his Independence Day speech on 17 August 1958 he was able to invoke the imperialist danger and rebuke the Constituent Assembly, which had been elected in December 1955, for its slowness in preparing a new constitution; he warned that the army, having put down armed rebellion, would no longer allow politicians to play with economic issues. About the same time Nasution spoke out in favour of the 1945 constitution. This instrument gave strong powers to the President, who was to form his own cabinet after being appointed for five years by a People's Consultative Assembly (MPR). The MPR, meeting at least once in five years, was to lay down the broad lines of government policy. All statutes required the agreement of parliament (DPR), although the President was not responsible to it. In the event of his disagreement with the DPR, the President, 'should exigency compel', had the right to make regulations; but these were to be revoked if the DPR did not agree to them 'in its next session'. The attraction of the constitution for Nasution was that it would enable him to reduce political instability by claiming a place for the army among professional and other groups that were to be represented in the MPR and DPR.

It became clear in June 1959 that the Constituent Assembly was determined to block proposals submitted by Sukarno. Nasution, with Sukarno absent abroad, then used his martial law powers to ban all political activity; soon afterwards he and Sukarno agreed that the 1945 constitution should be restored by presidential decree. In spite of its high-sounding, democratic phraseology, the constitution makes no provision for elections to either the MPR or the DPR; nor does it specify how members are to be appointed, although it guarantees that all social groups will be somehow represented. Sukarno was soon to clarify this issue. After decreeing the restoration of the constitution on 5 July, he appointed the members of the MPR and DPR himself. Guided democracy, which dates from his formation of the Djuanda cabinet, was thus consolidated.

Those who express dismay at this action are ignoring the social conditions that led to it. Sukarno cannot be said to have quashed democracy, because it had never existed in Indonesia in any valid sense. To criticize him and Nasution for restoring the 1945 constitution would be like reproaching the barons of England for not ensuring that adult suffrage was written into Magna Carta. Even Hatta, one of the main architects of the spurious parliamentary structure, had come to realize that his system was doomed. In June 1957 he said there were conditions in which a dictatorship was inevitable; and the wording of his statement suggested that he considered that he, not Sukarno, was the man for the job.[40] During the 1971 election campaign Hatta declared that elections would be futile until the people were educated, since only then would they be able to withstand intimidation. What he said at that time was true from the beginning; that is why the 1945 constitution, which left it to the articulate to form the MPR, obviously under strong guidance, was more suited to Indonesia than the semblance of Western democracy.

In backward countries the question is not whether a government is authoritarian, for authoritarianism is already endemic, but the way in which it exercises its authority and what effort it makes to enable the people to lift themselves from their poverty; for only they can do it. As will be emphasized in subsequent chapters, poverty in Indonesia is not an economic but a cultural issue. Nevertheless no cultural change, assuming it to be possible, is likely without revolutionary leadership. It was to provide the spearhead of a new society that in the guided democracy period Sukarno revived his 1927 attempts to unite the forces of secular nationalism, religion, and communism by raising the banner of his Nasakom (nationalism, religion (*agama*) and communism).

Sukarno had long believed that the causes of Indonesia's poverty were social; his caustic remarks about economists did not reflect ignorance of what they had to offer, but his conviction that their ideas were irrelevant to a backward country. In this respect, and possibly others, he was a man before his time; for few understood then the inapplicability of Western economic techniques that are now in evident disarray throughout the Third World. Sukarno's approach to the economy was dual. On the one hand his government took steps intended to keep the Western economic enclave alive; on the other – and this is what mattered most – he believed that the lot of the masses would never be improved until they themselves, in a further revolutionary stage, brought about social change that would lead to an increase in their productivity.

It is of no great importance whether or not the measures applied by his limited team of economists to the self-contained, Western-type sector were the most effective that could be devised. In the first place, as Geertz unwittingly shows, there was no possibility that Indonesians could develop within the foreseeable future an economy that the Dutch had initiated. More important was that such an economy, even if the Dutch had been allowed to remain, would never have fanned out into the hinterland to the benefit of the masses. The Dutch had been dismayed at the collapse of their vigorous attempts to stimulate indigenous enterprise; and where they had failed the Indonesians could never succeed by adopting the same Western methods. Sukarno had read Boeke (discussed in chapter 11), who was convinced that the Western-type sector would remain an enclave in a stagnant, pre-capitalist economy; and he knew of an official Dutch pronouncement in 1900 that Java was a 'chronic distress area' suffering from centuries of 'ingrained poverty', and that it was 'easier to demonstrate the presence of this disease than its cure'.[41] Attempts to blame Sukarno for what was and is a chronic condition may therefore be rejected as missing the point. The task was not for economists, but for social revolutionaries; and even their chance of success would have been slender.

Yet from early in the period of guided democracy Sukarno sponsored or approved numerous technical economic measures, which have been described and commented upon by specialists; in 1965 he was still trying to keep the tottering enclave going by strongly urging indigenous capital accumulation. But his longer-term policy, to which he attached overwhelming importance, was revolution in which something like the structure of China's communes would be established, without the godless ideology.

In his Independence Day address on 17 August 1963 he emphasized that the economic problem must be tackled not 'in a routine fashion', but as an 'instrument of the revolution'. In advanced countries, he said, 'persons of outstanding skills in the routines of economics' were perhaps required, but their ways were not suitable for 'a nation in revolution'. Sukarno affirmed 'for the umpteenth time' that the most important source of production was the workers and peasants. He added: 'It is not enough to say negatively that efforts to increase production must not be hostile to the workers and peasants. These efforts must develop the productive powers of the workers and peasants in a positive way.' This was no abstract slogan. Precisely what Sukarno meant had been clear since 28 October 1956, if not earlier, when he appealed for the burial of the parties. He said: 'Our situation with respect to the party system is one of complete disruption. It is not healthy; it must be transformed entirely. Especially, if we want to build as people have in other countries I have seen, for example in the Chinese People's Republic.'

Sukarno was compelled to make no more than oblique allusions to his quasi-communist goal because his authority was not secure. Far from being a dictator, he had to contend with both the army and the political élite. With their interests increasingly threatened by Sukarno's revolutionary declarations and ominous measures, they became more vulnerable to the whisperings, blandishments and bribes of Western diplomats and agents. Over drinks at garden parties in the heady, tropical evenings, they were intoxicated with ideas of parliamentary democracy, of which they had already proved such feeble exponents. Conspiracies abounded. Six attempts were made to murder Sukarno; and it is reasonable to suspect, although the evidence is only circumstantial, that the ever-present CIA played a part in some of them. The army's power in the early years of guided democracy has been described by the Australian journalist, Bruce Grant.[42]

Using the war emergency regulations, the army reached into the administrative life of the country. It banned strikes, broke up demonstrations, controlled the use of slogans, closed down newspaper printing offices, ran the former Dutch estates. In July–August 1960, it moved against the PKI, banned the party newspaper *Harian Rakjat* and interrogated the leaders (Aidit for eight consecutive days) to the extent of 190 typed pages of questions and answers. It cancelled the PKI's sixth congress. When Aidit challenged Nasution, declaring the congress would go ahead as scheduled, President Sukarno intervened and the result was one of his compromises. The congress was not cancelled; it was postponed. When it was held, army stenographers, like police, sat in and took a record of the proceedings.

The army's use as an instrument of authoritarian government was not, however, confined to the communists. It was generally tough on civil liberties during this period. In an effort to root out corruption it investigated thousands of charges, many trifling, without any noticeable result except that corruption appeared to spread to the army. With the responsibility of supervising import-export trade, rice supplies, government services, all forms of transport, to mention only some of its functions, the army began to develop as a duplicate administrative élite. An army signature was necessary in many daily transactions, and the citizenry began to complain about military interference.

Sukarno curbed this rampage by a combination of political skill and cunning. After setting faction against faction in the divided and disruptive armed forces, he neutralized Nasution in June 1962, when he deprived him of his army operational command by promoting him to Chief of Staff of the Armed Forces. His successful campaign to oust the Dutch from West Irian helped him to win the loyalty of many officers, large numbers of whom became ardent advocates of Nasakom. He packed the non-elected MPRS (provisional MPR) with supporters from various parties, and in May 1963 was strong enough to be appointed President for Life and to limit the army's powers by ending martial law.

✓ The guess-work that typifies much academic writing on Indonesia has produced differences about whether Sukarno or Nasution was the force behind guided democracy. Legge says Nasution became 'in effect a co-sponsor with Sukarno of the whole guided democracy idea': Lev saw the army as the 'prime mover behind guided democracy'.[43] In an interview with the author in January 1973 Nasution shows that both Legge and Lev have raised a false issue:

I proposed in the National Council in 1958 a return to the
1945 constitution. He [Sukarno] did not accept. He agreed
only after the Constituent Assembly came to a deadlock . . .
I had big power until the 1945 constitution was restored in
1959. Until then Sukarno and I were [in effect] the cabinet.
I was not afraid when we made our agreement to return to
the 1945 constitution, with a transition period of three years,
then elections. These were two of the three cabinet
programme points. The third was the elections . . . The
elections were to be more free than the last [1971]. Ninety
per cent of the members were to be elected and 10 per cent
appointed by the army and functional groups.

Explaining the difference between the 1945 constitution and
guided democracy, Nasution says:

A Father Figure [in guided democracy] presides over a
family of Moslems, communists, etc. If there is no consensus,
they ask the Father Figure to decide. This is a simplified
account. In effect, he was *lurah* [village head] of the whole
of Indonesia. That is why at first he opposed the return
to the 1945 constitution. That is why he set up Djuanda
as his First Minister, while he remained the Father Figure,
Great Leader, *Führer*. Djuanda, as First Minister, would
have to answer to congress [MPRS], Parliament and the
people, while the Father Figure was responsible to the
whole nation, but not through the institutions. He thus
manipulated the 1945 constitution, the original concept.

Individual officers were certainly the 'prime movers' in bullying
the people and exacting tribute; but this had nothing to do with
Nasution's desire to promote order within the 1945 constitution
or with Sukarno's concept of guided democracy. Apart from the
mechanical use of the word *Führer*, Nasution's brief description
of the principle of guided democracy is consistent with Sukarno's
thinking; but his accusation that Sukarno manipulated the
constitution, presumably by packing the MPRS, needs examination. An 'elucidation' published with the constitution emphasizes
that it is 'flexible'; and the absence of a provision for elections gives
the President an intended loophole. The elucidation says that
while the 'brief' rules are binding, it is not desirable to fix ideas

85

that circumstances may outmode; what is important is the 'spirit of the authorities'; and whatever is necessary to execute the 'fundamental rules must be left to statutes'. The hand of Sukarno in the 1945 elucidation is obvious. But in 1959 he found that the safeguards he had devised to ensure that the nation did not destroy itself by internal strife were not enough. That was why he sought to go beyond the rules into the realm of even stronger presidential leadership, in which he was certainly a *lurah* and not a *Führer*.

Communism with God

While Sukarno had no party organization at his command, his Nasakom ideology became a substantial weapon, despite inevitable internal strains, which were aggravated by Western subversion. Its most dynamic component was the PKI; and Sukarno seized upon the party's growing influence to help direct the Indonesian revolution, as he always called it, towards its next stage. Before independence Sukarno had emphasized that freedom from the Dutch would not in itself achieve social justice for the Marhaens, but that further revolutionary action would be necessary. He appears to have felt all along that the PKI would have to take the lead in bringing about the change, although he was convinced that to succeed it must make room for God. He had not dared to risk splitting the nation by lending too much support to what was only one of the three elements in his concept of the national family. But, convinced that the PKI was vital to the achievement of a better Indonesian society, he had long given it special consideration; even after the 1948 Madiun *putsch*, during which he urged the people to choose between the Sukarno-Hatta team (Hatta was Vice-President) and the PKI leaders, he blamed the insurrection not on the PKI, as a stream in the Indonesian revolution, but on its 'mistaken' leaders.

The PKI's surprising success in the 1955 general elections and its later pre-eminence in Java probably showed Sukarno that the time was ripe to move, however cautiously, toward the next stage. For the first time in Indonesia's history a force had arisen that might lead to the cultural revolution that was needed to end centuries of oppression – by feudal lords, the Dutch, the modern *priyayi* élite, the army, and, not least, the superstitions that had kept the people backward. The communists built huge trade unions, and organized peasants. Scientists, writers and university teachers, who did not wish to commit themselves to the whole Marxist ideology, but saw hope in the movement, joined Communist-inspired cultural and professional organizations. Sukarno, after a meeting with Chou En-lai in Jakarta in April 1965, secretly decided to accelerate this trend by creating a fifth force – a popular militia outside the control of the four branches of the armed forces, the Army, Navy and Air Force and Police; to this end he arranged for 100,000 rifles to be sent from China, without the army's knowledge. At the same time he seized upon the Malaysia Confrontation as an opportunity to train Nasakom civilian fighters at Halim air base, near Jakarta. Politicians and civil servants were obliged to attend courses in Nasakom ideology and Marxism. The government news agency, Antara, was put under the domination of Communists, and the only foreign news it distributed was from Hsinhua, the Peking news agency. Resentment mounted among those who wanted to preserve their privileges; and Sukarno came more and more into the open in denouncing those whom he saw as mere toadies among the élite, the 'double-faced', the 'hypocrites' and the 'pig-headed', who used his revolutionary phrases and symbols only to keep their jobs while they plotted to get rid of him. Yet he still felt obliged to move cautiously. He had what he believed to be evidence that both the United States and Britain were encouraging anti-Communist generals to overthrow him. Fear of provoking a coup almost certainly explains why he excluded Communists from his inner cabinet, despite PKI pressure; and it certainly accounts for the fact that his decision to import Chinese rifles was kept secret until after the *putsch* of 1 October 1965.

Strange comments have been written about this period. Sukarno has been accused of merely playing some sly, old-fashioned Javanese game of palace politics, trading favours in a so-called 'theatre state'; his use of symbols has been said to show that he was more interested in what the state was than in what it was doing.[44] The fact is that Sukarno knew that symbols were indispensable to the Javanese mind. It is true that the palace became the seat of political bargaining, in which Sukarno diminished opposition by playing off his enemies against one another with the manipulative cunning that some writers see as his dominant characteristic. But unscrupulous scheming is an old

87

Javanese weapon. His opponents had used it to push him aside
soon after the proclamation of independence and imprison him
in the presidency; if he used it better than others it was not that
he was less ethical by Javanese criteria but more skilful. Unsavoury though his intrigues may seem and much though he
possibly enjoyed them himself, failure to perpetrate them would
have left him with no chance of maintaining power and, what
was certainly no less important to him, of trying to lead the
nation in the direction in which he had always been convinced it
should go.

Sukarno's approach to politics was dual, as it was to the economy.
While he ruled rather like a traditional king at the palace, and
was venerated as such by most Indonesians, he was trying to
shepherd the Marhaens in a direction that would ultimately
bring down the palace political structure. His trading with the
élite was increasingly offset by his scathing denunciation of them;
and his purpose was clearly revealed in the revolutionary declamation that marked his speeches in the 1960s. Some commentators
have found no substance in his oratory of that period;[45] the
generalizations in his speech of 17 August 1960, when he spoke
of the 'romanticism of revolution', have been cited to show that
he had no precise plan of action. But Sukarno, with the typical
Javanese tactical prudence of which Suharto was also to be a
master, was preparing the people for more specific exhortations
that were to come. His first step was to impress upon the people
that the Father of the Nation identified himself with continued
revolution: 'Once we start a revolution we must continue that
revolution until all its ideals have been implemented.' Gradually
it became clear that the Communists had his full blessing as the
vanguard in the Marhaenist struggle. On 17 August 1964 he felt
strong enough to declare:

> I have been accused of bringing advantage to one group
> only among our big national family. My answer is also, yes.
> Yes, I am giving advantage to one group only, namely – the
> revolutionary group! I am a friend of the nationalists, but
> only the *revolutionary* nationalists! I am a friend of the
> religious groups, but only the *revolutionary* religious groups!
> I am a friend of the communists, because the communists
> are *revolutionary* people.

In May 1965 he put his aim beyond doubt when he said at the forty-fifth anniversary of the PKI: 'I love the PKI as my brother, and if it dies I shall feel it as the loss of a dear relative.' There was no empty symbolism, no theatre state in declarations such as those, backed as they were by an arrangement to import Chinese rifles for the fifth force. But Sukarno's statement in his autobiography that he was not, had never been, and could never be a Communist may be taken literally. His ideology was his own Nasakom, which was based on the ideas he formulated when as a young man he argued that 'historical materialism' could be separated from 'philosophic materialism', with which he disagreed.[46]

Kidney stones debilitated Sukarno in the last years of guided democracy, and he had been aware for some time that he was ageing; on the eve of his sixtieth birthday in June 1961 he wrote to his wife, Hartini, that he was old by Indonesian standards.[47] With characteristic self-mockery, he tells in his autobiography of a tendency to shout at people to relieve tension caused by bad news arriving 'every five minutes'. Overburdened with insoluble political and economic problems, disheartened, perhaps, by the gloomy prospects of his people, he became increasingly tired. Some of the excesses of his later years, both in his private life and public statements, are probably attributable to chronic fatigue and the beginnings of senility. Although he was careful not to force the political pace, it seems that towards the end of his rule he was trying feverishly to ensure the foundations of a new society for the Marhaens before he died. He told Dahm just before he was deposed that the PKI was the 'avant-garde of the revolutionary forces' and was needed to achieve 'social justice and a prosperous society'.[48] This does not mean that he had abandoned Nasakom, but that he regarded the PKI as the spearhead of a united movement that in the end would achieve what was obviously his goal, communism – an Indonesian version – with God, to whom he prayed five times a day, as required by Islam. No greater precision was needed. It was not because he was limited in himself, but because he understood the limitations of his people at the time, that he avoided a comprehensive blueprint. He believed that such a complex, backward society could not be moulded, but could only be changed gradually by continual revolution. As a young man Sukarno had sought to create among

the illiterate and primitively superstitious Marhaens the will to
independence; he left it to historic circumstance, which he
happened to predict correctly, to make possible the desire that he
fostered. Now he sought to inspire them with the even more
radical aim of social reconstruction, and to promote, step by step,
the instrument by which they might bring it about – a Communist-
led Nasakom. The precise shape of the new society was for the
future. Unlike Western academics who spoke recklessly of 'take-
off', he came to see that the 'prosperous society' of which he
dreamed would not be realized within a foreseeable period. He
says in his autobiography:

> Totally inexperienced Indonesia had to start from scratch.
> We still desperately need technical and managerial know-
> how, but this takes generations to develop. Then, too,
> most of our peasantry lives on Java, the most densely
> populated area of the world . . . Lack of adequate farm land
> makes for poverty and hunger, but the plain fact is that the
> Javanese want to live on Java. Transplanting them will
> also take time . . . there is no substitute for time.

Harry Benda says in his introduction to Dahm's book that
Sukarno was a tragically misguided man who led Indonesia to the
'brink of disaster'.[49] In fact, Sukarno nearly succeeded in setting
the Marhaens on the only course that has yet offered hope,
forlorn though it was, of raising them from their stagnation.
What stopped him was his overthrow by a military junta, which
seized power amid the applause of nations in the Western bloc
and with at least their moral support.

CHAPTER THREE

The enigma of the 'putsch'

The facts

It is typical of the unpredictability of events in Indonesia that the *putsch* which led to Sukarno's overthrow was intended, so its leaders claimed, to protect him. The precise origin of this curious incident remains a puzzle to most investigators. There are a few who, predictably, are sure that the Communists were entirely to blame; they support the Indonesian Army's assertion that the PKI plotted the coup and used discontented army officers to carry it out. Others accept the statement of the officer who led the operation that he acted on his own initiative. Another view is that the military rebels and the PKI took the initiative separately and became partners.

Some Indonesian intelligence men claim that Sukarno was behind the coup; on the other hand, W. F. Wertheim, the Dutch sociologist, is convinced that Suharto was in the confidence of one of the conspirators. The theme of this book requires no attempt to solve these enigmas or to find a way through the maze of contradictions that each tentative answer presents; nor is it proposed to undertake a complete summing up of the evidence. The extent to which the PKI was involved would not have influenced the army's decision to make the *putsch* at once a tombstone for Sukarnoism and the foundation of its own rise to power; and if a Communist had got himself mixed up in the plot against his leader's instructions, which is what one of them claimed, this would have been a sufficient pretext to wipe out the entire party. The aim here is to illustrate that the bizarre and haphazard, which have always played a part in the life of the nation, are a component of its tragedy and are not merely incidental to it. Indonesia was born after a kidnapping; it was to be reborn in a *putsch* and baptised with the blood of a massacre.

The *putsch* took place in a period of increased friction between the army leaders and the Sukarno – PKI alliance, which was complicated with repercussions of the great conflict between Western powers and their variegated adversaries in South East Asia and elsewhere in the Third World. Both Britain and the United States were engaged in what may now be seen as anachronistic and ineffectual meddling in the region, in which they were doomed to lose most of their influence. For Britain the main white man's burden was Malaysia, which had already split when Singapore left it; for the United States it was Vietnam, formerly French Indo-China.

Indonesia's confrontation with Malaysia is sometimes regarded as an adventure devised by Sukarno to divert the masses from economic problems and to foment the spirit of nationalism. While it is true that Sukarno was always seeking opportunities to make the nation conscious of itself, this view is too simple. When he launched the confrontation Sukarno was supported not only by all parties but by the army leadership, which at that time shared his fear of Western imperialism. General Nasution recalls (in an interview with the author in January 1973) that during the regional rebellions an American pilot, Allan Pope, had been shot down during a bloody bombing raid on Ambon in April 1958 after taking off from Clark, the US air base near Manila. Nasution said that the army had regarded British bases across the Strait of Malacca as a threat since the early days of the Republic. 'I got surface to surface missiles from Moscow in 1964', he said. 'With these we would have been able to blockade Singapore. At the end of 1964 I signed a contract with the Russians for missiles for two regiments. Sukarno would only agree to two, but they were not enough.' Nasution said that where he and Sukarno disagreed was on how to handle the threat. He regarded it as a technical matter, but Sukarno saw it 'as part of the whole global confrontation between the old and the new emerging forces'.

For Indonesia the formation of Malaysia as a client state meant the consolidation of British military power on its doorstep. Sukarno and military men suspected that the British, like the Americans, had already aided the regional rebels. The anxiety of the young Republic, which had only barely won its freedom, was understandable. Yet when Sukarno took action against the British and their allies along the border of Kalimantan (former Borneo) he was condemned in the West as irresponsible. Contrariwise, after the Indonesian Army had overthrown him and ended the confrontation, Western governments sympathized with the junta's alarm at the presence of a small number of Malaysian Chinese guerrillas in the same area.

The beginning of the confrontation in 1963 precipitated ugly outbreaks of mob violence against the British in Jakarta. The British Embassy was sacked; diplomats' houses were occupied and their cars set on fire. Farther afield, British plantations were confiscated. In 1964 Sukarno changed his target and launched his first public attack on the United States in his Independence Day speech on 17 August. Again the mobs went into action. United States buildings were damaged and despoiled; American citizens found themselves without water, electricity or post; and anti-American posters were stuck prominently in the streets. American aid, which had totalled nearly $700 million between 1949 and the middle of 1964, dwindled to a trickle.

In January 1965 Sukarno took Indonesia out of the United Nations when Malaysia was given a place in the Security Council. Peking applauded, and Sukarno spoke increasingly of the Peking–Jakarta axis. Sukarno's ties with the PKI, which clearly supported China in its clash with the USSR, became closer and more evident. He called in Njoto, the third man in the PKI leadership and a member of his 108-man cabinet, to help him draft his 17 August speech, in which he confirmed a previous statement that, alongside the Army, Navy, Air Force and Police, he might set up a 'fifth force' – a militia of workers and peasants, which had been urged by the PKI, ostensibly for service in Malaysia, but was opposed by the army. As usual, a huge crowd, estimated at 250,000, had assembled in Merdeka (freedom) Square to hear the President. But this time they were not given the usual comic relief. Before and during his speech Sukarno looked angry and made none of his customary jokes. He bitterly and sometimes

93

illogically attacked British and American imperialism, and rebuked the generals, though with tact. It was 'possible', he said, that some generals who had begun as revolutionaries had become counter-revolutionary.

The shrieks of Communist tub-thumpers had already reached a savage pitch. The generals were branded as 'capitalist bureaucrats', because of their corrupt management of enterprises seized from the Dutch in December 1957. A week before the *putsch* a youth front demanded that 'corruptors, capitalist bureaucrats, pilferers and charlatans' should be 'dragged to the gallows' or 'shot in public'. The Communist Party Chairman, Dipa Nusantara Aidit, said that counter-revolutionaries were cornered; and he warned the people to prepare to strike back against desperate, barbarous acts. While the mobs revelled in this orgy of vituperation, more serious business was being done in secret. It was revealed later that in the middle of September President Sukarno had secretly sent his air force chief, Air Vice-Marshal Omar Dhani, to Peking to arrange the delivery of 100,000 small arms for the 'fifth force', the initiation of which Sukarno had discussed with Chou En-lai in Jakarta in April. And in Jakarta and Central Java conspirators were planning the coup of 1 October. This pitiful bungle was to have a catastrophic sequel; it led to the army's overthrowing of Sukarno and to one of the most vicious organized massacres in the history of mankind.

X The main facts of the operation itself are not in dispute. In the early hours of 1 October 1965 six generals and a lieutenant were murdered after military rebels had raided their houses. Three of the generals were shot dead on the spot, either because they resisted attempts to kidnap them or because their killers lost their nerve; the four other officers and the three dead were taken in lorries to Halim air force base, close to Jakarta, where the rebel leaders had established their headquarters with the approval of Omar Dhani. Those alive were killed and the bodies of all seven were dropped into a well at a spot known as Crocodile Hole, on the edge of the base.

The rebels were under the command of Lieutanant-Colonel Untung, commander of one of the three battalions of President Sukarno's palace guard (Tjakrabirawa). They had set out from Halim in lorries at about 1.30 a.m., divided into seven squads. Six of the victims lived in Jakarta and the seventh in the satellite town of Kebayoran. The two most important men on the rebels' list were General Nasution, the only one to escape, and Lieutenant-General Achmad Yani. Nasution was Defence Minister and senior in rank to Yani, but Sukarno, with whom he had fundamental disagreements, had promoted him out of operational command in 1962. Yani, as Army Commander and Army Minister, had all Indonesian troops under his control; he wore the ring of Fort Leavenworth, in the United States, where he had undergone a training course; he had reiterated his opposition to a 'fifth force' immediately after Sukarno had announced that he was considering it.

The squads carried out their task with what seems to have been a mixture of cold-blooded ruthlessness and panic. The story of Yani's murder comes from his young children; for Mrs Yani, who had been upset since her husband had taken a young second wife, was spending the night with relatives. A squad of about 200 palace guards overpowered Yani's guard outside the house, and a small party entered through the unlocked front door. Disturbed by their noise, Yani got out of bed and found soldiers in the front room with his eight-year-old son, who had awakened a few minutes earlier. One of the guards told him that the President wanted to see him urgently. It is not known if Yani suspected a trap, but he replied that he must first put on a uniform. A sergeant told him there was no time for such a formality; the President was waiting and he could change at a toilet at the palace. Yani was enraged at such insolence from a non-commissioned officer; he knocked the sergeant unconscious and swept from the room, possibly to change, shutting a glass door behind him. A guard fired through the glass with an automatic weapon and Yani fell with several bullets in his back. Other children ran from their bedrooms and saw their father being dragged along the floor to a lorry that was waiting outside. Yani was mortally wounded; he tried to embrace his eldest son, aged eleven, but was pulled callously away and apparently died in the lorry on the way to Halim. His house, with its relics of the murder, has been preserved as a museum.

At Nasution's house some of the raiders disarmed the guards while others took up positions in the back garden to prevent him from escaping. The house was on one floor, characterizing the modest style in which the Nasutions lived. General and Mrs Nasution heard the raiders breaking in at the front. Mrs Nasution got out of bed, opened the bedroom door, and immediately slammed and locked it; she had come face to face with a palace guard, his gun at the ready. Nasution, a former guerrilla leader in the war with the Dutch, decided to investigate, and re-opened the door. The soldier fired at him, but missed when Nasution automatically dropped flat. His wife again shut and locked the door and both fled through another outlet and along a passage. Urged by his wife to escape, Nasution ran out through a side door and sprinted across the garden. Soldiers fired in the darkness as he pulled himself over a wall and landed in the Iraqui Ambassador's property, injuring an ankle. But there were two other casualties, one of which was to anguish him for a long time to come. Nasution's five-year-old daughter was shot three times in the back, while his sister was carrying her from a bedroom; she died a few days later. And one of Nasution's aides, Lieutenant Pierre Tendean, was taken to Halim, where he was murdered with the generals and thrown into the well.

While the seven squads were at work, other rebel units, consisting mainly of a regiment from Central Java and one from East Java, both of which had arrived for Armed Forces Day celebrations, occupied the national radio station and the telecommunications building, on two sides of Merdeka Square, and took up a commanding position opposite the Presidential Palace, on another side. With Untung's battalion of palace guards and the two from East and Central Java the rebels commanded only about 3,000 men in Jakarta itself, while at Halim they controlled the air force defence units and a few thousand Communist youths and girls, some of them armed with air force weapons, who had been training for the Malaysia Confrontation. Thirty tanks and armoured cars of the Siliwangi Division, expected from Bandung, several hours' drive away, had failed to arrive. With 20,000 troops already in the capital to celebrate Armed Forces Day on 5 October, the tanks were obviously essential if the coup were to be sustained for more than a few hours;[1] but the rebels blundered on without them, possibly hoping that the air force would help.

Soon after 7 a.m. Radio Indonesia broadcast the first news of the night's events. It made no mention of the murders, but said that a newly formed 30 September Movement had arrested a number of generals who had been plotting to overthrow Sukarno at the instigation of the American Central Intelligence Agency.

Those arrested, the radio said, were members of a council of generals, whose aim was to launch a coup just before Armed Forces Day; Untung's action had thus 'saved the life of the President'. The generals were described as power-crazed officers who had neglected their men while living in luxury, leading a gay life, insulting Indonesian womanhood, and squandering public funds. The army was not for generals, the radio said, but for soldiers who were loyal to the ideas of the nation's revolution.

Later that day Radio Indonesia broadcast what it called Decree No. 1 – it was also the last – of the 30 September Movement Command. This peculiar document set up a 45-man Revolutionary Council of Indonesia, which took over 'all the authority of the state'. Sukarno, whom the movement claimed to be protecting, was not mentioned in the six rambling articles; his cabinet was dismissed, but members were ordered to carry out routine instructions until further notice. The decree ordered the establishment of regional councils, rising in tiers from a maximum of seven members in the villages to twenty-five in the provinces. Apparently it was assumed that the whole nation would follow the lead given by Jakarta; for nothing had been done to ensure large-scale co-ordination of revolt throughout Java, let alone the whole archipelago. The council was to rule until general elections had been held for the MPR. Untung, a man of no political experience and limited intelligence, was announced as Chairman of the Revolutionary Council; four officers from the Army, Air Force, Navy and Police were vice-chairmen. The list of forty-five council members was beyond interpretation. It included at least two Communists, one of whom was leader of the youths at Halim, and Sukarno's pro-Peking Foreign Minister, Dr Subandrio; but also named were anti-Communist generals who were to help crush the rebellion. Militarily, the *putsch* had gone off at half-cock without the vital tanks and armoured cars; politically it was nonsensical. It is not surprising that some scholars have attributed its origin to frustration and puritanism among mystical officers in Central Java; nor is it surprising that its leaders were put to flight within twenty-four hours by the man who was to rule and subdue a nation of 135 million people, Major-General Suharto.

The rebels had left Suharto off their list. This was strange, because he was more important than most of those murdered.

In 1962 he had been entrusted with the task of driving the Dutch from New Guinea, a major operation with repercussions that led to tense meetings of the United Nations. At the time of the coup, he headed Kostrad (Strategic Reserve Command); troops under his orders were engaged in the confrontation with Malaysia. If he was not reputed to be among those who squandered money, led a gay life and insulted the nation's women, neither was Nasution. It is conceivable that Untung felt some loyalty to him. Untung had become a national hero when, under Suharto's command, he was the first paratrooper to be dropped into the West Irian jungle in 1962; and Suharto had attended his wedding in Yogyakarta, Central Java.

If the account given by his biographer, O. G. Roeder,[2] is correct, Suharto heard of the coup only by chance. A television technician, on his way home, it appears, had noticed 'some unusual activities' outside the houses of Nasution and Major-General Harjono, one of the six who were murdered. He informed an army captain, who was loath to disturb a general at such an hour and called on Suharto's civilian neighbour, Mashuri, who later became one of Suharto's ministers. Mashuri passed the information on to Suharto at 5.30 a.m. It seems there was nothing to indicate that generals had been kidnapped and murdered. But Suharto 'had a very unpleasant foreboding on hearing the first vague reports'. He had a shower, put on his battle dress and, since his driver was not yet on duty, drove his jeep to Kostrad HQ, close to the palace. He passed soldiers under his command on the road, but they did not salute him. Soon afterwards Suharto heard the news of the coup broadcast by Radio Indonesia. The radio said that Sukarno was under the protection of the 30 September Movement. But this was not true; Sukarno was missing when a leader of the movement tried to see him at the palace.

Sukarno, according to evidence given by his aides at subsequent trials, spent the night at the house of his Japanese wife, Ratna Sari Dewi. He was told about 6 a.m. of the shooting at Nasution's house, and immediately set out for the palace. While he was on his way a security officer at the palace radioed his escort that troops had surrounded the building. He then changed direction and went to the house of another of his wives, Hariati, in the outskirts of Jakarta, where he conferred with his aides about what should be done to protect him. One suggestion, according to his aides, was that he should go to sea in a warship; but Sukarno chose to go to Halim, from which he would have been able to fly in an emergency. While a plane was soon standing by, it would be surprising if Sukarno had been unable to establish that the *putsch* leaders were at the base and if that were not one of his reasons for going there. His aides said that he arrived at Halim about 9.30 a.m. He conferred first with Air Vice-Marshal Omar Dhani then, separately, with Brigadier-General Supardjo, who was deeply involved in the plot. Supardjo said at his trial that after hearing his explanation of what had happened during the night, Sukarno clapped him on the shoulder and said: 'That sort of thing will happen in a revolution.' Dhani said that Sukarno expounded the inevitability of such incidents in a big revolution like Indonesia's, but warned that there must be no more bloodshed.

While Sukarno was temporizing at Halim, Suharto was briskly taking action at Kostrad HQ. But for a time he was working largely in the dark. He knew nothing of the murders at Halim. Even the President's whereabouts was a mystery at first. Suharto did not hear from him until 10 a.m., when he received a message that Sukarno was safe 'at a place about two hours drive from Kostrad HQ'. He said later that he guessed that Sukarno was at Halim, and asked the messenger to inform him that he was dealing with the situation in Jakarta.

Suharto had to go carefully. Sukarno was at Halim, where the rebels had their headquarters. Omar Dhani was obviously supporting the coup. There were countless officers in the army who, for one reason or another, shared Untung's views on the generals. With Sukarno yet to declare his position, it was a situation that required all the resolution and shrewdness that Suharto was to show from that time on. Leadership of the counter-coup was not automatically Suharto's. He was not Yani's deputy, but, as a field commander, had acted in his place during previous absences. Nasution, as Defence Minister and the most senior general, might well have taken command, had he been willing and quick enough, even though he had no troops directly under his control; but Suharto had him shunted to the military hospital, and he did not appear at Kostrad HQ until 4 p.m. By this time Suharto was in a position to strike at the rebels. Nasution told him go ahead.

After having made careful soundings in the morning Suharto ordered the Siliwangi Division tanks and armoured cars, on which the rebels had been counting, to move to Jakarta under officers whom he could trust. He also called in para-commandos (RPKAD), led by Colonel (later Brigadier-General) Sarwo Edhie, who was to play a leading part in ousting Sukarno and wiping out the PKI. He said later that he could have routed the rebels in the morning, without the extra men and armour, but he did not want to plunge the army into internecine war. With the loyalty of the para-commandos and tank troops assured, he was in an overwhelming position when he opened negotiations through emissaries with the deputy commanders of the two battalions from East and Central Java, which were drawn up menacingly in front of his head-quarters. He told them they had been tricked into taking part in the coup; there was no plot against Sukarno, he said. The rebels played for time, but it was against them. At 3 p.m. Suharto warned the deputy commanders that if they did not parade their men and surrender within thirty minutes he would crush them. At least one company, it appears, slipped off to Halim, but most of the troops outside Suharto's headquarters surrendered. Soon afterwards, about 5 p.m., both the armoured troops and the para-commandos arrived. It was then a simple matter for Suharto to capture Radio Indonesia and the telecommunications building. He was in control of Jakarta by about 7 p.m.

It remained to clear out the rebels from Halim air base. Suharto had his tanks with which. to persuade them that they had lost. But in the afternoon Omar Dhani had issued an Order of the Day supporting the 30 September Movement and declaring that its aim was to protect the revolution and the President from CIA subversion. Suharto moved his headquarters to the sports complex built by the Russians at Senayan, a few miles from the centre.

It is hard to believe that Sukarno did not see or know of Dhani's Order of the Day before it was broadcast at 3 p.m. It might even have been a bluff, instigated by himself, to unnerve Kostrad, for Sukarno had already begun going through his palace routine of balancing acts. Cautiously he had conferred with the plotters one by one, avoiding any commitment to the conspiracy. As supreme commander of the armed forces, he summoned the police and navy chiefs for separate conferences. He also called for some senior army generals. But Suharto forbade them to go; he explained later that he could not risk losing any more senior officers. One of Sukarno's three deputy premiers, Johannes Leimena, went to

Halim; but neither of the two others was in Jakarta; Chairul Saleh was in Peking and Subandrio, who was both senior Deputy Premier and Foreign Minister, was in North Sumatra.

✓ Sukarno ignored Suharto's action to restore order, and did not at that stage condemn the 30 September Movement. At the same time he did not associate himself with the Movement's broadcast decree; and he may have insisted that neither his name nor his office should be mentioned in it. In the afternoon Sukarno issued an ordinance stating that, as Supreme Commander, he had taken over temporary command of the armed forces and had appointed Major-General Pranoto Reksosamudro to carry out the army's day to day tasks – the job that Suharto was doing. But the order was not broadcast, although it appeared in newspapers the next morning, 2 October. By this time Sukarno had left Halim.

After the vague message in the morning of 1 October Suharto had not heard from Sukarno until 7.30 p.m. on the same day, when Admiral E. Martadinata, the navy chief, had arrived from Halim to inform him of Sukarno's ordinance. Suharto's reply was to warn Sukarno to leave the base at once, because it would soon be under attack. Within a few hours Sukarno left by car for the palace at Bogor, sixty kilometres south of Jakarta, where another of his wives, Hartini, was waiting for him; he was escorted by his aide, Colonel Bambang Widjanarko, who had followed Martadinata to Kostrad.[3] With Jakarta under control, Sarwo Edhie positioned para-commandos, tanks, and armoured cars near the air base about 3 a.m. on 2 October, and began negotiations with the base commander, Commodore Dewanto. At Dewanto's suggestion the two went to Bogor to see the President, who sent an order to Supardjo that there must be no bloodshed. The rebels vanished after two air force men and one of Sarwo Edhie's had been killed in sporadic shooting.

Early in the afternoon Suharto also went to Bogor and took another step in the series of confrontations that were to end in ↵Sukarno's fall. Sukarno firmly declared that he had taken over leadership of the armed forces. He reiterated that Pranoto Reksosamudro would be temporarily in charge of day to day operations, but added that Suharto would restore order and security in accordance with a policy outlined by Sukarno. Suharto had no intention of weakening his newly gained power by sharing the command with Pranoto. But he avoided the issue for a time by asking Sukarno what had happened to the six generals. Sukarno gave him no satisfactory information. Suharto then reported in some detail on what he had done to restore order. At an appropriate moment he said: 'There is no such thing in military life as having two commanders, formally appointed at the same time.' By Javanese standards of politeness this was a blunt rebuff to the President. Having made his stand, Suharto needed only to ignore Pranoto altogether. He was sure of his officers at Kostrad; and Sukarno, while hesitating at Halim, had confused some who might otherwise have rallied to him.

A three-minute speech recorded by Sukarno was broadcast about 2 a.m. on 3 October. It was the first time that the people had heard their President in the forty-eight hours since the *putsch* began. In a tired voice he still referred to himself as Great Leader of the Revolution, a style accorded to him by the MPR, and repeated his order that Pranoto and Suharto should divide the command. But he knew that his power was seriously threatened. On 4 October he wrote to Dewi that he was calling a conference of all military commanders and deputy commanders in Bogor.[4] In another letter he mentioned a secret conference with the staff of the Siliwangi Division, which he described as his 'strongest rampart'. He said an intrigue was afoot to transfer the Siliwangi Commander, Major-General Adjie, to Jakarta, but that the regimental staff was opposed to it. Dewi had persuaded Sukarno to trust Nasution. He accepted her view that Nasution was reliable, despite Nasution's 'political immaturity'. 'I will trust him from now on', he added. Sukarno wrote that it was not yet clear whether a group of generals had planned a coup against him; evidence was conflicting.

Hard though he fought, nothing that Sukarno did after 30 September amounted to more than obstacles, formidable though some of them were, on Suharto's road to the presidency. For years Sukarno had been able to manipulate the political élite. But this was a game at which he could take his time; in the cumbersome politics of Indonesia nothing was very urgent. The situation that had flared up in Jakarta was foreign to his experience and beyond the scope of his talent. He was no longer faced with impotent politicians; his adversary now was a ruthless military strategist, who was to prove not only a manipulator of unexcelled patience, but, in the Javanese environment, a master of timing and devastating action. And Sukarno was ill and worn out; he wrote to Dewi from Bogor that because of heavy work and responsibility he was tired, but could not sleep.

It took considerable time to trace the six missing generals, because their killers had sealed and covered the well into which they were thrown. But by 4 October army investigators had found the spot and soldiers were lowered on ropes to bring up the bodies. Suharto was there and made a radio broadcast. His voice was angry. 'I am witnessing with my own eyes the cruelty of the barbaric adventurers who called themselves the 30 September Movement', he said. He pointed out that Halim base had been used to train Communist youth and women. The broadcast was followed by an exhibition of the bodies on television. Extraordinary accounts of what had been seen were circulated. One Western correspondent reported that the bodies had been decapitated and dismembered. But photographs provided by the army showed no dismemberment; and Brigadier-General Sugandhi, who saw the bodies when they were retrieved, said there was none, although eyes were missing and there were many slashes and bullet holes. John Hughes, *Christian Science Monitor* correspondent,[5] saw the photographs and wrote that it was difficult to determine how much damage to the bodies was caused by decomposition and how much by other means. A panel of doctors appointed by Sukarno said there was no evidence of mutilation.

The question of the PKI

The above sub-heading serves a double purpose: it marks not only a turn in the narrative, but a division between what is certain, or reasonably certain, and what is disputable – the question of whether or not the PKI or some of its members took part in plotting the coup. An unbiased attempt to get to the bottom of the affair has been made by Harold Crouch, who examined transcripts of evidence given at the trials of Communists and members of the armed forces.[6] What he has done, in effect, is to eliminate some of the contradictions and assume that the residue is largely true. My own view is that when witnesses have been proved untruthful, the whole of their evidence, not merely part of it, should be treated with greater suspicion than is apparent in Crouch's essay. Even after he has done his sifting, Crouch finds it necessary to put up various hypotheses. His thesis is spattered with phrases like 'the most likely resolution to these contradictions', 'the latter hypothesis', 'several possible interpretations', 'it seems', 'it is not clear'. I mention this not to depreciate a useful exercise, but to demonstrate the difficulties. In the end Crouch finds it is 'quite likely that the idea to purge the top army leaders originated among middle-level officers in Jakarta'. He believes that Aidit became directly involved after the plot had been hatched, but before 30 September. Not all investigators share this view: some think Aidit initiated the *putsch*; others that he was not involved at all.

Just as some writers begin with the idea that the PKI leaders had good reason to initiate the *putsch*, and then set out to prove their assumption, Anderson and McVey advance the hypothesis that the PKI had no reason to become involved, and try to demonstrate that they were not.[7] Both are scholars with considerable knowledge of Indonesia; McVey's *The Rise of Indonesian Communism*, covering the pre-independence period, is the standard work on the subject. Yet their supposition that the PKI was so successful in the existing political circumstances that it would not have initiated the plot has two weaknesses: it discounts what could well have been alarm in the PKI at the prospect that Sukarno's death would lead to a military coup; and, surprisingly, it disregards the fact that events that are irrational by any standards are recurrent in Indonesian politics. Anderson and McVey seem to overrate the calibre of the PKI leaders. Certainly, some PKI men were capable. But their achievement was merely relative; for any semblance of efficiency and foresight in Indonesia stands out against the traditional background of imprecision and muddle. Confronted with a critical situation like that created by Sukarno's illness, the Communists, with a few probable exceptions, would have been no less likely than any others to relapse into the irrationality that pervades the archipelago. Nikita Khruschev, an intuitive man, sensed that there was something odd about the party during his visit to Indonesia in February 1960. Commenting on the PKI's claim to have three million members, he said dryly: 'A Communist party is not like a grocer's shop. It does not follow that the more goods you have in your window the more successful you will be.'

One of the main difficulties in any study of the *putsch* is that at least some of those who confessed appear to have been beaten.

Another is that getting a reliable answer to a question in any circumstances is usually harder in Indonesia and other parts of Asia than in the West, where it is hard enough. Indonesians will more frequently represent as fact what they think might have happened, ought to have happened, or even what the questioner would like to have happened.

The 30 September Movement accused the generals, and the generals accuse the Movement, of being motived by the same aim – to seize power before Sukarno died or became incapacitated. Early in August there was a rumour that he had suffered a dangerous kidney attack. It is significant that the first substantial confirmation of this rumour came in the rebel broadcast on 1 October. The radio said that Sukarno had been 'gravely ill' early in August and that the alleged council of generals had expected him to die soon. This was an odd announcement. It suggests that the men behind the 30 September Movement attributed to the generals motives that were, in fact, their own. For if Sukarno had been about to die, there would have been no need for the generals to overthrow him. On the other hand the PKI would have had good reason to inspire a military coup against the generals: it could not have matched the army's tanks and trained troops in a fight for power that might have taken place on Sukarno's death, even if the 100,000 small arms had arrived from Peking in time. The army asserts that the only council of generals was a body formed to discuss matters such as promotion, and that there was no plot against Sukarno.

The army's case that the PKI was behind Untung's adventure rests almost entirely on suspect and often contradictory evidence. The only important, indisputable facts that it has presented are that Communist youths and women were present at Halim during the *putsch* and that the Communist newspaper *Harian Rakjat* (People's Daily) published an article supporting the 30 September Movement on 2 October – after the coup had been suppressed.

The presence at Halim air base of members of the Communist organizations, Pemuda Rakjat (Popular Youth), Gerwani (Indonesian Woman's Movement) and Sobsi, the PKI trade union, has been well established. They had been undergoing courses of one to two weeks since early in July with the approval of Omar Dhani, and were obviously the nucleus of the intended 'fifth force'. The trainees were told that they were being prepared for guerrilla warfare in Malaysia, as part of the Nasakom movement. While the PKI was more vigorous than the other two Nasakom components in organizing youth for this purpose, some national-ists had arrived at Halim, and Moslems were due on 1 October. At the trials of those accused of complicity in the *putsch* the army produced witnesses who said that Communist youths had taken part in the kidnapping of the generals. There is no more reason to believe this than to accept evidence that was transparently false; it would have been odd to increase the hazard of such an operation by including inexperienced youth in the military raiding parties, but no folly can be excluded in what was a hare-brained affair from the beginning.

The army made widely publicized claims that Communist women and youth hacked and slashed the generals in a frenzied ritual killing after their arrival at Halim. These claims have unfortunately percolated as fact, with a little cautious dilution, into the work of at least one scholar.[8] More than a year after the *putsch* John Hughes was allowed to question some of the accused women, using an interpreter provided by the army. One was a Gerwani leader, who was not alleged to have been present at Halim, but to have been informed of the murder plans. She insisted to Hughes that she had known nothing of military training at Halim or of a plot against the generals; her main job was to campaign for lower food prices. Of three young girls interviewed, two denied having been at Halim on 1 October, but admitted they had been trained there earlier for action against Malaysia. When shown their written confessions they said they had signed them because they were afraid. The third girl morosely withdrew into herself and said nothing.

At an interview a week later the girl who had been silent eventually broke down when interrogated by two women army officers, who said they had taken down her signed confession. She said she had gone to Crocodile Hole on 30 September on instructions from a village official; previously she had undergone 10 days training there. That night she and other girls were awakened in their tent. Gerwani and Pemuda Rakjat girls and youths gathered in a field, dancing and singing the movement's songs while pointing at three men who had been brought there, one in pyjamas, one in shorts, and another with his eyes bandaged. Someone shouted 'Kill the capitalist bureaucrats.' The victims, who were 'tied up', 'were beaten and smashed with rifle butts'. A girl platoon leader handed out razor blades, and the girls slashed the men and gouged out their eyes. The generals cried in pain. They were taken closer to the well, where the women shot them.

Hughes reminded the girl that she had refused to talk on the previous occasion and asked if she had been threatened or ill-treated in the meantime. He says she 'shook her head in the negative' (as, indeed, she would). The girl who was described as the platoon leader who had issued the razor blades was one of the three who had been interviewed earlier; she persisted in denying that she was at the camp on 1 October. The third was not present at the second interview. But another girl told a story similar to that of the one who finally spoke, although it differed in detail. Hughes says that 'from the demeanour of the women involved, from other information and from evidence as best as it can be gathered about injuries to the generals' bodies' he believes that the stories are 'substantially correct'. But those with experience of how adept the Indonesian Army is in putting on a show may prefer to suspend judgment. None of the girls who were supposed to have taken part in the Crocodile Hole murders has been prosecuted, despite the immense propaganda value that such a trial would have. Is this merely because of a shortage of judges? Or is it because the accusations are too absurd to stand examination, even in an Indonesian military court?

Another pillar of the case against the PKI is the alleged presence of Aidit, its Chairman, at Halim on 1 October. The evidence for this is not strong. There is no clear picture of when he arrived at the base or how long he was there. Some writers, picking up bits and pieces from the army's transcripts of the trials, say he was at Halim for twenty-four hours; but this is doubtful. Air Force Major Sujono, who trained the Communist youths and girls, gave evidence that he drove Aidit and Pranoto Reksosamudro to Halim on the night of 30 September. Yet Sukarno's aide, Bambang Widjanarko, went looking for Pranoto at Kostrad HQ after Sukarno had appointed him temporary army commander on 1 October; Suharto declared that Pranoto would not go to Halim.[9] It is therefore likely that Sujono was lying when he said he took Pranoto to the air base; and he may also have lied when he said he drove Aidit. Further, Aidit was said to have spent the night at an air force sergeant's house; there appears to be no evidence that he met any of the coup leaders that night. If he was so inactive, what was the point of his being there? It is possible that he did not go to the base at all on the night of 30 September.

After Suharto had put down the *putsch* in Jakarta, Aidit went to Yogyakarta, Central Java. Whether or not he had taken part in the plot, he would have been able to foresee that the army would now use the *putsch* to annihilate his party. He consequently hid from the army until, according to Hughes, a squad found him on 22 November in the small wooden house of a retired railway worker near Solo. The army made no announcement about his fate, but let it be known through journalists that he was shot. If Aidit's alleged presence at Halim for an unknown period during the *putch* is circumstantial evidence of his guilt, Suharto's failure to bring him to trial is circumstantial evidence that there is no proof of it. It has been suggested that Suharto had Aidit shot because he feared that Sukarno would come to his rescue and bring about his release. I find this an unconvincing explanation. Sukarno would have had no more success in saving Aidit than other PKI leaders. And if the army could have shown conclusively that Aidit was behind the *putsch*, it would have delivered a blow, not only at the PKI, but at Sukarno, who had sheltered it. The Communist leaders who faced the military court poured out a mass of contradictory confessions that were reminiscent of the Moscow trials; but if Aidit had been in the dock he might have been able to prove his innocence. Perhaps that was why he was murdered.

The army maintains that the PKI leadership hid in the background and avoided inclusion in the Revolutionary Council to escape blame if the coup failed. If this were so, it would be extraordinary if after having acted with such circumspection Aidit ran the unnecessary risk of showing himself at Halim. It is also hard to believe that the man who had made the PKI the third largest Communist Party in the world, after those of the USSR and China, was closely associated with such a badly planned operation; and a man of Aidit's intelligence, which was disciplined by years of political analysis and decision, would have needed to suffer an exceptional lapse to countenance grotesque and futile torture of the generals, which has been represented as a premeditated act preceded by a distribution of razor blades (an odd weapon to choose in a country abounding with lethal knives).

Even then one would expect that he would wait until success of the coup was certain.

The publication in *Harian Rakjat* on 2 October of an editorial and two cartoons supporting the coup was seized upon by the army to prove the PKI's involvement. But it could show the opposite. This material would have been prepared at the latest on 1 October, when Aidit was supposed to be at Halim. A relatively shrewd, quick-thinking man like Aidit would soon have seen the confusion among the coup leaders, with people going to and fro between Jakarta and the base and Sukarno wavering. If an editorial had been ordered before the coup, the obvious thing to have done would have been to send a message suspending it until victory was certain. The fact that the article appeared suggests that Aidit, at least, was not aware of it. In that event the action of the editors would be comprehensible. Rumours that the generals were plotting to overthrow Sukarno, with American backing, were widespread among both civilians and servicemen. When they heard Radio Indonesia broadcast that Untung had arrested six generals, the editors could have regarded it as consistent with party policy to give him moral support. Like other Indonesian newspapers, *Harian Rakjat* splashed the radio news on page one. The main headline was 'Lieutenant-Colonel Untung, Tjakrabirawa Battalion Commander, Saves President and RI [Indonesian Republic] from Generals' Council Coup'. The editorial called for no mass uprising, but emphasized that the coup was 'an internal army affair'. This was a restatement of the declaration in the decree that the 30 September Movement was 'solely confined to the body of the army'. On the other hand, the emphasis that the coup was purely military could have been planted in both the decree and the article by Communists, who were involved, but wanted to keep the party's name out of it; in that case the article's publication after the coup had failed could be explained very satisfactorily by an executive bungle that would have been a trifle compared with the botch of the 30 September affair itself.

While the purely circumstantial links between the PKI and the coup are open to different interpretations, the confessions of party leaders and military men at their trials are so confusing that at best they indicate what might have happened, rather than show it beyond reasonable doubt. Scholars are uneasy about the evidence. Bernhard Dahm puts together his tale of the plot from witnesses' statements, without interrupting its flow to warn the reader that there is explicit evidence against his incrimination of Aidit;[10] but he protects himself by stating at the end of a long note at the back of his book that much of the evidence at the trials is of 'doubtful authenticity' and that his 'judgements must be regarded as provisional'.[11] J. D. Legge properly indicates the pitfalls and says in a footnote: 'since the Tribunal was concerned to establish a particular case it cannot, in itself, yield a complete answer. Neither, however, can its massive accumulation of evidence be entirely brushed aside as representing an attempt to frame the PKI.' I am not as impressed as Legge seems to be by the sheer quantity of evidence that is often conflicting. The fact that there was a 'massive accumulation' of statements is of no importance whatever. The contradictory tales that incriminated the Communists may have amounted to little more than the invention of Indonesian intelligence men, who are notorious for muddling their scripts. In my opinion, no conclusions, tentative or otherwise, should be drawn from the trials; while no possibility should be ruled out, the only acceptable state of mind is that of genuinely suspended judgment. For the army forfeited its credibility at the outset by producing a confession that was proved to be as absurd as it was false; and what was done once could have been done a dozen times later.

The confession was extracted from Njono, a member of the PKI politburo and Chairman of Sobsi. It was published by the government news agency, Antara, early in December 1965. This trophy remained the foundation of the army's attempt to prove to the world that the PKI leadership took part in the coup until January 1966, when Anderson and McVey demolished it by circulating cyclostyled copies of their work.[12] They showed that Njono's account of the plot could not have been correct: among the inaccuracies was that Aidit and Njono were said to have attended crucial politburo meetings in July, when in fact they were abroad. At his trial in February Njono withdrew the confession, explaining that when he made it Communists were frequently beaten up during interrogation. Coincidentally with the trial, the Tokyo newspaper, *Asahi Shimbun*, published a confession that Aidit was said to have made after his capture. This was such a parody of what Aidit could have been expected to write that it might have been composed by the CIA. The army, without committing itself, gravely directed journalists' attention to it, but few people took it seriously.

The Communists whose evidence contributed most to the lore that has been built up round the *putsch* were: Sudisman, who was a member of the politburo and fourth man in the leadership; Peris Pardede, a candidate member of the politburo; Sjam, an obscure man with many aliases, who said he was head of a PKI special bureau formed to infiltrate the armed forces; Supono, or Pono, said to be one of Sjam's assistants; and Njono. Each of these witnesses told his story in great detail. Here we are concerned mainly with the most important contradictions.

Njono said at his trial in February 1966 that after Aidit's return from abroad the politburo met three times in August to discuss three matters – Sukarno's illness, information that a council of generals was plotting to overthrow him and the intention of a group of Sukarnoist officers to strike at the generals first. The question of whether or not to support the dissident officers was raised. At the final meeting on 28 August 1965 the politburo decided to adopt Aidit's suggestion simply to report the generals' conspiracy to Sukarno. (Sukarno did, in fact, receive information that the generals were plotting a coup; he raised the matter with Yani, who said there was nothing in it.) But the Sukarnoist officers decided to go ahead with their plans. Early in September they sent the General-Secretary of the Pemuda Rakjat, Sukanto, who had played a part in the recruiting of youths and women for training at Halim, to ask Njono for more volunteers. Njono said he agreed to this request, in spite of the politburo's decision. The recruits were told they were to fight Nekolim (neo-colonialism and imperialism), which was threatening to invade Indonesia.

Crouch's study of the trials shows that Pardede and Sudisman contradicted Njono and each other. Pardede said at Njono's trial that the politburo met 'a few days' after 17 August, Independence Day. Aidit told the meeting that 'progressive officers' had asked for his advice on whether to act before the generals could launch a coup. He recommended preventive military action, but when he asked the others for their opinions nobody replied. At Aidit's suggestion the meeting agreed to allow the four-man politburo standing committee to make the decision. Pardede said that about ten days later Sudisman, who was a member of the committee, told him that it had been decided to support the officers.

Sudisman at his trial in July 1967 contradicted both Njono and Pardede by stating that not only the committee but the politburo itself had decided to support the officers. His evidence was greatly confused. At one stage he corroborated Pardede's statement that the crucial politburo meeting was held a few days after 17 August; at another he said it was on 28 August. But, irrespective of when the meeting took place, Sudisman contradicted Njono's statement that the politburo decided against supporting the officers and Pardede's that it had left the question to the committee. It is conceivable that the politburo ratified the committee's decision after 28 August, but this does not appear to have been suggested. Sudisman incriminated the leadership further by stating that Aidit ordered Njono to recruit about 2,000 volunteers as a reserve for the military rebels. This contrasts with Njono's evidence that he received the request from the officers.

None of these three witnesses indicated any substantial link between the PKI top leadership and the officers. This was left to the mysterious Sjam, a self-confessed double agent, who was said to have been arrested in March 1967. Earlier this name cropped up in the interrogation of Untung. Hughes wrote at the time that it was thought to be an alias for Tjugito, a member of the PKI central committee; but this was not so, and at his trial Sjam appeared as an obscure party organizer, who, in addition to his known duties, had secretly worked for Aidit for many years. Since Aidit was dead, his story could not be contradicted. Sjam gave evidence at Sudisman's trial and was himself tried in February and March 1968. He said his real name was Kamarusaman. In 1957 he was given the task of winning over service officers to the PKI cause; at the same time he was acting as an informer for the Jakarta garrison.

The question arises as to whom Sjam was really working for. He said that his aim in informing for the garrison was to infiltrate it; but the garrison would obviously have expected him to provide information about the PKI. Sjam said that late in 1964 the politburo set up a special bureau for his infiltration work. He was put in charge, with two assistants, Supono and Walujo, and was responsible only to Aidit. On 12 August Aidit summoned him to his house, told him that a generals' council was planning to take over the country if Sukarno died, and ordered him to 'prepare a movement'. Sjam and his two assistants then saw Untung and other officers, who agreed to join them in an operation against the generals. He and Aidit drafted the decree issued by the 30 September Movement on 1 October.

If Sjam is to be believed, this was a remarkable situation. Under Aidit's leadership the PKI, which was the first Communist Party to be formed in Asia beyond the frontiers of the USSR, had become powerful in Indonesia. While the quality of its following was inferior, it claimed 3 million members, and those of its mass organizations of peasants, trade unionists, youth, women and various other groups were said to total more than 16 million; in the 1955 general elections it obtained 16 per cent of the votes, and in the subsequent regional poll became the strongest party in Java; it was represented in Sukarno's 108-man cabinet, and had a good chance of penetrating the inner cabinet. The party was not militant by Asian Communist standards; some foreign political writers said that Sukarno had tamed and domesticated it. Yet, according to the army, all this achievement of organization and prudence was risked in a stupid gamble; and, if Sjam's evidence is accepted, Aidit entrusted the dangerous task of organizing a coup to a minor party official, whose main work had been that of shady infiltration. Even Khruschev might have found this hard to believe. Nevertheless, an aberration provoked by fear of a generals' coup cannot be ruled out; and Untung confirmed that he and other officers had met Sjam.

Yet again there is contradiction. Untung said that, as an officer in Sukarno's guard, he had decided solely on his own initiative (not on Sjam's suggestion) to form a movement when he heard of the activities of the generals' council, and got in touch with Colonel Latief, an infantry brigade commander. A group of officers held their first meeting on 6 September at the house of a Captain Wahjudi, who later withdrew. Untung said Sjam and Supono were there, but that he had not met them before; Wahjudi said Latief brought them to the house. Sjam, according to his own and officers' evidence, was one of the main conspirators from that time. Latief, who seems to have met Sjam and Supono before Untung did, was never tried. After pointed references to this fact had been published abroad, he made a brief appearance at Supono's trial in 1972.

Some academics are impressed by Njono's revised statement, in which he again admitted PKI involvement in the conspiracy.

They ask what he could have had to gain by making such a confession. That question may be answered by three others. If he lied the first time, why should he have not lied the second? Why should his evidence be preferred to that of another Communist, Iskandar Subekti, who said at his trial in December 1972 that the PKI had nothing to do with planning the coup? More generally, what did Stalin's victims have to gain by their obviously false admissions?

I attended a hearing of Supono's trial. Grim-faced officers glowered down from their benches while Supono, a thin, shrewd-looking little man sat in a chair below them. Led by his counsel, sentence by sentence, he politely explained the details and motives of his alleged actions. A few months later it was announced that this meek figure had boldly refused to appeal to the President for clemency after his being sentenced to death and had defiantly affirmed his belief in the aims of the PKI. It seemed odd that he had not made his stand in court, when reporters were present to publicize it dramatically, rather than submit to days of tedious cross-examination that were certain to end in his conviction. At his trial he was certainly no Dimitrov. Perhaps both he and Sjam were involved in the army game. Indonesians who were released after having been detained following the riots in January 1974 said they saw the two men in prison. Far from having been executed, they were allowed out from time to time and wrote reports for the army on the political situation.

The army's record of fabrication and the unsatisfactory evidence of the trials does not, of course, mean that no Communists were involved in the plot. Whatever happened was almost certainly too bizarre for a Western mind to conceive; if the truth were told it would probably contain vital elements that no investigator has ever imagined. Perhaps there is some parallel between the events of September 1965 and the tragi-comedy of 1926, when Communists made sporadic, hopeless attempts at nationwide revolution.[13] In the 1920s a number of small, separated movements were pressing for rebellion against the Dutch. The Comintern advised caution in assessing their value; but some PKI leaders, including Alimin and Musso, were convinced that, as men on the spot, they knew better and believed that these purely local agitations could be welded into a revolution. In 1926 Alimin went so far as to accuse Moscow of slackness and to declare that

Eastern peoples would have to save the dictatorship of the proletariat in Russia from collapse.

Alimin sought approval of his proposed revolution from Tan Malaka, an exiled leader, who was living in Manila. Tan Malaka was dismayed; he warned that a revolt would fail and bring disaster to the party and the people; he urged Alimin to abandon a plan to seek support from the Comintern in Moscow. Alimin went from Manila to Singapore, where a meeting decided that he and Musso should go to Moscow, in spite of Tan Malaka's opposition. Tan Malaka hastened to Singapore in the hope of stopping the adventure, but the two had already left. After getting themselves mixed up with Zinoviev and other members of the doomed Trotskyist Left, Alimin and Musso saw Stalin. By this time events in China had brought the Comintern closer to the Trotskyist view that the Far East was ready for revolution. Stalin told Alimin and Musso that he was not unfavourable to revolution in Indonesia, but that he was against any badly planned action that risked failure. In other words, it seemed that Stalin thought that a revolutionary situation existed, but doubted if the PKI was capable of exploiting it. The upshot was that Alimin and Musso left Moscow in October, six months after their arrival, with instructions to call off the revolution and to campaign for radical nationalism and restoration of the PKI's legality.

The story now takes one of those unexpected turns, which, if more of them could be unearthed, would explain much that is mystifying in Indonesia. PKI leaders had agreed in Singapore that if Moscow opposed revolution they would launch guerrilla warfare on their own initiative. And before he met Stalin Musso sent a message to Batavia, instructing that this plan be put into operation; he managed to get his order out by pretending that the Indonesian delegate to the Comintern, Semaun, had authorized him to use a secret channel. Semaun discovered the trick, but thought it wise to say nothing about it. Thus Stalin was put to the trouble of delivering one of his painstaking analyses to his Indonesian comrades, while remaining oblivious of their capers.

It is not known if the message reached Batavia. But whether it arrived or not would have made no difference, because the Tegal branch of the PKI had decided to go on with the revolt, willy nilly. Their motives were scarcely Leninist; the branch leader was bent on avenging the death of his imprisoned brother and others were eager to even scores with police, who had wounded some of them in violent clashes. At a meeting of Tegal and other branch members in August, the Tegal men declared that once the revolt began it was certain to spread rapidly to other areas. There was some dissent, but Tegal went ahead. On a night late in September 1926 the revolutionaries took up position and awaited the explosion of a firework, which was to be their signal for attacking the police and taking over the area. But the man who was to have given the signal mistook the date and did not let off his firework until the next night. That, for the moment, was the end of the revolution. But the party's Batavia committee followed this abortive operation with a plan for a more widespread revolt, planned to take place in November, only two weeks after the meeting at which the decision was made. Uprisings did break out this time in both Java and Sumatra, but they were quickly suppressed. Dutch police had been in possession of the party's telegram code. There are, of course, great differences between the situation in 1926 and that in 1965, not the least of which is that the Dutch had imprisoned or exiled the best PKI leaders. But the mentality of the rest would have prevailed in 1965; for not all were Aidits.

The army frequently dropped hints that Sukarno was a party to the *putsch*, and on one occasion the officer who prosecuted Subandrio, the Foreign Minister, said the interrogations had proved it. But no proof has ever been produced. In 1972 Nasution said on television that Sukarno was behind the 30 September Movement. Some months later I asked him what evidence he had. He said that when Sukarno left a meeting he was addressing at Senajan on the eve of the *putsch*, for several minutes, his aide, Bambang Widjanarko, handed him a note; the next day Sukarno sent for his uniform and took a piece of paper from a pocket; the note was obviously about the coup. When I asked Nasution whether he had any other evidence to support his accusation, he said he could not remember and referred me to an intelligence captain, who, he said, had a file on the matter. I tried several times to see the captain, but he was always unavailable.[14] In my interviews with Nasution I had formed a high opinion of his discernment. It therefore came as a surprise that he should have defamed the founder of his nation without possessing evidence sufficiently impressive to remember. But I found repeatedly in

Indonesia that in juridical matters even apparently trained minds failed to distinguish between suspicion and certainty. There are other indications of Sukarno's possible complicity.[15] Supardjo, one of the *putsch* ringleaders, had gone to the palace from Halim on 1 October, apparently to report the murder of the generals to Sukarno, who happened not to be there. Omar Dhani saw Sukarno on 29 September, after having met Supardjo the day before.

The mystery would fall short of Indonesian standards if there were not at least circumstantial evidence that Suharto himself knew something about plans for the coup. And, in fact, there is: while Bambang was supposed to be handing a note to Sukarno, Suharto met Latief on the night of 30 September, a few hours before the rebels set out from Halim. W. F. Wertheim, who is noted for both his important sociological works on Indonesia and his hostility to the military rulers, has made much of this.[16] He quotes an interview in Arnold Brackman's *The Communist Collapse in Indonesia*, in which Suharto says:

Two days before September 30, our three-year-old son had an accident at home. He poured hot soup on himself and we had to rush him to the hospital. Many friends visited my son there and on the night of September 30 I was there, too. It is interesting to look back. I remember Colonel Latief dropped into the hospital that evening to inquire about my son's health. I was touched by his thoughtfulness. Of course, later Latief turned out to be an important figure in the events that followed. Today I realize that he did not go to the hospital that evening to check on my son but, rather, to check on me. He must have verified the genuine seriousness of my son's accident and confirmed my preoccupation with his condition. I remained at the hospital until about midnight and then returned home.

Wertheim comments:

How curious, that a man, who was one of the main plotters in the coup, and whose attention should have been fully occupied by the preparations for what was to happen that night, found time to go out of his way to inquire after the health of a little child! Suharto's explanation that Latief

probably wanted to know whether he, Suharto, the famous
fighting general who had led, on the first of March, 1949,
the raid on Jogja, then in Dutch hands, was so much preoccupied with the illness of his child that he could be counted
upon not to interfere is too ludicrous to be taken seriously.
What matters is that the plotters, far from finding
Suharto unimportant, on the contrary deemed him so
important that they wanted to make sure where he stood,
just before their action would start. What exactly was
discussed between the two at the military hospital will
remain a secret, I suppose, until Colonel Latief is free and
willing to speak. There is at least a reason to assume that,
through this meeting, Suharto got some information about the
plans for a coup. This could explain his efficient steps in
the afternoon of the first of October.

There remains one question: why did Suharto and
Brackman release this rather compromising story? I can
find only one plausible explanation. Maybe the visit of
Latief to the hospital, and his meeting with Suharto on the
night of September 30, had become known (Latief may have
spoken to some co-prisoners); rumours may have circulated
in certain quarters. There may have been some reason to
provide an explanation which sound [sic] rather harmless.
 . . . But through his contact with Colonel Latief a few
hours before the coup occurred he has, no doubt become
terlibat (involved) in it – and this a hundred time [sic]
more than all those thousands of small peasants who are
being innocently held prisoners for many years as being
terlibat, and who, when they are released do not find work
or land any more. According to the norms applied by his
own régime he would certainly belong to the 'B category'
political prisoners, and his exile to the island of Buru
would be much more justified than that of the present
inmates of the concentration camps.

There seems to have been an attempt to conceal Suharto's
meeting with Latief. Even the fact that he had been to the hospital
did not emerge for a considerable time. As late as 1967 Hughes
published:[17] 'Sources close to him say that he had, that night
[30 September], taken the advice of a seer to spend it at the

"confluence of two waters". So he had taken his son fishing at a spot where the rivers surged down into the sea.' The deliberate circulation of this charming anecdote in Western circles illustrates the way in which foreigners are taken out of their depth in Indonesia. To Westerners the tale was seen as evidence that the *putsch* surprised Suharto; but the Javanese who spread it about must have known that it was a *pasemon* – a device that exposes while being outwardly harmless. Certain Javanese believed that Suharto had provoked the coup to eliminate its victims and Sukarno at the same time. The seer in the *pasemon* was the *dukun*, upon whose advice, it was assumed, Suharto must have acted; to go to the confluence of two waters is to declare loyalty to opposing camps; to go fishing is to seek personal advantage. At least one highly placed military man appears to have concurred with the message of the *pasemon*. While driving in Jakarta with a European friend of mine one evening he asked: 'Has it ever occurred to you that it is strange that Kostrad escaped in the coup?' This pointed reference to the fact that Suharto was not on the rebels' list, coming from such a source, startled my friend, who cautiously replied: 'It is certainly an interesting question.' The military man said: 'He and Yani couldn't stand each other, you know.' The conversation then ceased.

Even if Sukarno, Suharto, or both, knew that the generals were to be kidnapped, there is no reason to suppose that either expected them to be murdered. Crouch has made some important points on how far the plotters meant to go. The only witness who said that they intended murder from the beginning appears to have been Sjam, who provided yet another contradiction. At one stage he said that the plan was to deliver the generals to the Revolutionary Council, which was to investigate what was believed to be their conspiracy against Sukarno; at another he said it had been decided to kill them. Crouch thinks it likely that the generals who were taken alive to Halim were murdered in panic when it was found that the others had been killed at their houses and that Nasution had escaped.[18] He says the evidence shows that the PKI did not intend to take over the government and that killing the generals was disastrously inconsistent with its [at most] purely defensive action. Crouch then raises the interesting issue of what would have happened if the operation had gone 'according to plan'. He says:

If the generals, including Nasution, had all been arrested
and accused of plotting against the President, it is possible
to believe that the President would have endorsed the 30
September Movement's action. With presidential
endorsement it would have been very difficult for the
remaining army leadership to move against the dissidents.
Most likely the matter would have been settled in the
traditional style of *musyawarah* (consultation) leading to a
compromise which weakened the 'hawks' in the army leadership
without reversing its fundamentally anti-communist outlook.

This seems to me to be a perceptive speculation. It may serve
to steady some scholars who have been put off balance by the
melodramatic propaganda that streamed from both the army and
Western embassies in the days following the recovery of the bodies.

The massacre

Most Indonesian soldiers and civilians, Western diplomats, all
those who loathed or feared Communism, believed automatically
that the PKI was to blame for the murders at Crocodile Hole.
The presence of members of PKI organizations at Halim was
evidence enough, and righteous wrath stifled further thought.
Nasution, anguished at his daughter's death, was seized by hatred.
'They must be smashed immediately', he said. 'Since they have
committed treason, they must be destroyed and quarantined from
all activities in our fatherland.' It was in this spirit that the army
set about exterminating the PKI to its roots. The scarcely necessary mandate to restore order that Suharto had extracted from
Sukarno on 2 October, after the *putsch* had virtually petered out,
became a licence to make countless arbitrary arrests and to provoke
a massacre that hundreds of thousands who were bereaved still
yearn to avenge. Estimates of the number killed vary greatly.
Hughes thought it was about 200,000. Adam Malik, the future
Foreign Minister, said a 'fair figure' was 160,000. A *Life Magazine*
correspondent, after spending several months travelling from
village to village, put it at 400,000. Any of these totals is credible,
for the highest is only 13 per cent of the 3 million members
claimed by the PKI.

The recovery of the generals' bodies from the well inflamed
anti-Communist emotions in Jakarta, but the army waited until

the funeral of Nasution's daughter before it unleashed the first of the riots that preceded the killing. At the funeral, as if by pre-arrangement, a high naval officer gave Moslem student leaders a one-word signal, *sikat*, which means 'sweep'. The next morning, armed with pistols, knives and clubs they raided and set ablaze the PKI headquarters, while soldiers blocked the approaching streets and firemen looked on. What had happened to the British and Americans was now happening to the Communists. Mobs ransacked the houses of Aidit and other PKI leaders. Some demonstrators called out, 'Long live America', as they drove past the United States Embassy. Because the Chinese Embassy failed to fly its flag at half-mast on the day of the generals' funeral, soldiers wrecked its commercial attaché's office. Traditional hostility to the 3 million Chinese inhabitants was roused and anti-Chinese rioting spread to many parts of the country. Ships came later from People's China to take away Chinese citizens who had been put in refugee camps in Sumatra.

From his own account to Hughes it was Sarwo Edhie who launched the massacre in Central Java, after asking Suharto to order him there.[19] Sarwo Edhie's task was not only to organize murder in the villages, but to deal with officers who had rebelled after hearing the broadcast announcement of Untung's operation. The rebels had taken over divisional headquarters at Semarang and brigade headquarters at Solo; and at Yogyakarta they had killed a battalion commander with a mortar barrel and his chief of staff with a large stone. They fled when the coup collapsed in Jakarta. Subsequently the three ringleaders were shot after having been captured near the Mount Merapi volcano. The fact that they were silenced, like Aidit, instead of being put on trial, may be significant. One of the three, Colonel Suherman, who was head of intelligence at Semarang, had recently returned from a training course at Fort Leavenworth. It is possible that his experience there gave him grounds for believing that the United States was, in fact, using certain generals in an attempt to overthrow Sukarno – a speculation that is consistent with Anderson and McVey's belief that disillusionment and frustration of officers in Central Java were a factor in the 30 September plot.

Sarwo Edhie and his para-commandos left Jakarta on 17 October. Within a week they had crushed such little resistance as Communist youths were able to organize. Some peasants, armed for the most part with only knives and improvised, bamboo spears, felled trees to protect their villages; but nothing they did could save them from the soldiers. At the approaches of one village women turned their bare bottoms contemptuously towards troops in an armoured car; it has been reported that they were members of Gerwani, but it is difficult to see how this could have been established with reasonable certainty while the soldiers rolled forward. The women persisted with their insult. Sarwo Edhie, who was directing the operation personally, ordered a gunner to fire. The women fell. Villagers rushed up to protest; they were also shot. The troops went from village to village, taking their victims away by the truck-load to be killed. Many were obliged to dig their own graves. It appears that those taken by the army were usually shot. But some military men gave anti-Communists a taste for blood by handing their prisoners over to be killed with knives or sickles. Sometimes an entire village population, excepting infants, was exterminated when the para-commandos suspected it of being wholly PKI.

Sarwo Edhie did not have enough troops to attack all the villages that were supposed to be legitimate targets either because the men had joined Sobsi or for any reason that an informer would offer. The solution was to train Moslems and others like hounds to smell out and kill anyone considered to be Communist. 'We decided to encourage the anti-Communist civilians to help with the job', Sarwo Edhie said. 'In Solo we gathered the youth, the nationalist groups, the religious organizations. We gave them two or three days' training, then sent them out to kill the Communists.'

Before the *putsch* a few clashes had occurred between wilder youths of the PKI and PNI (Indonesian National Party) and between the PKI and Ansor (the youth movement of the Nahdatul Ulama – Moslem Theologians' Council). The smouldering of these old feuds made it easy for the army to set village to destroy village, but sometimes non-partisan villagers were forced to execute the army's prisoners. Sarwo Edhie did not need to send a special force into East Java. For there the black-shirted Ansor youth were exceptionally strong and were able to slaughter without military help. Many private grudges were settled; and petty landlords seized the opportunity to rid themselves of peasants who, under local PKI leadership, had taken over fields in an attempt to enforce the government's ineffectual land reform. As in Central Java, thousands of bodies were hurled into rivers; bamboo barriers were put across the entrances of irrigation channels in the Kediri district to ward off corpses as they drifted down to the sea. In Surabaya the bodies became a danger to public health when ebbing tides deposited them on river banks. At Cirebon, in West Java, a guillotine was imaginatively erected to hasten the business of summary execution. And in some areas skewered, decapitated heads were left on display in the streets to symbolize victory and to warn others who might be tempted to transgress.

Possibly the savagery of the Moslem attacks was heightened in some areas by animosity between purer Moslems and the *abangan*, who, although nominally Moslem, hold ancient Javanese and Hindu beliefs that have no place in Islam. Whatever its cause, the enmity persisted long after the massacre. A Western diplomat discovered this when by accident he walked over some graves. 'It does not matter', he was told when he apologized to some passing peasants. 'They are only PKI.'

It was even more gruesome in Bali, where the massacre became so frenzied that paratroopers had to stop it before irreparable damage was done to the social structure. The Balinese are Hindus. This has led some to think that the lust to kill was inflamed by a desire to purge the land of evil. The religious, or mystical, factor can never be ruled out in any part of Indonesia: in Java some cunning land-owners who were *hajis* roused their simple-minded followers with the cry, '*jihat*' (holy war). But a European who has lived for many years in Bali said (in an interview with the author) that the main motive for the massacre was revenge. The PKI had won considerable support by promising land to peasants who were impoverished because the island could barely support its 2 million inhabitants. But its members were widely hated because they abused such power as they acquired by bullying and favouritism. The pro-Communist governor was a dictator; a PNI leader who accused him of violating the principles of Nasakom by favouring the PKI was imprisoned; it took Sukarno to free him. Bitterness between the PNI and PKI was widespread. Thus it was that PNI youth, also wearing black shirts, did in Bali what Ansor had done in East Java. In North Sulawesi (Celebes) the Christians were the executioners. In Sumatra the army did the job itself; troops under Brigadier-General Kemal Idris murdered about 20 per cent of rubber plantation workers after receiving an order from Suharto.

Legge attributes to G. J. Resink a remark that the Communists' tame submission to slaughter is explained by the *wayang*.[20] Resink is given to drawing vivid parallels between contemporary events in Indonesia and legends that both reflect and influence the Javanese ethos. He suggests that the Communists saw Sukarno as the *dalang* (puppet-player and narrator) in the *wayang*; when the killers swooped upon them they were seized with a sense of doom because they were on the left of the *dalang*, where characters who are to be vanquished are always ranged. The reticence of Indonesians in discussing their mysticism and the politeness that often causes them to express agreement with any speculations that foreigners offer would make it difficult to verify this theory. A possible flaw is that it would be remarkable if a significant number of the victims had been aware of the European political concept of left and right, although Sukarno used these terms. I should have thought that the peasants, who, Sukarno said, had been reduced to abject timidity by feudalism and the Dutch, simply collapsed when confronted with overwhelming force. But Resink's knowledge of the Javanese, from which I have benefited in conversations with him, entitles his idea to respect; he has lived in Java for most of his life, and comes from a family that has been there for three generations. Whether or not the linking of events with legends is valid in a particular instance, the approach in general is a good one, although it is now fashionable to overdo it; and those who seek clues in the *wayang* are likely to get closer to solving paradoxes than those who ignore it, provided they are scrupulously careful. A Russian journalist in Jakarta, who was frequently astonished by the mentality of Indonesian Communists, said those he spoke to before they were taken to prison showed no personal bitterness towards the army officers. 'We should have done the same to them', they told him. This attitude suggests that they might, in fact, have seen themselves as having lost in the *Bharāta Yuda*.

Resink's idea could also explain much of the public apathy to the massacre. If those on the left of the *dalang* felt themselves powerless when mighty forces suddenly appeared on the right, the spectators would also have seen destruction of the

Communists as inevitable and just. In the following years feelings about the massacre varied. Many Indonesians said simply that the PKI had to be destroyed to the roots for the nation's sake; some were ashamed; most avoided the subject. Of the civilians who murdered, a few had recurring nightmares in which their victims appeared before them like Banquo's ghost, and sought solace from doctors. But Indonesians of whatever ethnic group have a knack of blotting out what they wish to forget. Many of the killers might have taken refuge in fantasy, like the nineteenth-century Javanese migrants to New Caledonia and Malaya, who explained their desertion of their families by stating that they were in a trance when they boarded ships..

Albion and Uncle Sam

A possible element in the *putsch* and its aftermath, which deserves more examination than it has received, is foreign participation or influence. In May 1965 Subandrio, who in addition to being Foreign Minister and Deputy Prime Minister was head of the BPI (Central Intelligence Body), showed Sukarno what purported to be a copy of a communication from Andrew Gilchrist (later Sir Andrew), the British Ambassador, to the Foreign Office. The crucial passage was: 'It would be as well to emphasize once more to our local friends in the army that the strictest caution, discipline and co-ordination are essential to the success of the enterprise.' The copy was unsigned, but was on embassy paper, which, as Dahm says, may have been stolen when the British Embassy was looted in 1963. Subandrio said at his trial that it was found at the house of a departed representative of American film producers, Bill Palmer, who was at one time friendly with Sukarno, but was later accused of being a member of the CIA. Britain was heavily committed in Malaysia at that time and would have been delighted at the overthrowing of Sukarno; and British intelligence was very active in Indonesia. But this is far from proving that the document was genuine.

Of unquestionable authenticity, however, is a printed American document, of which I possess a photostat copy. Dated 16 February 1971, it is entitled 'Military Assistance Training in East and South East Asia' and is described as a 'staff report prepared for the use of the subcommittee on national security policy and scientific developments' of the House of Representatives Foreign Affairs Committee. To emphasize the virtues of the training programme in Indonesia the report recalls the part that it played in October 1965:

> At the time of the attempted Communist coup and military counter-coup of October 1965, more than 1,200 Indonesian officers, including senior military figures, had been trained in the United States.
> As a result of this experience, numerous friendships and contacts existed between the Indonesian and American military establishments, particularly between members of the two armies. In the post-coup period, when the political situation was still unsettled, the United States, using these existing channels of communication, was able to provide the anti-Communist forces with moral and token material support ...
> ... All the generals killed during the coup attempt, called Gestapu by the Indonesians, had been trained in the United States or had friendly relations with Westerners in Jakarta ...
> This success may be compared to the debacle which faced the Soviet Union. With its East European satellites, it had provided Indonesia with more than one billion dollars in military equipment between 1960 and 1965. Subsequently, Moscow was forced to look on helplessly as its equipment was used to suppress the Communist Party of Indonesia.

It is hard to see how this smug gloating over the annihilation of the PKI means anything else except that United States agents connived, at least, in the massacre. For the killing of defenceless villagers, and practically nothing else, is what the armed offensive against the party amounted to. There was no guerrilla fighting. The PKI was not like the Vietcong. It was represented in parliament and the government, and it possessed practically no guns, except the few lent by the Air Force at Halim. The reference to the Soviet bloc armaments is fatuous; these consisted mostly of warships and aeroplanes provided to help Indonesia wheedle West Irian out of the Dutch, and were not needed to wipe out ignorant peasants in regions considered to be under PKI influence.

It is possible that the Pentagon or CIA not only encouraged but inspired the massacre, by dropping hints through 'existing channels'; the experience of warfare against civilians in Vietnam might well have been applied in the form of 'moral and token material support'. Philip Agee, a CIA defector, said in an interview on the BBC in January 1975 that the CIA played a part in the massacre; the report to the sub-committee seems to corroborate his statement. 'Moral' support may also have been given in the silencing of Suherman, the rebel officer trained at Fort Leavenworth. The CIA had been busy in Indonesia for a long time; a congressional committee reported in April 1976 that it had studied CIA 'efforts to undermine President Sukarno in Indonesia'.[21] Such was America's blindness to its own interests at that time that no action which smashed the Peking-Jakarta axis would have seemed too ruthless or too costly.

The 1971 report does not say precisely when United States encouragement began; it could well be that messages received at Kostrad HQ early in October gave Suharto the confidence to risk disgrace by challenging the President. Nor does the report disclose to what extent 'existing channels' were used before the *putsch*. On 26 February 1966 Major Rhudito, a witness at Untung's trial, gave evidence that Sukarno possessed cheques from abroad that had been intended for the Generals' Council. Two months earlier Sukarno said that a foreign embassy had given $2 million to a leading Indonesian to 'divert the course of the Indonesian Revolution to the right'. According to the official news agency, Antara, Rhudito caused consternation in the court when he said he had heard tape-recorded evidence that generals had formed a cabinet to take over after a coup planned for 5 October 1965. In the transcript of the trial (p. 171) Rhudito says the recording was made at a Generals' Council meeting held at the Military Law Academy on 21 September 1965. He recalls that he heard the voice of Major-General S. Parman, one of the officers murdered on 1 October, listing the ministers; five of the generals killed in the *putsch* were included. Nasution was named as Prime Minister; Yani, First Deputy Prime Minister; Major-General Suprapto, Minister for the Interior; Major-General Harjono, Foreign Minister; Brigadier-General Sutojo, Minister of Justice and Parman himself, Attorney-General. Among the remaining ministers Ruslan Abdulgani, a member of Sukarno's Cabinet, was to be Second Deputy Prime Minister. When Rhudito mentioned the meeting, but before he spoke of the cabinet, the court president interrupted to say that the generals had met for a 'commanders' call' to discuss training.

It is difficult to know what to make of this evidence, as of the rest. The recording may not have existed, or it may have been faked, in which case it could have been circulated either by the CIA, to provoke the Communists, or by the Communists, to incite discontented officers; on the other hand, it may have been genuine. Rhudito's evidence is yet another reminder of the danger of drawing conclusions. In a written statement sent to the MPRS on 10 January 1967 Sukarno said three factors had coincided to bring about the 30 September Movement: the PKI leadership's being tricked, the cunning of Nekolim subversion and the fact that some people were 'not right' (in the head).[22] Sukarno did not reveal how the PKI was tricked or what Nekolim did. The reason was almost certainly that he did not know. In private life he insisted (as his wife Dewi said to the author) that the PKI was in no way responsible for the *putsch*. Dewi believes that any statements by Sukarno which imply PKI involvement could only have been made because of overwhelming political exigency – and even then only after the resurrection of the party had become impossible.

CHAPTER FOUR

The rise of Suharto

Organizing the students

While the 30 September *putsch* has received much attention from scholars, the ruthlessness with which Suharto overthrew Sukarno has been largely neglected or glossed. One reason for this is the disarming patience with which Suharto rose to the presidency; another is that some writers, looking at Indonesia through Western eyes, felt it was time that Sukarno went and that the means to such a desirable end were of little importance; not least is that scholars who have a vested interest in the subject are unwilling to risk being forbidden to enter Indonesia. Sukarno was not only a leader but a thinker whose ideas influenced much of the Third World, where he is still remembered with respect. He helped to give coherence to the aspirations of the New Emerging Forces – one of the numerous concepts that he originated. A conference (Conefo) at which he was to have tried to unite these forces, as he had done to a considerable extent with the diverse elements of Indonesia itself, was aborted by his downfall. This constituted a moral setback for the Third World and a victory for the United States, Britain and the West in general. For this reason alone Sukarno's fall was an event of historical importance.

It is sometimes said that Suharto rose to power 'the constitutional way'. This is fiction; Suharto first extorted a limited mandate from Sukarno with armed confrontation; then, in the President's name, and pretending to act under his orders, he set about demolishing the national structure, to which Sukarno had devoted his life. Supardjo, at his trial in February 1967, boldly accused the junta of rebelling against the legitimate government and of being responsible for the death of 500,000 Indonesians. The death-roll may have been less, or more, but the charge was essentially correct. It was, to borrow words that Suharto once used when accusing Peking of supporting the *putsch*, a 'historical fact'. Yet it is true that Suharto, once the initiative was securely in his hands, eased Sukarno from the presidency with incomparable Javanese finesse by means that passed for constitutional.

Sukarno's statements that the *putsch* was 'just a ripple in the ocean' of the Indonesian revolution and that 'such things happen' immediately provoked accusations of heartlessness. In fact, Sukarno was essentially a humane man and, although he would have been less resigned if the army had murdered PKI leaders, there was a considerable element of philosophy in his attitude. He was accustomed to observing events as history, with some detachment, while being emotionally and intellectually involved in them. As he was to point out later, he had forgiven Nasution for having directed guns at the palace in an attempt to force him to dissolve parliament in October 1952; and an air force officer, Daniel Maukar, who on another occasion had frightened the wits out of Sukarno by strafing the palace from a Mig, was reprieved, after having been sentenced to death, and allowed to leave prison periodically to visit his family. These incidents, too, were 'ripples in the ocean'; and the fact that the ripple of October 1965 became a disastrous wave was not Sukarno's doing, but the junta's.

At Halim on 1 October Sukarno would obviously have felt anxiety, which he expressed afterwards when warning the public that Nekolim would exploit the situation to 'divert the revolution to the right'. He had saved Indonesia at its birth from internecine destruction and had rallied it under the precarious banner of 'Unity in Diversity'; he knew that the nation was fragile and that only his hand could hold it together without destroying a vital part of it. As President for Life and Mandatory of the MPRS (Provisional People's Consultative Assembly), Sukarno had the right and the responsibility to deal with the *putsch* in his own way. He embarked cautiously on a procedure that should have ended in resolution by *musyawarah*, whatever might have been the temporary outcome of the collision between Suharto and the rebels of 30 September. But the junta, with 'moral and token material support' from the United States, adopted shock tactics that threw him off balance. Once it was clear that the junta was determined to oust him, he proposed general elections to form a new MPR. Had the people been allowed to vote freely, there is no doubt that the MPR would have confirmed his election as President. That is why no elections were held as long as he remained alive.

After the burning and ransacking of Communist property early in October 1965 there was a virtual lull in street demonstrations in Jakarta while the junta tried to cajole Sukarno into banning the PKI. Sukarno persistently refused; he would not betray the Marhaens by signing away what he believed to be their only hope of deliverance – Nasakom stiffened and led by a strong PKI. Not even the charms of his young Japanese wife, Ratna Sari Dewi, could sway him. 'I begged him to ban the PKI even temporarily', she was to say (in a conversation with the author). 'I said, "*Bapak*, the people need you. If you ban the PKI the generals will have to let you stay." But he wouldn't do it.' It did not take the junta long to realize that Sukarno would never yield to argument. They then set the students against him.

The social weight of the demonstrations against Sukarno has been exaggerated, and the point of Hughes's chapter heading, 'Children on the Barricades', appears to have been missed.[1] What is significant is that the demonstrators were, in fact, largely students and school children, whose parents were afraid that they might get themselves hurt. Sukarno had plenty of enemies among politicians, journalists, and business and professional men; but there were no mass demonstrations of workers and peasants against him, although attempts were made to organize a leaven of proletarians among the adolescents. One reason for the distortion in accounts of what took place is that information at the disposal of writers on acts of violence is usually limited to sporadic newspaper cuttings, although some scholars have access to diplomats' dispatches, which are not necessarily more illuminating. News agency files of daily reports that are often unpublished or cut are a more comprehensive source. At least one of these files shows that the demonstrations had a very small beginning, which was far from being wholly spontaneous.

A group of anti-Communist students had formed Kami (Indonesian Students' Action Front) late in October. From my experience of the way things happen in Indonesia, I doubt whether they would have done this without substantial backing. But whether or not they began on their own is of little importance; for Sarwo Edhie, back from the massacres in Java, was soon among them, enrolling as a student at Universitas Indonesia to legitimize his presence there with some of his officers.[2] A strangely mixed band worked in conjunction with Sarwo Edhie: they included Subchan Zainuri Echsan, a leader of the NU (Nahdatul Ulama – Moslem Theologians' Council), and the talented Chinese brothers, Lim Bian Kie and Lim Bian Koen, who had links with Catholic Action.

Subchan was a unusual man. Although he was a Vice-Chairman of the NU, which was in principle the political custodian of Moslem orthodoxy, his frequenting of night clubs, where he drank alcohol and danced with girls, won him the nickname of the dancing *ulama* (theologian). He had no university qualification, but for a time taught economics in an American business school. His American connexions were such that he was able to import a Cessna aeroplane for his private use in 1972, just before his death. Like Western diplomats, some of whom told correspondents only two days after the *putsch* that Peking was behind it, he quickly pinned the blame on Communists. On the evening of 1 October he and several other Moslems, none of whom were party leaders, formed an Action Command Against Communism. The same night he set up the KAP-Gestapu – Action Front for the Crushing of Gestapu (the 30 September Movement) – with the sanction of Major-General Umar Wirahadikusuma, a leading Jakarta officer, who promised him weapons. On 4 October a rally of a few hundred people organized by the front urged Sukarno to purge the cabinet and ban the PKI. These demands were reiterated on 21 October in a statement signed by Harry Tjan, Secretary-General of the Partai Katolik, and people who claimed to represent all parties except the PKI and the left wing of the PNI.

Lim Bian Koen was to lead raids on the Chinese Embassy in 1967, when, in the name of students, he demanded rupture of relations with Peking, a goal dear to both the junta and Washington. He and his brother, who was at that time a university lecturer in law, eventually emerged as the right hand men of two generals in Suharto's inner circle.

The first demonstration after the lull took place on 10 January. It began with a meeting of 500 Moslem and Catholic students in the seclusion of the university. The guest of honour at this rather exclusive gathering was Sarwo Edhie. The meeting carried a resolution demanding reconsideration of recently introduced price increases, 'retooling' of the cabinet, which meant purging of leftists, and banning of the PKI. After what has been described as a 'fiery address' by Sarwo Edhie,[3] the 500 clambered into lorries, which they could not have provided for themselves, and headed for the state secretariat building. Police, obviously acting on instructions, blocked entrances from side streets along the routes so that the procession could roll on without interruption. After argument a student delegation was allowed into the secretariat offices to present its resolution to the Third Vice-Premier, Chairul Saleh.

The framers of the resolution used oblique words like 're-consider' and 'retool', and did not mention Sukarno's name. But this was just a discreet beginning. When the crescendo of demonstrations mounted and the junta increased its grip on the government machinery, students were to bring out placards demanding the trial and even hanging of the President. By that time many Kami youths were wearing green and yellow uniforms, which, Sukarno said, were paid for by the CIA. When challenged, Sukarno could provide no proof, but several years later a business-man in Jakarta boasted to a correspondent that he had passed on to student leaders money provided by the United States Embassy. Those who set out from the University after Sarwo Edhie's harangue were merely the spearhead of the attack. Their resolution, known as the Tritura (People's Three Demands) became the rallying cry of mobs that were to go on the rampage until the junta got its way. As they cruised along the streets on 10 January, the 500 swelled to about 2,000 when other youths leaped into the ample lorry space. Later, when school children were formed into Kappi (Indonesian Pupils' Action Front), the junta could muster 50,000. Whether they were from the university or from the schools, the demonstrators were mostly of marked intellectual and emotional immaturity.[4] Many of them joined in the riots because their friends did, or for fun and excitement, like those who had volunteered to be trained to fight in Malaysia.

While it would be wrong to say that in 1966 there was no serious social unrest, it is more erroneous to assume that the riots of students and schoolchildren were a direct, let alone socially dynamic, expression of it. Certainly the demonstrators either had no loyalty to Sukarno or quickly lost it. Doubtless some were really concerned about prices, as most adults were, and believed that the confrontation was a waste of money, as some adults did; all probably detested the PKI, either because they believed it to be responsible for the Crocodile Hole murders or for deeper reasons; a few had genuinely liberal ideas for which they were to suffer when the army took absolute power. But this was not a basis for revolution against the President; and had it not been for the junta's exploitation of the *putsch*, the discontent with Sukarno, such as it was, would have remained inert at least for a very considerable period. Whatever their feelings were, the adolescents represented no coherent force that could provide a new social and political foundation; at most they could only provide a pretext for the generals' coup. They could never call the tune. The army conducted the orchestra; and if the players got off the note, as they sometimes did, they were quickly brought back into key. Later, when the army ruled and prices were still rising, students again demonstrated. This time they were driven from the streets. And the junta, doubting quite rightly from its own experience that the youth could act without external incitement, launched a witch-hunt for those who might be behind them.

Suharto began his confrontation with Sukarno on 1 October, when he issued two public statements, in which he ignored the President's announcement that he had temporarily assumed direct leadership of the armed forces and had appointed Pranoto Reksosamudro to carry out the army's daily tasks. Sukarno's announcement was made in his capacities of 'President/Supreme Commander/Great Leader of the Revolution/Mandatory of the MPRS'. Suharto's were signed by himself in the name of the 'Temporary Army Leadership'. His first said that the Army, Navy, and Police Force, had agreed to co-operate in overcoming the 'counter-revolutionary deeds' of the 30 September Movement. The second named the six abducted generals; it said that Sukarno and Nasution were safe and that the army's leadership was for the time being in Suharto's hands. There is already an element here of the deception that was to be perpetrated later on a much larger scale; for an impression was given that Suharto was ensuring the security of Sukarno, who had, in fact ensured it himself by going to Halim, from which he could have flown to safety if necessary. Suharto took his defiance a stage further with his refusal at Bogor on 2 October to share the command with Pranoto.

After the meeting at Bogor Sukarno made his tape-recorded statement, which the junta did not broadcast until the early hours of 3 October, when most people were asleep. Sukarno erred in saying that the air force was not involved in the *putsch*. The next day, standing beside the well at Crocodile Hole while the bodies were being hauled up, Suharto retorted in his live broadcast: 'It is impossible that these adventurers (the 30 September Movement) were not connected with individuals in the air force.' This was not a flat contradiction, because he did not accuse the air force command, but it was a useful thrust in Suharto's duel with Sukarno.

Sukarno lost the next round by default, when he failed to attend the generals' funeral; he wrote to Dewi on the same day that the security service, Subandrio and Leimena had advised him not to go, because nobody could predict what would happen in such emotional circumstances.[5] The army made the occasion one of national mourning, not without justification and doubtless not unmindful of the propaganda value. The bodies lay in state before being taken along streets bedecked with red and white Indonesian flags, flown at half-mast, to the Heroes' Cemetery. Diplomats, some of whom must have been as delighted at the turn in events as they were shocked by the murders, attended the burial ceremony. On the previous day Sukarno had posthumously promoted the generals by one rank and had declared them Heroes of the Revolution; but this gesture passed almost unnoticed and his absence from the funeral, with that of Chinese diplomats, laid him open to the charge that he was involved in, or approved, the 30 September plot. After the army's attack on Chinese property he ostentatiously invited the Chinese Ambassador for a talk and announced that relations between Indonesia and China would remain friendly, 'despite efforts to undermine them'. While this action did credit to his political integrity, it made him even more vulnerable to the junta; for Chinese are widely detested in Indonesia, irrespective of their politics.

On 6 October, the day after the funeral, Sukarno held a cabinet meeting at Bogor, which was attended by Njoto and Lukman, both PKI members. But he left it to Subandrio to inform the press that the President had condemned the 'barbarous' murders, and to emphasize that he had not approved the formation of the Revolutionary Council. Subandrio said that Sukarno was seeking a political solution; he recalled Sukarno's mercy to Daniel Maukar, and gave the impression that no severe punishment would be imposed on the *putsch* leaders; feelings of vengeance, he said, might lead to Indonesia's destruction.

By 14 October Suharto was in such a strong position that Sukarno appointed him Commander-in-Chief, shaking hands with him when he announced the promotion. Three days later Sarwo Edhie set out for Central Java to launch the massacre. Sukarno was aghast at the destruction of what he saw as one of the three pillars of the nation; he pleaded for an end to the slaughter. The public appeared largely indifferent, but it is my suspicion that some people were afraid that if they spoke up they would be included among the victims. On 21 December he passionately told a students' rally that he would carry to the grave his conviction that Communism was an indispensable ideological component of the Indonesian revolution; Nasakom must be saved at all costs. During the fight for independence, he said, the Dutch had imprisoned thousands of Communists and had exiled thousands more to the malaria-infested swamps of West Irian.

After Sarwo Edhie's student operation Sukarno invited Kami leaders to a cabinet meeting on 15 January, and three days later he gave some of them a 'fatherly talk'. But at a mass meeting on 13 February he praised the Sukarno Front, which Subandrio had organized to compete with Kami in the streets. He went further in his support of the PKI when he declared that no other party had equalled its sacrifices in the struggle against the Dutch. On 21 February he continued his offensive by dropping Nasution as Defence Minister Co-ordinator and Army Chief of Staff in a cabinet change.

This challenge to the army precipitated a series of violent, well-organized demonstrations. It took only one day to marshal transport and to arrange food supplies. On 23 February a mob estimated at 50,000, mostly adolescents, tried to storm the President's palace. Guards loyal to Sukarno repelled them, clubbing with rifle butts and lunging with bayonets. The next day, when fourteen ministers of the inner cabinet were to be installed, students blocked traffic by stopping cars and letting their tyres down; most ministers had to be taken to the palace by helicopter. In a clash outside the palace one of the guards shot and killed a medical student, Arif Rachman Hakim. This provided the students with a martyr, and led to formation of a Hakim Regiment, which fought Subandrio's youth bands with sticks and stones. Sukarno banned Kami on 25 February and closed the university. The result was an eruption of placards demanding, 'try Bung Karno' and 'hang Subandrio'. On 8 March students ransacked the Foreign Ministry and disfigured the walls with drawings of Subandrio, represented as a Pekinese dog.

The junta's coup

Despite murder in the countryside and violence in the streets, Sukarno continued to protect the PKI. His position was still strong and few observers were predicting his downfall. Most of the MPRS remained loyal. There were dedicated Sukarnoists in all branches of the armed forces: Sukarnoism was particularly strong in the Navy and Air Force and, above all, the Marines. With this backing assured, Sukarno summoned leaders of the nine political parties to a conference on 10 March. All of them signed a declaration that the riots were financed by the CIA to subvert presidential authority. With the initiative now in his hands, Sukarno called a meeting of his 108-man cabinet the next day. But the Suharto junta had decided it was time for armed troops to reinforce students in the streets and launched a decisive operation that must have gratified those who were providing 'moral and token material support' (see page 126).

Twenty minutes after the cabinet meeting began Sukarno received a message that unidentified troops had surrounded the palace. Later it was revealed that they were Sarwo Edhie's para-commandos, who had been ordered to remove their regimental badges. The unheralded arrival of this faceless band startled the cabinet. Sukarno, with scarcely a word to his ministers, it seems, made a dash for the door, followed by Subandrio and Chairul Saleh. So indecent was their haste that Subandrio, who had been sitting with his shoes off, was reported to have made his escape in his socks. The three climbed aboard a helicopter and immediately flew to the presidential residence at Bogor. The ministers left behind were stunned; the flight of their leader must have undermined their confidence in his power, and prepared their minds to accept his eventual overthrow. Yet while the incident had its comic side, the three men were legitimately afraid; for Sarwo Edhie said later that his troops had orders to shoot Subandrio on sight if he tried to leave the palace grounds. Having flushed his quarry in Jakarta, Suharto immediately sent three generals by car to trap him when he alighted at Bogor. After some hours of argument, Sukarno signed the document known as the 11 March Order, in which he made over certain tasks to Suharto. It is clear that Sukarno was under duress, but precisely how strong the threats were has not been established.

In my opinion Dahm is mistaken when he says that in the 11 March Order Sukarno 'signed the full powers [of government] in favour of Suharto'.[6] In the relevant clause, the first of three in the document (which Dahm does not quote), Sukarno ordered Suharto 'to take all necessary steps to guarantee security and calm and the stability of the running of the Government and the course of the Revolution, while securing the personal safety and the authority of the Great Leader of the Revolution/Mandatory of the MPRS for the sake of the Nation's integrity and that of the Republic of Indonesia and absolutely execute all the teachings of the Great Leader of the Revolution.' Guaranteeing the 'stability of the running of the Government' does not mean power actually to run the Government; the order, in fact, secures Sukarno's 'authority'.

The second clause confirms what appears to be the purpose of the first (to ensure security) by ordering Suharto to 'execute co-ordination in implementing this Order with Commanders in Chief of other Forces as best as possible'. (Sukarno might have hoped here that loyal officers in the Air Force, Navy and Police Force would eventually counter-balance the junta). The third clause obliged Suharto to 'report everything connected with this task and responsibility . . .' The phrase 'absolutely execute all the teachings of the Great Leader of the Revolution' could scarcely be interpreted as an order to take 'full powers' of government; Sukarno was clearly trying to protect Nasakom.

The formal situation was that on 2 October Sukarno had appointed Suharto to 'carry out directives for restoration of peace and order in connection with the 30 September affair'. That task was fulfilled with the arrest of the rebels; Untung had been sentenced to death at the beginning of March. The power that Suharto won on 11 March was, on paper, an extension in a new situation of what he had already received. But there were two differences: instead of acting, theoretically, under directives from Sukarno, he was now only obliged to report to him; and this time the stability that Suharto was empowered to ensure was endangered, not by the 30 September Movement, but by his own operations in whipping up student unrest and sending troops to raid the President's palace.

Sukarno must have known that Suharto, who had already committed what amounted to lese-majesty in a society marked by feudal deference, would interpret the Order in any way that suited him; but he had good reason to hope that he would not dare to go too far, through fear that Sukarnoists in the armed forces would revolt. The document was elastic; its significance was to be determined by future events. To assert with Dahm or to imply with Legge[7] that by exacting the 11 March Order Suharto was able to assume full powers of government is to underestimate Sukarno's position at the time and to miss some of the legalistic subtlety that accompanied Suharto's coercive actions. For, in fact, Suharto used the Order less as an instrument of power than as a wedge with which to attain it. At first he committed no overt acts of government, except those relating to security, without Sukarno's compliance. Measures like the dissolution of the PKI and the 'protective arrest' of ministers could all be interpreted as consistent with the order to guarantee stability. It was cleverly done and typically Javanese. Once Suharto had destroyed Sukarno's most militant supporters in the government, the residual terror of the massacre and the arrests was sufficient in itself to carry him forward. But even then he advanced gradually, never taking a step until he was sure that it could be achieved without provoking rebellion in the armed forces, which was the only physical challenge then possible.

After the 11 March Order he continued his policy of flouting Sukarno by abusing the powers that he possessed, rather than by assuming those he had yet to obtain. One of his first acts to 'secure' the President's authority was to send a platoon shooting its way into the BPI headquarters in the early hours of 12 March to search for Subandrio, Sukarno's most important minister, and to seize documents. Subandrio was not there, but twenty-one of his men, at least two of whom were wounded, were arrested. The same day Suharto executed Sukarno's teachings by dissolving the PKI, thus putting an end to Nasakom.

Suharto justified his actions in a series of cunningly worded announcements, in which he gave the impression that he was speaking with Sukarno's voice by using Sukarno's language. The announcements were mostly headed 'President of the Republic of Indonesia' and were signed by Suharto 'on his [the President's] behalf'. The first contained the substance of the 11 March Order. It also implied, although it did not state, that Suharto had full governmental powers, by pledging that the armed forces would 'implement the leftist People's Revolution of Indonesia, being anti-feudalism, anti-capitalism and anti-Nekolim'. But this was merely a device to create an atmosphere in which, a few months later, the MPRS could feel that it was doing little more than ratify a mandate that Sukarno had already given.

When he dissolved the PKI Suharto repeated the revolutionary slogans of his first announcement, with the exception of the word 'leftist', the retention of which would have seemed ludicrous even to the simplest minds. With superb cynicism he explained that the party had to be banned because its underground activities endangered, among other things, the 'crushing of the Nekolim project of "Malaysia" '. As late as 27 March he was still saying, in a broadcast, that the cabinet should have 'strength to continue our confrontation against "Malaysia"/Nekolim', although by this time he had begun secret negotiations with Kuala Lumpur, which were revealed two months later, when Adam Malik met Tun Abdul Razak, then Malaysian Deputy Premier, in Bangkok. He also emphasized the need to organize Sukarno's Conefo; but this, like the confrontation, was abandoned as part of the price of Western succour.

Borrowing liberally from old scripts, Suharto promised a 'prosperous society based on *Pancasila*, an Indonesian Socialist Society, blessed by Almighty God within the flower garden of the New World, without any form of oppression and exploitation'. Sometimes, with bland indifference to logic, he included expressions of love for 'Bung Karno' in announcements that were supposed to be coming from the President himself. That Suharto could get away with such a patently dishonest jumble sympto-matizes the mentality of the Indonesian public. Sheer gullibility was not the only factor. Those politicians who felt it was futile to oppose the army could easily rationalize their disloyalty to Sukarno by pretending to themselves that the announcements were his; some supported anything the army did because they believed it would bring about a more liberal system of government than Sukarno's guided democracy, or at least one in which they would play a more important part. With so many players willing to oblige for one reason or another, the junta was able to ensure the uninterrupted performance of a pantomime that was to go on throughout the coming MPRS meetings and long afterwards.

After the promulgation of the 11 March Order, Sarwo Edhie put on a spectacular military parade in Jakarta, with helicopters flying low over the procession. A crowd, estimated by the corre-spondent of the Dutch and French news agencies (ANP and AFP) at one million, came out to watch. There were plenty of cheers for the troops, but it would be mistaken to interpret the entire gathering as a demonstration; curiosity would have been sufficient to bring people into the streets in such uncertain times. The correspondent, a Dutchman, said the public impression was that Sukarno had merely made Suharto responsible for security – a very important observation, coming from a journalist who could not contain his detestation of Sukarno.

Suharto certainly did not act as if he had full powers, for on 14 March he began negotiations with Sukarno over cabinet reconstruction, which lasted nearly two weeks. Adolescents again came to his aid with demonstrations, in which students and children, from both secondary and elementary schools, careered round the city day after day in lorries, jeeps and, occasionally, armoured cars, at one stage occupying government buildings. Their main target was Subandrio, instrument of Sukarno's foreign policy, against whom the junta and British and American diplomats were waging a campaign of vilification. On 15 March Suharto, in Sukarno's name, ordered all leaders, cadres and activists of the PKI and affiliated organizations to report to authorities before the end of the month; he threatened stern measures against any of the eight remaining political parties that admitted PKI members.

Sukarno quickly acted to preserve his authority in matters that did not relate to security. On 16 March he made an announcement in which, he said, a 'wrong attitude' had emerged 'towards the position of the President/Supreme Commander of the Armed Forces'. The announcement was called 'Number 1', apparently to show that Suharto had exceeded whatever powers he had by issuing a 'Number 1' in the President's name. Outlining the constitutional position that had evolved since his decree of 5 July, 1959, Sukarno recalled that the MPRS had given him 'full powers' and asserted that he was 'only responsible to the MPRS and God Almighty' in carrying out the mandate. He insisted that he had 'the fullest freedom' to appoint his own assistants, and regretted that a 'section of society' had tried to change his team by means of an ultimatum. Obviously reproaching Suharto, he said he was always willing to take notice of thoughts 'conveyed according to the code of ethics and courtesies of our national identity'.

Suharto struck back at once, but within the limits of his security powers. On 17 March his forces seized control of the radio, all newspapers and the telephone, cable and telex services; they cut off Indonesia from the outside world by refusing to transmit communications overseas. The next day Suharto attacked on every front open to him. He went to the palace and increased his pressure on Sukarno to purge his cabinet, while Sarwo Edhie's troops surrounded the compound and blocked approaching streets with barbed wire, an operation that served the double purpose of intimidating Sukarno and controlling the demonstrations, which were developing their own momentum. At the same time he prepared the public for coming events with the repeated broadcast of a recorded speech over all networks. Listeners heard him warn that he had noticed 'indications of activities that might enable Nekolim to use them as a Trojan horse'. He promised 'firm action' to protect 'the course of the revolution and the leadership of the revolution's great leader, Bung Karno'. That Suharto felt obliged to resort to such hypocrisy in deference to public opinion is enough in itself to disprove suggestions that there was widespread hostility to Sukarno. The junta, in fact, seems to have feared that trouble would erupt in the armed forces at any moment. For on that same, busy day Suharto issued a statement that he was taking 'immediate and stern steps' to 'prevent uncontrolled troop movements'. Later large numbers of Sukarnoist officers and men were admitted to be under arrest, including 1,000 in the Diponegoro Division, which Suharto formerly commanded. Already the army had taken over all air bases, knowing that the air force was largely Sukarnoist.

The 'firm action' that was promised in Suharto's recorded warning was the previous arrest of fifteen cabinet ministers, which was officially disclosed immediately after the broadcasts. Subandrio was arrested at the President's palace by the commander of the Jakarta garrison, Brigadier-General (later Lieutenant-General) Amir Machmud, one of the three who went to Bogor on 11 March; Sukarno, who had been sheltering Subandrio, was obliged to leave the palace to avoid embarrassment, pleading, 'Amir, don't kill him', as he left. Subandrio was later sentenced to death for involvement in the *putsch*, on evidence that no Western court would have accepted. Suharto, after becoming President, commuted the sentence to life imprisonment; but by this time Subandrio, previously the most arrogant of ministers, had sunk into maudlin, religious mania.

Sukarno announced a new cabinet on 27 March 1966. Although he claimed that it was his own creation, the hand of Suharto was obvious. The 108 members were reduced to twenty-four (with deputy ministers under them), among whom was an inner cabinet of six vice-premiers, listed in order of precedence. The six included three of the junta's nominees – Sultan Hamengkubuwono of Yogyakarta, Suharto (ad interim) and Adam Malik. But they, in that order, were lower in status than Dr Johannes Leimena (the ageing leader of Parkindo – the Protestant Party), Idham Chalid (Nahdatul Ulama), and Roeslan Abdulgani (PNI – Indonesian National Party), all of whom were in the old cabinet. Sukarno remained Prime Minister and signed the announcement as President, along with his usual, other titles. As before, he styled the cabinet 'Dwikora', a word derived from his 'twofold command' to crush Malaysia; and he brought Nasution back into some prominence by appointing him as his deputy in the Crush Malaysia Command. Sukarno told journalists that his aim was to perfect the Dwikora cabinet. He emphasized: 'day to day government activities are carried out by me. Every member of the cabinet is my assistant.'

Meanwhile Suharto, with his excellent timing, had popped up on radio and television with a speech that is a gem of Javanese political deviousness. By asserting that the cabinet should be compact and defining its tasks he gave the impression that the armed forces were wholly responsible for the changes about to come. He skilfully usurped Sukarno's role of 'mouthpiece of the people' by declaring that the armed forces had carried out two of the People's Three Demands when it dissolved the PKI and arrested the ministers. He then said that the only way to achieve their third demand, for economic improvement, was to form a new cabinet. Thus he was able to give the impression that he was virtually running the government in response to popular request, without laying himself open to the charge that he had encroached upon the President's powers. This was not mere shadow boxing, but a calculated use of the wedge. The struggle was not yet over; and while Sukarno had obviously given ground under forceful persuasion, Suharto was still careful to emphasize in his speech that the army's policy was based on 'the teachings of the Great Leader of the Revolution, Bung Karno, who himself based his leadership on the strength of the people, and who serves the people's earnest demands'.

There is no evidence to suggest that by this time Sukarno had surrendered and was resigned to becoming a figurehead. Certainly, the PKI had been destroyed and his most sympathetic ministers had been arrested. But Sukarno still had overwhelming support in country areas and at least sufficient in Jakarta to make either victory for himself or a *modus vivendi* with Suharto possible, provided he was not arrested. That Suharto eventually overthrew him by means more subtle than arrest does not mean that at this stage he was bound to succeed.

Suharto had advanced; Hamengkubuwono was soon taking steps that led to Western backing for the economy. But the cabinet had not yet been shaped into the instrument Suharto desired. He therefore renewed and broadened his offensive with a campaign of punishment and intimidation, in which every sector of society was made to feel either the impact or the repercussions of the junta's growing power. Thousands of public servants who were more Sukarnoist than the average were dismissed on the ground that they sympathized with the PKI, thus putting thousands more in fear of their jobs; a purge of parliament, while pleasing politicians who felt that Sukarno had gone too far to the left, cowed those who wavered; and the junta disciplined many of those among its own ranks who were considered to be unreliable.

Yet for a time Suharto was still unsure of himself; and on 5 May 1966, he, Nasution and other service chiefs took the precaution of signing a pledge to 'safeguard the authority of the President, Bung Karno'.

The political struggle

While well-schooled adolescents chanted demands for even more drastic cabinet changes, Suharto intensified his efforts to control the MPRS. The arrest or murder of 120 of its members, who had totalled 609, had already ensured a certain amount of docility, but there was still much to be done. On 6 May 1966 Suharto surprised the political public by taking a plunge with his rare mixture of daring and circumspection. He announced that an MPRS session that was to have taken place six days later had been postponed because 'supplementary elements' were needed to 'fill the vacuum' left after the *putsch*. Playing his double game of pushing Sukarno aside while seeming to defer to him, he said that the armed forces wanted to 'place the head of state in his real position as stipulated by the constitution'. Implementation of the constitution had been put off course by the prologue and epilogue to the *putsch*, he said. Now the armed forces would set it right, 'in line with the intentions of President Sukarno and in line with the inner feelings of the people'. His action was unconstitutional, since Sukarno had insisted that he had not granted him governmental powers. But there was nothing Sukarno could do about it short of appealing to his supporters in the forces to wage a bloody civil war. Sukarno had packed the MPRS with a strong corps of supporters, after having reached agreement with leaders of political parties. Suharto now set about doing the same thing with less finesse. Sukarno watched impotently while Suharto 're-tooled' the constitutional machinery that was to grind down his authority; on 30 May he said he would 'remain silent in a thousand tongues' for the time being, but one day would speak out.

The complex process by which Suharto undermined Sukarno and manipulated the MPRS could not have been seen clearly at the time, even by those who were in Jakarta; it became more discernible when a pattern emerged in his subsequent elimination of all political rivalry. But much research is still needed to establish the balance of forces at given stages and to estimate the extent to which fear, rather than conviction, motived politicians. It is not claimed that the final assessment is being made here. But the emphasis given to MPRS resistance will certainly be nearer the truth than are works that represent Suharto as being swept forward by dominant, new social forces, of which the students are claimed to be an expression.

One of Suharto's methods, which he continued to apply after taking power, was to launch an offensive that served a triple purpose: to test the ground, to advance just as far as was proved safe and to soften up for the next attack. This strategy was manifest when the promised session of the MPRS took place from 20 June to 6 July. Five days after the opening a rally of 50,000, mostly adolescents, was staged outside the Russian-built sports complex, where the MPRS met in the basket-ball hall. The rally carried a resolution urging the MPRS to rule that Suharto would become Acting President if Sukarno should be unable to carry out his office. This was the first occasion on which Suharto's name had been linked with the Presidency. Thus, with the MPRS in session, Suharto was trying his strength by kite-flying, while creating an atmosphere that would be useful for the next meeting if he did not immediately attain his objective. Those familiar with the junta's stratagems would have no doubt that Suharto's men had set the demonstration in motion. And in the cleverly worded resolution they would suspect the hand of that impish master of political intrigue, Colonel (later Lieutenant-General) Ali Murtopo, who was later to dismantle all Indonesian political parties.

But the voices in the streets and pressure in the lobbies were not strong enough to ensure decisive victory at the MPRS meeting, and the junta had to fight hard to reach limited objectives on the road to Sukarno's defeat. The disappointment of Western diplomats at the MPRS's resistance to the junta and its allies was reflected in a report written on 30 June by the ANP-AFP correspondent,[8] who reproached members for a 'lack of rational thinking' when Sukarno's 'position as head of state is at stake'. They seemed to be 'emotionally involved where Sukarno is concerned', he lamented. The next day he reported that the Army appeared to have decided to 'wait for a more favourable moment'. He said: 'The army clearly fears that civil war would break out in Central and East Java if the "Bung" were to face an outright request to resign. There are strong rumours that the many supporters of "Bung Karno", as Sukarno is affectionately called by large numbers of the Javanese community, may start a "long march" on Jakarta if congress [MPRS] strips him of his powers.'

On 2 July Nasution predicted that the decisions of the MPRS, which met behind closed doors, would 'not be what Indonesians expected'. The MPRS was divided into two opposing groups, he said. Subchan admitted while the MPRS was still meeting that it 'failed to fulfil the people's demands regarding the many titles and functions of President Sukarno'. The resistance was so strong that the session was extended for a day while the junta and its supporters pressed and bargained to bring the MPRS into line. Meanwhile the official organ of the divided PNI, which was probably the largest party in the MPRS, despite the re-packing, had urged endorsement of a report by Sukarno, since it had answered 'all important questions that have arisen lately'.

When the decisions were announced, Nasution said that they were satisfactory to neither the armed forces nor the President. Sukarno remained President and Great Leader of the Revolution, and was applauded when he accepted the renewal of his mandate at the final session on 6 July. But as a first step in trimming his stature the junta and its allies persuaded the MPRS to revoke his appointment as President for Life. The argument that the title was in any case unconstitutional provided members with an acceptable pretext for giving in on that point. They also found nothing wrong in agreeing that Sukarno should elaborate his 33-minute progress report on his stewardship. The 11 March Order was made an MPRS decree, and was widened to give Suharto 'full discretion' in carrying it out. Sukarno's most obvious defeat was in foreign policy. The MPRS decided that Indonesia should re-join the United Nations, which it had left in the previous year, and put off the Conefo by declaring that it should be held when the world situation warranted it. General elections, previously promised by the junta, were postponed for a maximum of two years.

Sukarno was by no means beaten. In his acceptance speech he said he would refuse to form a Cabinet unless the government's policy remained not only to solve economic problems, as required by Suharto, but to fight Nekolim, hold general elections, and

preserve an active and independent foreign policy. Members cried
'Yes' when he asked if that was what they wanted. Earlier he
wrested a vital amendment from the junta. A motion had been
put up to *instruct* the President to order Suharto, as holder of the
11 March Order, to form a cabinet. After a conference between
Sukarno, the inner cabinet and armed forces leaders the motion
was altered to *request* Sukarno himself to undertake the task
'together with Lieutenant-General Suharto'. Only one member,
Adnan Bujung Nasution, protested at the change when the
motion was taken back to the MPRS; the fact that he was shouted
down suggests that the junta could push the assembly no farther.
Yet although General Nasution confirmed the change at a press
conference after the final session, the original motion appears in
some works as a decision. Both the original and amended motions
should be sufficient to show that the MPRS was not under the
illusion that Sukarno had transferred full governmental powers to
Suharto under the 11 March Order, in which case no further
authority to form a cabinet would have been necessary. The
army had gone as far as it could in trying to link cabinet formation
with the 11 March order, but had failed. Sukarno was still able
to assert in the MPRS on 6 July that only he had the constitutional
right to appoint ministers; there was no *formateur*, he said,
obviously referring to Suharto. The apparent contradiction
between the MPRS's loyalty to Sukarno and the rejection of his
foreign policy seems easy to explain. All members were concerned
about the economic débacle; a gesture had to be made to obtain
Western aid and advice, which, by orthodox criteria, were the
only means of averting total collapse.

It is possible that Suharto would have found ways of dealing
with the MPRS if he had not been afraid of Sukarnoists in the
armed forces, whose pent-up anger was an increasing threat.
While he could probably have crushed a revolt, he would not have
wanted the split to become more apparent. Three battalions of
the KKO (marines) had come from East Java to their Jakarta
head-quarters. Lorry-loads of them, armed with machine-guns,
had driven past Kostrad HQ and, on 1 July, the MPRS meeting-
place, shouting, 'long live Bung Karno'. Suharto concentrated
18,000 troops in the capital, including some that he brought in
from Sulawesi (Celebes) and alerted the Siliwangi Division at
Bandung, about 200 kilometres away. The Diponegoro Division

in Central Java and the Brawijaya in East Java had been purged. But neither the junta nor Western diplomats felt that these two regiments were yet completely reliable and feared that some units would rush to support the marines in any clash. Suharto ordered his men to ignore KKO provocation; for the time being it was enough that slogans should appear on walls, demanding, 'dissolve the KKO' and 'down with the KKO'.

Although on paper the junta gained less than it had hoped for, it had given the MPRS a salutary taste of what was to come, and Sukarno must have realized that continued pressure and blandishments would give Suharto full control in the end. Whatever his support might have been in a vote of the people, which he persistently urged while the army prevented it, there was no hope for him in Jakarta, where his immediate arrest would have followed any attempt to rally Sukarnoists in the forces. Sukarno was already virtually a prisoner: hostile troops were posted at both palaces to keep watch on him. In a conversation with Adam Malik he threatened to go to Central or East Java, where he would find both popular and armed support; Malik replied that he could try if he wished. There was a report that Sukarno did, in fact, attempt to 'escape by air' from Bogor to the KKO base at Surabaya on 3 July; it was said that officers at the palace intercepted him and 'talked him out of it'.

But Suharto still had to fight politically, and the struggle over formation of the new cabinet that the MPRS had agreed to order dragged on until the day of its announcement on 25 July. So dogged was Sukarno's resistance that the ANP-AFP correspondent reported in the morning the 'gloomy view' of 'usually well informed sources' that changes would be 'few and insignificant'. The previous day Sukarno told journalists after a conference with the old inner cabinet at Bogor that the list was not yet definite; and Suharto explained that it was still necessary to establish that the candidates would be 'the right men in the right places'. The struggle was obviously still going on. But when Sukarno announced the cabinet it was clear that he had lost heavily; Suharto became head of the inner cabinet, which was reduced from six to five members, and Sukarno's two associates, Leimena and Abdulgani, were removed. Sukarno was careful to point out that Suharto was not Prime Minister, but had replaced Leimena as senior minister. As Sukarno gave no indication that he remained Prime Minister himself, some correspondents took the liberty of reporting that the post had been abolished. Several appointments were made in the broader cabinet to suit Suharto. A change in its name from Dwikora to Ampera (from Sukarno's Message of the People's Sufferings), which the MPRS had authorized, expressed Suharto's emphasis on 'filling the people's stomachs' while preserving Sukarno's stamp.

After reading of these events in a news agency's files, one is dismayed at the treatment they have received by writers. Legge, for instance, says of the Ampera cabinet formation:[9] 'In the meantime Suharto continued to implement his own policies. In July he formed a new cabinet under the authority of the 11 March Order and in accordance with the instructions of the MPRS; it excluded the well-known Sukarno-men.' This unqualified statement seems, to put it moderately, an extraordinary simplification for a historian to make, particularly in what he calls a 'political biography' of Sukarno.

Sukarno was obviously rankled at having had to yield so much. At a cabinet installation ceremony he tried to show his power by promoting all service chiefs, including Suharto, who became a full general; but he revealed his weakness in futile retaliation, appointing Leimena, 'the greatest patriot in the country', to be his deputy as head of the Supreme Advisory Council and making Abdulgani chairman of the National Planning Council, the National Defence Institute and the Atomic Energy Commission. He angrily attacked correspondents who had reported that he had ceased to be Prime Minister. He was leading the cabinet, he said; and all the ministers, including the head of the inner cabinet, were his assistants. Sukarno was particularly bitter about persistent reports that he had handed over executive authority to Suharto on 11 March. At no stage had he done this, he said. Pointing his finger at foreign journalists, he shouted, 'I have been attacked by the imperialist press since I was eighteen years of age.' It was a fair accusation; and, unfortunately, it will take a generation to clear away the rubbish that has spilled over from newspapers into more durable works.

Two million people stood for two hours in Merdeka Square to hear Sukarno's Independence Day speech, entitled 'Never Leave History', on 17 August 1966. He condemned the *putsch*, and pretended to have taken the initiative in punishing its leaders by announcing that he had established the military court, which, in fact, Suharto had set up. With the PKI gone, he modified Nasakom to Nasasoc, replacing Communism with socialism. Nationalism, belief in God, and socialism were the need of every human being and every nation, he said. He reiterated his advocacy of Indonesian self-reliance, which eschewed begging, and co-operation with 'friends throughout the world'. Appealing to the United States to leave Vietnam, he offered to mediate, and warned: 'You will not be able to solve the Vietnam problem the way you are going about it; it is you who will be battered and torn.' Pathetically, he claimed that he had ordered Suharto to seek the end of the Malaysia Confrontation, which had taken place formally on 11 August.

On the eve of Independence Day he had delivered a vigorous speech to parliament. But it was clear that he was powerless. Suharto was indeed acting virtually on his own now, exploiting to the limit the 'discretion' given to him when the MPRS strengthened the 11 March Order. In both foreign and domestic policy he acted as if it were he, and not Sukarno, who had accepted the MPRS mandate amid applause in July. On 26 August, the new Information Minister, Burhanuddin Mohammed Diah, a shrewd man who has never been known to miss an opportunity, felt confident enough to tell journalists that nothing the President said was binding on the government.

On 5 October, Armed Forces Day, Sukarno addressed service-men, urging them to uphold *Pancasila*, which, he recalled, he had formulated twenty-two years previously. The junta then decided to strike again before he could rise. Through the MPRS standing committee, which it controlled, it ordered him to comply with the July request to make a supplementary progress report, dealing with the *putsch* and explaining the nation's moral and economic decline. Sukarno appears to have resisted this new attempt to humiliate him as long as possible. He did not make his statement until 10 January 1967 and then it was only in the form of a four-page letter, which he read at a press conference. He said that the *putsch* had come as a complete surprise to him. Responsibility for the economic crisis rested not on one person, but on the entire government apparatus and on society, which, as a whole, was also to blame for the moral decline – a reference to corruption. This homily, though logical enough, came oddly from a paternalistic leader who had claimed to be taking his people forward to a better life. Most Indonesians had always seen Sukarno as a kind of magician; his appearance as an impotent philosopher would not have helped him. While all policy-making had been snatched from Sukarno, he was dangerous as long as he remained President. Suharto therefore began a new offensive. Adolescents, who were never long off the streets in those days, came out immediately after Sukarno's letter was published and demanded; 'Hang Bung Karno'. As if to intimidate politicians, the impending prosecution was announced of certain PNI members on a charge of having taken part in the 30 September plot. Tension was built up by means of public statements and newspaper articles, which urged Sukarno to resign. Adam Malik, whose loquacity had made him a spokesman for the junta, said on 17 February that there would be no compromise: the President would be dismissed when the MPRS met again if he did not capitulate. The next day Suharto saw leaders of the eight political parties to sound out their views. But fears of civil war were revived when Lieutenant-General Hartono, commander of the 15,000 Marines, made a statement that was interpreted as support for Sukarno, to whom he was passionately loyal.

On 19 February Suharto went with other generals to Bogor and tried to bully Sukarno into resigning. But Sukarno would concede no more than a document transferring to Suharto the 'powers of government', which he had already seized, 'without diminishing the meaning and spirit of the 1945 Constitution'. Sukarno published the document, as a presidential announcement, but Suharto rejected it – a fact that seems to have eluded Legge, who says that the junta demanded it, and takes the trouble to speculate on why it did so. The 'compromise', as it was called, was clearly useless to Suharto. Under the 1945 constitution the President was answerable only to the MPRS, not even to parliament. This meant that any changes in foreign or domestic policy that Suharto introduced would remain unconstitutional unless Sukarno, who held the MPRS mandate, approved them. The document ensured Sukarno's control by obliging Suharto to report to him 'at every moment it is deemed necessary'.

Suharto's annoyance at the offer of what he already possessed was at once apparent. The next day Adam Malik said that Suharto would not side-track 'popular demands' for Sukarno's 'constitutional removal' from office. He said Suharto had refused to agree to the transfer and would accept nothing less than 'unconditional surrender'; nor would Sukarno be allowed to 'avoid his fate' at a trial by fleeing from the country. Suharto held a meeting on the same day with his senior military commanders to discuss the consequences of Sukarno's stand. Officers from the Air Force, Navy, Marines and Police, in which Sukarnoism was still strong, were significantly absent. It was reported that Suharto said he would use arms, if necessary, to enforce decisions of an MPRS meeting that was to be called in March. Suharto was obviously confident that he could persuade the MPRS to depose Sukarno. But he was less sure of his own forces; the navy commander, Muljadi, and police chief, Sutjipto Judodihardjo, were reported to have wavered in their reluctant support for Suharto on reading accounts of popular backing for Sukarno in the regions.

Nevertheless Suharto went ahead with his plan to depose Sukarno. A misleading broadcast on 23 February, in which he gave the impression that he had got what he wanted from Sukarno, was rectified on 25 February in a so-called government statement, which said that Sukarno had volunteered the transfer and that the struggle was not yet over. Suharto then ensured the complicity of the MPRS by building it up to 651 members with an infusion of reliable representatives of functional groups and a purged PNI representation. Sukarno's fall was now certain; and at a session lasting from 7 to 12 March 1967 the renovated MPRS cancelled his mandate and elected Suharto acting President. Suharto's appointment was to last until a new assembly was elected. But although elections were not held until 1971, Suharto's complete control of the MPRS ensured his appointment as President on 27 March 1968. The New Order, as it was called, had finally replaced the Old. Sukarno, though forbidden to take part in politics, was allowed a certain amount of freedom for a time, but this was increasingly reduced until he was placed under strict house arrest.

It had taken nearly eighteen months for Suharto to rise to Acting President and two and a half years to become formally head of state. If Suharto is to be admired for his patience in this epic Javanese duel, Sukarno should be praised for his endurance and political integrity. He fought to the end by every means possible, short of a direct appeal for civil war. At no stage did he concede anything that had not already been taken from him by force, whether it was security powers in March 1966 or governmental powers in March 1967. He spoke up for Nasakom, even after the PKI had been wiped out, and continued to campaign for Conefo, even when it was doomed. At times he pretended to retain more power than he had, but not to have done so would have invited immediate, total defeat. He clung to his mandate from the MPRS until the MPRS itself took it from him. He was beaten, but he did not surrender.

The new president

It took a long time for Suharto to eradicate Sukarnoists in the armed forces; Nasution said subsequently (to the author) that 'most of the army' supported Sukarno even after Suharto's election as Acting President. Hartono was exiled as ambassador to North Korea, and later died suddenly in Jakarta in suspicious circumstances after having been recalled for interrogation. The turning point in the armed forces probably came after the 'Vow of Yogya', by which six active military commanders resolved after a three-day conference at Yogyakarta, Central Java, in July 1967 to take 'firm steps' against all individuals and groups that favoured Sukarno's restoration to power. Dubious units were broken up; officers and non-commisioned officers were arrested by the dozen. The purge was not complete until 1971. But there was never a direct threat of rebellion. Suharto could be seen as a ruthless and capable military leader; those who were tempted to revolt were probably sobered by memories of his swift, efficient action in October 1965.

It would be interesting to know at what point Suharto decided to become President; probably it was very early. In February 1966 Murtopo, Mashuri and others urged him to dislodge Sukarno; he told them that if they wanted him to be leader they must accept his timetable. If any observer in Jakarta had been asked before 1 October 1965 who was the military man most eligible to be head of state, the answer would have been, if anyone, Nasution. Although Sukarno had promoted him out of harm's way when he made him Chief of Staff of the Armed Forces, Nasution was still influential and the only full general in the army. He was respected both for his intellect and, what was equally rare among the generals, his reputation for incorruptibility. He was the leading author of the army's tactical and political thinking. His book on guerrilla fighting had become a standard work in several countries and he had formulated and named the doctrine of *dwi-fonski* (double function), by which the army was seen to have a politico-social as well as a military role. At the time of the *putsch* he was not quite forty-seven, athletic in appearance and fit enough to be an excellent tennis player. Despite Suharto's ascendancy, Nasution was still referred to in news reports as 'head of the army leadership' as late as January 1966, if not later.

After the *putsch* Subchan urged Nasution to take over the government. Some say that he refused because, being a Sumatran, he would never receive enough support from Javanese generals. But Nasution said (in an interview with the author) that he did not even consider the idea; it was out of the question because he had no troops. Nevertheless, Nasution was active in highly emotional scenes that occurred after he arrived at Kostrad HQ on the afternoon of 1 October. He said:

[Admiral Eddy] Martadinata came from Sukarno at Halim and said that Sukarno had taken over the army with Pranoto as caretaker. I said it was an army matter; there was no need for this. Martadinata embraced me and asked me to forgive him. Muljadi [another admiral] and Hartono also embraced me. I told Martadinata to make a statement supporting Suharto; he did this the same night. Bambang [Sukarno's aide-de-camp] arrived half an hour later and reported the President's demand. I said: 'We are not opposing the President's order, but we cannot implement it during a military operation.' I asked Suharto to summon Pranoto. I told him: 'The TNI [army] is at stake. Report to the President that you cannot implement the order.' Our problem was to safeguard the army command, with the Kostrad commander as acting commander.

Nasution was unwilling to discuss whether he thought that Suharto had pushed him aside, except to say, 'perhaps I under-estimated him', which is certainly not an overstatement. But he did reveal a significant sidelight on Suharto's methods. When Suharto was pressing for the Dwikora cabinet reshuffle he proposed Nasution, representing the armed forces, as one of the three new vice-premiers, with Hamengkubuwono and Malik. Nasution said:

> The other three service chiefs were loyal to Sukarno. Sukarno said: 'Choose between Nasution and me.' A meeting was then held of the four service chiefs. I sent them a note telling them to cause a deadlock in the formation of the cabinet. I felt that this would strengthen our position and that time was on our side. A few days later, on a Saturday, Suharto came here [to Nasution's house] and reported that a deadlock could not be achieved because Sukarno was too powerful. He said he had been forced to become Vice-Premier, representing Hankam [the Defence Department], *ad interim*. He said: 'This is not for me; it is for you.'

But it was not for Nasution. In fact Suharto's next move was to take the post, not *ad interim*, of Senior Vice-Premier in the Ampera cabinet. Suharto, while avoiding the vice-presidency, which had been vacant since Mohammad Hatta resigned in 1956, quickly killed, with Nasution's complicity, a proposal that Nasution should be elected to it. Nasution was side-tracked into a blind alley as chairman of the MPRS, a post that was later abolished. Soon after his appointment Nasution declared in a television interview that Suharto would hand back the 11 March Order to Sukarno once its purpose had been achieved. This was probably an Indonesian way of trying to prevent Suharto from doing otherwise. Nasution's aim had been to save first the unity of the army command, then the original constitution, which had been born with the nation in 1945. Suharto's aim was, or became, to establish the army's rule over all and his rule over the army. After the day on which he was elected Acting President he and Nasution did not speak to each other again. (At least until January 1973, when the interview took place.)

Nasution was not the only person to underestimate Suharto; it took a long time for some diplomats to be convinced that he was capable of holding power. He looked so good-natured that his biography was entitled *The Smiling General*. At the MPRS meetings he read his speeches in an uninspiring monotone. It was easy to believe that this round-faced man had been merely swept to the presidency by some irresistible social tide. Early in 1969 a Western ambassador asked me who I thought was the real force in Indonesia; for it seemed possible that Suharto was only the junta's figurehead and that more powerful men were behind the scenes. When he grew used to speaking to small public gatherings Suharto relaxed into sheer frivolity, chuckling and joking amiably about what he saw as false solutions to Indonesia's problems. At Solo during the 1971 election campaign, standing with his weight on one foot and trailing the other lightly to and fro, he looked more like Laurence Olivier's Archie Rice, about to break into a soft shuffle, than the man who had crushed the PKI.

A tape-recording of an interview I had with him in November 1972 is enlivened by ripples of Suharto's spontaneous laughter. I pointed out to him that while Indonesia claimed that Peking Radio's attacks on his government were an obstacle to restoration of diplomatic relations, these were few compared with those from Moscow, with which relations were maintained. 'Yes', he smiled, 'I complain about that to the Russian Ambassador every time I see him.' He paused and his eyes shone as he laughingly added: 'But the Ambassador tells me it is not the Soviet government, but the Communist Party, which makes the attacks.' Suharto gave impressively quick and detailed replies to a number of questions about domestic and foreign policy; he could obviously hold his own among his ministers. But there was no sign of the qualities that enabled him to divert the course of Indonesian history.

Yet there are rare occasions when the man who overthrew Sukarno, and then brought to heel all the generals who helped him, shows himself for a second or two. The soft features suddenly sharpen and the kindly eyes glint menacingly. Few people have seen this steely transformation, but those who have are struck by it. I saw it only once, when Suharto suddenly turned and fixed his glance on a suspected general who was talking to a European at a reception. At this moment he immediatley appeared as a man who could not only lead, but rule, Indonesia.

While Sukarno's mind and heart were open to the world, it is doubtful if Suharto shares his more important thoughts with anyone except, perhaps, his *dukuns* and his wife, Tien. Possibly his reserve originated in his lonely childhood, spent among peasants in small villages of Central Java and in Solo. His parents, who were poor, separated two years after his birth in 1921 and he was brought up in various households, although his father ensured that he had primary and middle schooling. When he was fifteen he lived with a *dukun*, who was famed in the locality for his advice on personal and business problems and his ability to rid bewitched houses of evil spirits. He thus became imbued with Javanese mysticism, which was to influence him for the rest of his life; it was said that before he went abroad in September 1970, the head of a water buffalo was buried at each tip of the archipelago, on the advice of *dukuns*, to ensure that the nation held together during his absence.

Suharto joined the Royal Netherlands Indies Army in June 1940 and was quickly promoted to sergeant. Like many others who were to fight the Dutch in the struggle for independence, he served with the Japanese during the occupation. He became a staff officer of Peta, the Japanese-sponsored Volunteer Army of Defenders of the Motherland. After Japan's surrender on 15 August 1945, Suharto organized and led a daring attack on the Japanese garrison at Yogyakarta, Central Java, which capitulated after twelve hours. By the middle of 1946 he was Indonesian Army Regimental Commander at Yogyakarta, with the rank of Lieutenant-Colonel. On 1 March 1949 he led a successful raid on the town when it was occupied by the Dutch. He continued to rise; and in 1962 Sukarno promoted him to Major-General and put him in command of the forces that were massed to capture West Irian (Dutch New Guinea) from the Dutch. The following year Suharto was given the Kostrad command.

It is unlikely that a desire for power was the only motive in Suharto's decision to oust Sukarno. Probably *dukuns*, who often draw upon old Javanese prophecies, told him that the nation's history was about to take a new turn, and gave him a sense of mission; his wife's ambitions were also a likely influence. He was clearly convinced that Western aid was essential to Indonesia's economic development. His slogan, 'fill the people's stomachs', reflected his belief that Sukarno was only offering abstract political ideas and emotional exhortations that would never achieve the promised, just society. He knew, like Sukarno, that foreign countries were more interested in exploiting Indonesia than in helping it; but he believed that Javanese cleverness, rather than political awareness of the masses, would be sufficient to enable the nation to reap the benefits without paying the political and economic price.

Superficially it looked as if Suharto, for all his mysticism, was more practical than Sukarno, who had made his way intuitively through the works of Western political philosophers and sought to adapt them to his country's needs. Suharto's first aim was to stabilize the nation politically and economically before launching a programme of economic development. His policy was summed up in the phrase, 'development before politics'. To this end all political parties were virtually destroyed and all spontaneous expression of social forces was inhibited. The army and its technocrats took on the responsibility of bringing prosperity to Indonesia, in spite of immense cultural obstacles, without the participation of the people in either decision or discussion. This entailed repression on an unprecedented scale. All serious criticism and all protests, even those against manifest corruption in the President's circle, were eventually forbidden on the ground that they were a camouflage for some sinister political group, either Communist, Moslem or Socialist. Fear of Moslems led some of the President's advisers into the arms of Catholic Action, with the strange consequence that a Dutch Jesuit played a part in shaping the Javanese junta's political ideas. But before dealing with its remaining political rivals the junta busied itself with legalizing Indonesia's acquisition of West Irian.

PART TWO

The New Order

CHAPTER FIVE

The United Nations fiasco

The façade

Sudjarwo Tjondronegoro and I were sitting on a log in front of his new, unfenced bungalow, a few hundred metres up the timbered mountain that rises behind Jayapura,[1] West Irian's dilapidated little capital, which the Dutch had established on the coast, with the name of Hollandia. I had come across him by chance while walking down the road to Jayapura from an Indonesian Air Force hostel, where I was camping in one of the vacant rooms without permission. If I was a squatter, so in a sense were Sudjarwo and other Indonesian officials, for whose cars bulldozers had cut long, wide swathes in the bush, leaving fresh wounds of yellow clay, made sticky by the rains. For the Indonesians had not yet legally established absolute sovereignty over West Irian, and scores of thousands of Papuans had made it clear by revolt, protest and flight that they wanted them to go.

It was June 1969. The preliminary stages of the Act of Free Choice, which was to determine whether or not West Irian, formerly Dutch New Guinea, remained part of Indonesia, were well under way. Indonesia was carrying out the Act to honour the New York Agreement of August 1962, under which Holland ceded the territory to the Republic; the Dutch had insisted on a provision that the Papuans would be given the choice of independence by the end of 1969.

Sudjarwo, who had been Ambassador to the Netherlands in 1965–67, was Special Assistant to the Foreign Minister. He had been given the formidable task of rigging the Act, with the help of many thousands of troops, and the much simpler one of hoodwinking an obliging United Nations team, which was not unhappy to give the false impression that its presence would ensure fair play. Sudjarwo, I was told later, found the army's help embarrassing: he felt he could manage the show more to the satisfaction of international opinion, which was what mattered, without all the threatening, killing and looting; he was an old West Irian hand, well versed in the mummery of international politics. During President Sukarno's struggle to wrest this last piece of the Netherlands East Indies from the Dutch he had canvassed for votes at the United Nations. His opponent in the lobbies had been a Dutch Foreign Ministry official, Hugo Scheltema. Now Scheltema was Ambassador to Indonesia, the instrument of a sickening reversal of policy. The former antagonists, Sudjarwo and Scheltema, had become partners; and the Papuans, the darlings of the Netherlands when open West European imperialism was in its death-throes, were being dropped willy-nilly into Indonesia's lap.

As the government in Jakarta had forbidden visits of journalists and diplomats to West Irian since rebellion had broken out in the Wissell Lakes area in April, Sudjarwo was probably surprised to see me. For reasons that I could never establish with certainty an exception had been made to allow me in. Whatever his feelings were, Sudjarwo hid them behind the smile with which many Indonesians, particularly Javanese, express friendship or mask enmity at will. You can never be sure what that smile means; but even when you suspect danger you cannot resist it.

I sat down beside Sudjarwo. He was a tough but amiable man, with a gay laugh and humour in his eyes. I had already interviewed him a few times in Jakarta and had come to like him. Like many Indonesians with Dutch schooling, he was fluent in English.

'You can see it is all calm down there', he said, looking towards Jayapura.

I remembered the dozens of Papuans who, to the point of maddening irritation, had sidled up to me in the streets, protesting: 'Indonesia tidak baik (Indonesia is no good).' But since I had acquired a certain amount of Javanese obliqueness myself since my arrival in Indonesia the previous October, I said nothing about this for the moment. I thought of the blue harbour, with its tree-lined shore; it was one of the loveliest sights in the world, a daily joy to United Nations officials and other well-to-do, some of whom could glimpse it through trees from their houses on the slopes.

'Yes', I said, 'the sea is very calm.'

After some preparatory conversation I thought it good tactics to say: 'I have sent some reports that you will not like. You will have to get me expelled.' He smiled; we discussed one or two incidents, then dropped the subject.

The agreement signed by Holland and Indonesia at the United Nations on 15 August 1962 ended a dispute that had been going on since 1949, when the Dutch refused to cede sovereignty over West Irian along with the remainder of their territory in the Indies. It followed a threat by Indonesia to invade West Irian with 75,000 troops supported by warships bought on credit from Eastern Europe. Already the Indonesians had landed marines and dropped paratroopers in an operation launched by Major-General Suharto (now General Suharto, the President), who was promoted in rank for the purpose. A senior naval officer, Commodore Soedarso, became a national hero when he went down with his torpedo boat in a battle with a Dutch warship. Sukarno sought a diplomatic, rather than military, victory. Politically, he had manoeuvred himself into a strong position. Indonesia's purchase of one billion dollars worth of East European arms in 1961 was in itself enough to bring Washington running to his side, through fear of a successful, Soviet-backed military operation in the area. Soon Ellsworth Bunker, the American diplomat, was mediating on behalf of U Thant, then United Nations Acting Secretary-General. The Dutch, now virtually isolated, finally gave in and accepted Bunker's compromise proposals.

In its report on the Act of Free Choice, submitted to the United Nations in November 1969, Indonesia rightly described the 1962 Agreement as 'juridically probably rather a peculiar document'. It is beyond the scope of this book to investigate to what extent the amateurish draftsmanship was intentional. But there can be no doubt that the Agreement was deliberately vague on what had become the main issue in the dispute – the right of the Papuans to determine their own status. After a short transitional period of United Nations administration, 'full administrative responsibility' was to be transferred to Indonesia, whose laws were to apply. The presence of the United Nations in the subsequent Act of Free Choice was provided in Article XVII:

> Indonesia will invite the Secretary-General to appoint a Representative who . . . will carry out the Secretary-General's responsibilities to advise, assist and participate in arrangements which are the responsibility of Indonesia for the act of free choice.

These words were supposed to guarantee Papuan self-determination. Yet the idea of responsibility, used twice, was open to different interpretations; 'participate' was not defined; and there was nothing to ensure that the Secretary-General would be able to carry out his 'responsibilities' if the Indonesians were to insist, as they eventually did, that the sole 'responsibility' for the Act was theirs and that they were not even obliged to accept United Nations advice. At the signing ceremony the Dutch representative, Dr J. H. van Roijen, placed on record his government's interpretation of the Article. He said:

> The Netherlands Government has been, and is, most deeply concerned with the well-being of the Papuans. It is for that reason that the Netherlands has attached primary importance to the inclusion in the agreement of provisions safeguarding the further political, economic, cultural and educational development of the territory and its inhabitants, and guaranteeing for the Papuans, under active supervision of the United Nations, a genuine and valid exercise of freedom of choice with regard to their future.

Here the significant words are 'active supervision'. For in 1969 the United Nations officials repeatedly emphasized that whatever 'participation' was intended to mean it could never have been 'supervision'; apparently they had overlooked Dr van Roijen's speech. Whether Dr van Roijen meant what he said or whether his government, having changed its policy under pressure, was merely seeking to quieten Dutch opinion, is of little importance. For when the time came the Dutch looked the other way while the Indonesians made West Irian theirs by methods that broke both the spirit and the letter of the treaty. The Dutch Foreign Minister, Joseph Luns, whose touching pleas for the Papuans had marked his adamant refusal to cede West Irian in 1961, readily connived with Indonesia in the farce of 1969. But in 1962 the Dutch public were certainly given the impression that the Act would be supervised. Not only was there Dr van Roijen's assurance; the fact that the United Nations retained one of three signed copies of treaty, each bound in dark blue with the UN emblem in gold, seemed to sanctify the document and to ensure the freedom of choice that it purported to protect.

In his speech at the signing ceremony the Indonesian Minister of Foreign Affairs, Dr Subandrio, made no reference at all to the Papuans, but said that Indonesian unity had been restored and that the struggle for independence had been completed. At preliminary discussions on the Act of Free Choice held in New York on 3–5 June 1968 Sudjarwo told United Nations officials that arrangements for the Act were the 'sole responsibility' of Indonesia. The officials replied pointedly that the function of the United Nations was to 'participate', as well as to 'advise and assist'. But from the United Nations report on these meetings it appears that both sides thought it prudent merely to quote the treaty, without attempting to broach such an embarrassing issue as what 'participation' might mean.

The United Nations Secretary-General's interest in the Act of Free Choice dated from 21 September 1962, when the General Assembly authorized him to carry out the series of tasks that Holland and Indonesia had allotted to him in their Agreement. When the time for the Act drew near, U Thant chose as his representative in West Irian Fernando Ortiz Sanz, who gave up his post as Bolivia's permanent representative to the United Nations for the purpose. Ortiz Sanz subsequently reported to the United Nations that he was ready to leave for Indonesia as soon as he was appointed on 1 April 1968, but that the Indonesian government had asked him to postpone his departure. The Indonesians had good reasons for the delay: they had a revolt of Arfak tribesmen on their hands. Indonesian armed forces had delivered a decisive blow early in 1967, when planes bombed and strafed tribesmen who were threatening Manokwari town. But the fighting went on; and the government announced on 12 August 1968, after a special cabinet meeting held to discuss security, that 162 tribesmen had been killed and that more than 3,500 had surrendered, apparently since the operation began; the army had taken 138 prisoners and captured 123 weapons, all relics of the Second World War. While the rebellion had been virtually crushed, there was still mopping up to be done and the rebel leader, Lodewijk Mandatjan, remained at large with a band of followers.

Ortiz Sanz was a model of diplomatic correctness when he arrived in Jakarta on the day of this announcement. He told reporters that the best and most acceptable means of carrying out the Act of Free Choice had yet to be decided. He stuck to the book and defined his role as to assist, advise and participate, but said nothing to indicate that these words were a euphemism for utter impotence. The belief that the United Nations presence would ensure freedom of choice persisted for a time, and the Jakarta correspondent of the Dutch News Agency, Algemeen Nederlands Persbureau, referred to Ortiz Sanz both before and after his arrival as the 'UN supervisor'. But by the end of 1968 even the most wilfully blind could see that the Papuans were to have no effective say in their future; and educated Papuans were bitterly laughing off the self-determination procedure as 'the act free of choice'.

Suharto's Javanese gift for clothing an illegal operation with an elaborate semblance of legality, which he displayed after the *putsch*, was again evident. In overthrowing Sukarno he made it easy for his supporters at home and abroad to believe that he had acted constitutionally; in the same way, by going through the complex motions of the Act of Free Choice, he enabled those who wished to do so to shut their eyes to the fact that the Papuans had no choice at all. The pretence produced odd contradictions in official statements; for while the government wanted to keep alive the impression that the United Nations was some kind of umpire, it had to ensure control of West Irian by insisting that the Act was its exclusive business. In January 1969 the President's Adviser for Special Affairs, Brigadier-General (later Lieutenant-General) Ali Murtopo, said that U Thant had rejected an appeal by the President of the West Papua Freedom Committee, Nicolaas Jouwe, an exile living in Holland, that a one-man-one-vote plebiscite should be held. This announcement was intended to give the impression that U Thant was the final arbiter. But Suharto made Indonesia's position clear when he told a departing Reuters correspondent in an interview that anyone who opposed Indonesia's retention of West Irian would be guilty of treason.

This shaft of truth dismayed foreign diplomats who, for various reasons, were anxious that their compatriots should believe that a genuine plebiscite was being held. Attempts were made to explain away the statement as an error of interpretation from Indonesian into English. A British Embassy official went so far as to advise – and an American official to warn – the correspondent's successor to be more careful.

Suharto put his position beyond doubt in April, four months before the Act, when he told paratroopers at a ceremony near Bandung, West Java: 'The return of West Irian into the fold of the motherland is not at all a gift from outside, not just the result of cleverness at the negotiating table. It is supported by real military achievements and intensive preparations by the whole people of Indonesia.' The occasion was reported in the Indonesian press to be the presentation of a standard to a paratroop regiment that had dropped men into the West Irian jungle during the war with the Dutch in 1961; what was not stated at the time was that the troops were about to leave on a secret mission, the crushing of a new Papuan rebellion, wind of which had not yet reached observers in Jakarta.

Ortiz Sanz was not to be drawn on how these unequivocal statements might affect his task. He had set himself up in a house in the outskirts of Jakarta, where he worked with the gate locked and was rarely accessible to the press; he spent about half of his year's tour there and the remainder in a bungalow on the slopes above Jayapura. While foreign correspondents were badgering his officials for information about the Act of Free Choice, he was under instructions from U Thant not to provoke the Indonesians, whom no nation, in either the Eastern or Western bloc, wished to offend. Justice was not practical politics. The Americans, jubilant that the Indonesian Communist Party had been wiped out, had political, strategic and oil interests in Indonesia; the Russians were ingratiating themselves with the generals as part of their plan to penetrate the Indian Ocean; the British, fed up with the political recalcitrance of most of their former subjects, were nosing about for new markets and opportunities for investment and influence; the Dutch were seeking the return of Shell; the Australians wanted to be friends at any price with what they believed to be a potentially powerful neighbour; the French were looking for uranium in Kalimantan (Borneo), and saw in Indonesia the possibility of a link that would restore some of the presence in South East Asia that they had lost with Indo-China; and the Chinese apparently found little in it for them, and said nothing. The French were exceptionally zealous to keep on the right side of the Indonesians. Their Ambassador, Claude Cheysson, later a Commissioner of the European Communities, outsmarted his rivals with a statement that France had urged certain African countries – former colonies whose rulers were dependent on French aid – to vote in the United Nations General Assembly for adoption of the Secretary-General's report.

On 13 January 1969 Ortiz Sanz issued a statement on his consultations with the Indonesian government, which was obviously meant to reassure public opinion in Holland or wherever it might be interested. Apparently he considered it to be urgent, for it was delivered to correspondents late in the evening, long after normal working hours. Despite the obvious intentions of the Indonesians, Ortiz Sanz went out of his way to give a favourable impression of preparations for the Act of Free Choice. Along with a proud recital of the thousands of meaningless miles flown by his team in West Irian, he gave a short list of communications from the Indonesian government, which he described as a 'prompt and positive reaction' to his proposals. 'In view of these assurances and encouraging developments, the United Nations Representative is confident about the implementation of his various suggestions', he said. The communications from the Indonesians included an assurance that 'basic rights of the population' were 'guaranteed under the constitution of the Republic of Indonesia'. If this meant anything, it was that the government already considered the Papuans to be Indonesian citizens. Ortiz Sanz made no comment on this pronouncement. To have disputed it would have caused trouble; to have conceded it would have shown that his presence was useless.

Ortiz Sanz was in an uncomfortable position. Instructions received from New York, diplomacy and good manners dictated that he should be discreet about his negotiations with Indonesia; but questions were being raised in Holland about what the United Nations was doing. In March, without making any statement for attribution to himself, Ortiz Sanz let it be known that Indonesia had rejected his proposal that the one-man-one-vote principle should be applied in the more densely populated coastal areas, where the people were presumed to be more politically conscious and articulate than primitive tribes in the hinterland. Meanwhile the Indonesian government had announced that it would use the procedure of *musyawarah*, under which a consensus of elders is reached without a vote. The government claimed that this accorded with the traditions of the nation; but its reason for adopting *musyawarah* was that hand-picked assemblies of elders could be terrorized, as they were later, to choose Indonesia. Soon it became clear to all who were interested that the Act of Free Choice was to be a travesty. Protests in Holland reached such a pitch that in April threatened demonstrations obliged President Suharto to cancel a visit to The Hague, for which the Dutch government had been working since he came to power.

Rebellion

There was no mention in Ortiz Sanz's statement of the blood that had been shed in West Irian since his arrival – enough to have precipitated a meeting of the Security Council if any of the powers had had an axe to grind. Perhaps the United Nations team comfortably concluded that troubles had ended with the surrender of Lodewijk Mandatjan, who had held out against the Indonesians for years in the mountainous forests of Bird's Head. Mandatjan fled to the mountains in 1963, after Indonesia had taken over the administration of West Irian from the United Nations, pending the Act of Free Choice. According to the Indonesian Army Information Department, he returned to his village at one stage after having been promised a major's uniform and two jeeps, but resumed his leadership of rebellion in the mountains when the gifts failed to arrive. Doubtless this tit-bit of background was meant to reduce Mandatjan's stature in the public eye to that of a petty chieftain easily brought by baubles. It was the mistaken view of the army that Papuan revolt could be cooled off with inexpensive gifts; in January 1969 250 pigs and 200 fowls were flown to tribal leaders in Biak with a friendly message from President Suharto, but this gesture did not stop the rebellion that was to break out in the island a few months later. After his return to the mountains Mandatjan became a legendary fighter of such stature that Brigadier-General Sarwo Edhie, who had become West Irian military commander, announced his surrender on 1 January 1969 as the command's 'New Year present' to the government. At the height of Mandatjan's resistance the army put his followers at 10,000 members of the Arfak tribe, including women and children. Indonesian statistics, particularly those provided by local military commanders for their own purposes, are unreliable. But whatever the forces were, they made life unsafe at Indonesian outposts, using guns left behind by the armies of the Second World War.

The Indonesians gradually wore them down, bombing them, cutting them into isolated groups and starving them from their hiding places. Mandatjan became ill and could scarcely walk; his followers trickled back to their villages. Left with only about 500 scattered men and their 2,500 women and children, Mandatjan was reduced to mounting ambushes of no more than a few fighters at one spot. His rusty, obsolete rifles had lost most of their fire power. Even then he was too proud to surrender. But Sarwo Edhie provided a face-saver with that curious blend of bullying and sentimental appeal at which the Javanese excel. Among his officers was a Major Heroe whom, the army said, Mandatjan had adopted as a son when they fought together against the Dutch. After negotiations through intermediaries Major Heroe went to Mandatjan's headquarters and persuaded him to go back to his village, where he was put under some kind of medical care.

On 7 January Mandatjan arrived by plane in Jakarta to declare his allegiance to the Indonesian Republic. Looking ill and over-awed, he took the arm of an Indonesian army officer as he was quickly escorted to be whisked away in a jeep. He was wearing, at last, an Indonesian major's uniform. Major Heroe was with him; so was the former West Irian Governor, Eliezer Jan Bonay, who had been released on Christmas Eve after having been imprisoned for dissidence since February 1967. Arriving in the same plane were Mr and Mrs Ortiz Sanz.

Ortiz Sanz once said that some 600,000 of the 814,000 Papuans had no idea what the Act of Free Choice was about and that those who understood it were largely confined to the relatively well educated on the coast. Dutch missionaries did not share this view. They said that by and large the Papuans knew that they were being denied the right to determine freely whether interlopers would remain in their country or not: interlopers included the 'Javanese', by which the Papuans meant all Indonesians, whether they came from Java, Sumatra, the Moluccas or other islands, and all other foreigners.

There are few Papuans to whom the word 'primitive' could be
more correctly applied than the Stone Age people in the Baliem
Valley. They wear no clothes, but smear themselves with pig fat
to protect themselves from the mountain cold; the men cover
their penes in long, pointed sheaths made of gourd, not merely
from modesty but to give an impression of potency when the
sheath, or *koteka*, is held erect by a cord tied to the neck. One of
their chiefs, who boasts a record of cannibalism, knew enough
about what mattered to him in politics to say to a missionary: 'Yes,
it will be good when the Act of Free Choice is over and the
Javanese and all you people have gone.' It would be interesting to
know whether Ortiz Sanz would have classed this man among those
who knew what the Act of Free Choice meant. Interesting, too,
would be what Ortiz Sanz thought of Mandatjan's voting capability; and what the crestfallen Mandatjan thought of Ortiz Sanz
while he was travelling with him to final humiliation in Jakarta.

Mandatjan was not the last nor the worst headache for the
Indonesian rulers and for United Nations men and foreign
governments, particularly the Dutch, who were trying to convince
themselves that all was well in West Irian. On 27 April 1969
rebellion broke out at Enarotali, in the Wissel Lakes area of the
Central Highlands, and rapidly spread. The government announced that the rebels had dug holes in the airstrips at Enarotali
and four other places to prevent troops from landing to reinforce
the garrison. Papuan police had mutinied; on 29 April they fired
at Sarwo Edhie's plane, wounding a police inspector who accompanied him, when it flew over Enarotali. The army dropped
paratroops on 30 April and 4 May.

Ortiz Sanz flew to West Irian to investigate. On his return to
Jakarta on 19 May after a seven-day trip he told journalists at the
airport: 'Everything is quiet now.' He said he had been to
Enarotali, Jayapura, Wagete, Nabire and Biak; but he failed to
make the important qualification that at Enarotali he did not leave
the airstrip. Ortiz Sanz emphasized that Sarwo Edhie had assured
him that the Army had exercised restraint. 'I am very confident
that there is no cause for alarm about the future', he said. At a
press conference the next day Ortiz Sanz followed the government
line of minimizing the rebellion; he said the rebels consisted of
ninety-five police armed with rifles. Enarotali looked dead, he
said; he had been told that the people had fled to the woods during

the shooting. Ortiz Sanz said he was sure that if the army continued to show restraint and this was reciprocated by others, the Act of Free Choice would not be endangered. Having pronounced this favourable judgment on the army, he added that it was not his function to pass judgment on how the Act was performed. His task under the New York Agreement was simply to 'assist, advise and participate'. He could not do this work if he were to adopt a suspicious attitude or to question the honour of a sovereign government, which had been given the responsibility of carrying out the Act.

There was something desperate about the tone of this paradoxical statement. What Ortiz Sanz was saying meant that any suspicion on his part that justice was not being done would prevent him from taking action that might help to ensure it. This was an attitude far removed from that expressed by van Roijen when he spoke of 'active supervision'. Later I was to discuss the paralysing limitations of their vague mandate with members of the United Nations team in a cool bungalow on the slopes above Jayapura. There they had respite from both the humidity of the capital and the almost pestilential complaints of the people. All the team had sympathies with the Papuans, but they knew that to speak up would cost them their jobs. Army intelligence had already trumped up a charge against a senior official, Marshall Williams, who was saved from being declared *persona non grata* only by the good sense of the Foreign Ministry; a Dutch member of the United Nations development agency Fundwi, who was overtly sympathetic to the Papuans, was expelled on the absurd ground that he was plotting with the rebels. Against this threatening background the United Nations men took comfort in a discussion of semantics when I visited them in the bungalow. 'What does "assist" mean?', asked an old United Nations hand. 'We cannot do anything if the Indonesians don't allow it.' Another pointed out the difficulty of defining 'participate'. 'The French version could be said to mean something different from the English', he said. 'Certainly it does not mean "supervise".' A recently arrived member looked up sullenly and blurted: 'The whole thing is degrading to the United Nations.' But he was a callow young man, who had yet to learn the ropes.

Sarwo Edhie is a tough soldier, as he showed when he launched the massacre after the *putsch*. But Ortiz Sanz evidently succumbed

1 Public smiles mask power struggle: President Sukarno with Generals Suharto *(right)* and Nasution *(left)* at the Jakarta house of Sukarno's Japanese wife Dewi, 22 November 1965

2 President Suharto prefers a civilian image

3 Mrs Tien Suharto

4 Lieutenant-General Ali Murtrope

5 President Sukarno and his wife Hartini

6 President Sukarno, his Japanese wife Dewi and Chou En-lai

7 General Sumitro with the author at a foreign correspondents' lunch in Jakarta. *Extreme right* Vladimir Resanov, Soviet radio correspondent; *extreme left*: Brigadier General Marpaung, Defence Department spokesman

8 Pramoedya Anata Toer on Buru Island

9 D. N. Aidit, communist party Secretary-General

Dear darling Dewi,

I received your two letters. I am glad that you heard my speech, and thank you that you appreciate that speech.

Pramoto is rather weak, staff member of the Army-headquarters, but he is the only man in the M.B.A.D. who can deal with left and right. I appointed him as daily caretaker for daily management of the army temporality. The army-command I have taken in my own hand.

As soon as things are quiet again, I shall appoint the definitive army-commander. I don't know yet where Yani is, or what is exactly with him.

And as soon as things are safe, I shall return to Djakarta. Today's information was: "not yet".

I am constantly thinking of you. You know how I love you.   1000 kisses
                        Bachismo.—

10 Letter from President Sukarno to his Japanese wife Dewi on 3 October 1965

KANTOR BOGOR
TELEGRAM

Djawatan P.T.T. tidak membajar kerugian, disebabkan oleh tjatjat, tidak sampainja telegram dalam waktu jang tertentu atau hilangnja telegram.

Kantor berhubungan	No. lokal	Djenis	Kantor asal	Nomor	Bilangan kata	Tanggal	Djam	Petundjuk dinas.
ITX	6	ROMA	0456	30	13	1150	CW	=

= LT =

= MRS HARTINI SUKARNO PALACE BOGOBINDONESIA =

= AI ARRIVED YESTERDAY IN ROME COMMA TOMORROW WILL SEE THE POPE STOP AI AM THINKING OF YOU ALL THE TIME AND SEND YOU MY LOVE STOP KISSES TO THE CHIL-DREN STOP SUKARNO +

BOGOR

Diterima di: 14/5/19 59, 0859 Waktu Djawa
Oleh: E.

Diisjaratkan ke: ......, No. Lokal: ......
....../....../19......, ... Waktu Djawa
Oleh:

1604/O.—58

E. 1099-61-22 × 15 cm—12.700.000-65.

11 Telegram from President Sukarno to his wife Hartini

12 Political prisoners show infected feet

13 Soldier clubs youth in Jakarta riots, January 1974

14 The Indramayu famine

15 Dance of death for the political parties: Adam Malik, Foreign Minister *(right)* and Major-General Harun Sohar at a Golkar function during the 1971 election campaign

16 Syncretism: mosque beside a rice field on West Java coast with Islamic dome and Hindu roof

17 Villagers rounded up in a military exercise

18 Jakarta offices tower abover slums

19 Jakarta fish market

20 Bonfire of furniture from Chinese shop in Jakarta riots, January 1974

21 Village refreshment stall near Jakarta

to his charm; for he seemed as shocked as the general himself at reports that a Captain Harsono, flying a B 26 bomber, No. B267, had strafed the Papuans at Enarotali. 'I trust Brigadier-General Sarwo Edhie', he said. In fact, Sarwo Edhie merely said rockets had not been used; he made no mention of machine-guns. Adam Malik, the Foreign Minister, had said that the area might have been strafed to scare the Papuans, although he was sure that nobody had been hurt. A few months earlier, in December, the army had announced at a press conference that fighter planes would support 6,000 soldiers and marines who were to hunt the unfortunate Mandatjan. More recently, in February, four Papuans had asked President Suharto to take drastic action against 'violations' by troops in West Irian. In such conditions a United Nations official, who had accepted the task, however vague, of injecting a measure of justice into what was supposed to be an act of self-determination, would scarcely have exceeded his mandate by suspecting excesses, even if these announcements were all the information he had.

My inquiries in West Irian confirmed a press statement by the Governor, Frans Kasieppo, a Papuan, that the rebellion had the support of all the leaders of the 30,000 people in the Wissel Lakes area. Tribes that had been enemies for years were united in their hostility to the Indonesians. Police, it is true, were the spearhead of the revolt because they had rifles; and pay and other grievances provided a spark for the explosion. But the main issue was obvious from the outset, when Papuans seized a Catholic mission wireless transmitter on 27 April; on that and the following day they broadcast an appeal to army headquarters in Nabire to withdraw the local garrison and let the people chose their own future, 'free from Javanese pressure'. The Indonesian reply was to send in more troops. The Papuans then sabotaged the area's five rudimentary airstrips. Sarwo Edhie, after having been narrowly missed by bullets when he flew over to see what was happening, ordered paratroops into action.

At the first sight of this display of power from the heavens almost the entire population of 14,000 living in Enarotali and surrounding *kampongs* took fright and vanished into the bush. Plunging back into the more familiar security of the Stone Age, they cast off the veneer of an alien civilization and the clothes that went with it; men, stark naked, put on the traditional penis sheath;

among them were school teachers, who used nudity as a disguise, knowing that all educated Papuans were suspected of being rebel leaders. Among the last to flee was the houseboy of Father Tetro, a Dutch missionary; he was rowing his sister to safety across a lake when a patrol spotted him and shot him dead from the shore. This was the 'quiet' that the United Nations representative found on his brief visit to the region.

Having landed without food or blankets, many soldiers were forced to live off the country; they helped themselves to pigs and kept themselves warm in the mountain cold at night by burning house doors. Looters did not spare the mission stations. A pastor, John Schultz, bereft of most of his belongings, radioed his headquarters in Jayapura for clothes for his family. It is not, however, the policy of the Indonesian Army to loot. Military police in Nabire took stolen goods from men passing through the airport there and returned them to the owners.

Making their way along bush tracks between the deserted *kampongs*, Indonesian soldiers had an eerie time. Sometimes a shot would crack from the rifle of a rebel policeman hidden in the trees. But more sinister was the bow and arrow, which could kill or wound without a sound. No reliable figures of Indonesian casualties at this time are available; they were probably not many. But journeys that would normally last minutes sometimes took hours when troops slunk along the tracks, nervously seeking cover behind trees.

The rebellion petered out, for a time, against the superior fire power and organization of the Indonesian Army. With no battle and no specific confrontation, Sarwo Edhie made it his main task to get the people back to their homes so that the Act of Free Choice could be held. Early in May he sent out leaflets advising policemen to think of their wives and children. He assured them that they would not be prosecuted and that their families and property would be safe if they reported with their weapons to the nearest post. This was a nice application of an old Javanese formula: reassurance was blended with a partially concealed threat that the policemen would lose their property and that their wives and children would suffer if the general's advice went unheeded. On 5 June seven of ten who had surrendered publicly asked the general's pardon at one of those ludicrous, humiliating ceremonies that were becoming frequent in West Irian; the general patted them each on the back as a sign of forgiveness. About eighty men, women and children were all that the authorities could round up to express the people's joy that the wayward had repented.

Sarwo Edhie used ingenious tricks to get the people back. A Papuan dropped by parachute in the Wissel Lakes area told the tribesmen that he had seen large Dutch cargoes waiting to be shipped to them from Jakarta; all that was delaying the goods was a Dutch stipulation in the New York Agreement that they could not be shipped to West Irian until after the Act of Free Choice. The cynicism of this attempt to exploit the naiveté of the Papuans was surpassed when in leaflets dated 15 June the army cited the New Testament. 'Through your love of merciful Jesus Christ you should remember what is written in St. Luke's Gospel about the prodigal son', policemen were advised. 'Have you not pity for your wives and children, who are suffering because you left them?' It would be interesting to know where the West Irian Military Command got this idea from; the officers are not famed for their erudition in the Bible, or in the Koran either, for that matter. Possibly American Protestant missionaries lent a hand. They had already co-operated by passing on information given in confidence by Papuans that there would be serious trouble over the Act of Free Choice in the Enarotali area, but the army assured them there was only a trifling, local problem. Dutch Catholics also knew of the Papuans' plans to demand that all Indonesians leave, but they agreed to keep silent on obtaining a promise from tribal leaders that there would be no physical attacks.

Gradually some of the wandering, hungry population returned home. And Sarwo Edhie found time to express his regret to missionaries at the looting of mission tape recorders and other goods. He offered a special apology to Father Tetro, who had been slapped in the face by an Indonesian officer. But he said Father Tetro had provoked the officer by saying that looting Indonesian troops were as bad as the police; it was not proper to compare misbehaving Indonesian soldiers with Papuan police who had rebelled against constituted authority, he explained. On 9 June, Sarwo Edhie admitted that the revolt had been serious; but for the army's swift action, he said, the Act of Free Choice would have been jeopardized.

While the Enarotali rebellion caught attention because a Radio Australia man had the luck to stumble on it, pursuit and killing of

Papuans was taking place in other regions. Dutch Catholic missionaries, although they had no illusion that the people could govern themselves peacefully, were distressed at what they regarded as unnecessary repression. When I arrived at their headquarters in Jayapura at the end of May, I was told that the head of the regional hierarchy had become ill with worry and had gone to Europe to recuperate. Many of those left behind were consciencestricken. They felt they should protest; but they feared that if they made statements for publication they would be thrown out and that the schools they had developed down the years, sometimes at the risk of death from cannibals, would perish in a matter of months. I spent one evening with about a dozen of them at a tiny bungalow in the bush. We sat in the garden; it was almost pitch dark, but lamps gleaming through the front windows shed enough light to reveal the grotesque shapes of shrubs and trees. We drank *jenever*. There were a few jokes, but on the whole it was a sombre occasion.

The picture that emerged from my inquiries in West Irian made nonsense of the soothing utterances of the United Nations office. Indonesian troops and officials were waging a widespread campaign of intimidation to force the Act of Free Choice in favour of the Republic. They were gaoling the educated and terrorizing the primitive, pursuing them even into Australian territory, where they caught up with some and shot them. An uninformed tourist, if tourism had been allowed, might have been impressed in Jayapura by apparent displays of fervour for the Indonesian cause. Paper flags were stuck on the fronts of tiny dwellings, including the humblest huts on stilts along the shore; students were signing declarations of loyalty. But people were telling those they trusted that authorities had forced them to put up the flags; and students complained they had been threatened that they would get no education after the Act if they did not support Indonesia before it. After a demonstration on 11 May, when the army fired a shell from an armoured car over the heads of the crowd, students said that army officers forced them to stage a counter-demonstration.

The intimidation and the inevitable rumours that it inspired caused panic in many villages. In the Keerom area, south of Jayapura, a dozen Catholic schools were closed in the eighteen months to June 1969 because whole families had vanished. The flight of scores of thousands of Papuans confronted Indonesian officials with the danger that in some areas they would not even be able to go through the motions of the Act. In the first week of June Dutch missionaries at a boarding school refused to hand over three girls whom the army wanted to send to Australian New Guinea to call back their parents, influential tribal leaders, who had fled there.

This attempt to use children as emissaries is an example of the first element in the Javanese prescription of persuasion, intimidation and violence, to be administered as and where required. A typical use of the second element, intimidation, occurred when a Major Soewondo rounded up 200 village heads in the Lake Sentani area and ordered them to go into the bush and bring back their followers for the Act of Free Choice. The officially controlled Jayapura newspaper, *Tjenderawasih*, reported on 24 May that he warned the chiefs: 'I am drawing the line frankly and clearly. I say I will protect and guarantee the safety of everyone who is for Indonesia. I will shoot dead anyone who is against us – and all his followers.' The third element in the formula, violence, is generally reserved for use when the other two have failed. It is starkly illustrated by the killing of a youth, Julianus Joku, at Lake Sentani, near Jayapura's airport, on 18 May. Joku was a courier for the Free Papua Organization (OPM). Troops intercepted him when he tried to cross into Australian New Guinea, but he escaped to an island in the lake. When he heard a motor boat patrol approaching he swam to another island. He was wading ashore, waist deep, when the patrol caught up with him and riddled him with bullets at twenty metres range. Papuans said he had his hands up and was crying for mercy when he fell dead.

Villagers coming into Jayapura from neighbouring areas brought tales of looting, burning of houses, arrests and some shooting. About the time when Ortiz Sanz was issuing his reassurances, the army surrounded Dormena village, at Tanah Merah Bay, and arrested five members of the OPM, including two school teachers. The troops were hunting rebels who had kidnapped Petrus Jabausabra, a member of a regency council, who had spoken up for Indonesia. One Papuan was shot dead during the operation. Troops looted houses when people fled in terror from *kampongs* along the bay; they burned books, including a teacher's Bible. But near Merauke the Indonesians did not have it all their own way. Muju tribesmen from the foothills raided an Indonesian camp on the night of 27 April and killed three Indonesian soldiers with knives and axes. They were avenging the intimidation of the more timid Bupul tribesmen, who had fled with loss of life when soldiers threatened to shoot those who did not confess anti-Indonesian political activity.

The cruel illusion

The OPM was not, as an organization, the main factor in stirring up hostility to the Indonesians, although it played a part. On the contrary, it was unable to match the considerable revolutionary potential, which lay not only in the national aspirations of students and civil servants in Jayapura but in the more primitive rejection by the tribes of any outside interference. Some observers, and the Indonesians themselves, thought that much of the tribal unrest was provoked by local grievances, such as the authorities' failure to send a promised supply of nails or timber. But these outbreaks were mere symptoms of deeper resentment at the presence of foreigners, fired by an instinct of self-preservation that had been highly developed during centuries of ferocious intertribal warfare. Uniting the towns on the coasts with the tribes in the hinterland was the general desire of people to be left alone to preserve their culture or change it in their own way. The Papuans took no account of the danger that the withdrawal of the Indonesians would lead to destructive political intrigue in the towns and the resumption of bloody clashes in areas where cannibalism is not convincingly extinct. The desire for independence, however dimly its implications might have been understood, was shared by all. Among the more educated it was inflamed to hatred by the patronizing manner of the rulers, who obviously looked down on the Papuans as an inferior race. But strong though these feelings were, there was no chance of their being channelled into a disciplined force that would threaten Indonesian power: the educated élite were too few and the people as a whole, educated or not, were too childlike to produce sufficient leaders of the necessary calibre.

It was impossible to find out precisely what the OPM was in West Irian, even when speaking to youths and men who claimed to belong to it. Some had links in Australian territory with Nicolaas Jouwe's West Papua Freedom Committee, based in Holland. But this connexion seemed unimportant and the support from exiles and their private Dutch backers was more moral than practical: there were no bombs or guns being smuggled in. The movement had no single leader, nor even a unified command; it bore no comparison with the more mature fronts of the Middle East and Vietnam. But the actions attributed to it were not entirely sporadic; men from the coast, for instance, played a part in the Enarotali rebellion. A man in Jayapura told me that the OPM had twenty leaders and 5,000 registered members, and gave me the names of several key men in other towns, including that of an army sergeant. He was obviously taking part in planned operations; he made at least one trip to Australian New Guinea by canoe with a wounded man, and was able to tell me that two well-known rebels were going there through the bush two days before they arrived. Yet I was sceptical of his statement that there were 5,000 members registered in any sense of the word; for the Indonesians, who had spies everywhere, would have rounded up such a dangerous band. But there might have been twenty men who consulted one another from time to time about possible actions. OPM men threatened in a leaflet to sabotage water and electricity supplies if the Indonesians continued their intimidation; but no more was heard of the threat, although unguarded pipes and plant could easily have been blown up by determined guerrillas.

Yet the OPM, whatever it might have been, was an influence both for revolt and restraint. Fear of the OPM appears to have played a part in deterring tribesmen from giving in to Indonesian pressure. When Indonesian officials went to Arso village, south of Jayapura, to appoint members of the regency consultative council set up for the Act of Free Choice, they found only half a dozen passing crocodile hunters. The villagers had fled, and on their chief's door was a note reading 'Before me are bayonets [Indonesian troops], behind me are knives and arrows [OPM tribesmen]. It is better to live in the bush.' On the other hand, OPM leaders prevented reckless action. There were rumours that youths in Jayapura planned to begin 'killing Indonesians like chickens' on 10 June. An OPM man told me this plan had been quashed; he and friends knew that killings would bring reprisals, and argued that there should be no violence short of a full-scale revolt. For the present, they said, passions were not running high enough to ensure success; the people as a whole would not rise up until it became certain that the Act was turned against them; only then would their despair be deep enough to produce widespread fury. A Papuan pastor said that the OPM was not so much an organization as a movement. 'We are all OPM', he said. There was precision in this apparent vagueness. For the OPM was psychologically more complex than a political or guerrilla organization: it was a movement bearing some of the characteristics of a cult and brought to mind the cargo cult, which is widespread in Melanesia.[2] The cult has been particularly strong in Biak, where the army's invention of the myth of Dutch cargoes, which has been described earlier, appears to have been a crude attempt to exploit it (see page 177.)

At Madang, on the coast of former Australian New Guinea, the arrival of European cargo ships in the nineteenth century led Papuans to regard the heavens as a huge warehouse from which God distributed preserved foods, tools, guns and other goods to the people on earth. This belief began when they concluded that the first visitor, a Russian, was a god from the moon, after they had seen him carrying a lantern along the beach at night. Further experience of traders suggested that the whites were stealing cargoes that God meant for them. The desire to ensure that the cargoes were properly delivered gave rise to a cult that swept the area. Ceremonies, prayers and moral codes that conflicted with the traditional religion were created to rectify the cosmic dislocation. Christian missionaries, far from extinguishing the cult, provided it with a new impetus. From the Bible the Papuans concluded that God was punishing them for the sins of Noah's son, Shem, whom they saw as their ancestor. This prompted them to make friends with the missionaries; they hoped that if they renounced sorcery, polygamy and other practices that were evil in the sight of the god of the successful Europeans, the cargoes would come to them. They sent their children to Catholic schools, not so much to be converted as to act as spies who would find out the Christian secret. At the same time they killed their own pigs, laid waste their fields and destroyed their crops to arouse divine pity. Today they still scan the sea and sky, puzzled that the cargo never comes.

It is not suggested that the cult element in the fever that developed round the OPM symbol was either as deep in its origin or as bizarre in its manifestation as the cult of the cargo; but both were produced by the same kind of mind. Common to both was a pitiful belief in some kind of cosmic justice. The people in the

Madang area clung to the hope that a righteous god would ensure that they received his bounty once he had been propitiated. In West Irian there was conviction that freedom was assured by that Arbiter of Justice, that Omnipotent Power of Powers, the United Nations; if the Indonesians dared to remain in West Irian when it was clear that the people wanted them to go, then the United Nations would send in forces to fight alongside the OPM. Just as people along the coast near Madang waited in vain for the divine cargoes, so villagers in North Biak trudged to hilltops overlooking the sea, where, they believed, a United Nations submarine would bring them food and guns. Faith in deliverance was widespread: around Lake Sentani there were men who tattooed OPM on their bodies; children scratched the letters on one another's backs.

While magic had been renounced for tactical purposes in the cult of the cargo, belief in its potency flourished in West Irian, and fortified the rebels. I had experience of this when I spent a night in one of the huts built on stilts in the tangle of trees and vines lining the beach at Jayapura. Five young rebels and I had gone there after dark, with the intention of leaving by motor-canoe at dawn on an expedition, which did not come off. After drinking tea in the early hours of the morning, the students began to chew something; they told me it was the bark of a certain tree, the name of which I have forgotten. Offering me a piece, one of them said: 'If you eat this, no Indonesian bullet can ever hit you.' As there was a chance that we might be picked off by some zealous Indonesian patrol as we made our way along the coast, I hoped that the students would rely on stealth rather than the bark to ensure our safety. Noticing my lack of enthusiasm, the student said: 'I know you Europeans don't believe in magic. I am a Christian, but believe in magic, too.' I advised him not to put his belief to the test. 'You will get yourself shot', I said. He looked at me, his eyes gleaming with confidence that he possessed some superior truth. 'Never', he said. 'In Merauke they have great magic. They fly through the air as fast as the wind and the Indonesians cannot see them. That is how they killed those three soldiers.' Such a reassurance might have delighted an anthropologist; but my immediate concern was whether this deluded lot would be able to cope with an emergency, or even find the way through the jungle after the canoe trip. While I had been impressed by the imagination of Papuans, I had not expected such a flight from these lads, who were not fresh from the bush, but were students at what passes for a university at Jayapura. Yet the students' faith in bark did not seem to be absolute. Every time a leaf stirred outside they started in fear that their hiding-place had been discovered. Apparently they did not believe that the magic would make them arrest-proof as well as bullet-proof; and they had no desire to join friends among the political prisoners.

At the end of June the prisoners were numbered officially at 112. They included Mozes Weror, who for five years was a Third Secretary at the Indonesian Embassy in Canberra. Weror left the Foreign Ministry in February to go to West Irian and, as he said, 'help my people'. Like the other prisoners, all he asked for was a free vote. Ortiz Sanz said on 9 July that following his intervention the government had informed him that thirty-six prisoners had been released on 1 July; the remaining seventy-six would be brought to trial. But the trials were never held, and Papuans said that in the final stage of the Act of Free Choice prisoners in Jayapura alone totalled 250. A correspondent of the Dutch news agency, Algemeen Nederlands Persbureau, Link van Bruggen, reported from Biak that 200 political prisoners at a navy camp rioted on 30 July after ten Papuans, tied to one another with rope, had been flown in from the Wissel Lakes.

The events that led to our being in the hut illustrate how hard it is to establish facts among a people whose reason is dominated by imagination. Papuan pastors introduced me to a man who said that sixty-three women and children had been killed when Indonesians fired mortars from a beach at a camp established by the OPM on an overlooking mountain. The story was suspect: no men were among the dead, yet it was unlikely that all had been absent from the camp. The man told me that he had seen a mortar being fired. I asked him to describe the gun, but he was unable to do so; nor could he make a rough sketch of it. Eventually he convinced me that he had heard the gun going off; but I still lacked evidence that the bombs had hit anyone. After driving many miles I found at Lake Sentani a youth who, a pastor said, had seen the bodies of the victims before they were buried. He confirmed the story, but the wild look in his eyes and his excited prattle made me doubt his reliability. I took him back to Jayapura and asked the pastor to question him. The youth stuck to his story and, at my request, swore by God Almighty that he had counted the bodies. I then arranged with the students to take me to the spot, a journey of several hours by canoe and several more on foot. I insisted on leaving the following dawn, because I knew that, since no Papuan can keep a secret, the Indonesians would soon be on our track. When dawn came the students kept putting off our departure. Finally they told me that the canoe owner had been unable to get petrol and that an OPM leader near by wanted me to leave the hut at once because my presence might attract Indonesians. Later that morning this man, who was a civil servant, told me that there was no truth in the story of the massacre. It occurred to me that he might have been sent to put me off the trail. Indonesian bullying had so disturbed their minds that some Papuans were performing shabby little services for their rulers one day and vainly plotting their overthrow the next; they were not so much double-agents as chameleons, overwhelmed by the environment of the hour. Later I found reason to believe that the OPM man was telling the truth. But I shall never know for certain whether I missed one of the best news stories of the Act of Free Choice.

Not all the Papuans I met were as hazardously superstitious as the students in the hut. Yet the faith of all in the power and purity of the United Nations resembled that of the students who believed in the magic of the bark. United Nations officials in private talks found it difficult to convince even the most educated that their organization would not send troops to ensure Papuan independence if the Indonesians refused to grant it. To many Papuans the United Nations existed to protect 'human rights', a phrase they often used, with powers almost as great as those of the Christian god that missionaries had taught them to believe in.

One night I went to the house of an internationally known Papuan elder. The Indonesians had released him from prison on condition that he recanted his anti-Indonesian views; he went through the motions, but his heart was unchanged. This man assured me that West Irian would be free within a year. 'We are sending a delegation to the United Nations in September', he said. 'We have only to tell what is happening here.' The delegation was to make its way from Australian territory. The Papuan smiled indulgently at my lack of comprehension when I told him that the United Nations could not help. And he saw no significance in the fact that a small advance party, which had arrived in Australian territory, had already been interned on Manus Island, to which all Papuan refugees were taken if they did not renounce political activity. Asked how the delegation would obtain passports, he replied: 'The Dutch government will provide them. They are Christians.'

But the truth that they were alone, oppressed by Moslems and betrayed by Christians, was becoming clear to some. A few nights later a Papuan emerged from bushes at the side of a dark street, after I had left a Protestant hostel, where I used to eat sometimes. It was the civil servant I had met on the day of the abortive expedition with the students; he had been waiting for me. After an anxious glance along the road he asked me to join him in thicker darkness behind a tree. 'You told . . . the other night that the United Nations would never help us', he said. 'Why is that?' I explained the cruel politics. 'I understand', he said, and immediately vanished. I often wonder what became of him.

Some of the more educated fled the country. One very active rebel that I met went to Australian territory after the Act of Free Choice. When I last saw him he was still unconvinced that the United Nations would not come to the rescue; but, like the civil servant, he was beginning to see it. 'Then the Chinese will help us', he said. 'We had contact with them some time ago.' I told him that the Chinese could not send a single soldier. After arguing for a while, he exploded bitterly: 'Then we shall kill everyone.' In Australian territory this man qualified as an air pilot; his inexperience in politics and the immaturity of some of his emotions were no measure of his intelligence.

Sudjarwo's joke

After Sarwo Edhie had successfully glossed the rebellion for the benefit of Ortiz Sanz, Sudjarwo Tjondronegoro brought off a more astonishing feat: he carried out practically the whole of a vital stage of the Act of Free Choice without the much heralded participation and advice of the United Nations team. This was the formation of eight regency consultative assemblies, each of which was to have a final *musyawarah* on whether West Irian was to remain part of Indonesia. At his press conference on 20 May Ortiz Sanz had said he had emphasized to the Indonesian government that the constitution of the assemblies would only be democratic if three conditions were fulfilled: the assemblies should be sufficiently large, they should represent 'all sections' and they should clearly be elected by the people. He said that he had told the government that his staff were waiting to observe the election of the assemblies on the spot and to participate in the procedure as provided in the New York Agreement.

At the end of the month the staff were still waiting in Jayapura, while almost all the assemblies had been set up throughout the country. In an interview at Biak on 30 May Wiesber Loeis, an Indonesian Foreign Ministry official, told me that the United Nations office in Jakarta had been informed that the elections would begin on 7 May (it turned out later that the first was on 20 April) and would be completed by 6 June. Now nearly all had been finished. Loeis said he did not know why United Nations men had failed to attend any of them. But he said that when Indonesian officials learned that some UN men intended to come to Biak, they postponed elections in two districts and in half of Biak town for their benefit; they were still waiting for the UN men to arrive. Loeis said that in spite of the absence of the United Nations, the elections had been carried out democratically; and he supplied details of how this was done. A Western government official, one of two who had been allowed into West Irian for special reasons, who was present at the interview, told Loeis that many Papuans had been terrorized to fall into line with Indonesia. He cited an incident at Mulia, in the Central Highlands: a council member asked what would happend to him if he opted for in-dependence; the reply was that he would be shot.

Loeis's disclosure made a useful news story and its dispatch round the world by Agence France-Presse was a blow to the United Nations office in Jakarta. Accustomed to the protective devices of the world's most pampered bureaucracy, the team was thrown into confusion. The information officer said in reply to a newspaperman that the UN men had been unable to take part in the elections because the Indonesians had not supplied a timetable. Two days later he said that the mission had received a timetable, but he did not say when it arrived. Ortiz Sanz immediately rushed from Jakarta to Jayapura, denying himself the comfort of the usual overnight stop in Biak.

The United Nations team then began a comical scramble to participate. Without a single plane of their own, they tried to obtain mission transport to remote areas. The team of five men in

West Irian was increased by two from Jakarta, including the information officer; but it was still without interpreters, apart from one recently recruited member, who spoke Indonesian. Members of the team, working in pairs, were at the mercy of Indonesian officials when it came to understanding what was being said. The lack of seriousness of the entire operation then became apparent. Without planes the mission had no hope of observing this stage of the Act of Free Choice. Even if it had organized missionary transport well in advance, and it failed to take even this obvious precaution, it would not have been able to keep up with elections improvised in remote and mountainous areas devoid of roads. Without interpreters, the observers, or whatever they were, could make little contact with villagers who might seize a chance for a few words with them. No real participation of any kind was possible in these circumstances and this must have been clear from the beginning; there was no possibility of doing anything that would have any effect on the elections, rigged or not.

When asked about this débacle, the Indonesians were characteristically unruffled. Joost Rotty, the Foreign Ministry's chief representative in Jayapura, said that United Nations men knew the elections were being held and that there was nothing to stop them from going anywhere they wished. They did not need invitations, he said. Rotty explained that poor communications had made the operation difficult. Sometimes it had been necessary to hold elections, even without the knowledge of Sudjarwo Tjondronegoro. Trotting out Asia's favourite euphemism, he said it was all a misunderstanding.

Sudjarwo told me that in the last week of May the UN team had tried to charter a plane to observe elections fifteen minutes' flying time from Jayapura but could not obtain one. 'It is very hard for them', Sudjarwo said cheerfully. 'To get to some of the elections would take a three-day walk and a boat trip. I don't think it's quite in their line.' I had the impression that some Indonesians were laughing at the UN pantomime. And I admit that, despite my pity for the Papuans, I could not help enjoying the joke. At all events, the Indonesians completely outwitted the United Nations team. It was a clever manoeuvre, but not a bold one: the interests of the big powers, the indifference of the others, and the flabbiness of the United Nations presence ensured that there would be no serious complaints.

The team made their first appearance at the elections on 4 June, five days after I had sent the report that the show was virtually over. I attended one of these performances, which was held to elect representatives of the 15,000 inhabitants of Jayapura town in the regency's consultative assembly. Only nine candidates were nominated for the nine seats. It was impossible to tell exactly how many elders, said to be village and tribal heads, had been brought in to approve them, because voters could scarcely be distinguished from spectators. An Indonesian official told me there were between 100 and 150; I made it about 100; one of the two United Nations men present said he had counted seventy-four. There was no way of knowing whether these men were genuine representatives of the people. Probably they were; for by this time the entire population had been intimidated, and hand-picking of chiefs to obtain an affirmative vote was no longer necessary; any one of them would do what he was told as long as he remained under the eyes of the Indonesians.

The UN men did not speak Indonesian and had no means of asking the delegates questions or of understanding anything they might have wanted to say. I asked one of them, Marshall Williams, if he had been able to find out previously if those voting in fact represented the townspeople. He replied: 'We came in at this point.' A brisk-mannered Indonesian official asked the voters two questions in Indonesian. Each time only a few Papuans answered at first; but when the official gestured like an American cheer leader and called on the delegates to speak up, most of them responded. The questions were: 'Were you intimidated before coming here?. . . Were you subjected to any influence?' The answer was, 'No'. The United Nations men solemnly wrote notes. I did not embarrass them by asking what they thought of all this; perhaps they were thinking of the meeting held a few weeks earlier, when Major Soewondo threatened to shoot those who did not toe the line.

Ortiz Sanz showed no gratitude for the disclosure that the Indonesians had stolen a march on him. When I went to his Jayapura bungalow on 3 June and asked him the purpose of his hurried visit, he said: 'I do not propose to meet the press. They have been very unkind lately.' Ortiz Sanz then set about patching things up. On 9 July he informed the world in a statement issued in Jakarta that he had discovered on his visit to West Irian that most of the consultative assemblies had already been elected. He had therefore suggested on 13 June – eleven days after his arrival in Jayapura – that some elections should be held again, at least in areas where large numbers of representatives had been elected without the presence of the United Nations team. The statement disclosed that in a letter to the Indonesian authorities, dated 1 May, Ortiz Sanz had emphasized that members of the consultative assemblies should be 'clearly elected by the people'; he had said that his team was ready to take part and had asked for a timetable, which the Indonesians did not provide until 30 May (the day I saw Loeis) 'presumably because of transport difficulties'. Ortiz Sanz said he had also sought clarification of the functions of committees that were in charge of forming the consultative assemblies. (These were groups suitably composed to administer the dose of persuasion, intimidation and force.)

Ortiz Sanz's letter of 1 May is a good example of the skill of UN officials in keeping their files right, with the aim of forestalling future criticism and even salving their consciences. With this evidence of his probity Ortiz Sanz could blame his failure on the Indonesians' transport problems. He claimed that after his proposal of 13 June his team had been able to attend 'numerous elections' in June and July, of which details would be provided later. No further information was given until his report, submitted to the United Nations General Assembly in November, showed that altogether his team attended elections of 195 of the 1,026 assembly members (of whom about 136 regency council members were automatically appointed), or 21.9 per cent of those supposed to be elected. This might have been an adequate sample for a Gallup poll, but it was scarcely enough to ensure the integrity of the Act of Free Choice. Moreover, the United Nations men had no hope of knowing if those who approved the pre-selected candidates had been intimidated, or even if they truly represented the districts and organizations in whose names they were voting.

The re-staging of the six district elections was worthless. Bewildered Papuans were dragged out to go through the degrading business all over again. Link van Bruggen attended a re-election in the Bosnik area of Biak. He reported that 2–3,000 people watched seventy-five men confirm their vote for six candidates. After the vote the seventy-five applauded feebly. The crowd remained silent for a few moments, then burst into furious shouting. When the uproar died four men stepped forward with a petition asking, not for independence, but for elections on the basis of a one-man-one-vote. It is an unpleasant thought that the men, supported by the crowd, might have found courage to present their petition in the belief that the United Nations had at last come to protect them; it was in Biak that a hopeful band had awaited the submarine.

Rehearsal and performance

The eight regency consultative assemblies that were formed in this arbitrary fashion met on separate days in July and August to seal the permanent inclusion of West Irian in the Republic of Indonesia; they were of seventy-five to 175 members, each of whom was said to represent about 750 people. The first session, on 14 July, was in Merauke. Ortiz Sanz was there; so were the Australian and Dutch Ambassadors, Gordon Jockell and Scheltema, on whose complicity the Indonesians could rely, and the Thai Ambassador, Luang Phinit-Akson, dean of the diplomatic corps, a man valued for his habitual silence. The Indonesians made it a festive occasion. There was plenty of food and tobacco to draw a crowd and scented water to flatter the official party when it arrived to a ceremonious welcome. Improvised arches, banners bearing slogans, dancing, and singing of an Indonesian patriotic song enlivened the little town to a pitch that it had never seen before, and is unlikely to see again. The 175 assembly members, who represented 146,000 people, were unable to make the most of the gaiety. As soon as they came in from their villages they were guided into a heavily guarded housing complex and denied contact with the world outside except during official functions.

Nothing that could be called a *musyawarah* took place. Twenty members spoke and all declared themselves unanimously in favour of West Irian's remaining part of Indonesia. That splendid comedian, Adam Malik, immediately expressed his 'delight' that both the Dutch government and the United Nations had shown a 'good understanding' of the way in which the Act of Free Choice was being carried out. It appears that the people of the region were less pleased: Link van Bruggen wrote later that news had reached Jayapura, presumably through missionaries, that six of the unfortunate twenty had been killed by angry followers.

Meanwhile foreign correspondents, who had now been admitted into the territory, were reporting that serious trouble had broken out again in the Wissel Lakes area. A military spokesman in Jayapura was quoted as admitting that more than twenty Indonesians had been killed, but Link van Bruggen said a reliable source had put the death-roll at fifty. The reports were denied by the Information Ministry in Jakarta, which claimed that they were based on incidents that took place during the rebellion in April and that language difficulty had caused misunderstanding of what the military spokesman said. But evidence of a new revolt was too detailed to be dismissed; and the credibility of the authorities was diminished by their refusal to allow correspondents to go to places where the fighting was said to be going on. Link van Bruggen reported that 60,000 people had abandoned their *kampongs* in the Wissel Lakes area. Women and children were planting new vegetable plots in the mountains while the men were out ambushing the Indonesians. Papuans had surrounded troops at Moenamani, twenty kilometres west of Enarotali, and were attacking them with bows and arrows; Kepauke bowmen, famed for their resistance to the Japanese in the Second World War, were reported to have wiped out an entire Indonesian patrol of fifteen men near Kebo and eleven in a motor-boat on the Ara River, which flows into Lake Paniai. Another hazard for the troops was mantraps – deep, covered holes with spikes at the bottom. It looked as if the Papuans were preparing for prolonged guerrilla warfare. But once Ortiz Sanz and the three ambassadors had passed through Nabire, where they attended the *musyawarah* for the Act of Free Choice, Sarwo Edhie, with the spotlight removed from the region, swiftly established control of all settlements. When the three ambassadors returned to Jakarta, Jockell told correspondents at the airport that they had agreed to say nothing of their experiences, except that they had been well looked after.

Few, legitimate representatives from tribes in the Wissel Lakes area were present when Paniai regency's consultative assembly met at Nabire on 19 July: the vacancies were filled by men who were dragged from other areas, told what to do and confined to quarters until they were wanted. Elsewhere the Act went smoothly enough, with as few as twenty manageable members of each consultative assembly ostensibly engaging in *musyawarah* with Indonesian officials on behalf of as many as 175. Ortiz Sanz and the three silent diplomats attended all of the eight meetings; when other communications were impossible, they sailed along the coast from town to town in the comfort of a specially chartered 12,000-ton ship; it was at this time, perhaps, that they were best looked after. All was quiet whenever they arrived at a regency centre: at Biak and Jayapura scores of students and others likely to speak out were placed under preventive arrest in good time and detained until the Act was over.

The Act ended with a gala performance in Jayapura on 2 August. There were more diplomats and triumphal arches than at the seven earlier meetings, and there was more whipped-up rejoicing. As soon as they arrived the 110 regency representatives were bundled into an unfinished technical school and kept under guard for up to ten days before the *musyawarah*. They were allowed to go to church on Sunday, but armed soldiers kept watch on them. They were given clothes, shoes, wireless sets and other presents; and it was reported that they were promised money if they behaved themselves.

The Indonesians, who are masters of anything theatrical, thoroughly rehearsed the Papuans in singing, dancing, cheering and voting. It was reported on the eve of the Act that the Papuans had practised carrying Indonesian leaders shoulder-high; and certainly, on the day, there were no slips when Sarwo Edhie, the weighty Major-General (later Lieutenant-General) Amir Machmud, Minister for the Interior, and Sudjarwo were jubilantly hoisted. It was a commendable performance. But politically it was an anti-climax. Taking no chances, the ever-nervous Indonesian government had already announced, on 19 July, that unanimous decisions in Merauke, Jayawijaya (which includes the Baliem Valley) and Paniai – areas in which the greater part of the population live – meant that West Irian was already part of Indonesia. The elaborate drill in the remaining five regencies was therefore no more than a formality within a formality.

At the height of the excitement in Jayapura on 2 August Sarwo Edhie added a slight but sobering touch of fact. He told the Indonesian news agency, Antara, that there were still problems in West Irian that would have to be settled by military force. He said that a band of 150 armed rebels led by Awom was still to be reckoned within the Manokwari area; forty-seven police deserters near Enarotali and Wagete had not returned to their posts. This was an understatement of the seriousness of the situation, but it prepared the nation for reports of brutal actions against Papuans that were to come from West Irian for an indefinite period. And the reference to Wagete and Enarotali strengthened earlier reports that trouble round the Wissel Lakes was not yet over.

Ortiz Sanz's report was submitted to the United Nations General Assembly by the Secretary-General in November, 1969. A small delegation of Papuan exiles, led by Nicolaas Jouwe, tried hard to have the Act of Free Choice condemned; but they could not compete with the lobbying of Holland, the United States and France, to name only those who were conspicuous in their efforts. Holland made it clear to its friends that it wanted no trouble with the Indonesians. Since the Act of Free Choice had been carried out under a bilateral agreement, the Dutch attitude gave others the pretext for washing their hands of the affair. The Americans whispered in Latin American ears, while the French concentrated on the blacks from their former colonies.

On 19 November the assembly adopted by eighty-four votes to none, with thirty abstentions, a resolution submitted by Holland, Belgium, Luxembourg, Indonesia, Malaysia and Thailand, noting the report and acknowledging with appreciation the fulfilment by the Secretary-General and his representatives of the tasks entrusted to them. But a small group of nations headed by Ghana refused to co-operate. Ghana proposed an amendment declaring that a fresh Act of Free Choice should be held by the end of 1975, '*bearing in mind* Article XVIII of the Agreement, which, *inter alia*, calls for an act of free choice in accordance with international practice'. The amendment was tactfully worded to take 'note of the report of the Secretary-General and his representatives on their *efforts* [my italics] to fulfil their responsibilities under the Agreement of 1962'. It was rejected by sixty to fifteen, with thirty-nine abstentions.

The guilty men

Those whose passions respond automatically to a particular political colour will find it hard to pass judgment on the Act of

Free Choice. Indonesians of all political complexions regarded West Irian as theirs, and the Communist Party, before its extinction, was no exception. If Sukarno had remained in power the Act of Free Choice would probably never have been held at all; he had declared in November 1962 that he did not want a plebiscite.

While Indonesia was the main perpetrator in violating the Act, it was morally the least of the offenders. Since declaring their independence on 17 August 1945, the Indonesians had claimed all territory 'from Sabang [on the extreme tip of Sumatra] to Merauke', an emotive phrase born of the struggle for nationhood. Holland's refusal to cede West Irian until 1962 did not lessen what they believed to be the justice of their claim. The Indonesians rightly felt that the agreement to hold the Act of Free Choice had been forced on them in the last days of colonialism; to them the provision in the New York Agreement was an ember of Holland's inflammatory proposal that it would grant West Irian independence after ten years of preparation. Indonesia had seen the earlier scheme as an attempt to maintain a springboard in the region. For it was obvious that the Papuans would be incapable of governing themselves in ten or even twenty years; and the presence of the Dutch and the example of the Papuans would have encouraged dissidence in other parts of the archipelago. But in 1969 even the ember was dead; the Dutch had re-established relations with the Indonesians and were leaving it to them to determine the fate of the Papuans. In these circumstances Indonesia saw no more sense in conducting an Act of Free Choice in West Irian than in the Moluccas or Sumatra, where there had also been separatist movements. But they were prepared to put on a show to keep the record straight at the United Nations.

The military operations and the excesses that inevitably accompanied them should not be confused with this point of view. Nor should it be assumed that the army was insincere in its efforts to try persuasion before violence or that it was as ruthless as it might have been once force was used. Sarwo Edhie, for example, had a hard time putting down the Arfak revolt; but instead of shooting Mandatjan, as he could have done without it being known, he tried to make an ally of him. Nor was he unaware of the need to speed development to reassure the Papuans that the central government would supply their needs. When I saw him in Jayapura in June 1969, I mentioned the slowness of Fundwi, which had $30 million of Dutch money to spend on development. Already it was clear that a large amount of this was to be wasted through muddle; at that stage all Fundwi had done since making a survey in 1967 was to build fifty houses, in addition to twenty-five supplied by the government, for an extravagantly paid band of international bureaucrats, few of whom would have been given comparable jobs in private enterprise. 'If only they could get a sawmill started in Jayapura, it would help', Sarwo Edhie said. These were not the words of a sadist, but of a professional soldier doing a difficult job.

The rebellions in West Irian were not the first in the archipelago and the Indonesians considered them an internal affair. They felt that the Dutch had put ideas of independence into the heads of simple-minded Papuans when they proposed their ten-year plan; before then some Papuans had fought alongside Javanese against Holland. It required no great self-deception for Indonesians to believe that most of the revolt was fomented by agents of colonial die-hards. Nicolaas Jouwe was, in fact, supported by variously motived Dutch, who were unsympathetic to the Third World in general; but his few links with West Irian had little, if any, effect on events there.

The behaviour of the Dutch government was to some extent matched by that of the nations who voted with it, or abstained, in the General Assembly. But it was shabbier, because in 1962 Holland had declared that it remained 'most deeply concerned with the well-being of the Papuans'. While the misconduct of Indonesia and Holland may be condoned to the extent that it was not inconsistent with the standards of governments in general, the connivance of the United Nations secretariat must be condemned. The wrangles, intrigues and hypocrisy of the General Assembly and the Security Council make no departure from long-established international habits and in themselves add nothing to the gloomier side of mankind's prospects. But more is expected of the secretariat; and hope for a better world will be diminished if the organization set up to help bring it about is staffed by time-servers. It should be possible to assume that those who accept high positions in the United Nations have the integrity to ensure that its charter will become more than a miscellany of claptrap. But in West Irian the secretariat lacked the courage to lift itself above the makeshifts of politics; it thus missed an opportunity to assert itself as an authority to be reckoned with when the moral basis of the United Nations is threatened. The charter badly needed fortifying; it had been damaged in the 1950s, when the American-led West abused its control of the General Assembly. The failure of the secretariat to strengthen the charter by making an issue of West Irian had more than a negative result; it affirmed the pervading cynicism, which so overcame the Assembly that in 1974 Afro-Asian and Communist nations could laugh at attempts to moralize when their turn came in questions involving Israel and South Africa.

While Ortiz Sanz, as the man on the spot, inevitably becomes the main target when the United Nations operation is critized, it should not be assumed that he was wholly to blame, since he acted on instructions from U Thant, who showed himself to be unsympathetic to the Papuans when their delegation visited New York. If Ortiz Sanz's suggestion that one-man-one-vote be allowed in the more densely populated areas had been adopted, the Act of Free Choice would still have gone in Indonesia's favour, as most of the population live in the bush; but an over-whelming vote for independence in the coastal areas would at least have cast suspicion on a unanimous pro-Indonesian vote in the remainder of the territory. The Indonesians, however, would obviously never have accepted such a proposal; and only Ortiz Sanz would know whether he realized this when he submitted it, doubtless with U Thant's approval.

Ortiz Sanz was handicapped from the beginning. Indonesia's departure from the United Nations at the end of 1964 had stopped the secretariat from carrying out the provision of the agreement that it should prepare Papuans for the Act of Free Choice. Further, his staff was cut from an agreed fifty, first to twenty-five and then to sixteen, including typists and clerks; the appointments of eight observers and a second interpreter, who were to have arrived in March and June, were cancelled. In his report Ortiz Sanz explained that both parties to the agreement wanted to keep the budget, which they shared, at a 'minimum level – a request reiterated by the Indonesian Government'. But it is not necessary to be an old Asia hand to see that the real reason was to cripple the operation. The secretariat should have insisted that it would withdraw its mission unless it had enough observers; it must have known that poor communications would make it impossible for such a small staff to ensure a free choice, even if the Indonesians had accepted supervision.

Doubt about the meaning of 'participation' created a problem, but Ortiz Sanz resolved it with astonishing ease. In groping for a definition, he might have been expected at least to refer to van Roijen's assurance that there would be 'active supervision'. But in his report he merely said that as 'participation' was not defined in the agreement, he had assumed it to consist of two elements: first, the United Nations presence in West Irian; and secondly, an effort 'to improve the democratic conditions of the exercise'.

But much more effective participation was possible. In his report Ortiz Sanz said:

> I regret to have to express my reservation regarding the implementation of Article XXII of the Agreement, relating to 'the rights, including the rights of free speech, freedom of movement and of assembly, of the inhabitants of the area'. In spite of my constant efforts, this important provision was not fully implemented and the Administration exercised at all times a tight political control over the population.

This conscience-salving postscript contradicted the public assurances that Ortiz Sanz had given in Jakarta about the restraint and co-operation of the Indonesian government; but it came much too late to be of use. The peoples who, through their governments, had expressed concern about West Irian in the United Nations in 1962, were entitled to have this information before the Act of Free Choice had become final; the statement would certainly have received strong publicity if it had been made early in 1969. Whatever 'participation' had come to mean, it could not have precluded the right of the Secretary-General's representative to point out in good time the violation of a treaty with which the United Nations was associated. But the lateness of the disclosure was part of the general conspiracy. Another section of the report, which deals with what was, in fact, the pursuit and killing of terrified Papuans who fled across the border, contains this discreditable understatement: 'the recurrence of border crossings during my mission to West Irian seems to show a certain degree of political dissatisfaction on the part of some of the inhabitants.'

There was an even better opportunity for the UN team to act fruitfully than that afforded by the direct violation of the treaty; this was the surreptitious appointment of the consultative assemblies. Ortiz Sanz had plenty of warning that the Indonesians were likely to manipulate this operation. For, although they promised him on 24 May that 'United Nations participation . . . would be effectively secured', they ignored his request for the essential planes. The discovery that they had broken their promise and appointed most of the assembly members without even informing him should have constituted an intolerable provocation. Ortiz Sanz then might well have declared his presence pointless and taken his men back to New York. If he had done this, the white-washing session of the United Nations General Assembly could not have taken place. The Papuans would have been no nearer freedom of choice; but the secretariat would have given a useful lesson to all who flout the principles that the UN was formed to uphold.

CHAPTER SIX

Mopping up

In November 1969 the Indonesian Defence Department announced that it was about to launch the first large combined forces exercise since General Suharto came to power. The operation was called *Gala Yudha* (Big War). Four thousand men of the Army, Navy and Air Force were to resist an invader who would land on the northern coast of West Java at Cirebon to set up a Communist government with an Indonesian fifth column. The invaders were assumed to come from the 'China Sea' (apparently either the East China Sea or the South China Sea) and to have established a base in Western Malaysia; but while all concerned regarded the enemy as China, he was discreetly named *Musang* (civet-cat), a term that expressed the army's feelings about Communist China without directly creating new friction with it. Siliwangi Division troops would defeat *Musang* when he attempted to thrust south-west to Bandung, the West Javanese capital.

The announcement mystified foreign military attachés. This was a time when a self-confident United States had convinced itself and its friends that it could contain Communism in South-East Asia; in any case, a Chinese invasion was out of the question in the foreseeable future for obvious reasons. Yet apparently the Chinese were to land 'two or three divisions' at Cirebon – after their warships had sunk the US Seventh Fleet, for that would have been necessary, and survived attacks from heavy bombers based in Thailand. Several curious military attachés asked the Defence Department if they might observe this strange exercise, but were told that 'logistic problems' made their presence impossible and that there was no suitable accommodation for them. 'But I am an old soldier', one attaché persisted. 'I can sleep in my car; I can take my own food.' He was again refused.

The Defence Department did not want foreign correspondents at Cirebon either, but could hardly exclude them when arrangements had been made for a large number of Indonesian journalists to go there. This dilemma was easily resolved. Soon after they had applied for accreditation correspondents were told that they could not travel in their own cars. Some immediately withdrew their applications, because they thought they would see little of interest if they were pinned down at any spot chosen by the army; apart from that, the news value of the exercise was too small to be worth suffering a ten-hour trip from Jakarta in a crowded old press coach with springs that had long succumbed to rough roads. On the eve of the operation, doubtless disappointed to find a few names still on the list, the army sent correspondents a circular warning that the battle area was cholera-ridden and that the quality of neither the food nor the accommodation was assured. Only two correspondents had sufficient curiosity to survive this discouragement and leave in the coach next morning: they were the inevitable Japanese and myself. We had loaded ourselves with tins of rations, but they were not needed. With the Indonesian journalists we were put up in a former Dutch plantation director's mansion, where we ate splendidly and slept in immaculate beds, each set in a spacious cube of wire mosquito netting.

The reason why the army wanted to keep foreigners away soon became apparent. It had nothing to do with fears that the real *Musang* beyond the seas might use attachés or journalists to spy out tactical secrets; it was simply that this was no ordinary military exercise. Certainly there was some spotting of planes, one of which was reported to have crashed, with radar equipment that did not appear to work; a submarine from the rusting naval force harassed *Musang* until it broke down; and, contrariwise, well-trained squads that landed in an Alouette helicopter rescued wounded with speed that would have done credit to any crack regiment. But the main army operation was aimed less at vanquishing *Musang* than at impressing upon the people that the

Siliwangi Division ruled West Java. There was good reason for this. The poorer areas along the coast, where the mock battle was staged for four days, had been Communist strongholds; Cirebon was where the guillotine was established during the 1965 massacre; and the resentful survivors were engaging in passive resistance to army development projects. Some of those who were considered to be ringleaders had already been dealt with; dozens of their corpses, including that of a beheaded woman, had been seen drifting down the Ci Losari River, south-east of Cirebon, in September 1968; Antara News Agency reported that the dead were presumed to be underground Communists murdered by people upstream.

At press briefings officers explained that the *Gala Yudha* was not so much a normal exercise as a 'field test' of various factors, including co-operation between the army and the people. In preparing to resist invasion, journalists were told, the army considered not only the geographic but the demographic and social situations. An officer added privately that many people were still under Communist influence and objected to the army's posting of one soldier in each village to 'advise' the village head – a practice enforced throughout Indonesia. 'We tell them that martial law has been lifted and that we are only there to help, but they don't like us there', he said. 'We want to modify the social structure of the villages. We are trying to win support by building roads and bridges and helping with rice production.'

It required little knowledge of Indonesian anthropology to see that any attempt to tamper with village society, or even to reduce its jealously preserved isolation, was bound to meet with stubborn resistance, whether or nor Communists were whispering in people's ears. The army's attempt to set up new leaders more amenable to its wishes led in some places to a dual structure, in which the traditional heads enjoyed the respect of the villagers while the officials were ignored as much as possible. The *Gala Yudha* seemed to be aimed at breaking what was left of the people's morale. Troops in one area surrounded villages and stood outside individual houses, guns at the ready; officers explained that this was an exercise in stopping fifth-columnists from slipping out to join *Musang*. Not a face showed at any tiny window or door; one could imagine terrified families huddled inside, wondering if night would bring death as it had in 1965 and more recently. In another manoeuvre 5,000 people were 'evacuated' from their houses at dawn; most of them were put into the grounds of a mosque, where a grim-faced soldier, armed with an automatic weapon, watched over them; it was impossible to find out whether this ragged, skinny herd were meant to be saved from *Musang* or prevented from joining him, but their dejected faces showed that they were not enjoying the experience, whatever it was. This was supposed to be an exercise in co-operation, but at no stage was there any apparent communication between the troops and the people. Few came out of their houses when the army transports rolled by; there was no waving and there were no cheers. To an innocent eye from another planet the Siliwangi Division would have looked like an army of occupation; they were as estranged from the people as Sarwo Edhie's men were from the Papuans and from the Javanese murdered in 1965.

The Cirebon exercise was linked with what the army called mopping-up operations, which had been going on incessantly throughout Indonesia since 1966. While these were to continue indefinitely, their peak was in 1968, when the army made concentrated military attacks on Communists and Sukarnoists or anyone who looked like them in Central and East Java. At this time the generals were still having trouble with their own forces: officers and men were going over to a few newly formed Communist guerrilla bands, some of which made occasional raids on military posts. At the beginning of 1968 the generals resolved to intensify both the hunt for Communist cells and the purging of the armed forces. Newspaper correspondents first suspected that the campaign was under way when they were refused permission to enter Central and East Java.

The operation to which the Defence Department gave the most publicity began in June 1968 in the Blitar region of East Java, where overwhelming support for Sukarno, who was now under house arrest, was enlivened by sentiment about his mother's grave in the local cemetery. A melodramatic note was struck with the announcement that the army had used flame-throwers to drive out Communists who had established a mountain base in a network of Vietcong-style tunnels; but some, if not most, of the tunnels were natural caves formed in limestone. The East Java Command said on 9 August that 1,350 Communists had been arrested in the region up to that date; 500 of them, including a 'few hundred' army deserters, had been found in tunnels in the South Blitar area.

It is difficult to establish the relative importance of the three obvious components of this prolonged operation: a military action in which tanks and flame-throwers were used against men carrying small-arms; a police action against Communists who had fled to the relative safety of friendly families after the *putsch* in an area where the local command might well have shut its eyes to their presence; and the usual rampage against all and sundry that was launched wherever the ruling junta encountered hostility. A West Javanese parliamentary commission reported that the army had been impeded by the fact that 90 per cent of the population supported the victims. Some of those arrested were tried and sentenced to death. It is not known how many people were killed on the spot; newspapers put the number at 'scores'. In his MPR speech on 12 March 1973 Suharto named two Communist leaders who had been killed at Blitar and seven others who had been captured with 'thousands of their henchmen and followers'.

While the caves and tunnels at Blitar provided colour for a propaganda story, there were innumerable other campaigns that were less publicized. A few of them had the elements of a genuine military operation, to the extent that the victims had firearms, but most were aimed at unarmed peasants who disliked the army. The true nature of the killing and detention was revealed in the words of an army friend of mine who praised a certain commander in East Java for 'the great job' he did in 'cleaning up the villages'.

In July 1968 my predecessor at Agence France-Presse reported that a 'well-informed military man' had disclosed that a 'bloody fight' had just taken place in the Wonogiri area of Central Java against 'advancing communist units and underground communists and communist supporters'. The informant said that 'no quarter was given' when the 'enraged soldiers' killed an undisclosed number of Communists and army deserters. This report provides an example of the army's frequent use of military jargon to give the impression that it was fighting forces organized like the Vietcong, whereas most of its raids were on houses in barren, poverty-stricken areas, not on guerrillas hiding in jungle. But often there was no attempt to dress up the actions with military trappings. Simple announcements revealed, for instance, that more than 200 people were arrested in July near Semarang, the main town of Central Java, and 500, including army officers, in the Yogyakarta and Kedu regions. The sweep extended throughout the archipelago. It was announced in January 1969 that in one small province alone – Lampung, South Sumatra – arrests of 'underground communists' had totalled more than 4,000 in the previous year; doubtless these arose as much from the local commander's desire to win promotion as from any serious attempt by Communists to form the 'Red Army' mentioned in the announcement. In Jakarta arrests of up to a dozen or more were frequently announced. On 18 July 1968 the capital's Military Commander, Major-General Amir Machmud, (later Lieutenant-General and Minister for the Interior), reaffirmed his standing order to his troops to 'shoot disturbing Communist elements on sight'. This, however, was largely part of the general's game to prove his zeal. Communists, who were working underground in Jakarta, were hardly likely at that stage to create disturbances, and it is improbable that the order was ever carried out, although it might have been used to settle a private grievance or two.

There was one particularly successful operation that was not published at all until journalists unearthed it – the massacre of at least hundreds of people in Central Java in November and December 1968, when the horror of 1965 was revived. This grisly affair was finally exposed by the Vice-Chairman of the Indonesian Institute for Human Rights, Johannes Princen, and two Dutch journalists, who went to the area in February 1969 to investigate unconfirmed reports that had been leaking out. Princen, although born a Dutchman, had become an Indonesian citizen after deserting from the Dutch Army in 1940; he was a member of parliament until Sukarno's men imprisoned him for having opposed guided democracy; later he was detained twice by the junta. A Javanese Catholic priest, Father Sumarto, had pieced together an account of the massacre from the confessions of conscience-stricken Catholic members of the Civil Defence Corps, who had been forced to take part in it. Tormented by his secret, he told Princen and the Dutch journalists what he knew. A Civil Defence Corps man, who remained in a separate room to hide his identity, answered the journalists' questions through the priest and amplified his story.

Princen said he was convinced that about 860 had been murdered with blows on the head from iron bars, but that the total
was probably much higher. The massacre took place after a two-
months rounding up of alleged Communists, who were put into
detention camps at Purwodadi, Gundi and Kuwu town. Interro-
gating officers of the 404th and 409th Battalions had applied
electricity to prisoners' genital organs to extract information about
the underground. One man who was being beaten to death
appeared to want to be put out of his misery; for he screamed: 'I
am not dead yet.' It was cries like these that haunted the Civil
Defence Corps men and sent them running to their priest.
Princen said his informants claimed that the Purwodadi military
commander, Lieutenant-Colonel Tedjo Suwarno ordered the
massacre. When religious leaders threatened to complain to the
Central Java Command in Semarang, Tedjo Suwarno warned
them to keep silent. The army in Jakarta denied that any massacre
had taken place. But the Central Java commander, Major-General
Surono, went so far as to admit that some prisoners had been 'shot
while trying to escape' and that others had committed suicide
after having been captured in bunkers.

I have no doubt that Princen and the Dutch journalists established that a massacre had taken place. I could not obtain independent proof, because all witnesses had vanished or were silent
by the time I got to Purwodadi. But there were significant signs.
The priest had fled to sanctuary with the hierarchy in Semarang,
and efforts to interview him failed. At a convent where I called to
see what I could find out, excited European nuns told me that
one of their number had spoken to the priest and heard the entire
story. I asked to speak to her; but the Mother Superior had heard
of my presence and forbade the meeting. On the way to Purwodadi
in a locally hired car, I was struck by the absence of people as
we drove through what was generally one of the most thickly
populated areas in Indonesia. There were houses at intervals
along the road, but few women and children and practically no
men. I asked the driver why this was. He replied dully: 'Semua
mati' (all are dead). Apparently he was referring to what had
taken place in 1965 and later; for this was far from the scene of
the latest massacre.

I spent the afternoon with Tedjo Suwarno and had supper
with him and his family. He insisted that there had been no

killing, and took me on an inspection of three Purwodadi prisons – not the camps where the massacre took place – to show that all was well. One was an open yard, with sleeping accommodation in buildings at the sides; escape would have been easy, but the prisoners looked too old and demoralized to care. Tedjo Suwarno said they would not leave because they had nowhere to go; the people in their villages were hostile to them.

The two other prisons were large, galvanized iron sheds, each holdings a few hundred prisoners, who had little more room than was needed to enable them to lie side by side to sleep. One prisoner, a tall man of obvious breeding and education, was threading his way through the others, soothing a baby of about twelve months, which he carried in his arms. The baby had been brought to him for the evening; the Indonesian Army can be humane when it feels that it is in full control. Tedjo Suwarno said the prisoner was an 'intellectual' who had been arrested along with others that the Communists were using as Trojan horses. I should have liked to speak to this man, but did not ask permission for fear that he might burst out with something that would get him into worse trouble; he was tense as he paced to and fro, occasionally glowering at us. At one side of the shed a group of thin, prematurely aged men were praying. They were Moslems who had again seen the light, Tedjo Suwarno explained; they would be released when their rehabilitation was completed.

In a corner of the other shed two young women wearing *sarongs* and *kebayas* stood proudly, their eyes flashing, when I walked in with the commander and his party. Whether they were really Communists or not I do not know. But there was more character in their faces and in those of some of the men in the prisons than could easily be found outside. And I was angered that people of such calibre could be arrested at the whim of men like those who were escorting me.

It was not that I found Tedjo Suwarno so contemptible, even though I was convinced that he was lying when he denied the massacre. It was simply that he was not fit, any more than, say, the leader of some Communist band in Indo-China, to have a decisive say in who should die or go to prison. He was an introverted little man, deeply versed in Javanese mysticism. The generals must have had confidence in his ability and toughness, for he was responsible for security in a desolate area in which

200,000 ill-nourished people were breeding faster than rice could grow. His anti-Communist ardour inspired him to study Chinese and Vietnamese guerrilla tactics, possibly in material supplied to the army by the Americans, so that he could spot early signs of infiltration. At his headquarters he showed me a large map, with the areas still considered to be under Communist influence ringed in red and those that were 'rehabilitated' in blue. Tedjo Suwarno said that 40 per cent of the people in his area were 'Communist-orientated' compared with 65 per cent in 1965; but he did not explain how he had arrived at these figures. The Communist Party had now formed a front including fellow travellers and people discontented with the government for one reason or another. Twenty-three front leaders had been arrested in December. 'The Communists are infiltrating at all levels – the civil servants, the farmers, and the army', he said. 'People in Jakarta don't realize how serious the situation is.'

It was obvious that anyone who criticized the government, which meant almost any landless peasant and any thinker, would fall under suspicion and easily find himself in one of the big tin sheds, like the tall man with the baby. Some would doubtless be tortured in futile attempts to make them reveal the names of others in some imagined conspiracy; the army's habit of suspecting a plot and then finding characters to fit it would have prevailed here as in other districts.

Despite his low colonel's salary, Tedjo Suwarno lived well enough. His house was commodious and he kept a small grocery store in his front garden, which, no doubt, people from the half-empty town who were not in prison would have been well advised to patronize. But it was not merely his baronial position that he was defending: he was fighting for his culture, which was some-thing deeper than could be denoted by the word 'religion'. After supper, in the light of a kerosene lamp, he showed me a book in which traditional beliefs were written immaculately in Javanese and illustrated with diagrams that could have been Hindu in origin. Translating from this book in a mixture of Indonesian and English, Tedjo Suwarno earnestly explained the mysteries of creation and the sources of good and evil in the world, which was, in fact, Java. The volume, he said, had been given to him by his grandmother; he wanted to pass it on to his children. It was clear that Tedjo Suwarno, military commander of Purwodadi and local grocer, would fight to the end to prevent this ancient wisdom from being eclipsed by some new-fangled atheistic ideology contained in a little red book compiled, worst of all, by a Chinese. The army tried to cover the Purwodadi murders with a statement that there had been armed clashes with losses on both sides; but my interrogation of Tedjo Suwarno convinced me that there had been no fighting worth mentioning. A tiny museum housing weapons captured in operations against the Communists contained nothing more fearsome than eight old Russian handgrenades, a box of ammunition and home-made rifle butts fitted with springs to fire bicycle spokes a distance of twenty-five metres. Tedjo Suwarno said a bottle of snake venom, in which the spokes were to have been dipped, had been sent to Semarang headquarters. Certainly poverty was continuing to produce its crop of Communists; but the home-made rifles and the sharpened bicycle spokes were symbols of despair rather than a sign of strength. Later the army announced that Tedjo Suwarno had been transferred to another post, clumsily adding that this had nothing to do with any massacre; his successor was the commander of one of the two battalions that were accused of having perpetrated the murders.

A military operation that was certainly genuine was carried out in West Kalimantan (former Dutch Borneo) against Chinese guerrillas. It took until 1972 for the Indonesians to drive all the guerrillas back into the Malaysian province of Sarawak, whence they had come to be trained and armed by Sukarno's forces during the Malaysia Confrontation. The campaign cost the Indonesian Army 195 dead up to November 1972, when I visited West Kalimantan; guerrilla losses were put at 655 dead and 1,860 captured. Indonesia and Malaysia conducted a joint operation against the guerrillas along the Sarawak border, with an understanding that troops from either side could cross into the other's territory when necessary.

The West Kalimantan Command attributed its success in ridding itself of the guerrillas partly to its skill in winning support of the indigenous people, the Dyaks. Officers felt that the Malaysians' inability to wipe out guerrillas whom the Indonesians had virtually driven into their arms arose from their failure to adopt similar methods. The Indonesians applied their 'Doctrine of People's War', the adoption of which they were urging throughout

South East Asia as more effective than bombing and shelling techniques copied from the Americans. An officer said:

> We convinced the Dyaks that the Communists were their
> enemies. We mobilized some of them into a Civil
> Defence Corps and armed them with Lee Enfield rifles.
> They killed many guerrillas. Now they guard the frontier
> while we help them with civic action; every soldier who
> comes here is trained in rudimentary agriculture, medical
> aid and construction work. We have only two battalions of
> our own to guard the border (about 1,300 kilometres). Do
> you think we could have driven out the guerrillas without
> Dyak help?

In Sarawak I found that the Malaysian Army kept relatively aloof from the people; squads sent out to win over the Dyaks consisted of civilian experts, with police and troops usually playing only a security role. An Indonesian official commented: 'You can't win over the Dyaks that way. The troops must fight, eat and sleep with them as equals. That is what we mean by People's War. The guerrillas could not hide in the mountains without help from the local people. That is why you must have the Dyaks on your side.' The Indonesians obviously exaggerated the possibilities of People's War in parts of South East Asia where Communists could point to China as having done more for peasants than American-backed military governments had. But the doctrine worked in West Kalimantan; and in 1973 the central government showed faith in it by making a special $1,750,000 grant for development work along the Sarawak border.

Excluding West Irian, where rebellion continued, and West Kalimantan, the army's actions generally diminished in violence after 1968, although they were no less widespread; in January 1969 Suharto decreed the lifting of the state of emergency in Yogyakarta and Central Java 'because of favourable results in the restoration of law and order'. From that time the mopping up usually consisted of arrests of small batches of men and women, who were said to be part of underground movements that appeared to be springing up, often spontaneously, in widely separated areas. Thousands were arrested, but limited prison accommodation, even of the most primitive kind, kept the total fairly stable, with prisoners that were classed as less dangerous released to make room for new-comers. Generally those arrested on a single occasion numbered from one to a dozen or so; arrests of this order became so frequent that they ceased to be news, and most correspondents stopped reporting them except in special circumstances. Occasionally firearms were seized, but resistance was rare, and when it occurred it was pathetically feeble. In March 1969 three alleged Communists were killed in an army raid at Tangut Serdang, in Lampung province, South Sumatra. The official news agency, Antara, reported that they had tried to defend themselves with spears before being shot; one was a woman.

The purge of the civil service and armed forces also continued. In February 1969 the Governor of West Java disclosed that more than 1,100 administration staff had been dismissed on the pretext of having been involved in the 1965 *putsch*; 1,400 others who were suspected of Communist sympathies were put under surveillance. In May eleven of the MPRS secretariat in Jakarta were arrested on the invented charge of having taken part in the *putsch* conspiracy. It was officially stated in the same month that arrests in the army alone had totalled 2,250 since 1965. In April 1969 it was announced that all naval officers were being screened in a new purge.

The vast suppression of leftist and near-leftist forces was part of Suharto's plan to stabilize the nation not only politically but economically and, it would not be too much to say, spiritually. Economic stabilization was to be followed by development, which would lead to a 'flower garden' of prosperity and justice. Harmony in society was not a mere goal, but a *sine qua non* of progress; there could be discussions about details, but no opposition to the basic decisions of the wise rulers; discordant notes would be silenced. In other words, the Javanese philosopher-king attitude of Suharto was not unlike that of Sukarno; the difference was only in the wisdom offered and the way in which it was enforced.

Suharto's imposition of order by arrest and murder was matched by rigorous economic measures, including cuts in government expenditure sufficiently large to balance the budget without running the printing presses. The plunge of the rupiah, which had become one of the world's most delinquent currencies, was halted. It had gone from 120 to the dollar in February 1967 to 500 in October 1968; but two months later, largely because of an inflow of dollars in the form of Western aid, it had recovered to 420 and later was to improve further, for a time. Rice prices were kept temporarily in check by establishing a reserve, which reduced speculation, on the advice of an International Monetary Fund team that had set up an office in Jakarta.

These were encouraging signs for those who believed that, given initial capital and advice, Indonesia could develop a Western-style economy that would generate its own power. But this was an illusion. The army's vast repression campaign had already killed or paralysed many of those minute buds of initiative that are indispensable to the development of a country almost devoid of modern skills. Now its allies, the American-educated economists, were laying the foundations of an economy dependent on foreign capital, which could never be sufficient for the needs of a rapidly rising, widely scattered population, already close to 120 million. Some Indonesian economists, one of whom was later cast into prison, saw this. So did some politicians. And at the beginning of 1969 Suharto warned his cabinet that he would not tolerate ministerial or other opposition to the five year development plan, *Repelita*, which, financed by the West, was to begin the following April.

The junta's exclusive exercise of power was already being criticized by some who could safely protest and a few who could not. General Nasution, who was still Chairman of the MPR, told students undergoing military training in July 1968 that Indonesia was threatened by a form of Latin American-type militarism, which was anti-democratic and could give rise to a privileged class; he added that the army's green uniform had become a symbol of corruption. Two months later Subchan, who had hoped that the army would share power with suitable political parties in a 'realistic democracy' freed of Communists, said that so far democracy had not been achieved, 'apparently because it would be awkward for the leaders'. This remark was made in a jocular tone, but later Subchan was to challenge the junta with incredibly audacious, bitter attacks, for which he was to pay dearly.

In 1969 there were still a few with courage to speak up, but the number dwindled down the years. Sjafruddin Prawiranegara, a former Finance Minister and Central Bank Governor, who was Prime Minister of the PRRI, said Suharto had not kept his promise to bring about democracy. The government had won confidence in the rupiah, but not in itself; if it tried to raise a loan for economic development, it would fail. 'The government relies too much on the force of arms and on statements of support from party leaders who were not ashamed to be Sukarno's lackeys', he said. He warned Suharto to be wary of foreign praise, adding: 'It is impossible for foreigners to know us better than our own people do.' The government, he said, had not won the support of Moslems, who comprised most of the population. The statements of Nasution, Subchan and Sjafruddin Prawiranegara were serious; but few people in the new establishment took any notice of them. Among the deaf were the so-called technocrats, the tamed economists, who were later also to be silenced, side-tracked or dismissed in Suharto's process of achieving harmony by elimination.

During 1969 a leading Jakarta lawyer, Adnan Bujung Nasution – who had spoken up against Sukarno in the MPRS – waged a campaign to preserve vestiges of the rule of law. His doomed efforts reached their peak when he defended one of nine youths who were sentenced to eight months' imprisonment after they had opposed the election of a mayor in Medan, North Sumatra. The remarkable charge was that the youths had deprived members of an army-backed youth front of their freedom by forcing them to withdraw their support for the mayor; the enforcement was said to have been brought about by bribes, which the accused denied having given. On his return to Jakarta in October Nasution said that Kopkamtib (the command set up to restore law and order on 11 March 1966) was abusing its powers so wantonly that it appeared that North Sumatra was in a state of war; university lecturers, journalists and others who expressed even slight differences with official opinion risked being branded as taking a Communist line. A few months earlier Nasution had said that the time was not ripe to start the development plan in South Kalimantan (former Borneo) because the people were 'living in a constant state of fear'; the military commander was 'maintaining the position of absolute ruler, exercising authority like a war administrator'; the recent arrest of students had left the region in a state of apprehension.

Nasution's statements were published by Antara News Agency, in whose bulletins no criticism of generals was allowed without approval by the army's supervisor, as he was officially called. It looked as if Suharto was taking advantage of Nasution's efforts, to support his own campaign against unseemly warlord activities, including smuggling and the exaction of tribute, among his far-flung commanders. Nasution was non-political; he had opposed Sukarno vehemently and was now fighting the army with the same motive, which he expressed in a letter to a newspaper with the tag, *fiat justitia ruat coelum*. But while the junta was vulnerable to Western economic ideas, it was unscathed by European principles of justice. And Nasution inevitably landed in prison some time later after further campaigning for civil liberty.

While journalists were bullied and occasionally imprisoned in the provinces for no more than reporting what they believed to be facts, a show-case free press was maintained in Jakarta, partly to beguile observers, whose comments could have provoked opposition in Western countries to providing Indonesia with soft loans. But even there army pressure on newspapers was apparent in the sixties to all except some academics, writing from a distance, and diplomats on the spot, blinded by expediency; and in the seventies the closing of newspapers and detention of editors made the repression apparent to everybody.

CHAPTER SEVEN

Corruption and beyond

The oil kingdom

A view implicit in later chapters is that Western economic aid, with its wrong emphasis and encouragement of unsuitable technology, impedes indigenous development in Indonesia. But even if this were not so, the present administration of funds provided by foreign taxpayers could never achieve what is said to be its main purpose, which is to generate a widespread, self-sustaining economy – and thus prevent the rise of peasant communism. The rulers and their Chinese partners are building up huge financial interests beyond the control of even the administration that the junta has set up. With this separate economy, this enclave within the enclave, far-reaching economic planning is impossible. To call such a vast purloining of the nation's productive resources and bank credit mere corruption is like describing Alexander the Great's conquests as an act of petty larceny; it goes far beyond what is normally understood by corruption, which, rife though it is, has become only a red herring in Indonesia.

The first serious assault on the junta's financial empire was made by Mochtar Lubis, who made good use of the relative press freedom in Jakarta while it lasted, but later was to share with Princen the distinction of having been detained by both the Sukarno and Suharto governments. In November 1969 he launched in his doomed newspaper *Indonesia Raja* a prolonged, slashing campaign against Lieutenant-General Ibnu Sutowo, head of the state authority, Pertamina, which controls all of Indonesia's considerable oil. He pointed out that Pertamina published no balance sheet, was beyond the control of the National Planning Board (which was responsible for the Five Year Plan), and had borrowed millions of dollars overseas without government sanction. Lubis accused Sutowo of turning Pertamina into a private financial and industrial complex for which he was accountable to neither parliament nor, in practice, the government. Sutowo, he said, was frittering away loans and oil revenue on irrelevant ventures including a mosque at the University of Indonesia, a $2.5 million sports stadium at Palembang, South Sumatra, a travel office and two hotels in Jakarta and a restaurant in New York. Sutowo was making big profits from the Tugu Insurance Company, which he had set up privately in Hong Kong to insure Pertamina's tankers; described as a merchant, he was one of the company's three directors. Lubis said Sutowo had sold large oil mining concessions for nominal sums to friends, who resold them at a high profit; he gave details of four contracts, copies of which were supplied to him by a disgruntled official, which named foreigners who had virtually been given presents estimated to total at least $60 million. Later Lubis published complicated contracts under which, he said, Indonesia was losing money by selling oil through Japanese trading companies. He listed the names, prices, and market values of five secondhand tankers, which, he said, Pertamina had bought for more than they were worth on Sutowo's instructions.

I have no doubt that Mochtar Lubis would not have published details of the benificent disposal of oil concessions, the dubious overpayment for tankers and other unsavoury matters unless he had evidence of their authenticity; I verified Sutowo's connexion with the Tugu Insurance Company by obtaining its balance sheet from Hong Kong. The investment in enterprises totally unrelated to the oil industry was well established; in fact, Pertamina documented its extravagance with cyclostyled copies of the speech that Sutowo made when he opened his New York restaurant. Investments that were to provide windfalls for Sutowo's foreign and Indonesian friends continued on an increasing scale, but it was impossible to obtain an official list of them; for just as it published no accounts, Pertamina kept most of its activities secret. Before leaving Indonesia in January 1973 I asked the

Pertamina public relations officer if he would give me a list of all its undertakings in Indonesia. After a pleasant lunch he handed me a large, sealed envelope, saying: 'This is what you asked for.' When I opened it later I found it contained only scanty information, which had already been published.

The malpractices of Pertamina were known to foreign oil experts. I was shown inferior tankers in Tanjung Priok harbour, near Jakarta, which Pertamina had bought from Japan. 'The Japanese will make you good tankers or not so good', my informant said. 'It depends on what you pay. These will start breaking down in a few years. But Pertamina paid for top quality. Somebody got a kickback.' Corruption also led to the installation of low-grade pipes at two waterside pumping stations, which I visited. A British firm had offered pipes guaranteed to stand the pressure of pumping at the normal rate of 400 tons an hour for fifteen years; but it suited Pertamina to pay an excessive price for Japanese pipes, which after two years were so leaky that the rate had to be cut by half, while tanker captains demanded written instructions to discharge so slowly. Despite the reduced pressure, frequent stops had to be made to repair leaks when the automatic alarm bells rang at the stations; the result was that it took up to four times the normal period to pump oil ashore. As Pertamina was chartering tankers on a time basis, the cost to the country of the directors' pickings was immense.

In May 1972 more than eighty people perished in a fire that broke out near one of the installations I had visited, and swept across a vast oil streak to fishing boats. Antara News Agency said that the fire was believed to have begun when a fisherman's lamp ignited oil leaking from a pipe through which a small tanker was discharging. Pertamina denied that its pipe had leaked, but, as is usual in Indonesia, no public inquiry was held. A blaze at Semarang, Central Java, killed more than fifty destitute people who had crept out at night to salvage petrol leaking copiously from a pipe that ran from the harbour to the town. Children had held flaming torches to illuminate the leak while their parents eagerly filled buckets with petrol, which they hoped to sell easily following a 49 per cent price increase. The petrol burst into sheets of flame; and screaming men, women and children were burned to death as they tripped over full buckets. This time Pertamina could not deny that its notorious leaks had led to a fire. But, again, there

was no public inquiry, and the victims received neither compensation nor sympathy; they were mere stragglers in the junta's
great march to modernity, and should not have taken the petrol
in any case.

Sutowo, then in his fifties, had been a medical practitioner,
but had abandoned his profession for a military career; he was
put in charge of oil installations when the army seized control
of Dutch property in 1957. He made no attempt to avoid outward
signs of his vast wealth. In Jakarta he was driven in a Rolls Royce
with gold-plated fittings. He had his own security force, which
was virtually a private army, and an intelligence service to spy on
his enemies. Guards wearing elegant, light-blue uniforms,
contrasting with the drab but practical green of the army proper,
formed up and presented arms when he arrived at the gates of his
Sumatran oil enterprises. Although his trim, wiry body suggested
that his habits were abstemious, he entertained lavishly when he
thought the occasion demanded it. The large sums spent on food
and display at his daughter's wedding aroused public bitterness.
Invitation cards were booklets like a princess's *carnet de bal*. The
cover, unsullied by printer's ink, was heavily embossed in Javanese;
inside, bound with gold braid, was a coloured miniature of the
couple, with the invitation printed in gold. When Sutowo was
made a Doctor of Economic Science (*honoris causa*) at a university
in Surabaya, which he endowed, the invitation cards were less
expensive; but each was also a ticket to travel free by air to the
ceremony. Sutowo extended the grounds of his heavily guarded
mansion in Jakarta by buying and pulling down neighbouring
houses; when I measured the two frontages of his growing corner
block with eighty-centimetre paces in January 1973 they totalled
208 metres in an overcrowded city of 5 million people.

Sutowo behaved so much like a feudal king that it was not
unreasonable to wonder if he was Suharto's master. The fact
was that while Sutowo's control of Indonesia's oil wealth enabled
him to buy loyalty from individuals in the armed forces, the
ultimate power could only be exercised by a man with troops
under his command and the ability to lead them in the field.
This was Suharto; and although a necessary and calculated
delegation of some of his operational military authority put him
in danger from other generals at one stage, he had little to fear
from Sutowo.

In seeking cheap credits from Western countries the junta pointed to the national budget to show that it was cutting military expenditure to a minimum, so that the maximum could be devoted to economic development. But some Western diplomats estimated in 1972 that the budget provided only 60 per cent of money spent on the armed forces; the rest came from Pertamina, which provided houses for officers and men, roads, amenities and perquisites. Air force officers said: 'If we want a helicopter we ask Pertamina.' Suharto could scarcely have relished Sutowo's being continually hailed as a distributor of largesse; and when he entered his office in a luxurious conference building that Pertamina erected for the nation, he probably felt no gratitude when he found on his desk an inkstand inscribed as a gift from Sutowo. Occasionally there were signs that Suharto was displeased with Sutowo. Criticism of Pertamina appeared in Antara bulletins; the palace spokesman went out of his way to publish details of the Semarang petrol fire; and Sutowo was absent from Suharto's party when he visited Japan in May 1972 to negotiate, among other things, credits for Pertamina. But under the military government it was inevitable that some general would run the oil industry and become rich and powerful by doing so; Sutowo, with his long experience, was the obvious choice; and when it came to a point Suharto defended him against criticism until finally it became impossible to do so (see chapter 12).

Suharto and the cukongs

While Ibnu Sutowo had established a firm hold on Indonesia's oil since before the *putsch*, rich opportunities were still open to the Suharto circle. In January 1970 Lubis followed his attack on Sutowo with an accusation that Suharto's personal adviser on financial affairs, Major-General Soerjo Wirojohadipoetro, was involved in swindling the government of $711,000. I saw photocopies of incriminating documents, and subsequently interviewed an official who revealed what was one of the most remarkable stories in the history of fraud. The swindle was perpetrated by representing that a state company, PN Aneka Niaga, was paying $711,000 for a non-existent cargo of insecticide that was certified to have been transported in a non-existent ship. The seller of the cargo was a company registered in Liechtenstein and partly owned by a Chinese, Ong Seng Keng, who had adopted the Indonesian name of Arief Husni. I was shown a photo-copy of a letter in which Soerjo asked the Bank Negara Indonesia, the central bank, to open a letter of credit to pay for the insecticide. Photo-copied documents included a faked bill of lading issued by a firm in Singapore and a Dutch surveyor's certificate that the cargo had been loaded in Hong Kong in a ship named the *Tonaga*, which was proved not to exist. In a handwritten letter Soerjo asked PN Aneka Niaga to iron out certain difficulties that had arisen when the Swiss Bank Corporation questioned a clause in the contract of sale. There was not the slightest doubt that a grave crime had been committed. But Suharto ignored demands for a trial. It was officially stated after a cabinet meeting that the matter had been 'settled out of court'; the money had been refunded, the government said, and there was nothing more to worry about.

Soon afterwards Ong was accused of having attempted to obtain $5,500,000 for 20,000 tons of fertilizer that was certified to have been shipped from Taiwan in Japanese vessels, but never arrived in Jakarta. Again, it was said, false surveys were used to obtain letters of credit. It was reported that Ong had been arrested this time; but he was never brought to trial. This was not surprising: his links with the President had been established when at the opening of Ong's Ramayana Bank Soerjo read a speech on Suharto's behalf. The only persons punished were two Bank Negara Indonesia officials, who had referred the papers to the Attorney-General's Department when they discovered irregularities; they were quietly removed from their posts. One was an army officer, a graduate of the Rotterdam School of Economics; his victimization heightened discontent among other young officers who felt that Indonesia's affairs should be conducted differently.

In a society in which the state oil company published no accounts and criminals were protected by the President, it was clear that there were few curbs on the junta's opportunities to rake in funds for its collective and individual purposes. But following a leak to newspapers in March 1970 that certain officers had been involved in gun-running to Biafra, a show was made of trying Major-General Hartono Wirdjodiprodojo, officer in charge of construction at army headquarters. He was accused of having falsely certified that arms handled by a named London dealer were for the Indonesian armed forces; the dealer required certificates to ship the arms from England. Although it was never mentioned in court, knowledgeable sources said the arms went to Biafra. Evidence was given that Hartono received $130,000 for signing the certificates, but it might well have been more. A Dakota plane that he was alleged to have bought with the proceeds for an air line in which he had an interest was confiscated. It is inconceivable that Hartono, the only man brought to trial, was engaged in such an affair on his own. Since he was said to have been under 'house arrest' for twenty months, he had only four months of his two-year sentence to serve; he gave notice of appeal and served none at all.

Soerjo's associate, Ong, was one of a group of about twenty powerful Chinese known as *cukongs*, or financiers, a term that has become bitterly pejorative in Indonesia. One of the most notorious was Lim Siu Liong, who had connexions not only with some of the generals, but with Mrs Suharto. According to army officers in a position to know, Mrs Suharto used a charity organization, the Yayasan Harapan Kita (Our Hope Foundation) as a cover for her operations with him and others. This body, with Mrs Suharto as its chairman, maintained an excellent school for backward children, but did little other charitable work.

The officers said that Mrs Suharto, as chairman of the foundation, received 40 per cent of the profits of PT Bogasari, a flour milling company, under its articles of association, while Sudwikatmono, a son of Suharto's aunt, Mrs Somoprawiro, was a director. It appears that Lim saw his chance when Prima, a flour milling company in Singapore, applied to the Investment Board for permission to set up three factories, one in each of Surabaya, Makasar (now Ujung Pandang) and Jakarta. All the necessary signatures for the permit had been obtained except Suharto's. Lim then obtained an investment credit from the Bank Negara Indonesia to float PT Bogasari, and the Prima application was refused. Subsequently Prima established a plant at Makasar but was not allowed to sell in Java, Lesser Sunda Islands or Sumatra, which were reserved for PT Bogasari, except during the 1972 rice shortage, when the Suhartos' territories were opened to it.

The Suhartos had been in business in one way or another for a long time. In 1958, when he commanded the Diponegoro Division in Central Java, Suharto was accused of exporting and bartering state plantation sugar, an operation he claimed to be carrying out for the benefit of his unit. Before leaving Jakarta I asked General Nasution why no action had been taken against Suharto. He said:

> When I was Chief of Staff Suharto was interrogated for importing and exporting activities in Semarang [Central Java]. I signed an order not to put him on trial. What he did was not big compared with what others were doing. He exported sugar to Singapore and Hong Kong in exchange for other goods. They even used sugar from East Java after taking it to Semarang. But I thought that if we did not attack the big ones it would not be just to prosecute Suharto.

According to an Indonesian who specializes in *cukong* affairs, one of the 'big ones' would have been Yani, from whom Suharto inherited Ong Seng Keng, the Chinese who had collaborated with his personal assistant, Major-General Soerjo, in the fertilizer cargo fraud and other affairs. Soerjo, who had been in charge of army finance since 1945, introduced Ong to Suharto in 1966. The pretty woman whom Yani had taken as his second wife shortly before his murder in the *putsch* married Brigadier-General Herman Sarens Sudiro, who at one time was associated with the Yayasan Harapan Kita. Sudiro was widely believed to be involved in a large-scale smuggling racket, in which cars were imported duty-free by means of passports bought from Indonesian students overseas and altered to bear the names of fictitious temporary visitors. The Chinese inevitably involved in the affair was imprisoned, but Sudiro, whose complicity is vouched for by intelligence men and police, escaped prosecution. Sudiro's business connexion with Mrs Suharto was close. There is a well-authenticated case of a man who wanted to sell equipment to a certain department (I prefer not to mention what it was); he was told that he must first see Sudiro. While discussing the deal, Sudiro, who has a wireless transmitter at his house, picked up a microphone and talked it over with Mrs Suharto. Sudiro was executive chairman of the new racecourse, with its totalisator and air-conditioned stand, for which horses were fed on oats flown at great expense from Australia while millions of children had no more flesh than was needed to cover their bones; as far as I know he had no link with the modern dog track, which was also established after the *putsch*.

Revealing though Lubis's newspaper campaign was, it took army officers to uncover the extraordinary scope of the *cukongs'* operations and to establish to their satisfaction that Suharto himself was involved in them. These investigators concluded that People's China was using the *cukongs*, some of whom undoubtedly had links with Peking, to foment discontent in Indonesia by further enriching the élite. Whether or not one agrees with this theory, the officers are responsible men whose opinion is worthy of respect and it must be said that the Suharto circle's associations with the *cukongs* is the greatest single cause of urban, civilian bitterness towards the junta and of potential rebellion within the armed forces.

Among documents that came into the officers' hands is what is claimed to be a letter to Soerjo from a private detective, A. David, formerly of 101 Groot Hertoginnelaan, The Hague. There is no reason to doubt the authenticity of this letter. David certainly existed; a Dutch colleague of mine knew him well. One of Soerjo's officers engaged him to trace funds remitted illicitly to Holland before the *putsch*. At the beginning David was told that the money was to go into a special national fund, but it soon became evident that this was not the destination intended. After a dispute David sued Soerjo in Holland for his fees and expenses, but died in October 1973 before the court proceedings had ended. The letter, dated 16 September 1972, is written in a menacing tone, and carries an implied threat that Soerjo's own vast operations will be exposed if the case is not settled. It begins (in Dutch):

Re law suit

Dear General Soerjo,

    To my great regret I have not received any reaction to all my letters. I have really tried my best to resolve the conflict between you and me – not wished by me – amicably, outside the court.

    I have the fullest right to claim fulfilment of agreements and if you ignore all my letters then – again much against my will – I shall be obliged to find other ways to seek satisfaction.

    Possibly you think that I am only using bluff methods. I have been working for many years together with the judicial apparatus in Holland and with fiscal and economic

inquiry and tracing services here and elsewhere. I am
therefore really not alone. You are making a big mistake
if you think so.

The letter is about 2,000 words long. It gives minute details of
contracts, which, it says, were entered into by Soerjo and his
Chinese associates, who are named, in which secret commissions
amounted to millions of dollars. 'Enormous amounts', it says,
were made from Koti (Supreme Operation Command) orders.
Two of the Chinese received 15 per cent commission from the
supply of parachutes worth $12,500,000. Other lucrative deals
were the 'notorious LST transaction via INTERMECO
UTRECHT N.V./RUBIN-New York'; a contract for Bailey
bridges; and 'the supply among other things of 125 rubber
pontoons (via Lindeteves-Jacoberg-Amsterdam) with a profit
percentage of as high as 550 per cent. The pontoons were pur-
chased from American dumps, but put on the bill as "brand new".
This is pure swindle.' After detailing other, similar transactions,
the letter continues:

You see that you and I keep meeting each other, while
a conflict between you and me was not even necessary if
you had kept to your agreements.
I am working in a team – a team of very sharp, first-class
detectives – with branches in Hong Kong, Singapore,
Tokyo and New York.
We can, of course, name quite a few other matters. I
name, for instance, the order you gave on 6 December 1966
to a certain Mr H. Roestam (see annex II) to found a
business (DOLIMEX GmbH) in Dusseldorf, Western
Germany, for the execution of a contract to supply five ferry
boats for the Indonesian navy (L/C No 80664 dated 25.11.65
of US $3,750,000 – opened by the Bank Negara Indonesia
via Indoverbank N.V. Amsterdam/Deutsche Bank AG
Dusseldorf) . . . It is known exactly how things were
manipulated in this transaction. A big amount disappeared.

The letter recalls that David met Soerjo on 7 December 1966
at the house of one of the Chinese at Wassenaar, Holland, to
hand him an advance on his share in the 'PN GULA transactions',
in which 'again very big amounts for so-called "over-prices" and

commissions were kept aside and cashed'. After reminding Soerjo of further shady affairs, the letter says:

Why did you really break off the contact with me, which was once so good? I took seriously the task given to me and considered it an honour to lend good service to the Republic of Indonesia. Was not everything going on in an official manner?

Only later did living and learning show that I had brought a hornets' nest about my ears.

The letter ends with a postscript: 'Annex III concerns your private bank account at the COMMERZBANK-Dusseldorf'.

With this document in their hands, the Indonesian officers made further inquiries and produced one of their own, also in Dutch, with David's evident collaboration. Ominously typed at the bottom is the word *merdeka* (freedom), the battle-cry of the Indonesian revolution. The report repeats and amplifies some of the David letter, and provides fresh allegations. Previously critics of the rulers had avoided direct mention of the President, partly because of traditional deference; but the report says that Suharto himself is a partner of the *cukongs* in a huge financial empire. It claims that he has a close association with Lim Poo Hien, at whose Wassenaar house David was said in the letter to have met Soerjo.

The report says that the capital of both Lim and Suharto is administered by Rubin, Rubin, Weinberg and Dipaola, solicitors, of 375 Park Avenue, New York. The firm's premises are also the registered offices of Greater Southeast Financial & Development Corporation Ltd, which has close ties with Waringin Finance Ltd, Singapore [in which, I was told by another source, Suharto's brother, Probo Sutedjo, has an interest]. Waringin's directors include Lim Poo Hien and Lim Siu Liong [Mrs Suharto's associate], owner of a large number of companies, including Tarumatex.

Tarumatex, a Bandung textile company, is well known in Jakarta. Early in 1971 Frank N. Hawkins, Jr. Associated Press correspondent, revealed that the army had given the company a $1,700,000 contract at the end of 1970 in dubious circumstances. The Ministry of Industry had advised that the company could not meet the terms – 1,020,000 yards of cloth in six months.

Corruption and beyond

Tarumatex was paid 675 rupiahs ($1.67) a yard; soon after the deal was signed it farmed out most of the work to larger companies for 525 rupiahs ($1.38) a yard. The disclosure that generals were involved in this and other *cukong* activities caused immense embarrassment in the Suharto circle, but no denial was issued.) The report continues:

> Among others, the notorious LST transaction – extremely old, converted landing ships – in which about F1 [guilders] 12,000,000 just disappeared – was executed by Rubin's mediation.
>
> The order for the execution of the above notorious transaction – which caused a lot of commotion in the Indonesian and foreign press, but was hushed up by the military, was given on 7 April 1968 by President Suharto to Jantje Lim Poo Hien alias Harjanto [many Chinese have adopted Indonesian names]. One of the directors of the above-mentioned company [Greater Southeast Financial and Development Corporation Ltd] is Mr R. Ibnu Hardjanto, a close relative of President Suharto.
>
> According to a power of attorney given on 7 April 1968 to Jantje Lim Poo Hien by President Suharto, Lim Poo Hien is the only one who – although merely a private person and on top of that of Chinese origin – conducts business transactions for and in the name of President Suharto *personally*.
>
> Waringin Finance Ltd in Singapore is one of the very biggest financing companies in South East Asia, led by Chinese who maintained very close relations with a number of generals and advisors of the President, including General Soerjo Wirojohadipoetro.
>
> PT Seragam Technical Supply, of 40 djalan Raya Krekot Bunder, Djakarta, is led by Jantje (Jany) Lim Poo Hien alias Harjanto – living at Djalan Tjendana 15, opposite President Suharto – and his younger brother, Willy Lim Poo Giok alias Surijadi . . . Shareholders are: General Suharto, President RI; General R. Soerjo Wirojohadipoetro; General R. Hartono, TNI [Indonesian Army]; and General Sri Martojo, Auri [Indonesian Air Force]. All four above-named high authorities were already shareholders of PT

Seragam Technical Supply during the 'Sukarno régime',
and important orders for the Indonesian forces and police
were channelled via this firm. . .

The Waringin *cukong* group has enormously big interests
in banks, shipping, air lines, import-export companies, travel
agencies, restaurants, industries, rice mills, and export
concessions for tin, rubber, and other products.

The report says that part of the Waringin capital was obtained
from the smuggling of rubber, cinchona, tin and other Indonesian
products. A tin smelting plant bought in West Germany for use
at the national mines on Bangka Island is *'so-called* unsatisfactory
and therefore about one third of the production of tin ore has to
be processed and traded in Singapore [by Waringin]'. The report
adds that this business is extremely profitable; the refining
produces a rare material, seltine earth, which is in great demand
in the colour television industry. Waringin handles 8,000 tons of
tin yearly.

The officers who circulated the report had no politics, as far
as I could tell. Their aim was less to denigrate the Suharto circle
than to warn against what they saw as a danger from Peking. The
main purpose of their investigations seemed to be to establish
how strong was what they called the *cukongs'* 'grip on the President'.
The report ends with a brief strategic analysis. It predicts that
within foreseeable time China, 'the world's third nuclear power',
and Japan, 'the third industrial nation', will co-operate economically on a scale that will make China 'a power of the first order in
South East Asia'. Meanwhile, the report says, Peking aims to
strengthen the social, political and economic position of overseas
Chinese to the detriment of indigenous entrepreneurs; an end
must therefore be put to the 'economic and potential political
influence of the *cukongs* in the army and the presidential palace'.

A junta as enterprising as Suharto's was unlikely to miss the
pickings offered by Lockheed. The US Senate multinational
corporations sub-committee reported that the CIA had found
that the Lockheed representative in Jakarta was 'definitely well
connected with the Suharto régime'. According to a 1968 Lockheed memo, a general described as 'closely related' to the representative and who 'controlled considerable funds, at once made
those available to Suharto'.[1]

Apart from the hidden, mammoth concerns, there are groups of companies openly run by the armed forces to supplement the needs of various units and their leaders. Some of these lack sufficient Chinese help to ensure their success, and in 1972 Lieutenant-General Mokogenta, a Sulawesi Moslem of good reputation, was given the impossible task of putting them in order. Outside the main groups are companies run by generals, including air lines that take badly needed business from the national line, Garuda. One of the air lines collapsed after having stranded passengers for some days in Bali, when its failure to pay bills to Pertamina left it without petrol; Ibnu Sutowo, who was also interested in air traffic, thus taught his rivals a lesson. Lieutenant-General Ali Murtopo's Opsus (Special Operations) was given a timber concession in West Kalimantan, and co-operated with the Jakarta garrison in establishing a steel mill with Taiwan capital. Opsus was subsequently dissolved, but doubtless its business interests remained in good hands. Army officers also run state enterprises, including plantations and a hotel chain, not entirely in the national interest. With all these operations – covered, open and remaining to be disclosed – it is clear that a huge part of the nation's productive resources is in the hands of the generals and their *cukongs*, who are accountable to nobody. Many of the companies are floated with bank credit, often unsoundly, with a consequent inflationary increase in the money supply. Large amounts of capital, instead of being devoted to domestic development, are exported for the benefit of a few. In such conditions there is no possibility of developing a widely based, virile, indigenous economy, or of foreign soft loans achieving the purpose that is claimed for them.

Student accusers

The government was unlucky in Lubis's timing of his attack on corruption and mismanagement in Pertamina; for, less than two months later, it felt obliged to raise the price of kerosene by 100 per cent and of petrol by 49 per cent. The announcement of the decision over radio and television on the evening of 5 January 1970 was a blow to most people, for whom kerosene, used for both cooking and lighting, was already a big item in their meagre budgets. At least one newspaper had the courage to make this point. And after an absence from public activity since May 1967, when they had demonstrated briefly against corruption, students flocked into the streets again.

Contrasting with the quick reactions of their predecessors during the struggle against Sukarno, it took ten days for the new crop of students to organize their first protest; during this period a group of them formed the Accusing Students' Movement. On 16 January 600 from universities and high schools began a series of demonstrations that were to continue on and off throughout the year. They forced an interview with the Mining Minister, and jammed traffic by stopping cars to plaster them with stickers condemning the price rises and corruption. But the demonstrations were never as big as those in the sixties, when students were incited and supported by the army and some of its political allies; troops were easily able to disperse them.

The reason for the slowness in getting the demonstrations started was that student organizations, having served the junta's purposes in the sixties, had broken up. Kappi, which consisted not only of high school children, as some writers appear to think, but thousands from elementary schools, had dissolved as soon as the excitement had died down. Kami, the university students' body, was divided in so far as it remained at all and had no properly elected leaders. The articulate few at the top had gone their various ways. Some of those who had hoped that the New Order would make Indonesia more democratic in a Western sense had turned to journalism and continued to fight for their beliefs as long as it was possible; others had become servants of the junta and were appointed members of the DPR and the MPRS. In February 1969 there were signs of life in the Kami rump when students from Bogor, Bandung and Surabaya joined some in Jakarta to debate what role, if any, the organization should play. Some students accused those who had joined forces with the junta of having betrayed the ideals of the movement, and the conference ended without taking a decision.

Army intelligence believed that a group of disenchanted politicians led by Subchan was behind this attempt to revive Kami and turn it against the army to strengthen the case for a genuine civilian share in government. Although I confess that I never got round to proving it, I believe that the intelligence men were right. I find it extremely unlikely that students from as far as Surabaya converged on Jakarta without the backing of some well-established organization. And had the anti-Pertamina demonstrations been purely spontaneous, one would have expected them to break out as soon as the price of kerosene went up. That they did not take place until ten days afterwards suggests that they were belatedly organized by some other group with, incidentally, the resources to supply printed stickers. But this is not to suggest that the student leaders had no ideas of their own.

Troops were always present, but took no action, when small student bands strutted into the Finance Ministry and Trade Department, or squatted on the floor of the Attorney-General's office to tell Lieutenant-General Soegih Arto that he should prosecute government leaders on the ground that their obvious wealth could only have been acquired by corruption. The students ignored Suharto's appeal to stay off the streets, and on 22 January 1970 about 10,000 blocked traffic in a renewed car-sticker campaign. This time a fresh note was heard; younger demonstrators had come on the scene to cry: 'Kappi lives again', which sounded suspiciously like an adult slogan uttered with a piping voice. The army, which had found children difficult to manage in the anti-Sukarno demonstrations, was determined to stand no more nonsense from this reckless lot; it immediately announced that all demonstrations were banned. The next day troops were posted at schools while officers summoned the University of Indonesia students' council to give it fatherly advice in the form of persuasion and veiled threats. Attempts to defy the ban with brief demonstrations, which vanished before the arrival of security forces, petered out when on 26 January troops broke up a gathering of 200 pupils at a school. Student leaders, a few of whom had been interrogated and released, then agreed to obey the army. But this was a tactical move, and a few weeks later they used the annual commencement procession to parade satirical devices, such as a coffin draped in military green and inscribed, 'The Aspirations of the New Order'.

A pantomime followed which displayed the students' humour, the army's strength, the pathetically low level of political discussion, and the Javanese gift for either compromise or face-saving humbug, depending on how one sees it. The students announced that they would call for a procession of 500,000 people who were concerned about corruption. But, they emphasized, it would be a *malam tirakatan*, a night of meditation, not a demonstration. Army officers feigned sympathy with this laudable project, but advised against it on the ground that wicked people might exploit it. Adam Malik, with obvious contempt for the students' intelligence, said that a street procession could impede the nation's economic development; he recommended meditation at home, in mosques or, better still, at the Heroes' Cemetery. When persuasion failed, the army forbade the gathering, meditative or not. It looked as if a nasty situation might develop until the Governor of Greater Jakarta, Lieutenant-General Ali Sadikin, offered an ingenious solution. Everyone was concerned about corruption, he said. So why not ask all citizens to turn out their lights for fifteen minutes and pray for an end to it? The students agreed, but not until six of them had been interrogated by intelligence men for thirteen hours until early in the morning; and on 15 August Jakarta was in almost total darkness from 11 to 11.15 p.m., when most people were asleep. A leader of the newly formed KAK (Committee Against Corruption), Husni Sabirin, a student of international law, said: 'We have won. The governor is supporting our campaign.'

Although the generals could smile, the night of the blackout was tense enough. Armed troops patrolled Jakarta's main street, Jalan Thamrin, and arrested Indonesia's leading dramatist, Willy Rendra, and eleven other writers and artists, who were meditating on a grass strip, along with seven newspaper reporters. While five were still being questioned, Suharto delivered next morning an Independence Eve address to the DPR in which some humourless speech-writer made him promise to build a nation 'free from fear' and to 'lead the fight against corruption'. But the atmosphere of Jakarta had been better expressed by newspapers in bitter condemnation of threats that had been made several days earlier by Lieutenant-General Sumitro, Deputy Commander of Kopkamtib (Command for Restoration of Order and Security). The still outspoken newspaper *Harian Kami*, which originated as the organ of the students' organization, said editors and students 'went home panic-stricken' from a conference with Sumitro. The Catholic newspaper, *Kompas*, said editors were 'shocked' at the army's threat to 'enter directly into the press world'.

Kept off the streets for the time being, the students found other means of making their point. On 27 August a delegation waited on Soegih Arto to present him with a yellow star on a red background – a medal, they called it – and a 'charter of merit' for having upheld laws against corruption. The charter eloquently praised Soegih Arto for having just prosecuted nine very minor electricity officials, one of whom was accused of having misappropriated 150 rupians (less than 50 US cents). Soegih Arto, whose humour at the expense of political prisoners will be recalled, found this joke too much to bear and stalked indignantly from his office. The junta, whose crassness seemed to be unlimited at times, had launched its trifling prosecutions as part of a campaign to convince the people that it was dealing with corruption. But nobody was deceived. The newspaper, *Pedoman*, expressed the views of all when it said: 'Big men who have enriched themselves by using their positions and connexions and have scooped up state funds amounting to millions of dollars – not rupiahs – are scot-free.'

In his 16 August speech Suharto had already surpassed Soegih Arto's cynicism with remarks that could only have come from a leader who had guns to protect him from public anger. Although David had not yet written his letter, and the disgusted officers were yet to circulate their report, many of the political public were aware of the manipulations of the generals and the *cukongs*. Lubis had exposed Soerjo, and it was not only the editor of *Pedoman* who knew that the state was being robbed of huge sums. Yet Suharto, though closely surrounded by corruption as he evidently was, dared to pose as a protector of the nation's funds. Totally without relevance to what everyone knew to be the real issue, he said that since 1969 ninety-four civil servants had been convicted of corruption and 506 disciplined. With this evidence of strong action, he turned to the corruption commission, which he had set up at the height of Lubis's campaign, but whose report would never have been published if it had not been leaked to the Protestant newspaper, *Sinar Harapan*, whose version of it is the only source of its contents to this day. Suharto made no comment on the commission's findings that Pertamina had failed to pay its very substantial income tax, an important factor in the national budget; instead, he embarked on a sickening defence of Sutowo. Nor did he mention the commission's confirmation that the finances of the state rice authority, which was run by a general, were 'out of order', and that there had been 'deviations' in the sale of lucrative timber concessions to foreign companies. He said: 'From the various steps taken . . . it is clear that most of the commission's suggestions run, as a matter of fact, parallel to what has been done by the government.' He overlooked the fact that one of the proposals was that Waringin Finance Ltd, whose directors included two of the Suharto circle's *cukongs*, should be prosecuted immediately for irregularities.

Newspapers did not dare to criticize Suharto's speech, but some occasionally reminded the public that the real corruption was in the highest places. On 12 December 1972 *Harian Kami*, which was later banned, reported that a university graduate, Deddy Hamid, had been detained for eight months after having exposed a relatively small $150,000 fraud in the Air Force, for which he worked. His wife, a university lecturer, had been threatened with prosecution for leaking state secrets when she asked a lawyer to help him. While the army had put an end to overt war-lord activity, the war-lord spirit lived on.

Whether or not the students had been provoked by politicians when they began their demonstrations, some of them emerged from their campaign seasoned and independent. The army forced them to dissolve KAK, but they expressed both their determination and their disillusionment in a sad document entitled 'Report to the People'. Recent meetings with Suharto had left them unsatisfied, they said; their complaints of abuses by his personal assistants had met with the 'lamentation of a President who said he was willing to resign if the people did not give him their confidence'. Politicians had not helped because they were confused through being in a precarious position. The students said that their fight against corruption had taught them a 'bitter political lesson'. They added: 'We have been accused of being egged on by certain political forces, of being against the armed forces, and against Suharto. We were, in fact, manoeuvred into a position sufficiently dangerous for us, which was out of proportion to our aims.' KAK was finished, the students said, but its members would fight on as individuals.

The student leaders could easily see through the puerile attempts at demagogy that were meant to fob them off. They had been unimpressed when Suharto told them: 'I do not want to spend 2,000,000 rupiahs ($5,000) on a corruption case worth only 1,000,000. That would mean a deficit.' And they had smiled when the Planning Board Chairman, Widjojo Nitisastro, gravely told them that the kerosene price rise was needed to pay for the next year's general elections – in which the army was to use force to ensure its rule – and to reduce dependence on foreign credits – which were to continue their accelerating rise.

CHAPTER EIGHT

Split and rule

A lesson for the PNI

The junta did not repress the students simply to protect its financial manipulators, but to ensure its grip on every social and political force. Suharto had decided towards the end of 1969 to go through the motions of general elections in July 1971, and some of his security generals had been in a state of nerves ever since, through fear that popular movements would get out of hand under the cover of an election campaign. In the first few months after the coup Suharto had the support of strongly anti-Communist and anti-Sukarnoist members of the political parties, notably certain Moslems, Catholics and what may be called, very roughly for convenience, the right wing of the PNI. But he felt that even these were unreliable and set about balancing one against the other. In the critical period early in 1967, when revolt in the marines and navy was still a possibility, he had sent Major-General (later Lieutenant-General) Sumitro to East Java to curb the Sukarnoists while leaving them sufficiently strong to prevent the Moslems from becoming too powerful in the province; Sarwo Edhie was removed from the North Sumatra Command to West Irian because, with his characteristic enthusiasm for such operations, he did too good a job in crushing the PNI.[1]

But this pursuit of the old political game was only a stop-gap to be retained until the junta had found a means of retaining power while seeming to observe the 1945 constitution. Various ideas were considered, the most notable of which was that of the Siliwangi Division commander, Major-General Dharsono, that political parties should be reduced to two groups, one supporting the government and the other a 'loyal opposition'. Suharto rejected this idea. Presumably he thought that the two-party system, as it was called, would leave civilians with too much room for manoeuvre. In any case he would have been reluctant to endorse the political initiative of another powerful general, particularly the commander of the Siliwangi Division, which already enjoyed enough prestige as an élite corps. When Dharsono persisted in advocating his idea in public, Suharto sent him off as Ambassador to Bangkok.

While Suharto had strengthened his control of the constitutional machinery by packing the MPRS and DPR, he still sought a more stable and reliable instrument. In May 1968 Brigadier-General (later Lieutenant-General) Ali Murtopo, Suharto's Adviser on Special Affairs, proposed formation of a new development group, which would work on projects in the villages and later become a political party;[2] to that end he gave some support to a new group led by Omar Khajam, who had been connected with the Indonesian Socialist Party (PSI), which was banned by Sukarno. But Suharto said that the army would not accept such a party because it would lead in effect to a revival of the PSI, which was anathema because of its association with regional rebellion; he told Murtopo and civilians who accompanied him, that they must take control of Sekber Golkar, an almost defunct organization, and work through that. The civilians, who included Murtopo's assistant, Lim Bian Kie, Sumiskum, who was later DPR Vice-Speaker, Soegih Arto (not the general) who became DPR majority leader, Murdopo and Sulistro, said the task would be impossible because Golkar was infested with Sukarnoists. 'That is why I need you there', Suharto replied. 'This is the only vehicle acceptable to the army. If there is an election, you must be ready.'

Sekber Golkar (known as Golkar) had been represented in Sukarno's National Front, which included leaders of the three components of Nasakom. It was a body consisting mostly of professional and other organizations (so-called functional groups) that had no party ties. After his conference with Murtopo, Suharto ordered Major-General (later Lieutenant-General) Darjatmo, a special deputy of the Army Chief of Staff, to reorganize Golkar and admit the men who were to be the spearhead of the army's election campaign. Murdopo and Sulistro were already members; by October, after certain resistance had been overcome, a new group within Golkar, the Gerakan Pembangunan (Development Movement) was formed to admit Lim Bian Kie and others.

By this time party leaders were expressing misgivings that Suharto might not carry out the decision of the March 1968 MPRS meeting to hold elections not later than July 1971. They had good reason to do so; for Ali Murtopo and all Suharto's other advisers were still strongly asserting that the country was not sufficiently under control to take the risk.[3] But Suharto was deeply concerned that the army's rule should wear the clothes of legality, to convince, not only the outside world, but possibly himself, that he was the people's chosen leader. During a discussion with his advisers in October 1969 Suharto retorted: 'If I wait for you I shall be old before the elections are held.' Realizing that Suharto had made up his mind, one of the new Golkar members warned: 'If we are to win we shall need your support.' It appears Suharto said nothing; but when the time came Golkar received all the military help that it needed to ensure victory.

After the sudden passage of election bills in the DPR, Suharto called in his civilian team on 31 December 1969 for a meeting that lasted from 8 p.m. until 11.30 p.m. and told them to prepare a campaign. An election committee was then formed with the following post-election aims: (1) no ideology except *Pancasila*; (2) political parties to be based on development programmes, not political ideas; (3) the number of political parties to be reduced; (4) villagers to participate in development between elections, but not in politics; (5) mass organizations to be divorced from political parties; (6) civil servants to be excluded from joining political parties and to be loyal only to the government. This programme was summed up in the slogan 'development before politics', and was the exact opposite of Sukarno's view that the masses could not be mobilized for development until society had been reshaped to inspire them.

The army forced civil servants to leave political parties early in the election campaign, and herded them into a single organization, Korpri, which was established to support Golkar. This measure was considered vital, for, as one Golkar leader put it (to the author), the civil service was 'the only real political infrastructure in Indonesia – from the top to the grass roots'. Patronage had given the PNI, divided though it was, vast influence among civil servants, which extended down to school teachers and heads of remote villages, who were able to capture the votes of simple people dependent on them for favours and even their livelihood. Similarly the Nahdatul Ulama (NU – Moslem Theologians' Council) wielded power through religious leaders and teachers, and bought support with the corruptly managed funds of the Department of Religion. If Golkar was to win without the application of unmitigated military force, this machinery had to be dismantled.

In this picture of a new Javanese ruling élite searching for ways to consolidate and extend its power, it would seem strange to find the figure of Catholic Action hidden among the shadows in the background. Yet it was there in the person of a Dutch Jesuit, Father Beek, who had been in Indonesia since the fifties. After the *putsch* the foreign element in the Catholic hierarchy quickly made up its mind about whom to support. As one of them said (in a conversation with the author): 'With the Communists no longer a force, there were only two possible governments, the Moslems or the army. We preferred the army.' Father Beek exerted his influence largely through Chinese Catholics, of whom Lim Bian Kie was one. There is no evidence that he went so far as to advise them on the specific aims of Golkar, although he might well have done so, for he was closely in touch with Ali Murtopo's circle. What he certainly did was to discuss such matters as how far democracy was possible in a developing country; and he wrote an article, circulated in the Defence Department, in which he warned that Moslems were using Communist-type tactics to bring about an Islamic state. There are only about 2 million Catholics in Indonesia, but the activities of Father Beek and of others equally gifted in political intrigue gave them an influence greater than their numbers indicated.

Having appointed his own election squad, Suharto immediately set about crippling the old political parties, with the intention of emasculating them completely after the poll. The first to be dealt with was the PNI, which had already been subjected to some vigorous softening up, with the arrest of some of its more vital members, the killing of leftist cadres along with Communists after the *putsch*, and an enforced change of leadership. The party's increasingly leftist trend had led to a split in August 1965, when the Central Leadership Council suspended a group of anti-left leaders. The purged men proclaimed their loyalty to Sukarno, but after the *putsch* they formed a splinter PNI and supported Suharto, although some were later forced out of politics altogether when they resisted the junta's moves towards dictatorship. The original PNI, which with the veteran Ali Sastroamidjojo as its General Chairman retained the bulk of popular backing, continued to support Sukarno. According to Sastroamidjojo (in an interview with the author in January 1973; he has since died), Suharto invited him to his house early in 1966 and said: 'I am worried about the situation in the PNI. It is the only national party and could be a counter-balance to the Moslems.' Sastroamidjojo agreed to Suharto's suggestion that a conference should be held to reconcile the two groups..But when the conference took place in Bandung in April 1966, armed troops stopped Sastroamidjojo's supporters from entering the hall; Sastroamidjojo was howled down when he tried to speak; and Osa Maliki, head of the splinter group, was elected General Chairman of what was supposed to be a reunited PNI. Sastroamidjojo immediately wrote to Suharto: 'I am obliged to report to you, because you took the initiative in the convening of the congress. It has worked out that there is no real unity and no real restoration of the strength of the PNI.' After a political career that began in the 1920s, when he was arrested by the Dutch in Holland and acquitted of a charge of subversion, he then retired from politics.

After Osa Maliki's death a conference was held in Semarang in April 1970 to elect a new General Chairman. A week earlier Suharto had expressed his goodwill to the party and had given an assurance that there would be no interference in its affairs. But the army broke Suharto's promise and gave delegates a foretaste of the intimidation that was to mount as the general election campaign got under way. Ali Murtopo had decided that Hadisubeno Sosrowerdjojo, and not the Acting General Chairman, Hardi, should be the new PNI leader, although both had belonged to the Osa Maliki faction. Murtopo personally set up a post near the conference hall; and his officers, dressed in civilian clothes, visited delegates in their hotels and forced them to sign away their votes. Some PNI members put up a strong resistance; at least one was interrogated all night and threatened with arrest on the ground that he had belonged to a Communist-controlled student organization in 1955; several had their party cards torn up; others were forbidden to enter the hall. After eight days the conference chairman announced that Hadisubeno had been elected; he did not take a vote, but said that 230 out of 238 delegates had signed in the new chairman's favour. Later it appeared that Murtopo had made a mistake in backing Hadisubeno, who proved to be one of the most intransigent of the few politicians who confronted the army in public; but the PNI had been taught a lesson, which most of its influential members did not forget.

Far though the junta had advanced on its march of political extermination, one very formidable obstacle remained: Sukarno was still alive. Before his overthrow Sukarno had challenged the junta to hold elections, the outcome of which would be either to confirm or reject him as president. The generals justified his continued detention on the ground that they were investigating his involvement in the *putsch*. To hold the elections without first trying him would not only appear irregular, but might be exploited by elements in the PNI, which had drawn some of its symbols from the party founded by Sukarno in 1927.[4] But the junta had only circumstantial evidence against Sukarno, which was much less convincing than that against Suharto, whose meeting with Latief on the eve of the *putsch* would have been sufficient to incriminate anyone on the other side. Unable to convict Sukarno and unwilling to free him, and always nervous and prone to over-react, the junta would have been loath to hold the elections while he lived.

The death of Sukarno

Sukarno obliged the junta by dying in Jakarta central military hospital at 0710 hours on 21 June 1970. The officially stated cause of death was his chronic kidney disease, but relatives said that his end was hastened by the almost total isolation that the army enforced upon him after his overthrow in March 1968. No less grievous, it seems, was a broken heart; in an outburst to Hartini, one of his wives,[5] he made a bitter comparison between the treatment he had received as a prisoner of the Dutch, who allowed him freedom of communication and discussion within the limits of his place of exile, and his merciless confinement by his own people, for whom he had 'done so much'. An Indonesian doctor told a Western diplomat that another factor in the timing of his death may have been cortisone, which had apparently been administered over a considerable period to maintain his blood pressure; this drug, it was thought, produced the moon face observed by those (including the author) who saw him when he lay briefly in state.

Sukarno's last two years were a tragic finale to the life of the man who had done most to infuse Indonesians with the sense of national identity that led to their independence. His detention was called house arrest, but imprisonment would have been a better description. At first he was allowed to move under guard between his house, Batu Tulis, at Bogor, where he lived with Hartini, and another in the outskirts of Jakarta, formerly occupied by Ratna Sari Dewi, who had returned to Japan. But in September 1968 the army confined him to Dewi's house, a large, rambling bungalow, set deep in a high-walled, overgrown garden. There, apart from limited family visits, he was only allowed the company of military interrogators, thirty guards and servants.

Accustomed to comings and goings at the palace and the applause of the millions whom he had harangued, Sukarno became increasingly depressed by his incarceration. For a time Hartini was allowed to see him three times a week, from 10 a.m. to 4 p.m.; on Sundays she took their two sons with her. The five children of his marriage to Fatmawati, whom Hartini had superseded in 1954, also visited him occasionally. Early in 1969 neither Hartini nor any of his children could obtain permits to visit Sukarno. Hartini says they were given no explanation; she adds:[6]

After about four months we were allowed to see him again. He wept like a child as soon as he saw us. His health and spirit were irreparably broken. His hair had turned completely grey. He looked very pale. The loneliness of those four months had been more than he could stand. It tipped the balance in the battle against his illness.

The children of his previous marriage and I were later given permits to see him once a month, all together. This was soon increased to twice, and then to three times a month.

In the last six months of his life he rarely spoke. All he
said was a few words about his daily needs and other
essential matters. Even those words were incoherent.
Perhaps he could have spoken more if he had wished to do
so. But he did not seem to care about anything. He
appeared to be indifferent to whether he was alive or dead.

Sukarno was admitted to the military hospital on Suharto's
orders on 16 June. His approaching death raised the problem of
where he was to be buried and whether he was to receive a state
funeral. Technically, he had been under detention pending
Suharto's decision on whether to prosecute him for involvement
in the 1965 *putsch* – a holding charge on which people were
arrested even in the seventies. Some generals were opposed to his
being accorded state honours, partly because of his alleged guilt
and partly because the junta's enemies could use the occasion to
whip up public feeling. The army was extremely nervous; within
a few hours of Sukarno's death all troops in the Jakarta garrison
were put on the alert. But not to make some gesture to the founder
of the nation might also have caused an outcry. Suharto, with his
impeccable judgment on such occasions, found the solution. He
decided to hold a state funeral that would be quick, safe and
meaningless. Sukarno was allowed to lie in state at Dewi's house
until the morning after his death, when he was whisked off by
plane to Malang, taken by road to Blitar, East Java and buried
next to his mother.

This clever device was represented in foreign news media as a
magnanimous act. On the day of Sukarno's death the BBC
World Service announced that Suharto was to give a funeral
oration. This is the oration, which Suharto delivered outside
Dewi's house: 'According to the decision of the government, you
[General Maraden Panggabean, Deputy Commander-in-Chief
of the Armed Forces] are hereby assigned as inspector of ceremony
for the funeral of Haji Dr Sukarno. I therefore hand the late Dr
Sukarno to you for burial at a state funeral.' That is all Suharto
had to say about the man who had striven since his youth, first to
create and then to guide Indonesia. On the day Sukarno died a
mean tribute was paid to him in a frigid government communiqué.
After announcing his death the communiqué immediately made
the point that Sukarno's declining health had interrupted

investigations into the 'legal affair' (his alleged involvement in the putsch); for this reason his case had not been brought to court. Nevertheless, the communiqué said, it was 'proper to pay respect to the services of the late Dr Sukarno towards the struggle of the Indonesian nation, particularly as the independence *proklamator* of the Republic [the least of his services]'. It had therefore been decided to hold a state funeral and to hoist the national flag at half-mast for seven days.

Thousands of people filed passed Sukarno's coffin when he lay in state in Dewi's house. Men and women of all ages, some wheeling huge wreaths in little carts, made their way down the drive and packed the verandah as they waited their turn for a last glimpse of the man who had been a president to all and a king to most. Many of the mourners were young; some carried babies. About fifty people, mostly old women with a mystical air, sat cross-legged on the floor, gazing silently at the coffin. Clouds of white incense drifted across the room.

Scores of thousands lined the route when the body was taken to Halim air base next day to be flown to Blitar. At the airport Sukarno's coffin was carried across the tarmac to the beat of muffled drums. It was all in perfect taste. But it was clear that the junta was despatching Sukarno to the farthest possible place in the shortest possible time. After pall-bearers representing all services had lifted the coffin into an air force plane, a young woman rushed forward and shrieked hysterically: 'Where is Bung Karno? Is this all they are doing for him?' Struggling and screaming, she was gently dragged from the tarmac by a group of young men, who tried to stifle her cries; some of them were sobbing. Crowds estimated at half a million paid tribute to Sukarno in East Java; many people had made their way from Central Java. Hundreds of thousands were at the roadside when the coffin was taken from Malang to Blitar; they were kept in order by soldiers, who stood at intervals with fixed bayonets.

For a while both the army and Moslem political leaders were more afraid of Sukarno dead than alive. They thought the PNI was certain to exploit Sukarno's death in the election campaign; but more dangerous was that a Sukarno cult, which had been in evidence for some time, would grip the peasantry and lead to frenzy akin to the Ratu Adil phenomenon. There were rumours that mystics planned to seize Sukarno's body and take it to a secret place, where it would become a shrine for cult leaders. The generals put a heavy guard on the grave and ordered provincial governors to report on public feeling. The army newspaper, *Berita Yudha*, said that the outcome would be unpredictable if Sukarno's fanatical followers were influenced by 'poisonous rumours spread by those who instigated the *putsch*'. Within a month of Sukarno's death the East Java military commander ruled that nobody could visit the grave without giving two weeks' notice to military authorities; he warned that if the PNI made trouble it would have to face the army.

The generals tried to obliterate Sukarno's name even beyond Indonesia. In 1973 it was announced in Karachi that a small monument to Sukarno, consisting of a building with three minarets, was being built at Lakarna, Pakistan, near the house of the Prime Minister, Zulfikar Ali Bhutto, on Bhutto's orders. The monument was completed, but the Indonesian junta applied pressure and prevented its inauguration.

Legge writes:[7]

> With his death it was possible for President Suharto's government to soften towards him and a decision was quickly made that he would be given a state funeral. Official spokesmen remembered his achievements as well as his failures and he was viewed once again as the father of his country.

This report needs correcting. I do not know to which spokesmen Legge is referring. But, whoever they were and whatever they said, the junta's continued hostility to Sukarno was clear from its communiqué and its actions, the most heinous of which was to stain his memory with the unsubstantiated implication that he was involved in the murder of the six generals in 1965, and that but for his illness he would have been brought to trial. The generals' chronic nervousness and the political climate of the time ruled out any softening of policy. Sukarno was not restored as 'the father of his country'; he was buried in an unmarked grave, with nothing to show that he lay there. He was not even restored as the father of his family; his children, who had been obliged to obtain army authorization to see him during his detention, now required permits to visit the cemetery.

Sukarno did not ask to be buried next to his mother, much though he loved her. He said in his autobiography that he wished his 'final home to be the cool, mountainous, fertile Priangan area of Bandung', where, he recalled, he had met Marhaen. He asked that his casket be 'wrapped with the flag of the Islamic order, Mohammadiyah'. There must be no imposing monument, proclaiming his various high offices of President, Commander-in-Chief, etc. All he wanted was a 'plain little stone' inscribed: 'Here lies Bung Karno, the mouthpiece of the Indonesian people.'

Indonesian history is one of recurrent surprise. The least surprise of all would be the fulfilment of Sukarno's wish before this century was out.

The Golkar campaign

With the Sukarno problem resolved and the elections only a year ahead, the junta intensified its onslaught against the remains of the political structure. The Minister for the Interior, Major-General (later Lieutenant-General) Amir Machmud, bluntly expressed the attitude of the generals when he said he would use 'foul play' if it was needed to 'preserve the nation's stability'; he proved as good as his word when forcing civil servants to break up their old associations and join Korpi, which owed 'mono-loyalty' to the government. His fellow officers went further in a brilliantly co-ordinated campaign, which ranged from the splitting of political and professional bodies to sheer terror. Local military commanders used such methods as they found necessary to ensure Golkar's victory; some chose torture and, occasionally, murder. As General Nasution put it (in an interview with the author in January 1973): 'If the top [Suharto] says it wants 51 per cent [of votes], the [provincial] governor says 60 per cent, the *bupati* [regent] 70 per cent and the *lurah* [village head] 90 per cent, to be safe.' In the year preceding the elections I reported the arrest of more than 1,500 people who were said to have either violated the election laws or to have been involved in the 1965 *putsch*; what they had done, in fact, was to refuse to desert their political parties in favour of Golkar. The arrests were all published in Jakarta newspapers as having been announced by military commanders, doubtless as a warning to others; the total number was probably much larger, for there must have been many arrests that were never disclosed. Most, if not all, of those arrested were released in time to advise their villages that it might be better to vote for Golkar after all.

The army was not only engaged in the use of brute force. Everywhere the Golkar team spread the message that there could be no more politics in Indonesia until after a period of economic development optimistically estimated at twenty-five years, during which it was hoped to overtake Japan; politics were a luxury that could not be afforded in the hard struggle that lay ahead; only Golkar, which was said to be non-political, could be entrusted with the tasks that faced the nation. On the face of it this was a good argument. Ever since independence politicians had frittered away their energies with insane wrangling and had done virtually nothing to lift the people from their poverty. Now a new era was promised, in which economists and the armed forces would strive together to lay the basis of an economy that would bring prosperity. In Jakarta, at least, most journalists and senior civil servants, who were relatively prosperous under the New Order, supported Golkar. Many who joined, endorsing the intimidation as a necessary evil, believed that they were to be given an opportunity to play a vital part in reconstructing the nation. Later they were to be disillusioned. But for the time being an editor who said, 'all the intellectuals support Golkar' was not far off the mark. On the other hand, there was a trace of truth in the rejoinder of a foreign journalist who said: 'There are no intellectuals in Jakarta: they are all on Buru Island.'

The PNI's role as patron made large-scale desertion to Golkar inevitable, even without the ever-present intimidation. For many years, despite cabinet changes, PNI ministers had run the departments of information, the interior and education and staffed them with their supporters. While some of the party's members were dedicated to such coherent ideas as it possessed, many saw the PNI as little more than a protector of jobs, and had few qualms of conscience when they switched their loyalty to a group associated with the new and powerful master. At the same time the generals felt it necessary to continually emphasize their might.

The junta made no attempt to conceal its use of government equipment for electioneering purposes, since in Indonesia there are no legal niceties like those that brought Mrs Indira Gandhi to trial for malpractice in India's 1971 elections; it used the Ministry of Information, radio and television for its propaganda. Throughout the archipelago the Golkar teams worked hand in hand with the army; they frequently travelled in army jeeps and lorries, although many were given Honda motor cycles on which, wearing brand-new sun glasses, a prestige symbol, they made a sinister impression as they roared into villages when roads were good enough. In Jakarta Golkar raised $250,000 for its campaign at a single cabaret dinner when 500 business men, mostly Chinese, paid $500 a ticket; a Japanese, who bought five tickets, was rewarded with a seat next to the Trade Minister, Sumitro Djojohadikusumo.

The actions against politicians in the towns and common people in the villages were accompanied by a series of nasty announcements that were obviously intended to cow the ignorant. The first was made as early as September 1970, when Amir Machmud said that 400 sharp-shooters would help to 'safeguard the elections'. Several weeks later it was announced that 11,000 tear gas bombs and smoke grenades were being made at the government arsenal in Bandung, although no mention was made of the arsenal's stock of light missiles, which, an officer told me, could be useful for breaking up crowds. The Defence and Security Department then said that it would hold 'joint combat exercises' throughout Indonesia from 8 to 19 December. This time there was no nonsensical attempt to invent an enemy like *Musang*, who was supposed to have invaded West Java a year earlier; the exercises were frankly and ominously named Operation Authority, and doubtless thousands upon thousands of villagers were made to feel the army's might, as in Cirebon. It was claimed that in one manoeuvre a brigade of troops was flown from Bandung to North Sumatra.

In March 1971 Major-General Yoga Sugomo, an intelligence chief, told a conference of newspaper editors that a large-scale operation against Communists was to be carried out. He said the situation was 'boiling' and predicted that inter-party bitterness would increase. 'Do not be surprised if later you hear reports of many arrests', he said. What he meant was that the army would be arresting many of Golkar's opponents; his aim at this stage was to condition the minds of editors to accept the increased use of force. The newspaper, *Harian Kami*, commented that the 'terrifying psy war' reflected in the generals' statements gave the impression that Indonesia was preparing for battle, rather than a general election. Unnerving though it was for the people, some of the threatening was probably a pretext to incur expense on security. The total cost of the army's purely military election measures was officially stated to be more than $8 million in addition to $50 million allocated for normal polling expenses. In a country in which auditing is virtually non-existent, these sums must have provided many a plum for those disbursing them at various levels.

There has been speculation among academics about whether Golkar could have succeeded without the army's widespread intimidation of voters, but this unanswerable question becomes less interesting when it is seen that Suharto was determined to win at any cost; the people, whether they voted in fear or not, were certain to find themselves with a Golkar majority. The candidates to be elected on 3 July 1971 were not only to be members of the central, provincial, or regency parliaments, but would provide the majority in the MPR, the supreme governing body. In March 1973 the MPR was to decide whether or not Suharto would continue as President for a further five years, and to lay down the national policy lines for that period. The result of the elections was therefore vital, and Suharto would not have taken the slightest risk with them; it was inconceivable that the junta would relinquish power after having seized and consolidated it so ruthlessly. Suharto required a constitutional cloak, to satisfy his Javanese quest for harmony no less than for more practical reasons; but if the electorate had proved less manageable than he had estimated, he would certainly have postponed the elections, as he had done before, on the ground of either security or the exigencies of economic development. Since 1966 the junta had tightened its hold on the MPRS by packing it with new allies and offering perquisites to some of the older professionals. Now it was poised for a final leap to unchallengeable rule through an assembly, which, though technically elected by the people, would be pliable in its hands. There was nothing new in the attacks on the parties and the terrorizing of villagers, which merely extended the progressive destruction of political rivals that began with the confrontation of Sukarno, the 1965 massacre, and the mauling of the PNI in 1966.

Disfranchisement, which may be regarded as the limit of political intimidation, short of imprisonment or murder, was

certainly a substantial factor. On 30 October 1970 the General
Elections Institute, which organized the election machinery,
announced that 1,900,000 would not be allowed to vote on the
ground that they were involved directly or indirectly in the 1965
putsch or had been members of organizations that were now prohibited. The number eligible was given as 57,038,347, later
adjusted to 58,179,245. In the closing days of the campaign
institute officials said they did not know the number disfranchised.
The total of votes was said after the poll to be 54,696,887, excluding those in West Irian.

The junta also purged the candidates of the nine political
parties. It attempted to conceal the severity of this measure by
announcing the disqualifications in three stages in March and
April 1971: the final list did not mention the number submitted
in the first. Golkar, which was in fact a tenth party despite its
protests of being non-political, emerged as the biggest contestant
in the field with 538. The PNI, the biggest loser, was cut by 171,
a large number of whom were school teachers, from 677 to 506;
the NU was permitted 397 candidates of the 421 nominated and
the other important Moslem party, Parmusi, 327 out of 468; the
PSII (Moslem) came through the sieve with 309 candidates,
IPKI (National) 295, Murba (leftist national) 193, Parkindo
(Protestant) 182, Perti (Moslem) 150 and Partai Katolik (Catholic)
115. The government explained that those disqualified had not
complied with regulations obliging them to produce health
certificates, biographical information and documents exonerating
them from involvement in the *putsch*; as the *putsch* clearance
could be withheld from anyone whom the army disliked, it was a
useful tool for weeding out some of those who had minds of their
own. The army was too shrewd to include military men among the
Golkar candidates; officers were, in any case, to be nominated
to both the DPR and MPR. Nevertheless, several newspapers
protested that wives of ministers, governors and military commanders were on the Golkar list.

The assault on the Moslems

While the Communists had been virtually annihilated and the
secular nationalists mortally wounded, the army had so far
left the Moslems largely unscathed. Islamic roots in the nation's

political and social life were so deep and widespread that the army prudently deferred its open assault on the Moslem parties until it had exploited their active help or moral support in reducing the others. Indonesian Islam is a complex and sometimes contentious subject, which contains enough pitfalls for the scholar, let alone the layman. Yet some attempt to grasp its significance has to be made, for no study of Indonesia's problems is of use unless this significant force is taken into account.

It will be enough here to deal briefly with Java. Although for the most part the Javanese are nominally Islamic, their religion is permeated with Hindu and pre-Hindu beliefs and practices, syncretically mixed in proportions that vary from region to region and person to person. Seen as in a spectrum, the Islamic component is scarcely visible at one end, but it becomes increasingly pronounced towards the other, where it attains relative purity as the Hindu and primitive elements fade away. Among Sundanese in West Java Islam is said to be about as pure as anywhere in the world. Geertz's widely copied division of the various combinations of beliefs and attitudes into three classes is considered by Dutch scholars to be unworkable.[8]

Javanese whose beliefs and practices are much less Islamic than Hindu and pre-Hindu are called *abangan* (the red ones), not usually by themselves but, in a depreciatory sense, by purer Moslems (some of whom call themselves *putihan* – the white ones). They often speak of themselves as subscribing to *agama Jawa*, which is translated as Javanese religion, although the word *agama* at once falls `short of and goes beyond the Western equivalent; these people refer to themselves as 'statistical Moslems', which means that for the purposes of official records they are Islamic, rather than, say, Hindu or Christian. But purer Moslems would not call them Moslems; nor would their diverse beliefs be easy to categorize. In the middle of the spectrum it is difficult to distinguish clearly between beliefs that could be called *abangan* and those that are relatively pure Moslem. While there is a certain amount of antipathy between the *abangan* and the purer Moslems in some areas, Islamic religious leaders and teachers in the villages are sometimes sympathetic to *abangan* beliefs. With the *ulama* (Moslem theologians), their hold on the peasants has always given them a potential power that no ruler has been able to ignore. The peasant following of the NU, for instance, is substantially *abangan*, although the party is loosely described in some books as orthodox Moslem.

Before the arrival of the Dutch the *ulama*, whose hearts were in Mecca, had annoyed some rulers in the archipelago. From the seclusion of the *pesantren* they challenged the heresies and materialism of the aristocracy; they wielded power over the people with threats of hell and promises of paradise; and they spread Islamic law to the detriment of the *adat*. In the second half of the nineteenth century war with Aceh, where Islam is strong, caused the Dutch government to appoint the renowned Arabist, Christiaan Snouck Hurgronje, as adviser on Islamic affairs in the Indies. During the Second World War the Japanese army sought to make allies of the Moslems by setting up the Masjumi, an Indonesian Islamic council, and permitting it to have its own armed corps.

After independence Darul Islam movements, which were established outside the Moslem political parties, made separate attempts to set up Islamic states. The first rebellion broke out in West Java in 1949 and was followed by others in Aceh and South Sulawesi. In West Java the Indonesian Islamic Army was said to have killed about 1,000 people a year in raids on government posts up till 1955; in Aceh the rebellion took place mainly in 1953; in South Sulawesi it continued intermittently until it was crushed in 1965. But Darul Islam was an extreme movement. Under Sukarno's guided democracy the Moslem parties formed the bulk of the religious pillar of Nasakom, although Sukarno forced the Masjumi, which had been newly formed after the defeat of the Japanese, to dissolve itself along with the PSI. While Sukarno had accepted the political role of Islam, Suharto did not; and his confrontation of the Moslem parties revived the formidable problems that had beset the old Javanese rulers, the Dutch and the Japanese.

In 1955, when Indonesia held its only general elections before those of 1971, the combined votes of the four Moslem parties far exceeded those of any other group. The Moslems won 43.5 per cent, the two secular national parties (PNI and IPKI) 23.7 per cent and the PKI 16.4 per cent, with minor parties making up the rest. The Masjumi alone polled 20.9 per cent compared with the PNI's 22.3 per cent and the two parties were equal in winning fifty-seven seats each, the greatest number won by any party.

Substantial though the Moslem vote was, it did not indicate the potential strength in 1971. With the PKI destroyed and the PNI under attack, there was a strong possibility that large numbers of the masses would rally to the already powerful Moslem parties with their far-reaching affiliated bodies. The army was aware of this danger. It was easy enough to ensure the loyalty of the small PSII and smaller Perti; but the NU, which obtained 18.4 per cent of the votes and 45 seats in 1955, and the Parmusi (Partai Muslimin Indonesia) required more drastic treatment.

Suharto set up the Parmusi by decree in February 1968, knowing that it would include former members of the Masjumi, which had been defunct since Sukarno forced it to dissolve. Dahm's statement that Suharto took this action, 'evidently hoping that this would content the adherents of Masjumi' provides an example of the difficulty of interpreting Indonesian politics from a distance.[9] Suharto, in fact, limited the Masjumi influence when he excluded certain former members of it from the Parmusi executive board. The Masjumi, like the banned PSI, was detested by many Javanese officers for its involvement in the Sumatran rebellion. Some of its leaders favoured a theocracy, and the most moderate wanted to temper the secularism desired by the army and the non-Islamic parties; all were regarded as dangerous and Suharto knew that they would not be satisfied to sit back and rubber-stamp army decisions. Suharto's aim was not to content them, for there was little they could do without a political organization, but to use the Parmusi to help pack the MPRS, which was to elect him President in the following month. It was a daring move, but it showed Suharto's confidence that he could handle any political problem that arose. Inevitably, some of the Masjumi leaders began to show their old spirit. And just as inevitably Ali Murtopo followed up his undermining of the PNI at Semarang with an operation against the Parmusi; his first target was the party General Chairman, Djarnawi Hadikusuma, who was considered insufficiently resistant to Masjumi influence.

This time Ali Murtopo artfully concealed the bludgeon by putting on one of those political playlets of which he is master. He chose as his opening character John Naro, whom he had been schooling in various strategems for some years. Naro, known as Johnny, was a neat, sly man who, like Ali Murtopo, had close American connexions; he was a leader of the Vietnam lobby,

which intermittently clamoured for Indonesian recognition of
South Vietnam, and he frequently visited Saigon. Murtopo had
planted him as one of the six chairmen of the Parmusi when
Suharto established it by decree in February 1968. On 17 October
1970 Naro called a meeting of selected executive members and
announced that he had been obliged to take over the leadership,
because the established board was acting against the party's
interests by opposing the government. With the dumbfounded
party members thrown into confusion, Amir Machmud – the
Minister for the Interior – stepped on to the stage. It was most
regrettable, he said, that discord should have arisen in one of the
great religious parties; the dispute must be settled in the national
interest. This was Suharto's cue to enter gravely and declare that
since the party was created with his blessing he would favour it
with his mediation; he must be impartial, he said, and not show
prejudice by choosing either Djarnawi or Naro; he therefore ruled
that Mintaredja, one of his ministers of state, should be chairman.
Mintaredja was a member of the Parmusi, but, like Naro, had
never been conspicuous in Moslem politics. It appeared that he
had been kept in the sinecure of Minister of State for Liaison
Affairs for use on an occasion such as this; he fought the elections
with the slogan, 'Golkar's victory is Parmusi's victory.'

Meanwhile, behind the public scene, Djarnawi had refused to
accept the President's mediation from the moment it was proposed.
With courage that is rarely shown by Indonesian politicians, he
resisted both blandishments and threats. Five visits from Ali
Murtopo and one from Major-General Sutopo Juwono, the head
of Bakin (Intelligence Co-ordinating Body), who seized all his
branch membership lists, failed to weaken him. Immediately the
President's ruling was announced Djarnawi's board met and
rejected it. On 20 November 1970 Djarnawi was still defying the
decision on the ground that it did not bind the party, and he
refused to hand over the administration and offices to Mintaredja.
When Amir Machmud accused him of breaking the law he
retorted that Suharto had appointed him chairman by decree.
The next day Suharto simply issued another decree, establishing a
new board with Mintaredja as chairman.

Djarnawi's stand made such an impression on me that I went
to see him at his house. I expected to find him in one of the
commodious bungalows, set in spacious gardens, which fell into

the hands of many politicians when the Dutch were forced to leave. But this was not Djarnawi's style; I traced him to one of a row of tiny houses that lined both sides of an unmade road, which was just wide enough for my car to pass through without running over children who played at the side. When I entered the house, white-robed girls briefly appeared from the back; apparently they had been at prayers. Djarnawi's wife came into the barely furnished sitting room with soft drinks. Djarnawi, after cautiously parrying some of my questions by making jokes, said he had been deposed because he did not get rid of the old Masjumi leaders in the party branches. While he had agreed with the army that new blood was desirable, he thought that the pace should not be forced. But he must have known that the main issue was that the army did not want any party that it did not control or, in the end, any party at all.

My encounter with Djarnawi cured much of the disgust I had come to feel about Indonesia. The plutocratic, bullying generals, economic mismanagement, the low level of public discussion, corruption in all walks of life including religion, and the ignorance of the masses had induced a feeling that Indonesia was drifting beyond help. But now I saw just a spark of hope. I felt that in meeting this brave, incorruptible respresentative of the better side of Indonesian Islam, I had at last glimpsed a sterling trait in the nation's make-up.

Suharto's liquidation of the old board was not immediately effective. Djarnawi insisted he would carry on at the Parmusi headquarters; Mintaredja, he said, would have to find other premises; the nine members of the 35-man executive who had supported Naro would be excluded from board meetings. Djarnawi was fighting from a solid base: the Parmusi's offices were provided by the Muhammadiyah, which claimed 9 million members, ran 6,000 educational establishments ranging from kindergartens to what were classed as universities, and drew revenues from printing works, the sale of books, and gifts from the well-to-do. At a special national party conference on 22 November men who claimed to represent 12 million Moslems belonging to the Parmusi and affiliated organizations rejected the appointment of Mintaredja and decided to hit back at Suharto by boycotting the elections. Djarnawi, however, was careful not to use the word 'boycott', which would have made him liable to five years' imprisonment for 'undermining or obstructing' the elections. Instead he announced that from that date all party branches would be 'inactive'. But before many weeks had passed Ali Murtopo and his men, backed by Bakin and with the decree in their hands, had worn down all resistance. The old board, or part of it, met on 12 April 1971, and agreed that Mintaredja should be chairman; some held handkerchiefs over their eyes to hide their tears when they voted. Djarnawi did not consent, but disappeared from politics. When I called to see him before leaving Indonesia at the beginning of 1973, neighbours said that he, his wife and the children who had appeared in white robes at our first meeting had all moved to Yogyakarta, whence they had come.

The Masjumi and its inheritor, the Parmusi, were usually said to be the political wing of modernist Islam, which had found social expression in the Muhammadiyah, while the other large Moslem party, the NU, was considered to represent orthodoxy: the modernists leave themselves open to fresh interpretations of the Koran and Hadith in refusing to be bound by those that the orthodox accept. But research is needed into the extent to which it has become necessary to qualify this distinction between the two parties, which were united until the NU broke away from the Masjumi in 1952. While the NU leadership clung in theory to orthodox Islam, it was permeated with *abangan* beliefs. It is said that true, or relatively true, Moslems were more likely to be found in the Masjumi than in the NU; the modern thinking that opened their minds to new interpretations of the Koran also protected them from the full force of *abangan* superstition. Politicians who were not greatly concerned with theological hair-splitting were found in both parties; the NU's First Chairman, Subchan, the 'dancing *ulama*' referred to in chapter IV, had little in common with the introversion of the *pesantren*; and in East Java I found members of the party's youth organization, Ansor, whose education and outlook were broader than one would expect to be obtainable from *ulama*. 'What do you think of Golkar's slogan, "development before politics"?', I asked one of them. 'It is a political statement', he said. This answer might have been given on the bank of the Seine.

The NU was especially dangerous. Most of its timid leaders would have quickly succumbed to the army, as they had done to Sukarno; but among them was Subchan, dogged and irrepressible, who forced even some of the opportunists to support his militant actions through fear that they would lose influence in the branches if they opposed him or remained silent. The explosive mixture of Islam, mysticism and social discontent in the NU-dominated villages was thus not merely in the hands of the *ulama, kyahi,* and decrepit urban politicians; it could be ignited by a man who understood American methods of political campaigning and was determined to fight the army's rule. Subchan had seen early that the Suharto junta was bent on establishing a military dictatorship; that was why he urged General Nasution, who wanted a genuine return to the 1945 constitution, to take over the presidency in 1965. He was disappointed, almost to the point of contempt, at what he believed to have been Nasution's weakness. 'Nasution dribbles well, but he will never score a goal', he once said (in a conversation with the author). The junta had seen Subchan's capability during its brief alliance with him in the over-throwing of of Sukarno; it now regarded him as its most implacable enemy.

It appears that Ali Murtopo planned to deal with the NU from the inside, much as he had done with the PNI at Semarang, but that Subchan forestalled him by ensuring that the party congress at which the coup was to have taken place was postponed until after the elections. But the junta still had terror as a weapon, and used it to force villages in NU areas to support Golkar. In April 1971 an NU leader, *Haji* Hisbullah Huda, Vice-Speaker of the East Java Provincial Parliament, said that arrest and torture had reduced almost all villagers in East Java to constant fear. His disclosure that several NU members had committed suicide reflected the dread of countless simple people that they would be consumed by hell fire if they deserted the *kyahi* and punished by the army if they did not; for some the choice was too terrible to make, and the only way out was to kill themselves. But the fears of the more easily frightened were matched by the anger of the more courageous. And Huda warned that hundreds of thousands of Ansor youth and millions of NU members were only awaiting the command to launch a *jihat* (holy war). The NU Second Chairman, Achmad Sjaichu, called on Ansor members to be prepared to die. This was probably little more than electioneering, for Sjaichu's public reassurances of loyalty to Suharto suggested that he did not share the fighting spirit of men like Subchan. But there was no question that in rural areas NU passions were intense; and Nuddin Lubis, the NU leader in the DPR, expressed the feelings of many Moslems when he said: 'Force and intimidation are raging in almost every province of our country. People are pleading for help, yet the government insists that there is no intimidation.'

In May the NU executive board began publishing branch reports containing details of the army's campaign. They were a catalogue of beatings, bleeding noses, fainting under torture and murder. A village elder was asked by a sub-regency official to name the *kyahi* who had delivered a certain sermon; he declined to answer and was hit on the head and threatened with dismissal. Military police alternately ducked Ansor youths and baked them in the sun; ninety-three villagers were forced to stand in the sun and were beaten until they put the Golkar symbol, a banyan tree, on their identity cards. Villagers were warned that if they did not join Golkar they would be sent to Buru Island; others were threatened with transportation to West Irian; and another group were told that they would be shot. Troops fired over the heads of villagers during a prayer meeting. A villager was beaten when he refused to disclose who had made a Golkar symbol from cow dung. In each case the place of the atrocity was given. Ten thousand workers at a state plantation at Jember, East Java, were told they would be evicted from their homes if they did not vote for Golkar. To the Western newspaper reader, hardened to the shocks of large-scale massacres, bombings, train crashes, and even his own fear of atomic annihiliation, these incidents may seem trifling. But, multiplied many times, they comprised a wave of terror that caused anguish in Indonesia.

It is impossible to be sure to what extent the army's violence spread along the archipelago, because correspondents could not justify travelling great distances to obtain news that was not of world interest. After a tour of Central Sulawesi Ischak Moro, a member of the PSII and Deputy Chairman of the Parliamentary Legal and Home Affairs Committee, said Golkar had threatened that people who did not vote for it would be hanged or shot and that the mouths of politicians who talked too much would be 'stuffed with bullets'. The official news agency, Antara, reported that police had killed two 'Communists' and arrested several others in a 'mopping up operation' in North Sulawesi. In South

Sulawesi the military command said that six army officers were under arrest for intimidating electors; but it was hard to judge the significance of this, for according to the same announcement 125 officers and men had been arrested in the previous month for involvement in the 1965 *putsch*. Parkindo, the Protestant Party, complained of intimidation in North Sumatra, but predicted that people would have courage to resist it. Antara reported that 30,000 NU members in Maura Sabak, Jambi, had 'defected to Golkar'.

There was widespread interference with the village structure. I found by chance that the army had changed all of the 543 village heads in West Sumatra between 1966 and 1970. The Governor, Harun Zain, explained that many of them were under PKI influence. This excuse was part of the army's policy of branding its opponents as potential or actual Communists. West Sumatra is overwhelmingly Islamic; in the 1955 elections Moslem parties received 80 per cent of the votes and the PKI only 10 per cent.

In areas in which the political parties were weak, the army met with few difficulties. In Aceh, for instance, it appears that Golkar was able to win over the *kyahi* by promising mosques, which were rarely built, and handing out Honda motor-cycles. But the Governor admitted on 14 May that thirty people had been detained for political offences; some had been released. Generally it may be assumed that the junta used whatever measures it considered necessary to ensure Golkar's victory. In April it forbade diplomats to leave Jakarta without permission, obviously to ensure that only those who could be trusted not to pry too much went to areas where the worst was happening. Foreign correspondents were warned in writing 'to avoid conduct that can affect or hamper the election situation'.

In May 1971 I made an eight-day tour of East Java and Bali. The stories on the spot were similar to those published by the parties in Jakarta. At Wajak, East Java, a youth who was foolish enough to protest that Golkar was an even greater enemy of Moslems than the PKI spent four days in hospital after military police had beaten him up; village heads had been told that if they did not join Golkar they would lose their identity cards and be treated as security risks; farmers refusing to yield had difficulty in renewing their cards, without which they could not sell their produce in the markets. At Probolinggo 90 per cent of the 200,000 Moslem population had succumbed and transferred their allegiance from the NU to Golkar, but I had the impression that the local *haji*, who feared losing his business, had connived in the desertion; military police had seized all loudspeakers in this area. In their homes in widely scattered towns and villages both humble and well-to-do told of intimidation in hushed voices. They said that the army sometimes blocked roads leading to rallies for which permits had been granted.

In the village of Karangploso, near Malang, East Java, which I visited, seventeen Moslems were arrested after having been tricked into a bizarre conspiracy by an ex-Communist, whom the army forced to act as *agent provocateur*. The *agent* approached them after they had persistently refused to desert the NU for Golkar; he told them that if they went through a certain ritual with a magic knife that he possessed, their persecutors would die. The men gathered at a place indicated by the agent and were all arrested for having conspired to murder Golkar leaders. Karangploso is a tiny village, but its few small houses are overshadowed by an ugly military post; as I left, an army lorry drove up, loaded with armed soldiers. This episode struck me as a useful sample of rural life in areas where the NU had predominated: the men who took me to the place were educated Ansor leaders; the peasants, although supporting the so-called orthodox Moslem party, believed in magic; and the army ruled over all.

In Bali, which is almost entirely Hindu, the PNI was the army's main danger. In the 1955 elections it had won fourteen of the provincial parliament's twenty-six seats. Following the ban on the PKI (eight seats), PSI (two) and Masjumi (one), it could not fail to win again unless the army intervened. The Balinese peasants, who speak their own language in their homes, are at best indifferent to the Javanese, and have little enthusiasm for the idea of Indonesia, despite the fact that Sukarno's mother came from Bali. There was no chance that they would abandon the PNI, which had trusted regional leaders in Bali, for the Javanese-controlled Golkar, if allowed to choose freely; the fact that Golkar won in the island is one of the certain signs that the elections were not genuine. The Golkar team, headed by a Brigadier-General, opened its campaign with the usual bullying. On 23 March PNI leaders complained to the local military commander that since

November their followers had suffered 124 assaults on themselves or their property. The banyan tree threatened to become as prolific as the island's coconut palms; it was painted on boards outside the innumerable military posts, indicating that these were also the offices of Golkar, and was stuck on houses, shops, offices and cars. PNI leaders were afraid to make public statements about intimidation. One of them explained: 'The best we can do is to concentrate on going into the villages to reassure the people that they will not break the law if they vote for the PNI. We tell them that we are one of the nine parties permitted by President Suharto to contest the elections. Many village heads are very simple people. They are easily frightened when army officers threaten to treat them as security risks.'

In June 1971 the Protestant newspaper, *Sinar Harapan*, published the result of its inquiry into the NU's accusation that military police had murdered Moslems and tortured others in Indramayu regency, West Java. It quoted the Indramayu Deputy Police Commissioner as saying that the number killed was about twenty. A named man said that on 13 December 1970 his son had been shot dead by a Lieutenant Otong at the side of a freshly dug grave in front of a forcibly assembled crowd. Before pulling the trigger, Otong had warned: 'This is what will happen to all who do not join Golkar.' Another of the victims died after Lieutenant Otong had towed him along the ground behind a motor-cycle. Killing was not an official part of the junta's election campaign, and Otong was sentenced to imprisonment after having been shot through the ear by an outraged officer, who complained that he had shamed the army. There were few other murders; but those that took place were a significant, if extreme, expression of the army's determination to win.[10]

The army's toughest opponents were Moslems in the island of Madura; in May the entire military command in Surabaya was ferried across to try and get them under control. The Moslems' faith, blended with belief in various forms of magic, was no more potent than that of the people in East and West Java; but they are a fierce and courageous people, whose favourite sport is bull-racing, in which drivers perch precariously on low, wooden chariots. On the night of 17 June troops surrounded and broke up an NU election meeting of 20,000 Madurese at Sumenep; an armed soldier leaped on to the platform, told Mohammed Hartono,

Chairman of the NU group in the national parliament, to stop his speech, and ordered the crowd to go home. Earlier in the day the army paraded light cannon and patrolled the streets in armoured cars and lorries when 50,000 people gathered in the town square; troops blocked roads and turned back other Moslems who were on their way to the rally. A few days earlier military police had stabbed to death a man they mistook for an NU leader. The cumulative repression provoked anger and hate. Ansor youth began to talk of a holy war and said they would do whatever the *kyahi* asked of them; and there were whispers in some areas that certain *kyahi* were charmed against death and would lead the people to victory. This was dangerous stuff, and the army knew it. Either to force people into Golkar or to rig the election could lead to bloodshed. Eventually the exasperated military command accepted that in Madura the NU must be allowed to win.

Less than a month before the elections Subchan decided it was time for the NU to stop merely protesting and go over to the offensive. In a widely published statement he said he had evidence that the poll would be rigged, and threatened to appeal to the United Nations Human Rights Commission against Golkar's 'killing and violation of human rights'. Making the first personal attack on members of the junta's establishment since the election campaign began, he branded Amir Machmud as a 'tool', who had broken his own election laws; he dismissed the Education Minister, Mashuri, a Golkar member, as being 'devoid of moral values'. Unkindest of all, he pooh-poohed Indonesia's recent economic improvement as being merely the result of 'huge assistance' that the junta received from the West in return for banning the PKI and overthrowing Sukarno. The army apparently feared that the accusation of a conspiracy to rig the elections could lead to riots in areas where the NU failed. Two days after the publication of Subchan's statement Suharto warned that the armed forces would 'join hand in hand with the people' to fight 'certain leaders' who had decided to launch a holy war if they lost. Meanwhile sixty-five active NU members, including the Second Chairman's secretary, had been arrested in the previous three weeks; the Parmusi Central Java Chairman in Semarang was also arrested.

If the PNI suffered less violence in the field than the NU did, it was because if had already been battered. Many of its leftist cadres and followers had been swept up with the Communists and either killed or put in prison. These represented a relatively new party stream, which Ali Sastroamidjojo had fostered, not because he was under Communist influence, as some generals pretend, but to compete with it (so he told the author in an interview in January 1973). The party's older base, in the civil service, was easily disposed of by drafting members into Korpri. Here the army was able to work from the top downwards; and once the higher officials capitulated, their subordinates and people in the villages that the PNI controlled often followed. Nevertheless there was intimidation enough; and on 30 March 1971 the party secretariat said it had a file thirty centimetres thick of complaints from intimidated members.

To the army's chagrin Hadisubeno showed no gratitude for having been pushed into the PNI chair at Semarang, and vied with Subchan in heated campaigning. At a PNI meeting in Surabaya a life-size portrait of Sukarno dominated a small one of Suharto. On another occasion Hadisubeno caused a sensation in the close atmosphere of military repression when he burst out with: 'Ten Suhartos, ten Nasutions, and a cartload of generals do not add up to one Sukarno.' His party revived the inflammatory cult of Marhaen, the poor peasant whom Sukarno had made the symbol of the people's sufferings and hopes. The army talked of banning all Sukarno's teachings, but when Hadisubeno challenged it to ban the PNI as well it retreated and only banned Nasakom and certain other doctrines, not Marhaenism.

Yet there was something weak in Hadisubeno's bluster, which was accompanied by his reassurances that the PNI, in spite of all, supported the Suharto government. Possibly he felt obliged to make concessions to hold his position in the party. There were reports that attempts were made to displace him at a central board conference in Bandung early in April, but that the plot failed when members could not agree on his successor. The conference put out a resolution expressing concern that actions taken by 'certain political groups' would hamper the government's development plans, while pledging itself to maintain 'harmonious relations' between Suharto and the PNI masses. The same kind of caution was shown by PNI Third Chairman, Hardjantho, when he attributed intimidation of his members in Bali to 'enemies of the PNI who have infiltrated Golkar'; with an eye to the inevitable future, he did not blame the army or Golkar itself.

But Hadisubeno fought on, warning that the people might rise against local military commanders if violence continued. Apparently safe in his position of General Chairman, he became an increasing nuisance to the generals. And it must have been a great relief to them when he died suddenly at the height of the campaign. His death was announced by the PNI central board on 24 April. The board said that he had died the same morning in a Semarang hospital, to which he had been admitted the day before after having fainted; the cause of his death was diabetes and the effects of a kidney operation, which he was said to have undergone a month earlier. The bitterness between Hadisubeno and the army and the speed with which the cause of his death had been established inevitably aroused suspicion. On 28 April Mohammad Isnaeni, First Chairman of the PNI, who was later to become party leader, felt obliged, after a talk with Suharto, to deny that Hadisubeno had died from 'mysterious causes'; he said he had met the 'team of doctors' who had treated him and was satisfied with their diagnosis. Yet it seemed strange that a team should have been brought in at such short notice when a politician merely fainted during the rigours of electioneering. After the elections Subchan told me he was sure that Hadisubeno had been murdered. 'I was afraid they would kill me, too', he said. 'When I became ill I went into the Catholic hospital; I thought it would be safer.' While I have my suspicions, I retain an open mind on this matter. I mention Subchan's view for the benefit of historians, who may like to make further inquiries. A Moslem politician taking refuge in a Catholic hospital for fear of being killed by a secular army is in any case a vivid indication of the political climate at the time.

Such fire as there was in the PNI campaign dwindled when Hadisubeno died, but revived when Sukarno's eldest son, Guntur, and second daughter, Rachmawati, joined in the fight. Although she was only twenty, Rachmawati was harder-hitting than her 26-year-old brother, and did not fear to make bitter accusations of intimidation, although she, too, as far as I know, never mentioned the army by name. But Guntur was an electrifying speaker and roused crowds to a frenzy when he spoke in poetic language that not only recalled his spellbinding father but had a style of its own. At a rally in Semarang PNI supporters carried pictures of both Sukarno and Guntur. The army then forbade the use of

Sukarno's image in the campaign and confined Guntur to meetings in Jakarta, where his guitar-playing and declamation drew crowds of several thousand. At the final PNI rally of 14,000 in Jakarta he put on an oratorical performance that his father could scarcely have bettered. He told his listeners: 'When George Washington proclaimed American independence in 1776, there was a fighter named Paul Revere. To announce the proclamation he rode on horseback, and went from house to house knocking on the doors of the people. I want every Marhaen to be a Paul Revere to himself and to let his heart tell him what to do on the third of July [election day].' If, in fact, Paul Revere made his midnight ride in 1775, not to announce independence but to warn that the British were coming from Boston, the audience did not know or care. Here was Sukarno's handsome, romantic son giving them hope, which, if it was all that Sukarno had given them, was not less. The crowd responded like an orchestra to a conductor. When Guntur reached a climax they cheered; when he lifted his hand they were instantly silent and listened motionless until he provoked them to cheer again. At the end of the evening Guntur's mother, Fatmawati, who had made the red and white Indonesian flag that was hauled up in Jakarta on 17 August 1945, joined him on the platform.

But it was all entertainment; there was no depth to it, no political substance. The emotions that were inspired that night might have been useful to start a riot, but they were not the kind to give people courage to go out alone and vote against the Indonesian army. One sensed the feebleness of the PNI, with a rabble roused too easily while the beneficiaries of a doomed patronage looked on with apprehension.

More impressive was the NU final rally. The mob element, conspicuous at the PNI meeting, was absent; for the NU's poor live in rural villages, not in the congested *kampongs* of Jakarta. The tone of the speeches was serious, the applause civilized. And there were prayers, including one for a seventy-year old man whom a soldier had just shot at Slateng, East Java, when he refused to set an example by signing a Golkar form; a picture of his body, with a bullet hole in his chest, had been published in the NU newspaper. The prayer, doubtless, was part of the political stage-managing. But there was strength in this quieter meeting. The Islamic faith, one felt, would be more proof against pressure on election day than the legend of Marhaen, touching though it was.

The elections

In May and June two small organizations sprang up and tried to fight for a clean election; the Indonesian Committee to Uphold Democracy, formed by twenty-one students, and the White Group, headed by the lawyer, Adnan Bujung Nasution. The White Group dissolved under pressure after having issued leaflets urging the people not to yield to force on election day; the students were interrogated and their activities banned after they had appealed to Dr Mohammed Hatta, the former Vice-President, who declared independence with Sukarno in 1945, to help them. Hatta had long been of the opinion that polling was meaningless and intimidation inevitable in an uneducated society. Nevertheless he told the students that he would not have thought the present situation in Indonesia could have arisen. He advised them to report intimidation to the President, so that no charges would be preferred against them. At the same time he said he was glad to know that there were still people living in Indonesia who were willing to struggle. 'Don't be afraid to take risks', he said. 'I myself took risks [the Dutch sent him to the malaria-infested prison camp at Boven Digul, New Guinea] and was even betrayed by friends.' After having given this advice, Hatta was summoned with his wife to see the Suhartos. Mrs Tien Suharto then announced that Hatta would leave two days later for Holland, ostensibly to undergo medical treatment, accompanied by his wife, a daughter, his doctor, and two secretaries. A month earlier the government had sent Mohammed Daud Beureueh, who had led the Darul Islam revolt and was still the unofficial leader of the Aceh people, on an overseas tour. He had declared loyalty to Suharto, but the junta apparently feared that dissidents would draw inspiration from him, as the students were to do when they appealed to Hatta; it paid his expenses and those of one of his sons, his doctor and a servant on a trip to Singapore, Kuala Lumpur, Bangkok, Beirut, Jedda, Cairo, Istanbul, Bern, Bonn, Paris and places in the United States. It was not disclosed who paid Hatta's expenses. Both men stayed abroad until after the elections.

After a meeting on 3–5 June the Supreme Council of the Guardians of Indonesian Churches in a statement signed by Cardinal Darmojuwono called on the government to ensure that there was no 'manipulation' or intimidation. The Protestant Council of Churches then warned President Suharto that election tension could split the nation, and urged him to ensure a free, secret vote. In South Sulawesi twenty youth organizations representing Moslems, Christians and secular nationalists issued a joint protest against 'torture, beatings, arrests and illegal interrogation'. In different areas the repression produced the same telling phrase, that the authorities were behaving like the 'Japanese army of occupation'.

The army made it clear that it would crush any dissent. On 17 June it said that four combat battalions and four armoured car companies had been training for six months to 'safeguard the elections'; they were led by Brigadier-General Jasir Hadibroto, whose men had caught and killed Aidit in Central Java. In addition three battalions of sharp-shooters (*jangos*) wearing civilian clothes would mingle with crowds. Three days before the elections it was announced that all troops in Indonesia were on the alert and that 190,000 Civil Defence Corps men would be stationed at polling booths. Eight warships and twelve patrol boats would also be used to ensure security, by means that were not explained. Members of the former Communist railway union, SBKA, who were among those disfranchised, were confined to warehouses, canteens and other railway buildings on 1–4 July; their families were expected to provide them with bed-clothes and take meals to them. The men were told to continue working, but not to go near polling booths. This measure was obviously aimed largely at emphasizing the army's authority in the eyes of the frightened electors, for without the necessary card the railway men could not have voted. In West Kalimantan the military commander ordered Chinese not to travel on election day and told his men to shoot on sight anyone who made trouble. By this time, according to the newspaper, *Harian Kami*, the parliamentary committee appointed to keep watch on the elections was unable to function because some members had suffered nervous collapse. On election eve *Harian Kami*, which was born amid hopes of greater democracy after the *putsch*, was banned along with the NU organ, *Duta Masjarakat*.

This was the atmosphere in which Indonesians went to the polls, which some commentators have hailed as either a triumph of democracy or step towards it. The predictable result was a sweeping victory for Golkar, which won 236 of the 360 elective seats, including nine representing West Irian, where a special election procedure was enforced. The four Moslem parties won a total of ninety-four, with fifty-eight going to the NU and twenty-four to the Parmusi. The PNI, with only twenty seats, was smashed. The Protestants won seven and the Catholics three.

The poll was not declared until 7 August, but the result was apparent on election night when unofficial figures were broadcast several hours after polling had ended. Two days later the NU, followed by the demoralized PNI, launched a series of protests against widespread intimidation of voters. Party branches reported arrests totalling many hundreds that had taken place on or just before election day, including 400 NU men in the Lamongan sub-regency of East Java. Accusations of extreme violence in certain areas received some corroboration when the official news agency, Antara, quoted the East Java police chief as saying that he was investigating an unspecified number of murders.

I have reliable, independent evidence that in Bali Civil Defence Corps men took some voters forcibly by the arm as they entered polling booths; even an Indian citizen was among those rounded up and told to vote for Golkar. On election eve tales of torture and beating were being whispered throughout Denpasar, the capital of Bali; even if only a fraction of them were true, this would have been enough to convince the simple community that to vote against Golkar would bring punishment to them all. My informant said next day: 'These people are so terrified that I pity them.' In this former PNI stronghold Golkar won seven of the eight national parliament seats – a result that would have done credit to any dictatorship.

To the accusations of brutality Subchan added that of ballot-rigging. This was possible even in the polling booths, he said, because party scrutineers, although permitted by law, were often either driven away or afraid to take their places. Where this did not happen – mostly in big towns – the junta was still able to falsify the poll by altering the record of votes sent from the booths to district counting centres. 'This was easy because the validity certificate, signed by party scrutineers, if they were allowed to be present, was on a separate sheet from the figures', he said. One did not have to go far to find at least the possibility of rigging. I chose for my sampling the hamlet of Cilandak, in the outskirts of Jakarta, where intimidation of NU supporters was reported to be particularly vicious. After driving through forest along a rough, dirt road I found an isolated kiosk, which was being used as a polling both, with no other building in sight. As I walked towards the door an armed Civil Defence Corps man stopped me and, although I showed him the special card issued to correspondents for the elections, said I could not enter. Eventually after some talk inside the booth I was allowed in. Voting had finished and counting was going on. While I sat there every vote that was counted except two in this intensely Moslem region was for Golkar. When the counting stopped I asked an official who were the party scrutineers at the counting table. He indicated one man, and said he was a *haji* who represented the NU. I pointed out that the law provided that each party could nominate two scrutineers, but received no reply when I asked where the others were. According to the regulations, I said, the result should be announced to an assembly of voters; I asked where the people were. They had all gone home, the official replied. I asked if he intended to obey the law and announce the results. He said that the *lurah* (village head) had told him not to do so. Outside an army jeep was waiting to take the ballot papers with their certified count to the district centre. If, for some reason, the initial intimidation had failed, there would have been nothing to prevent tampering with the votes on the way. What had happened at the booth earlier in the day I cannot say for certain. But even if the vote had been declared, as it should have been, only the trees would have been there to acclaim the Golkar victory.

While the secrecy of the ballot was violated in outlying areas, as far as I know this did not happen in the towns. But it is my opinion that a subtle and successful attempt was made to convey the impression to a largely superstitious and easily intimidated people that somehow Big Brother was watching. In the first place even small *kampongs* were divided into sections, each with its own polling booth. Ostensibly this was to speed voting, but it gave voters a feeling that they were being individually supervised. With the total numbers of booths officially put at 793,036, the average was one for 69 voters.

At a *kampong* I visited near Jakarta airport only a few voters were present in any one booth while I was there. The procedure was laid down by regulation. At the booth entrance the elector showed his voting permit to an official, who gave him a number. He sat on a bench until his number was called, when he exchanged his permit for a folded ballot paper, while 'mentioning loudly and clearly his name'. He then went behind a screen, where he could not be seen, and punched a hole through the symbol of the party he had chosen. But he did not drop his ballot paper straight into a box. Instead he went out and showed the folded paper not only to the chairman but to member number five of the election committee; it was no coincidence that five was Golkar's number, placed next to its symbol on the ballot paper. As the regulations put it, he then placed the paper in the box, 'after being allowed to do so by the chairman/member number 5'. Since the paper was folded and the punch mark invisible there was no way in which the officials could tell whether the vote was in order. The only possible reason why it was shown to them was to make the elector fear that by some means the chairman and the mighty Golkar would know how he had voted; this was also the purpose of giving him a number, which impeded rather than increased the flow of votes. Not all the voters were simple enough to believe in such occult phenomena as the magic knife that was offered to the NU men at Karangploso; but those who were illiterate would certainly have feared that their number was on the paper and those who could read would have been likely to wonder whether it was there in code or hidden by some means known only to the rulers. In a country pervaded by belief in ghosts and fear of black magic, intimidation by suggestion is a powerful weapon. Sitting on the bench in the polling both, sometimes alone for a considerable period, the elector, his number in his hand, would have become increasingly unnerved while officials looked at him and jotted down notes. At the Ministry of the Interior I saw a civil servant nervously hold his paper to the light before voting, apparently to make sure that there was no identifying mark on it.

I have no documents to prove that the government intended the effect that it undoubtedly achieved. But K. E. Ward[11] came across evidence that such methods were in the official mind in a booklet issued by the Malang Resident, Soehardjo. Explaining how to intimidate political parties, Soehardjo said: 'Before a campaign meeting, assemble the speakers at a local government office and warn them about the limits they must observe in campaigning. The official giving them the warning need only be a subordinate one, but he should be very loyal to his superiors, be well-built, and have a rather awful appearance' (Ward's translation).

All government and quasi-government workers were obliged to vote at their offices, while their superiors prowled about. Here, too, numerous polling booths were set up in each large office. Amir Machmud had already told civil servants that they must 'vote for the banyan tree, like it or not'. And most of them did. At the Ministry of the Interior I asked Amir Machmud's right-hand man, Brigadier-General Wang Suandi, why there were so few party scrutineers at the tables that were spaced along the sides of a courtyard, where the miniature booths had been placed. 'I think they are short of manpower', he smiled. I had the feeling that by election day there were few civil servants who dared to say openly that they still supported their old parties.

The essentials of the junta's election strategy may now be seen. The instrument was Golkar, which as far as possible used legitimate campaigning methods to attract support for the programme of economic development freed from politics. Many educated people saw hope in this policy; and others, who had always sought patronage, found it in their interest to vote for a party that was backed by the invincible junta, just as they had used or bowed to the PNI when it was influential before the *putsch*. But there remained a multitude who either felt and thought otherwise or were influenced by those who did; to these people the army applied various kinds of intimidation. On election day those who wavered or continued to resist were subjected to further force in some rural areas; and all voters were finally put through a voting procedure that was designed to awe them; always in reserve was the option of easily rigging the ballot if the earlier methods failed. To crush riots that might break out because of either intimidation or rigging, the entire army, with troops specially trained for the purpose, was on the alert; some were stationed at Halim air base, ready to be flown to the outer islands if a local military commander appealed for help; in Bali private inter-island calls were forbidden on election day, when the army kept the lines open for an emergency. Thus while the army made its announcement of military preparations early in the campaign merely for propaganda, there was genuine anxiety towards the end; and the atmosphere at the Defence Department in Jakarta remained tense until the elections were over.

In the face of such might an elector required more than ordinary political conviction to sustain him as he walked into the polling booth, particularly outside the towns. Moslems who remained strongly under the influence of the *kyahi* often had this; generally the PNI masses did not. On election morning a man closely connected with army intelligence said to me with great emotion: 'These people are unbeatable; they have been praying all night.' The faith of the Moslems explains more than anything else the remarkable performance of their parties in winning ninety-four of the 360 DPR elective seats compared with the shattered PNI's miserable twenty. Or, looking at it another way, it could be that in Indonesia on election day fear of the army was greater than fear of hell, except among the more devout or superstitious. The Balinese Hindus, with neither belief in hell nor any substantial political awareness, had nothing at all to fortify them as they were driven whimpering to the polls. The Madurese, fired by faith, superstition, and their own hot blood, did best of all. Political analysts may take over the subject from here.

Nevertheless, many PNI men showed exceptional courage and like Moslem party members lost their jobs in consequence; the NU claimed that 3,000 teachers had been dismissed from government schools in East Java alone. The Indonesian Council of Churches and the Catholic Archbishop of Jakarta, Monsignor Leo Sukoto, SJ, both supported the appeal by the NU and the PNI to review all dismissals of civil servants.

It took some time for the army to unwind its intimidation. Nearly two weeks after the elections the PNI central board urged the government to stop 'arrests, destructive actions and threats'. Vengeful army officers were still pursuing villagers who had insisted on putting their scrutineers in polling booths and had defied orders to vote for Golkar; 700 Moslems took refuge in a *pesantren* at Sukerjo Asembagus, East Java, after troops had burned down some of their houses. In the middle of July Antara reported that Colonel Harun Suwardi, military commander of Malang and Besuki, had ordered a halt to 'arrests, fomenting of trouble and flight of people afraid of arrest'. The colonel explained: 'The elections are over and the situation should return to normal.'

CHAPTER NINE

The end of politics

Packing the MPR

The new MPR, which the junta set up after the elections, was reported by news agencies and praised by commentators as the first in Indonesia with an elected majority. One Western agency, which has a reputation for old-fashioned reliability, said: 'President Suharto appointed 207 of the 920–member congress . . . and others won their seats in general elections last year.' In fact the number of MPR members who had not faced the electors was considerably more. An obvious omission from this report was that the 920 included 100 appointed members of parliament, in addition to the 207, making a total of 307. But the junta did not end its puppeteering operation there, and devised the election laws so that by various means it could select up to 61 per cent of members. The compliance of the entire MPR was ensured by packing it with 276 armed forces officers, of whom half were generals, senior naval men and marshals, with colonels comprising most of the others. Confronted with this redoubtable array of military brass, only a civilian of exceptional spirit would have offered serious opposition to the junta's measures.

The composition of the MPR was laid down in Law No. 16, officially described as having been promulgated by President Suharto (in November 1969) 'with the approval of the Dewan Perwakilan Rakyat Gotong Royong (DPR – parliament)'.[1] Dahm,[2] like more popular writers, takes at its face value the provision in

Article 1 that the 'number of appointed MPR members is fixed at
one-third of the total number of MPR members'; but it is at
once necessary to add the twenty-six governors and other provincial heads, whose automatic appointment is provided in
Article 8, to the 307 that were considered to be one-third of 920.
After that the picture is ingeniously concealed; and to obtain a
full view of the junta's manipulative powers it is necessary to hop
from article to article in both the law and the implementing
regulation that was gazetted in 1970, after Dahm had completed
his history.

The MPR was made up of: the 460 members of the DPR
(360 elected and 100 appointed by the President, of whom seventy-
five were armed forces and twenty-five Golkar); 207 appointed
by the President (155 armed forces and fifty-two Golkar); 130
representing the provinces; 121 appointed from Golkar and the
political parties; and two from parties that contested the elections
but did not win a seat.[3] The implementing regulation, which did
not require the approval of parliament, gave the junta powers of
selection that could be missed by those unfamiliar with its ways.
Article 6 provided that provincial parliaments should elect the
members who were to represent them in the MPR; but there was a
vital reservation that the candidates 'may or may not be' members
of a provincial parliament and that a 'technical committee' would
examine their qualifications. This meant that the army, which
controlled the technical committee in every province, could pre-
select the entire provincial representation in the MPR. It could
make its choice from appointed members of the parliaments,
who in each province numbered more (at least eight) than the
quota of MPR representatives (at most seven); or it could choose
from Golkar, from relatively trusted members of political parties
or from preferred outsiders. As a stiffener, the twenty-six provincial
governors or heads were included by law. The result in practice
was that the 130 provincial representatives included forty-six
armed forces officers, but only seventeen carefully screened
members of political parties; politicians comprised 13 per cent of
the provincial representation in the MPR, compared with 34 per
cent of DPR seats that the parties won in the elections.

The junta was also able to control the appointment of the 121
extra members who represented the parties and Golkar in proportion to their election successes. Law No 16 stated simply that

they would be included among the components of the 920, but did not stipulate who was to appoint them. Party leaders naturally presumed that they would make the choice; but when the implementing regulation was published they found that the nominating procedure was to be 'further regulated by the President', who could delegate his authority to the Minister for the Interior. Thus the junta, with 307 members directly nominated by the President and the controlled selection of 130 from the regions and 123 from the parties (two from the unsuccessful parties), could, if it wished, choose up to 61 per cent of the MPR, apart from the 236 Golkar members who were included by virtue of their election to the DPR. It would be impossible to ascertain to what extent the junta availed itself of this premeditated opportunity. Doubtless it went as far as it found necessary. But this did not mean that the generals felt secure. They did not trust any politicians, whether they selected them or not; nor did they trust Golkar.

A useful weapon in the hands of the junta was the right of the parties and Golkar to replace after the election candidates who were listed before it. Disappointing Golkar members from Sumatra were disposed of by this means. In Sinkawang, West Kalimantan, I found that the replacement right had been used against the oppressed Chinese majority in the area. Chinese community leaders had dutifully joined Golkar, which received an overwhelming vote. Golkar, directed by the army, replaced most of the candidates with non-Chinese, with the result that only one Chinese sat in the local parliament of forty. I suggested to a military officer that it would have been wiser to allow about a dozen Chinese members to sit in the chamber. 'You need not have included any of them in the MPR', I said. He agreed that a mistake had been made, and said it was to be rectified later. This is another point at which political analysts might like to take over.

The battering of the political parties and their impotence in the supreme governing body brought neither peace of mind to the generals nor stability to the nation. The ever-anxious junta, fearing that its plans for Suharto's re-election might go awry at the critical MPR meeting in March 1973, was gripped by an extraordinary infantile neurosis, which provoked the contempt of educated civilians, probably without exception. This attack of March nerves, as it might be called, not only produced repressive acts that were unnecessary by any criteria, but appeared to paralyse some of the generals themselves. It even had repercussions in Indonesia's diplomacy. I asked Adam Malik how feelers for a resumption of relations with China, which were suspended in 1967, were getting on. 'Sumitro [the general most concerned with security] says we can't do anything until after March', he replied. Lieutenant-General Ali Sadikin, Greater Jakarta's energetic governor, was invited to address the Foreign Correspondents' Club; but one of his aides made it clear that the general must remain silent until after March. Other leading citizens were invited to speak; the reply always given or implied was 'not until after March'. General Nasution was told to discontinue his academic lectures to Moslem students until after March. The Film Censorship Board postponed the release of thirteen American, Hong Kong and Indian films until after March; scenes of demonstrations and mass opposition to government policies shown in the films might cause social unrest, the board ruled; the films could be shown in the first week of April.

One of the first victims of the army's jumpiness was Guntur Sukarno, who was interrogated by Kopkamtib in Jakarta two days after the elections. It looked as if the aim was to ensure that Sukarno did not add his eloquence to protests against the polling abuses. His interrogation was preceded by a menacing announcement in Bandung that he was to be asked about his presence at a meeting of student organizations, which included Communists, in December 1965. An indication of the pressure exerted on him is that Sukarno issued a written denial that he had been interrogated. But the next day his intrepid sister, Rachmawati, disclosed that when Sukarno went to a local Kopkamtib office, accompanied by his mother, he was questioned about anti-Suharto slogans, which had appeared on walls; she said that a man produced by Kopkamtib broke down and admitted that he had been forced to make a false confession implicating her brother. After this incident Guntur dropped out of the scene, and the Marhaens were left to struggle on without his help.

The junta did not miss a proposed discussion of an old Dutch law against 'hate-sowing' by the Law Faculty of one of Jakarta's universities. The law had been dragged out of the colonial archives to prosecute Tengku Dzulkafli Hafas, the perky editor of the newspaper *Nusantara*, for making pungent jokes about the junta in his column. Hafas was sentenced to a year's imprisonment, but was freed pending appeal. The university discussion was begun by liberals who were concerned about press freedom, but there was also a pure academic interest in the law. Some lawyers held that it was no longer valid; one argument was that while the body of Dutch law still applied in Indonesia, the 'hate-sowing' articles were invalid because they did not exist in the original Dutch Penal Code, but had been inserted in it by the Dutch East Indies government, whose measures were no longer enforceable. Harmless and interesting though the debate at the Law Faculty would have been, the junta took no chances and banned the meeting. It also banned a discussion on juvenile delinquency on the ground that it could be exploited for political purposes. By these and other similar acts the junta deepened the gloom of more intelligent citizens in and outside the academic world, whose spirit and initiative were essential to the nation's development.

There were times when some of the generals appeared to have lost their reason. Amir Machmud made a statement that under-ground Communists would try to change the constitution at the MPR meeting in March; they had sent pretty girls from Central Java to infiltrate the civil service for this purpose, he said – without explaining why the girls had not been arrested. Not satisfied with looking for trouble among Indonesian civilians, the generals turned their attention to foreigners. General Sutopo Juwono, head of Bakin, made a special survey of tensions that might arise before March and predicted that foreign subversion would be intensified. In a wave of xenophobia, which aroused comment in the press, an American businessman who unwittingly got himself mixed in rival military factions was expelled for subversion and financially ruined; several foreign academics who wanted to visit Indonesia were refused visas. Nor did the junta spare its own forces: at the end of July 1972 it was officially announced that an undisclosed number of senior and junior officers had been arrested for investigation for their involvement in the 1965 *putsch*; in August Sumitro said that a purge of the armed forces and civil service was continuing; and the next month three air marshals were interrogated about possible past association with Communists. After the July arrests the sober, observant editor of the newspaper *Pedoman* wrote: 'News about detention of high ranking military officers reminds us once again that while things might look stable and fully under control on the surface, there are restlessness, tensions and conflicting groups underneath; all of which gives the impression that the present stability is artificial.'

Into this cauldron of intrigue and repression the President's wife, Mrs Tien Suharto, an overbearing and ambitious woman, tossed a fresh ingredient that set it bubbling and spitting for months: this was her Indonesia in Miniature project, then estimated to cost $26 million which was widely condemned as a waste of the nation's resources. There is no better example of the political and social ineptitude of Suharto's circle than this affair, which was to become the main preoccupation of security men and a worry to the National Planning Board for a considerable period. The polite protests and small student demonstrations that followed Mrs Suharto's announcement of the scheme in November 1971 could have been handled easily. But the melodrama with which the junta attached sinister motives to even the most reasonable protests created a tense atmosphere in which Suharto emotionally defended his wife in public and savagely threatened hidden plotters, whom he accused of trying to overthrow him. This episode may seem trivial at a distance, but when Suharto eventually goes, either gracefully or otherwise, it may be seen as marking the turning point in his career as President. What is certain is that it fomented further discontent with him, not only among civilians but in all ranks of the armed forces, and helped to precipitate a threat to his power from inside the army. It also increased the unpopularity of Mrs Suharto, whose association with *cukongs* was more widely known than her husband's at that time; her name, being unfortunately the same as the Dutch word for 'ten', had already been coined into 'Madame Tien per cent'.

The plan was for an exhibition of Indonesian architecture, arts and crafts over an area of 1,350 by 580 metres near Jakarta, with a miniature of the archipelago set in a lake in the centre. It included a 'tall and dignified monument, which reflects the spirit of the philosophy of *Pancasila*, and depicts the great character and personality of the Indonesian people'. In an expensive brochure Mrs Suharto emphasized that her aim was to 'develop and deepen the love of the Indonesian people for their fatherland'; but first on her list of promotion points was the attraction of tourists. Now it is just possible that the expenditure of $26 million on a tourist attraction, instead of on badly needed village industries and schools, could have been justified, since the linkage effects of tourism are considerable. But it must be said bluntly that for all Suharto's stereotyped talk about the economy, the need to examine the scheme's profitability and to balance its benefits against those of other forms of investment would not have entered his head when he signed his approval and gave his patronage; the mind of the 'development President', as he is sometimes called, does not work in that way. The land was bought and the plan announced before any attempt was made to estimate whether tourist traffic would enable the scheme to be soundly amortized over a given term. It was stated that finance would come from outside the national budget; but the National Planning Board, who were not consulted, were aghast to read in the brochure that both domestic and foreign capital would be sought. Nor was the public reassured when Mrs Suharto and Amir Machmud asked a conference of provincial governors to raise money for the venture.

The first to protest were the 300 families whose miniature houses and gardens were razed to make room for the scheme; they complained that compensation, fixed by the sponsors at 100 rupiahs (about a quarter of an American dollar) per square metre was inadequate. Adnan Bujung Nasution's Legal Aid/Public Defence Institute took up their case, but no more was heard of it. Ali Murtopo saw it in his interests to defend Mrs Suharto's project, and in a comical over-reaction he urged Kopkamtib to take firm action against the newspaper, *Sinar Harapan*, whose reports, he said, 'could create public disorder, endangering the security of the state and even the leadership of President Suharto'. At the height of the protests, limited though they were to voices that could never prevail, Mrs Suharto declared that she would go on fighting for her project as long as she remained alive. But she detracted from the lofty tones of her brochure by adding: 'The men [meaning, in particular, the generals] have their massage parlours [virtually brothels, in which the more active girls were examined regularly for venereal disease]; we women [her committee] should have something for ourselves.' On 6 January 1972 Suharto, speaking without notes at the opening of a hospital built by Pertamina, made an incredibly ferocious speech. Recalling the *putsch*, he said that in those early days the one who supported him was his wife, whereas the Pancasila Front and the 1966

Generation (two anti-Sukarno movements) were not yet born.
Suharto said he would not tolerate abuse of the democratic system.
'I will smash whoever tries to violate the constitution, and I will
be supported by the armed forces', he said. 'If they do not understand what I mean by "I will not tolerate", I mean I will eliminate
them.'

Suharto's gibe at the Pancasila Front and the 1966 Generation
were aimed at Subchan and other civilians who had turned
against him since 1965 and were thought by intelligence men to be
behind the protests and press criticism. The junta could never
believe that criticism could be the spontaneous expression of
independent minds, and it was always looking for cloak and dagger
operations similar to its own. In the words of a young dissident,
Arief Budiman, who was arrested, Kopkamtib had a habit of
'writing melodramatic scenarios and looking afterwards for the
facts to fit them'. Suharto's speech was followed by a Kopkamtib
warning to newspapers not to report the statements of 'street
parliaments', that is, any critical statement made outside the
well-controlled DPR. Four organizations that had been formed to
fight the project were dissolved; they were the Savings Drive
Movement, People's Money Safeguarding Movement, and
Common Sense Movement, all named with typically cautious
irony, and the surprisingly blunt Anti-Miniature Movement.
Students who tried to present arguments to various people,
including Mrs Suharto, were hounded from the streets, although
they limited themselves to small groups in an attempt to defeat
the ban on demonstrations. In January 1972 eight students,
including a girl, squatted on grass outside police headquarters and
vowed to remain there until Budiman, who led them, and two
arrested students were released. Nobody asked them to leave,
but after they had maintained a vigil for five days and nights, a
squad of police, armed with electric rods and idiotically protecting
themselves with riot shields, darted out and dragged the students
fifty metres down the road; one student fainted and was taken to
hospital by his comrades.

Johannes Princen was arrested on 20 January because he
frequently accompanied students on their missions. The Managing
Editor of *Sinar Harapan*, Aristides Katoppo, its defence correspondent and a member of its board, were detained after the
newspaper had published a report that Suharto had instructed

ministries not to aid Indonesia in Miniature; Suharto had in fact given the instruction, apparently to appease the Planning Board and other critics inside the administration; but the junta claimed that the information had been given to newspapers at a confidential briefing – at which *Sinar Harapan* was not represented. Katoppo was interrogated for twenty hours, almost without interruption. Among questions put to the newspaper's defence correspondent was whether he had read Plato's *Republic*. In February I invited Katoppo as my guest at a Jakarta Foreign Correspondents' Club luncheon, which was addressed by Lieutenant-General Sumitro, Deputy Commander of Kopkamtib; I was naive enough to think that it might be a good thing if the two had a chat in an informal atmosphere. I do not know whether the ever-suspicious Sumitro thought there was a plot to kill him, but twenty of his security men began searching the restaurant, including the kitchen, where I suppose poison might have been laid, at 8 a.m. on the day of the luncheon. Half an hour before guests were due to arrive, I received a note from Katoppo that Kopkamtib had again detained him for questioning. I told Sumitro I was disappointed that this day had been chosen for the interrogation. Sumitro smiled and asked if I saw Katoppo often. Here, after all, was a possible link with foreign subversion. Katoppo's second interrogation began at 10 a.m. on 4 February and lasted until 1 p.m. on 5 February, with four hours allowed for sleep; one of his interrogators consoled him by recalling that it took many years to clear up the Dreyfus case and that nobody yet knew who was behind the murder of President Kennedy.

By 24 February 1972 Princen and the three students were released; the longest detained was Princen, who had been interrogated for a month and freed on condition that he remained in Jakarta. Critics of Indonesia in Miniature were given an opportunity to express their opinions to a parliamentary committee, which produced a meaningless report; after that they were silent. University professors never renewed their briefly expressed concern about the arrests, and the Bar Association left in the air its request for clarification of Kopkamtib's powers; poets who had gathered to read poems of protest against repression, including some written in colonial days, were not heard again for some time. Mrs Suharto's project was carried out at a final cost that was never disclosed. What it cost her husband in prestige and power has yet to be assessed. But Indonesians, who have a habit of propagating self-fulfilling prophecies, were saying in Jakarta before the end of 1972 that centuries ago a Sundanese soothsayer had prophesied that Java would one day be ruled by a king who would be brought down by his wife's misdeeds.

In January 1972 the double wedding of Suharto's eldest son and a daughter took place. It was denied that seventy gold-plated kris were presented to important guests, but the published figure of $20,000 for the total cost, which might have been on the low side, was never disputed. Although the ceremony was that of commoners, Mrs Suharto, who is descended from minor royalty, saw to it that her children wore lavish costumes worthy of a prince and princess; she had already furnished a palace reception room with yellow, the colour associated with royalty in Java and other parts of South East Asia.

Winding up the parties

Comical though it was, the hysteria with which Suharto and some of his circle handled objections to the Indonesia in Minature project had a practical cause. At that time the junta was busy with a new stage in its plan to castrate the political parties, a delicate operation, which was one of the causes of the March nerves; it feared that if public indignation were allowed to rise politicians might be encouraged to show fight. At the MPR session in June–July 1966 the junta had put through a resolution calling for simplification of the parties. On 2 February 1970 Suharto suggested that the parties be divided into two groups, with the 'functional group' (the army and Golkar) as the third. He reiterated his idea at a cabinet meeting on 3 March, pointing out that his aim was to 'guarantee maximum security' at the elections. But although motions were made to oblige him, nothing came of his proposal in practice. Suharto did not press the matter, apparently thinking it better to be let the parties remain separate until after the elections, when his certain victory would make it easier to deal with them.

In May 1971 Ali Murtopo made an ominous announcement, one of several, that the 'political structure' would be reformed after the elections. Familiar as they were with Murtopo's methods, those leaders still interested in preserving their political identity were unnerved rather than reassured by his statement that the parties would not be dissolved, and they anxiously awaited the day when their fate would be clear. They received their first inkling on 6 October when Suharto summoned selected leaders of the parties by telephone in two groups, with which he conferred separately. It was at once obvious that these were the groups into which the seven parties that won seats would be marshalled when the new DPR met for the first time on 28 October. Two days later Suharto conferred with leaders of each party separately. He then announced that the parties would sit in parliament in two strangely named groups, the Spiritual Material (consisting of the Moslem parties, NU, Parmusi, PSSI, and Perti) and the Material Spiritual (the PNI, the Partai Katolik, and Parkindo). The armed forces and Golkar were also to sit separately. Ali Murtopo had been talking for some time about the Spiritual Material and Material Spiritual groups or *fraksi* (from the Dutch *fractie*). Just before the elections I asked him what was the difference in the meaning of the names and whether the Christians, lumped with the secular PNI, were considered to be less spiritual than the Moslems. 'They are just names', he said with a smile. He seemed to feel that since the political parties were of little account it did not matter what they were called. On the suggestion of some of the parties Material Spiritual was changed to Democratic Development (Demokrasi Pembangunan) and Spiritual Material to Development Union (Persatuan Pembangunan), the names that had been proposed in 1970.

While the parties retained their identity, each of the two groups was required to reach agreement within itself before issues came up in the DPR. A passing political analyst might have asked whether transferring wrangles from inside to outside the house would achieve the commendable aim of speeding parliamentary business. But there was no problem here; for Suharto had formed the groups merely as a brief step towards squeezing the last breath from the parties by means of enforced mergers. He made this clear when he suggested to party leaders during the discussions that began on 6 October that to simplify politics only three symbols, including that of Golkar, should be used in the 1976 elections.

By this time Murtopo had organized support for the mergers inside the parties. The PNI was too weak to fight, and the resistance of a few of its members was nullified by the acquiescence of most of its leaders. Idham Chalid, General Chairman of the NU, had fallen into line with the junta long before the elections. A former advocate of Nasakom, well described by a newspaper as a chameleon, he had found no difficulty in sliding from Sukarno's inner cabinet into that of Suharto in 1966; during the elections he remained aloof, apart from reproving Subchan for having criticized Suharto. Suharto's nominee in Parmusi, Mintaredja, was so dedicated to the party's political suicide that during the elections he had said that a victory for Golkar would be a victory for Parmusi. But there was still opposition, led notably by Subchan and by M. C. Ibrahim, General Chairman of the PSII, who dismissed leaders of branches that had merged under pressure. Suharto had excluded each of them from his palace meetings, while inviting lower-rank representatives of their parties; he now left it to Murtopo to get rid of them. Subchan was ousted from his position of First NU Chairman at an engineered board meeting in February 1972. In a letter to party branches he protested that the move was illegal and contrary to the party congress's decision in the previous December to re-elect him; he said that he would consider himself to be in office until the next congress. But whatever support he might have had in the branches he had lost to Murtopo in Jakarta, and was powerless.

Resistance in the PSII was strong; the party, though small, derived from the Sarekat Islam, which at one stage had dominated the struggle for independence. Murtopo intervened, split the party, and in December organized a take-over similar to the one brought about by Naro in Parmusi. He first sent in a band of youths calling themselves 'The Team to Save the PSII' to seize the party office; the aim, however, was not to save the PSII but to liquidate it politically. A few days later an 'emergency leadership' was set up under Anwar Tjokroaminoto, who had been defeated in elections for the chairmanship, but had attended the palace meetings in October after having conspired with the junta for some time. Ironically, Tjokroaminoto was the son of the famous leader of Sarekat Islam, whose imprisonment by the Dutch had led Sukarno to suspend his studies in order to aid the family. Anwar's support for the enemies of his father's *protégé* and his slaying of the offspring of his father's party was an event of Oedipus proportions; he died in November 1975, aged sixty-six.

Murtopo also dealt with Murba, a small but influential, socially conscious party that had been disrupted since the death of its leader, Sukarni, at the age of 55 on 7 May 1971, during the election campaign; Murtopo set up a new board headed by a man who, the old board said, was not a party member.

Despite its gains after the palace meetings of October 1971 the junta was cautious in its advance towards the complete merger of the parties into two groups. In April 1972 Lieutenant-General Sutopo Juwono, head of Bakin, said the issue could 'produce tensions' before the March MPR meeting. There were fears that if the pace were too rapid politicians who actively resisted would be joined by those who hesitated. But Suharto's patience was not unlimited; and during a conference with Democratic Development leaders at his private house in September he ominously mentioned the possibility that only one political group would compete against Golkar at the next elections. The hint was not missed; on 25 October leaders of the four Islamic parties announced after a conference with Suharto that the Development Union would fight the 1976 elections under one flag. Through Mintaredja, who forecast further 'consolidation', Suharto made it known that he would not be satisfied with the new confederation and would insist on a full merger.

But Suharto had already brought off a great victory. Mintaredja disclosed that it was on Suharto's suggestion that the parties had decided not to give themselves an 'ideological name, such as Islamic Group'. This meant that Islam had abandoned its right to campaign under its own banner, which had been a rallying point for its followers since colonial days and before. In place of the old, battling Moslem parties was a single, innocuous group, indistinguishable in its permitted aims from Golkar, but without Golkar's electioneering resources. This one fact makes nonsense of statements that the Moslems would gain from their enforced unity; the junta's aim was not to strengthen them but to destroy them politically.

Vanquished though they were for all practical purposes, some Moslem leaders, under pressure from their following, tried to avert full abdication; but on 5 January 1973 the four Moslem parties converted the Development Union group into the Development Union Party (Partai Persatuan Pembangunan) and said they would merge all their political activities, while continuing their social work separately. The five parties of the Democratic Development group also tried to stall the issue. They cited a 1966 MPRS decision to support their view that simplification of the political structure should be carried out by legislation. Meanwhile they pointed out that the group had already succeeded in uniting the principles and objectives of its five members 'on the basis of *Pancasila*' – a typically meaningless statement, which reflects the low level of Indonesian political discussion. But this weak manoeuvre was of no avail; and late on the night of 10 January 1973 the group followed the Moslems and became the Indonesian Democratic Party (Partai Demokrasi Indonesia) with the PNI's Mohammad Isnaeni as its General Chairman. As with the Moslems, the individual parties were to merge politically, retaining their own organizations only for social activities.

Suharto thus achieved his goal of bringing about the mergers before the MPR March meeting with two good months to spare. As the newspaper *Kompas* euphemistically put it: '. . . force outside joined in playing a role, at least in creating the momentum'. The so-called simplification of the political structure meant no more than simplification of the junta's stranglehold: two parties, formed by pressure at the top, could be more easily managed than seven. As for the bottom, this was eliminated altogether under the 'floating mass' principle, which forbade political activity between election campaigns below the district level, that is to say, in the villages. Since most of the people lived in villages this meant there were to be virtually no politics at all. This idea had been aired by the generals for more than a year; in September 1971 it provoked protests from PNI and NU leaders; now it had become a reality. The villagers, the theory was, would be better devoting their energies to development than politics. At election time the two new parties would be free to compete for the 'floating mass', the junta promised. But in reality they would be without organization and their new, unfamiliar symbols would be lost in proliferation of the Golkar banyan tree.

The destruction of the nine parties that had contested the elections effected a final break with the nation's political past. Some of them, notably the PSII, PNI and NU, had links going back to colonial days. To pull down their election banners was like breaking up some regiment, rich in tradition, and consigning its emblems to the rubbish heap. That their demise passed off so smoothly, with scarcely more than whispered protests, was not only the result of Suharto's ruthlessness and superb tactics and the weakness and opportunism of most of the leaders. There was no real political structure. The parties had no deep social base; they were like fungi clinging to an artificial tree. Neither the PNI nor the Moslem parties possessed mass support in the generally accepted sense of the word; their followers were for the most part people devoid of aspiration, who in the elections of 1971, as in 1955, did not respond to appeal so much as yield to fear. In such an environment the armed forces were bound to win a total victory. The junta could have got rid of the parties earlier, but wanted to give an appearance of consensus, not least to protect its Western governmental backers from criticism at home. The conspiracy to pretend that Indonesia was a democracy was as deep as that which attempted to disguise the West Irian fiasco.

While winding up the political parties, the junta made sure that the MPR executive machinery could never be used to rally opposition. Nasution, as Chairman, and Subchan, one of the four Vice-Chairmen, who occupied adjoining offices in the MPR secretariat building, were regarded as a danger. Their removal once the elections were over was certain, but filling the vacancies remained a problem. To put one of the junta at the head of the MPR would not only create a bad impression overseas, but would provide a possible base for a rival to Suharto; and civilians, Golkar or not, were all distrusted. There was speculation in newspapers and among diplomats about who was to be appointed. A few weeks after the elections I asked Murtopo who would be the new Chairman. He gave an unexpected reply. 'We are not going to have one', he laughed. 'That's a good one, isn't it!' I had to admit it was. The junta decided that the speaker and Vice-Speaker of the DPR would hold office in the MPR, but only during its rare sessions, between which the administration would be run by faceless clerks. Murtopo always enjoyed his manipulations and relished the comedy of this one. He was in exceptionally good spirits that day, with the election success just behind him. I told him that I had found the feelings of Moslem youth extremely strong during my recent visit to East Java, and asked him whether he expected trouble there. 'No', he said. 'The Jihat (holy war) Brigade are mostly my men. They tell me what is happening. When I hear that Subchan has given some instructions, I ring him and say:

"What's this you are up to?" ' Typically, Murtopo had set up a little band to act as both informers and *provocateurs*. But Subchan was not yet finished; he and Nasution were busy preparing a report on MPR affairs from 1966 to 1972, which included letters from the President on various matters. Police seized most of the copies in January 1973, but a few survived, including one given to me by Subchan with the remark: 'This shows how Suharto has failed to carry out the MPRS decisions.'

The junta chose 1 October 1972, the seventh anniversary of the *putsch*, for the MPR's first meeting. The day began with a dawn visit to Crocodile Hole, where a modest, well-designed shrine had been erected in memory of the six generals and junior officer who were murdered. The session seemed to serve little purpose other than to emphasize the junta's authority and to rehearse both procedure and elaborate security precautions for the more important performance that was to follow in March 1973. The members, who were supposed to 'hold the sovereignty of the state', according to the 1945 constitution, were ordered to be in Jakarta not later than 24 September, after which they were issued with new suits and given instructions. As President Suharto explained in his opening speech, the MPR had 'absolute power', but it needed 'guidance'. Idham Chalid, as Chairman of the DPR, was elected MPR Chairman, in accordance with Murtopo's formula; among the four Vice-Chairmen was the equally obliging John Naro.

Suharto's men had long been setting up a chorus of fictitiously spontaneous demands for his re-election as President. As early as May 1971 Mintaredja was announcing that Parmusi proposed to nominate him, although not that the party would dissolve itself in the meantime. Antara published a series of requests from regional parliaments, party branches and other organizations that Suharto should agree to remain President. This evident engineering was drily described in the Moslem newspaper *Abadi* as 'computerized democracy', in which a hidden programmer automatically obtained the result he wanted. The campaign reached its climax after the opening of the main MPR session on 12 March, when Isnaeni joyfully announced at a press conference that Suharto had agreed to the Indonesian Democratic Party's plea that he should continue as President. Suharto had told the party's board: 'I accept if the people wish it.' He was elected unopposed on 22 March, with the Sultan of Yogyakarta, Hameng-kubuwono IX, as Vice-President.

I was not able to see this ceremony, because intelligence men had blocked the renewal of my visa, although they knew that I was to leave the country just after the MPR meeting to take up a post in Pakistan. I had particularly wanted to stay because in December Subchan had advised me: 'You must wait until after the MPR meeting. There may be a surprise.' He told me no more, except that there were several possibilities. Whatever the surprise was to have been, it did not come off at the MPR meeting, possibly because Subchan was no longer there to help bring it about.

I had only just got to know Subchan, but learned much from him in three long interviews. In January I was to have spent a weekend at his cottage in Bandung where, in the relative cool of the mountains, he was to have given me a detailed account of the repression of the Moslem parties, for use in this book; I also hoped to find out more than I knew about his anti-Communist activities just after the *putsch*. After Subchan had failed to keep his appointment to go to Bandung, I telephoned his house and was told he was ill. When I telephoned again some days later his secretary said he had gone on a pilgrimage to Mecca. I remembered his views on the death of Hadisubeno and wondered if he had gone to Mecca for the same reason that he had entered a Catholic hospital during the elections. Just before leaving Indonesia at the end of January, I telephoned his house again. This time I was told that he had just been killed in a road accident in Saudi Arabia.

Subchan was 42. When he was pushed out of the NU leadership, the newspaper, *Harian Kami*, wrote that political life would be dull indeed if the 'humorous bachelor' disappeared permanently from the scene. Now he was to receive an even higher tribute from the Catholic newspaper *Kompas*, which said, with admirable daring and integrity: 'He was courageous at a time [the elections] when most of us were intimidated.'

CHAPTER TEN

The power struggle

General Sumitro, Deputy Commander of Kopkamtib, was one
of those many Indonesians whose complexity may only be
glimpsed by the Western mind. He was proficient enough in
German to graduate creditably from the military staff college in
Hamburg and in English to address the Foreign Currespondents'
Club; but the education that made these accomplishments possible
did not extinguish the beliefs that had been taught to him since
childhood, and he was said by a military colleague to seek power
from occult practices in East Java, whence he came. A short, very
plump, choleric man, he had a habit of clenching and unclenching
his fist during conversation that displeased him; he was suspicious
and authoritarian, and was reputed to break up chance gatherings
of officers in the corridors of his headquarters; his junior officers
seemed frightened of him. Yet he was not without charm; and
some Western diplomats found him agreeable and exceptionally
intelligent in discussion.

In Sukarno's time, when the Central Javanese clique of generals
made few concessions to officers from other regions, Sumitro's
career was retarded. When he commanded the infantry school
advanced course at Bandung, as a colonel, some of his pupils
were senior in rank to him. After the *putsch* Suharto sent him to
maintain order in East Java, where Sukarnoism was particularly
strong, a task for which his East Javanese origin and former links
with the PNI especially qualified him. When he had pacified the

area to the extent consistent with balancing the Moslems against the PNI and avoiding a physical clash with the marines, Sumitro was recalled to Jakarta, where, now a Major-General, he succeeded in displacing Lieutenant-General Kartakasuma as Chief of Staff to the Minister of Defence. Suharto, who made a practice of exiling dangerous or disgruntled generals to diplomatic posts, first tried to get rid of Kartakasuma by naming him Ambassador in Bonn; but Kartakasuma rejected the appointment and clung to his post until Suharto rebuked and removed him.

Sumitro then carried out a radical reform of the command structure. Under the system inherited from Sukarno each of the three services, Army, Navy and Air Force had its own operational commander. In the new structure, which Suharto announced on Armed Forces Day, 5 October 1969, the commanders were replaced by chiefs of staff, who had no operational function; a similar change was made in the Police Force. All four services were placed under the direct command of Suharto, as Commander-in-Chief of the Armed Forces, or his deputy; none could be mobilized for any purpose without his orders. As Sumitro, who by that time was a Lieutenant-General, said the following day, the reorganization would 'prevent the occurrence of situations like those in Latin America, where the seizure of power is always accompanied by activities on the part of one of the armed forces or individuals from the armed forces'. In the preceding weeks, when it became known that the reorganization would take place, there was speculation about whom Suharto would trust with the potentially dangerous new position of Deputy Commander-in-Chief of the Armed Forces. Many observers, including diplomats at the German Embassy, thought that Sumitro would be appointed. But the man chosen was General Maraden Panggabean, former Army Chief of Staff. Sumitro became Deputy Commander of Kopkamtib, with General Panggabean as Commander; he abolished his own post of Chief of Staff to the Defence Minister, thus kicking aside a useful stepping stone for other ambitious generals.

It was said in the army that Sumitro himself proposed that Panggabean should be Deputy Commander-in-Chief. As an East Javanese, who still had to win support from Central Javanese in various strata, he did not yet feel strong enough to occupy the post with the kind of power he desired. Meanwhile Panggabean could be little more than a cipher: as a Sumatran and a Christian, he had little influence in the now-broadened Javanese clique; since he was approaching retiring age, he could be removed elegantly at any opportune time. Suharto probably also found it desirable to neutralize the post; he must have seen that Sumitro had already advanced far enough. But meanwhile Sumitro was able to extend his influence throughout the provinces; for as a vigorous day-to-day leader of the powerful Kopkamtib, with its virtually unlimited powers of repression and arrest, he was in constant touch with local commanders on the matters that counted most in maintaining the junta's rule.

Sumitro's nationalistic fervour, dating from the Sukarno period, was well exemplified by his loathing of the PSI for the part it had played in the Sumatran rebellion. He hated anything that threatened national integrity and undertook his security task with Teutonic earnestness and thoroughness. The responsibility for maintaining public calm during the period of party mergers preceding the MPR meeting was largely his. He was therefore exasperated, so I was told, when Mrs Suharto added to the causes of March nerves by clumsily launching her Indonesia in Miniature project and engaging in other activities, which confirmed public belief that she was in league with hated Chinese business men. One of Sumitro's jobs was to keep demonstrators off the streets; now the President's wife had given the army's more active enemies a pretext for encouraging them to come out at a critical time.

Sumitro, too, worked with a *cukong*, who adopted the respectable name of Bob Hasasan; he also had an interest in at least one foreign company, to which his only contribution was his influence. In addition to his commodious residence, which after alteration gave an impression of being fortified, he had a mansion, said to have been built by Pertamina, which would have yielded him a monthly rent of $1,500 or more. Since the early Sukarno days the army had been expected to supplement its budget with profits from enterprises. This principle became corruption when officers acted as individuals, rather than on behalf of their units. But Sumitro considered his sidelines to be modest, legitimate additions to his small salary, which was insufficient to maintain and educate his family in the way he desired; on the other hand he felt that such practices as placing trading permits in corrupt and inefficient hands were a danger to both the economy and public order.

People were restless when Suharto's brother built a mansion on a large corner block in the centre of Jakarta, lavishly using imported materials, with profits from a cloves monopoly and his other enterprises. They were not reassured when they heard that Mrs Suharto's brothers were making a muddle of business for which they should never have been licensed.

Sumitro saw himself as having to handle security problems that were aggravated by a clique to which he did not belong; for the inner circle, as it was called in the army, consisted only of Suharto, Soerjo, Murtopo and Major-General Sudjono Humardani, the President's Personal Assistant for Economic Affairs. On the assumption that the Indonesian economy is little more than a glorified *pasar*, it would be hard to find men more suited to have the final say in its management. Suharto was experienced in barter; Soerjo had begun his career as a book-keeper and boasted a long record of shady deals with the Chinese; Humardani, after running his Humardani Shop in Solo, had picked up a smattering of business training at Fort Benjamin Harrison, in the United States, and had acted as a go-between in various deals, mostly with Japanese; and Murtopo could wangle anything. Looking at the picture from a distance, there are times when that shabby image is all one sees. But Suharto's three closest assistants exemplified three of the hall-marks of his rule: political ruthlessness, in Murtopo; corruption, in Soerjo; and mysticism, in Humardani, who exercised an influence so profound that he was known to Indonesian journalists as Rasputin, although he worked through the President, not his wife.

Humardani was a weird man. He once received a Western ambassador in a darkened room, with objects that appeared to have occult significance looming up in the dimness; he was wearing a kind of Javanese costume and glided about in bare feet. At an international conference on regionalism in Jakarta in October 1974 he rapidly scribbled notes while Adam Malik was speaking. At the end of the speech he said: 'Bapak Malik, there is one question I want to ask you. Do we eat to live or live to eat?' Malik characteristically replied: 'A bit of both.' Astonished delegates learned later that Humardani was prompted to ask the question by a dream about a famine. In his capacity as Presidential Assistant Humardani made several visits to Japan, where his hosts left no appetite unsatisfied. I put it to one of Humardani's associates that the Japanese were bribing him. 'Humardani has taken nothing', he said. 'He does it all for Indonesia. All he has got out of it is a car.'

After Suharto had visited Japan in May 1972 it was announced that among credits that Pertamina would receive was one of $40 million from a consortium headed by the Sumitomo Bank. The rate of interest was to be that of Asian dollars, then about 6 per cent for six months, but this was not disclosed in Indonesia. Since Indonesia was borrowing from countries in the IGGI (Inter-Governmental Group on Indonesia, consisting of Western bloc countries committed to aid the Suharto government) at the specially low rate of 2½ per cent subsidized by their taxpayers, the higher rate caused concern in the planning Board and among some of the creditors. I had never managed to interview Humardani, but in August I spotted him at Suharto's Independence Night reception in the palace garden and got myself introduced to him. Before he could slip away I asked: 'What is the interest rate for the Sumitomo credit, general?'

'IGGI rates', he automatically replied.

'But the bank says it is to be the same as for Asian dollars', I said. 'That's 6 per cent, not 2½.'

Humardani gave a startled look as if he had been confronted with a fact for the first time in his life. 'Ooh! I don't know anything about that', said the President's Assistant for Economic Affairs.

'But I thought you were the big man in these deals with Japan, general.'

'Ooh, not now; maybe later', he said with a little cackle, hastily withdrawing into the shadows.

Was it possible that the President's assistant, after his frequent visits to Japan, did not know the credit terms? Or was he a liar, as well as a charlatan? Either way, it made no difference to the tragic fact that such a shifty nonentity could have so powerful a voice, or any voice at all, in the fate of 120 million unfortunate people. Suharto's reliance on him appears to have been inspired by special insight attributed to him by *dukuns*, whom they both consulted. It was *dukuns* who encouraged Suharto to visit Japan in May, against the advice of the Foreign Ministry, which found it unnecessary and humiliating for the President himself to go on a loan-raising trip; it was *dukuns* who, in the opinion of an expert at the German Embassy, prevented Suharto from receiving the biggest trade and industrial delegation ever to have left Western Germany. Humardani, a kind of *dukun* himself, helped to fell two Cabinet Ministers – Slamet Bratanata, a man of exceptional integrity, and Sumitro Djojohadikusumo, who had considerable ability. He was the only general present, apart from the cabinet secretary, when Suharto began his operation to merge the political parties at the palace in October. Apparently Suharto needed him more than anyone else on that critical occasion.

It may be assumed that the grotesque contradiction between a mystical quest for harmony on the one hand and unseemly corruption on the other displeased the relatively tidy mind of the German-trained Sumitro. It also unsettled other officers who, like those who launched the *putsch*, were disgusted, envious or both. On one occasion, purely out of politeness, I told a junior officer, whom I had just met, how much I admired his commander's mansion. 'Yes', he said, 'it is very good, very big. I live in a small house. It is very hot. And I do not like it.' It is rare for an officer to speak so frankly to a foreigner, and on such an occasion one merely nods ambiguously, since the voice may be that of an *agent provocateur*. But whether this man was trying to set a trap or was particularly reckless in his speech, his terse remark vividly amplified the hints of some whom I knew better.

While the Suharto circle gave privileges and a free hand to their *cukongs*, they created bitterness by ending many of the illicit practices of their subordinates. Suharto stopped a band of officers from smuggling through Tanjung Priok harbour and ruled that army enterprises must pay customs duties; armed forces smuggling in the Outer Islands was also curbed, in so far as it was possible; local commanders were repeatedly forbidden to exact taxes for their own benefit, although Chinese still found themselves paying protection money in various places. These attempts to mask the junta's essentially war-lord face were extended to the ranks. After a series of ugly incidents in Jakarta, the Defence Department announced in May 1970 that any serviceman who deliberately ran down and killed a civilian with a vehicle would be instantly dismissed. Gradually troops were brought under control; they ceased to attack bus conductors who insisted on their paying fares and cinema staff who would not admit them without tickets. But this enforced morality filled them not with virtue, but resentment, when they saw the growing opulence of those at the top.

It should be recorded that there were provincial commanders who were not aspiring war-lords, but were concerned only to serve their country. I do not know whether they were in the minority or majority. But Chinese in Pontianak, West Kalimantan, told me in 1972 that the commander was perfectly correct in his relations with them and exacted no tribute. This was an impressive compliment; for the Chinese in this province, who are confined to the coast to keep them out of touch with guerrillas from Sarawak, have no cause to be generous in their comments on the army. All the officers appeared to live simply, and those of the rank of major and below were housed in a row of sparsely furnished cottages that were, indeed, small and hot. These officers, under-equipped and under-manned, had the task of holding back what they and the Defence Department believed to be a threat from Peking. It was out of the question that any of them should complain in the presence of a passing foreigner; but it would be surprising if some did not occasionally compare their hard, monotonous life, far from their native Java, with that of the prosperous generals in Jakarta.

It was Subchan's opinion that most provincial military leaders and most officers of the important Siliwangi Division, but not their commander, were dissatisfied with the Suharto clique for one reason or another. He saw them as elements in a power struggle that was developing, although not planned, between the ruling élite and discontented senior officers, of whom Sumitro was the most important. Politically, Subchan said (in a conversation with the author), there was no difference between the two groups; both were totalitarian. But whereas the discontented would have been satisfied with full political control and limited personal luxury, the rulers wanted to be not only military dictators but merchant princes, and were trying to build private financial empires with the Chinese. The Suharto men were founding an Indonesian capitalist embryo. The others were either luke-warm towards capitalism or opposed to it; but they did not want Communism and were angry because the rulers' corruption and ostentatious display of wealth were helping to foster its revival. To these dissident forces, and overlapping with them to some extent, were officers who felt simply that the ruling clique was dishonouring the name of the TNI (Indonesian National Army) and those whose faith in Nasakom had been repressed but not destroyed.

While the ruling group is obviously well described in Subchan's analysis, its more diversified opponent needs elaboration, which Subchan could certainly have provided. But even in its rudimentary form the analysis is worth preserving. For it gives a broad picture of the forces which, although they were not organized, gave Sumitro confidence to increase the momentum of his career and press for more power; and it enabled Subchan to predict, before anyone else whom I met, important developments that lay ahead. My inquiries, discreet though they were, into the possible consequences of this situation probably caused the refusal to renew my visa. Malik's explanation to journalists was that I had 'too many contacts'; Murtopo told me with a grin on my last day that I had to leave 'just for sentimental reasons'. But there were hints that the real reason was that I was getting too close to the secrets of the embarrassing power struggle, using the key that Subchan had given me.

Sumitro's first evident strike was against one of the *cukongs* of Suharto's circle, Kwee Som Tjok, a textile manufacturer, who in the Sukarno days was a leading member of Baperki, a Communist-sponsored organization of Chinese Indonesians. Kwee's considerable interests included batik sold under the trade-name, Keris. Mrs Suharto had opened an exhibition of this product in August 1972. While Suharto's spokesman denied that she had any business association with Kwee, a military officer told me that this was merely a technical point, because the link was effected through the Yayasan Harapan Kita. After the opening of the exhibition a journalist, acting in tune with the rising public resentment of the partnership between the Suhartos and the *cukongs*, questioned Kwee about his association with Baperki. Kwee's wealth and his connexion with the Suhartos had apparently given him more arrogance than sense; he boasted that if he were arrested he would be freed within twenty-four hours. Sumitro took up this challenge: the Semarang military commander, acting in his Kopkamtib capacity, arrested Kwee and put him under interrogation about Baperki. On 10 September Antara News Agency reported the Semarang Kopkamtib command spokesman as saying that Kwee had made his boast 'on the assumption of having obtained sympathy from senior officials for his success in popularizing batik as a national product'. This veiled sneer at the Suharto circle was a sure sign of Sumitro's rising influence, since Antara, a government-supervised agency, clearly showed that it had nothing to fear from security men. The spokesman added that the Semarang commander had taken measures to 'maintain the operation of the batik industry' while Kwee was under detention. This was an incredible affront to the Suhartos. With the co-operation of Kwee and others, they had developed their batik interests to such an extent that Suharto had opened a batik market, which was in fact a vast complex of unnecessary, modern showrooms, in Solo in 1971; now one of Sumitro's men was saying that he had ensured that the industry was 'still running smoothly'.

The arrest of the *cukong* upon whom Mrs Suharto had beamed her approval at his batik exhibition was a brilliant, resolute stroke, which Sumitro could not have attempted but for the background of army discontent so well observed by Subchan; it would have at once consolidated and increased the tacit support of which he must have become aware when he conversed with local military commanders and other generals, with that subtle indirectness in which Javanese excel. And it won the open acclaim of non-Chinese business men and other civilians.

With newspapers gleefully reporting that Kwee was still under arrest, Suharto instructed Sutopo Juwono, head of Bakin, to summon newspaper editors and tell them that action was being taken to prevent Chinese subversion. But nobody believed this hocus-pocus, and Sumitro cleverly retaliated by calling a conference of his own. In the presence of eleven generals, he told seven selected newspaper editors that he needed their support in a dialogue on security and other national issues. Two newspapers would be allowed to write about anything that the editor chose, including Communism. But, for a start, only one, *Nusantara*, would be given this freedom. This was an astoundingly bold manoeuvre. *Nusantara* had been waging an incessant campaign of invective against the *cukongs*, and had clearly indicated their connexion with the Suharto circle. It was *Nusantara's* editor, Hafas, who had been prosecuted by Murtopo's instigation under the Dutch law against hate-sowing. Hafas, with his appeal still unheard, was now being told by Sumitro that he could write anything he liked. Since Sumitro controlled the only effective security force, this gave Hafas full protection from Murtopo; no less important, it put him beyond the reach of Humardani, who bragged that he had brought about the dismissal of a Defence Department spokesman because he was a friend of *Nusantara's* proprietor, Hassan.

Sumitro's challenge was thus aimed at the entire inner circle. Since no attempt was made to dislodge him, it appeared that he commanded powerful military backing, which was no longer merely tacit. A foreign military attaché, who made a special investigation, said that Sumitro, despite his East Javanese origin, had the support of more than half the officers in the Central Java Diponegoro Division, formerly commanded by Suharto; this did not mean that they were planning a coup, but that they preferred Sumitro as a leader. With rumours of an anti-Suharto army conspiracy spreading in the civil service, an official asked me: 'Have you heard that Sutopo Juwono and Sumitro are now working together?' I had no information about this; but I established later that Sutopo, whose intelligence activities reached as far as Peking, considered the Suharto circle's *cukongs* to be a danger.

The temperature behind the scenes became more apparent when another civil servant, after fulminating against corruption, blurted: 'Do you think that Sumitro would make a better President than Suharto?' I had never expected to hear such words in Jakarta, and was completely taken aback by the question; had I not known the man well, I should have been sure that he was an *agent provocateur*. All I said in reply was that any unconstitutional act would be bad for Indonesia. 'It would be done constitutionally,' he said. Soon afterwards an internationally known Indonesian with good contacts in the army told me: 'Sumitro will be President within a year.' Rumours that Sumitro's influence was increasing reached the embassies, and there was a significant increase in the flow of those fair-weather friends, the diplomats, to his office. Whatever people might have been expecting from Sumitro, I do not think it was ever in his mind to become President. Subchan thought that Sumitro knew he did not have the right personality for a head of state. Sumitro's ultimate goal, he said, was to become Defence Minister and Commander-in-Chief of the Armed Forces; with this power in his hands, he could rule through a puppet President, possibly a civilian. For the time being he aimed simply to become full Commander, instead of Deputy Commander, of Kopkamtib. As events showed, Subchan was on the right track. But he underestimated the potential of both Sumitro and the rest of the discontented group. For after the MPR meeting, when Suharto announced cabinet and other changes on 27 March 1973, Sumitro was appointed not only Kopkamtib Commander but Deputy Commander-in-Chief of the Armed Forces. Suharto abandoned the post of Commander-in-Chief and handed it over, with the portfolio of Defence Minister, to Panggabean.

Thus Sumitro had created a situation in which he could make his next moves at his own pace, as he had done in 1969, when Panggabean was made titular Kopkamtib Commander. Suharto was virtually out of the army, while Panggabean, whose retirement was near, could exercise no more control over the armed forces than he had over Kopkamtib. Sumitro, now virtually in full command of both the armed forces as such and the security network within the army, was well poised for a further advance; he had converted to his own use the structure that he had devised, ostensibly to protect Suharto, in 1969. Under the 1945 constitution the President held 'the highest authority over the army, the navy and the air force', but Sukarno had found it necessary to secure this authority by appointing himself Commander-in-Chief. Now the head of the military junta, although faced by an ambitious rival, had abandoned a position considered indispensable by his civilian predecessor. To those few who had been watching Sumitro's career since 1969 the significance of Suharto's abdication was clear. But others thought that Suharto's withdrawal to a purely civilian function meant that he was in such a strong position that he could rely on others to do the security work while he attended to more important affairs of state. Doubtless this is what almost any of Jakarta's smiling generals would have told questioners, to preserve an appearance of unity; they might, indeed, have adopted this face-saving device among themselves in the tortuous negotiations that preceded the changes. But the view was utterly mistaken. Yet Suharto, although his position was weak, had not become weak himself; he remained the strong, ruthless man who overthrew the founder of the nation. As will be seen, his yielding to Sumitro was not a surrender but a tactical retreat, executed with his superior cunning.

Suharto's plight might have been even more serious had Subchan been alive. The surprise development of which Subchan spoke could well have been a plan of his own to defy Suharto at the MPR meeting, relying on Sumitro's support. This was by no means out of the question; he had the courage, and had already made a start with his provocative MPRS report. The preponderance of Golkar and nominated members did not in itself guarantee support for Suharto. The junta as a whole obviously distrusted Golkar, and when I asked a general early in 1972 to explain why, he said simply: 'There are too many Moslems among them.' The Moslems remained a potential danger even after their parties had been demolished.

Subchan had some useful ammunition, of which other civilians were also aware. He told me that Chinese associated with the Suharto circle had received 82 per cent of 56 billion rupiahs (about $135 million) domestic investment credits granted by Indonesian banks in 1970–71. Some of this capital, instead of being used for economic development in Indonesia, had been invested overseas. Waringin Finance Ltd owned a jute mill in Singapore in addition to the smelting plant mentioned in the officer's report (see chapter VII). The Suhartos shared with Ibnu Sutowo the Robin Shipyard, Robin Air and an office building, all in Singapore, with Robin Low, a Chinese, as nominee. The Suharto circle's interests are obviously so vast that I have no compunction for publishing these allegations without proof that they are authentic. However, inquiries in Singapore established that Low, whom Subchan described as the Pertamina agent, does exist. A former taxi driver, he is now one of the wealthiest men in Singapore. Companies that bear his name are Robin Air, Robin Construction Company, Robin Development Company, Robin Dredging, Robin Shipbuilders, Robin Shipyard, Robina Advertising and Robin department store, all housed in a building of more than twenty stories. What is relevant here is that had Subchan flung such inflammatory material across the floor of the MPR under Sumitro's protection, which he might well have been able to obtain, there could, indeed, have been a surprise. A link, however transient, between the Moslem parties and Sumitro was all that was needed to bring the Suharto clique down at that critical time.

Fortunate though it was for the inner circle, Subchan's death did not diminish the danger that widespread civilian and military discontent would encourage any purposeful dissident, such as Sumitro. Before I left Jakarta there was already an upsurge of bitterness and contempt. The junta had ridden roughshod over numerous groups and individuals, who, whatever their failings had been in the past, thought themselves more qualified than the generals to decide how the country should be run. The technocrats were unhappy. Though nominally in charge of the economy, they were faced with the Suharto circle's haphazard and irregular use of credit, Pertamina's serious over-borrowing and a host of other anomalies that made comprehensive planning impossible. Golkar was still rigidly directed by the junta, whose officers occupied its main executive positions and were planted in the advisory board. For most members the groups' election victory was a mockery. The generals, fearing that any initiative other than their own would have political consequences, suppressed every attempt of the rank and file to propose reforms that were vital to the economic enclave; only a small coterie, which had worked with Murtopo from the beginning to make Golkar the junta's instrument, had any say whatever in governing the nation.

In January 1973 I invited Lim Bian Kie, who was one of the coterie, to produce evidence of any initiative that Golkar had taken in parliament. He arranged a meeting with some leading members, but after a long discussion it appeared that all they had been able to achieve was to present a report on the 1972 rice crisis. Measures such as making Pertamina accountable to parliament, bringing all the army's revenues under strict parliamentary control and the setting up of a commission to examine the Suharto circle's financial empire had not been considered. The powerlessness of Golkar, the majority group, reduced parliament to less than an advisory council. I asked a retired politician, who had taken part in the fight for independence, whether he considered that the DPR had more authority than the Volksraad, an advisory body with limited legislative powers set up by the Dutch to appease nationalists. 'No', he said, relishing the irony of the situation. 'The minutes of the Volksraad make refreshing reading these days.' He saw no prospect of improvement until the nation had somehow got rid of 'this footling gang'.

But others were not as resigned. One non-political professional man of ability and integrity, who impressed me with his common sense, said:

We have three big problems: one, the population explosion; two, unemployment; three, we are immobilized by the sea [between the islands]. To solve them we need men of zeal, passion. The severest critics are those who overthrew the Founder to put this regime in power. They wanted a more pragmatic approach . . . They [the army] have had seven years. Where the country needs men to inspire the people, now we have leaders who have aroused contempt. This is perhaps their greatest crime. It is not only the educated, the intellectuals who are disillusioned, but the common people. My mother is illiterate. Yet she asked: 'What is this lady [Mrs Suharto] doing, buying up land and dealing with financiers?' . . . Then there is the cosmopolitan capitalist. It does not matter to him whether his factory is here or in Taipeh or Hong Kong or New Orleans. For him the most important aim is to have Indonesia as a market. That is why the world is keeping us not too poor, but not too rich, not wanting us to build our economy faster. This is why we have not [in power] a Moslem party with a progressive Moslem programme, or a nationalist party with zeal, or a socialist party driven by socialist idealism. You must have passion to fight injustice. They want to keep us servile, docile and mediocre.

This man's eloquence in a language that was his third (he was speaking in English; normally he spoke Indonesian or Dutch), like the eloquence of the ex-politician with his ironic nostalgia for the Volksraad, indicates the quality of minds that the junta was suppressing. His ideas were shared by large numbers of people who felt that the junta was not only corrupt, but the instrument of neo-colonialism. His last words to me were: 'What we have to do is to convince the youth of this country that it is no disgrace to be arrested by this gang.'

This was an unwitting statement of despair; for despite the legends, the young had never played an important part in social change in Indonesia and were not likely to be effective against the scores of armoured cars parked at vantage points in Jakarta or against the American M-16 automatic rifles with which some security forces were armed. The few who were continuing their protests at that time were easily handled. Early in December 1972 thirty-five students tried to present a statement to the State Secretary, Major-General Sudharmono, about the rice shortage, which was so acute that people in some areas were eating leaves.

After Sudharmono had refused to see them, police arrested twenty-one and detained them for interrogation.

One of the first overt signs of deep anger among civilians and in sections of the armed forces was the anti-Chinese riot in Bandung, West Java, on 5 August 1973, when more than 1,500 shops were damaged. Violence began about 4 p.m. The failure of the Siliwangi Division to intervene until late in the evening suggested sympathy with the rioters, and recalls Subchan's statement that most of the division were opposed to Suharto. Nineteen officers and men, including two Lieutenant-Colonels, were later arrested on the usual ground that they were influenced by the underground Communist Party. In Jakarta students at the University of Indonesia issued a 'Petition of 24 October', in which they condemned 'violation of the law, raging corruption, abuse of authority, rising prices, and unemployment'. On 11 November the newly-formed Indonesia for Indonesia Student Movement handed the visiting Dutch Minister for Development and Co-operation, Jan P. Pronk, a statement declaring: '. . . we do not take pride in the results of foreign aid in the form of high buildings and hotels, Coca-Cola, night clubs etc. . . . more people are without jobs, homes and land; our small textile industry has died; our forests have become barren and our oilfields depleted.'

Sumitro then appeared vividly on the scene with visits to universities in West, East, and Central Java in November. He promised a 'new pattern of leadership' and extended to students the offer of 'two-way communication' that he had made to selected editors fifteen months previously. More significantly still, he made an approach to the Moslems. In September several hundred Moslem students had forced their way on to the floor of the DPR when the Minister for Religion, Mukti Ali, was speaking on a bill to unify marriage and divorce laws for all religions. The bill, like any other that went before parliament, had the backing of Suharto, who saw it as part of his plan to bring about the complete secularization of Moslems. The alliance between Sumitro and Sutopo Juwono now became evident when the two approached Moslem leaders and offered them a new bill, which, with modifications, became law when it was passed with Moslem support in December.

This was an ominous setback for the Suharto circle. The entire armed forces, Sumitro included, had been mobilized to wage an election campaign of unprecedented ruthlessness, in which the

Moslems had been seen as the most dangerous opponent; measures had been enforced to control both the DPR and MPR; the Moslem parties, along with the others, had been virtually banned from politics and forbidden even to call themselves by their own names. Now, after all this elaborate repression, Sumitro and Sutopo Juwono had joined forces with the enemy, bringing together Moslems inside and outside Golkar. The danger to Suharto was obvious.

A new threat then emerged. As early as October 1972 I was told by what turned out to be an exceptionally well-informed source that Sumitro was beginning to form an alliance with Nasution, who had more links with the Moslems than any other general. On 11 January 1974 the two generals went to Magelang, Central Java, where the Military Academy is situated. Sarwo Edhie had been languishing there since Suharto had shunted him into a *cul-de-sac* as Governor of the Academy after the West Irian operation. While there appears to be no proof that the three generals met, it seems highly improbable that Sumitro and Nasution had any other purpose in visiting Magelang than to confer, if not to conspire, with Sarwo Edhie.

Whatever the plans of Sumitro and his allies were, they obviously included at least connivance in student demonstrations, which led to ferocious riots that broke out during the visit of the Japanese Prime Minister, Kakuei Tanaka, five days after the Magelang trip. Ostensibly the riots were directed against Japanese economic penetration; but it was obvious that this was merely a pretext, inspired by similar outbreaks in Bangkok, and that the real target was the Suharto circle. Before Tanaka's arrival on 14 January Sumitro's security forces did not prevent students from demonstrating outside Ali Murtopo's office and burning effigies of Sudjono Humardani, as well as Tanaka, in Jakarta and Bandung. Leaflets distributed by thousands of students who paraded through the city on the morning after Tanaka's arrival demanded the dismissal of Suharto's three special assistants – Humardani, Murtopo and Soerjo – a reduction in prices, and an end to corruption. They called their demands Tritura 74, echoing the People's Three Demands formulated in the 1966 campaign against Sukarno. Correspondents were surprised to find that Sumitro, instead of suppressing the demonstrators, was amiably chatting with them from a jeep outside the Japanese Embassy.

Mobs from the poorer quarters joined the students, and for two days Jakarta was shaken by violent rioting. The showrooms of the Astra motor company, a Japanese concern in which Mrs Suharto was believed to have an interest, were heavily damaged; more than 100 shops were burned and looted; 650 Japanese and other motor cars were set on fire or battered; a crowd of several thousand blocked a six-lane road while youths ransacked massage parlours and burned the furniture in the street. In some areas of the city security forces fired on the mobs. By the time the riot had subsided at least eleven civilians had been killed and about 130 injured.

The sudden appearance of the mobs and the conversion of the student demonstration into a large-scale riot needs explanation. The mobs consisted of *becak* drivers, youths and even children from the poorer quarters; they certainly would have had no organizational link with the students. It is inconceivable that Sumitro, who was responsible for security, would have set such an uncontrollable force in motion; his aim was evidently to intensify civilian and military pressure on the Suharto clique, not to try and overthrow it violently from the streets. The newspaper *Indonesia Raya* hinted that Ali Murtopo had organized the provocation of the mobs in order to bring discredit upon Sumitro; certainly Murtopo's organization, Opsus (Special Operations), was the only one in Jakarta with a team capable of doing such a job.

Whoever was behind the violence, Suharto turned it to his advantage: he dismissed Sumitro and took over the post of Kopkamtib commander himself. Once again Suharto had displayed an uncanny patience, which could only have arisen from complete confidence in his ultimate victory over all adversaries. Ten months previously he had yielded the powerful security command and exposed the control of the entire armed forces to Sumitro, an obviously dangerous rival. He then sat back and watched while Sumitro increasingly over-reached himself; always the military strategist, he possibly even encouraged support for Sumitro here and there, to tempt him to advance too far. During those ten months Suharto awaited, and possibly arranged, his opportunity. When the riots broke out he struck.

Koptamtib, the Order and Security Restoration Command, was the organization Suharto had established under Sukarno's 11 March Order in 1966. His resumption of the command reminded everyone that this was the man who had overthrown Sukarno. Generals and other officers who had begun to look to Sumitro would have been disillusioned and alarmed when the outcome of his operation against the Suharto clique led to riots that threatened the entire military structure. With the boat perilously rocking, they were doubtless relieved to see the old captain back at the helm. Suharto, therefore, had no difficulty in disposing of his opponents. With his usual solicitude for the appearance of unity in the junta, he offered ambassadorships to Sumitro, Sutopo Juwono and Sarwo Edhie. Sumitro declined, but Sutopo Juwono became Ambassador to the Netherlands and Sarwo Edhie Ambassador to South Korea. Some less important officers were also significantly transferred.

Since the official statements denied that there had been any friction in the armed forces, a scapegoat had to be found for the riots. After the 1965 *putsch* it had been possible to blame the PKI for a rebellion in the army carried out by officers, some of whom had motives similar to those of Sumitro and his supporters. This time people connected with the banned Masjumi and PSI were made to carry the cross of the army power struggle; their parties' role in the Sumatra rebellion was dragged up and they were accused of again trying to subvert the Republic by overthrowing the President. In the inevitable witch-hunt more than 200 were questioned; of these forty-two, including university lecturers, students, lawyers and politicians, were held for trial on subversion charges. The junta claimed that the ringleader was an economist, Professor Sarbini, who was a known critic of the government's economic policies. Eleven newspapers and magazines were banned. It was announced in February that seven of the publications, including the English language *Djakarta Times*, *Indonesia Raya*, *Harian Kami* and *Abadi*, would not be allowed to resume publication; the fate of the other four was to be decided later. Mochtar Lubis, the Editor of *Indonesia Raya*, who had launched the campaign against Ibnu Sutowo in 1969, was arrested in February, but released in the middle of April.

It is a fact that some members of the PSI, despite the ban that had been in force since Sukarno's time, met at intervals and considered their party to be still functioning secretly. It is also true that contact between some army officers and political leaders, including former Masjumi and PSI men, was growing before I left Jakarta in January 1973. But to claim that the civilians were trying to overthrow the military government is absurd. At the most they would have done no more than incite to riot, and even this is doubtful. Probably the few who were involved with Sumitro, Nasution, Sutopo Juwono and Sarwo Edhie hoped for no more than a change of government brought about legitimately by the MPR. But men like Sarbini, a thinker of integrity who had refused to become a tool of the junta and its *cukongs*, were to be sacrificed to maintain the fiction of army unity. Fortunately for the alleged conspirators, an acute financial crisis came to their rescue in 1975 by emphasizing the junta's dependence on foreign aid; Western social democrats, particularly in Holland, were able to exercise pressure for the release of their political kindred in the PSI, and others with them. Sarbini was freed on 3 April 1976 after two years of his life had been wasted in prison.

When Sumitro was at the peak of ascendancy, some Indonesians thought he saw himself as a Gajah Mada, the Prime Minister who restored the East Javanese Majapahit kingdom in the fourteenth century. Suharto, on the other hand, was said to believe that God had decreed his rule in accordance with the Islamic dogma of *takdir* (predestination). Divinely chosen or not, Suharto had now reached the highest attainable summit of power. With regal disdain for popular intelligence, he dismissed his three special assistants, Murtopo, Humardani and Soerjo, without in any way reducing their influence. His rule seemed assured. The armed forces had been purged of Sukarnoists as far as was possible; the political parties were as good as dead; and the dismissal of Sumitro stood as a warning to aspiring young Turks. But the harmony for which Suharto longed was as far off as ever; for the beheading of poppies never means that the ground that nourished them has ceased to be fertile.

PART THREE

The shaky bastion

CHAPTER ELEVEN

The cultural barrier

The spirit world

The Javanese have been oppressed and humiliated by either their own rulers or Europeans throughout almost their entire history up to the present; they have had one short, partial respite, when Sukarno inspired them with hope and vaingloriousness. But there is another, more powerful tyranny, which has been unremitting: that of the demons who have pursued and tormented them from generation to generation. With the exception of a minority who are Westernized or can be said to be truly Islamic, although even some of these are apt to lapse, the Javanese live in a world of spirits and dark magic, with which they feel constantly obliged to reckon. Thus servants of Europeans may ask that lights burn outside their rooms all night; for spirits can only approach in darkness. As extra security they will tune a wireless set to a station that broadcasts *wayang* music from dusk to dawn, since this, too, keeps spirits away. Even then, a servant is afraid to sleep alone in a house. There are other hazards: an enemy may acquire from a *dukun* the secret of murder by effigy; an antique kris, bought by an unwary European for his collection, may house a giant, which, unless counter-magic is applied, will loom up in the night. Certain types of kris are believed to be protective. An Indonesian diplomat refused to enter Australia until customs officials revoked their ruling that he could not take his weapon with him. After Sukarno's fall a rumour spread that he had lost a kris that had saved him earlier from assassination; during the 1971 election campaign a newspaper published a report that a woman, who was then said to be meditating in a remote cave, had given it to the PNI leader, Hadisubeno. But the Sukarno family said there was no truth in this story. Belief in the dark arts is not confined to the illiterate; a high government official, who was much travelled and commanded two European languages, assured me that Hartini won Sukarno from Fatmawati with black magic, a device that her beauty, charm and shrewdness would seem to have made unnecessary.

The old conflict between the extremes of the two main religious currents, *abangan* and purer Moslem, persists. When a modern hotel was built at Samudera Beach, on the south coast of West Java, room 308 was reserved for Ratu Kidul, the green-clad sea goddess, whose wrath was held to account for frequent drownings. But in 1967, when Moslems predominated among the hotel staff, the pagan shrine became the site of Islamic prayers. Belief in spirits, although rejected by the more educated Moslems, predominates among the masses, who classify and name them with familiarity.[1] There are some that frighten, some that merely play jokes and others that cause illness or madness. A useful spirit for people who can win him over is the *mentek*, who looks like a child; he will pick the grain from a neighbour's rice and fix it to another's stalks. A demon will put himself at the service of those who go through the appropriate ritual at some ancient, sacred ruin and promise to deliver four dead human beings to the spirits, a contract that is renewable annually. The success of misers, with their accumulated wealth, and certain *hajis*, with their political and spiritual power, is sometimes attributed to this practice. Geertz[2] reports that in 1951 a man trained thirty-three students to carry out counter-magic against a *haji*, who was said to have made such a pact. The students wore black spectacles to see the spirits and torches to repel them. The battle appears to have been going on every Friday night when Geertz left the district.

In 1970 Bandung police used *dukuns* to try to solve a murder. One *dukun* directed the spirit of a dead woman into the body of a youth, who was suspected of having killed her, so that it could make disclosures through his tongue; but the spirit of the youth's dead father entered his body just in time to defeat the other and stop him from talking. Police then continued their inquiries by other means. Elsewhere in West Java, in the Sumedang area, seventy people were arrested for the strangling, burning and shooting of seven suspected practitioners of black magic. The Catholic newspaper *Kompas* said that villagers blamed witchcraft for a series of local disasters, including an earth tremor that destroyed more than 100 houses.

Belief in spirits is inevitably accompanied by extraordinary gullibility. As Raffles wrote about 160 years ago, since when nothing of consequence has changed in Java, the people are easily duped by religious fanatics and quacks. 'Nothing is so easy as for an artful man to persuade the Javans that he possesses supernatural power', he said. In 1970 Antara News Agency reported that a man was to be prosecuted for fraud after selling a ghost that failed to turn up. His victim paid $1,000 in the expectation that the ghost would appear every Friday night; properly asked and with God's help, it was to have brought him 1 million rupiahs (about $2,500) each visit. Suharto, Adam Malik and Nasution were among many who were deceived by an apparent miracle, when a woman claimed that she was eighteen months pregnant and that her unborn child could recite the Koran. She went to Malaysia with this tale, enabling Tunku Abdul Rahman, the Prime Minister, to wonder at the miraculous voice. In Jakarta Nasution prostrated himself in prayer when he heard the words of the Koran. The hoax had been going on for weeks when sceptics persuaded the Attorney-General's Department to investigate. The woman fled, after being told that she must submit to an X-ray examination. When she was arrested, police found a small tape-recorder and a recording of a child's voice, which she had concealed in her clothing for the recitals.

The primitive fears and superstitious nature of the masses are reflected in propaganda methods that Indonesian Communists found expedient in the twenties. With the message of the Russian revolution still echoing throughout Asia, the Communists waged an apocalyptic leaflet war, suited to the temperament and ignorance of the people. There was no nonsense about workers of the world uniting, a formula devoid of meaning for the peasant, who habitually resisted any social co-operation beyond the smallest village unit. Instead, myths were invented about the paradise to come and, above all, the dreadful fate in store for those who were not found on the side of the Communist angels on judgment day.

Before the Russian revolution, one leaflet said,[3] the emperor had sentenced Lenin's brother to a terrible death; two horses, each tied to one of his legs, galloped in different directions and tore him apart. When the time of revenge came, Lenin seized power; the emperor was arrested and his body burned. The leaflet said Communism was now spreading over the world; it warned:

> When the time has come we may no longer join. Therefore
> we must enter now, so that we shall be able to help drive
> away the Dutch . . . The faithful may take no *kafir* for
> their ruler . . . It is better that we become communists,
> for communists will come here from Russia to drive out
> the present Dutch government. Whoever is not a communist
> will be killed immediately by the Russians. To become a
> member of the Communist Party you need only pay F1
> [guilder] 0.83. What would you rather do, brothers,
> pay F1 0.83 or be killed by the leader of the communists?
> If you join the Communist Party you will live freely and
> pleasantly, and you will be safe. You will need pay no
> more taxes to the government and the village.

Along with these threats and promises were warnings that ships and planes were coming from China and planes from Kemal Ataturk; in the Moluccas people were told that they would be thrown into the sea if they had not joined the party by the time the Russians arrived.

The missing entrepreneur

Some sociologists are troubled by what seems to them to be history's remissness in failing to provide Java with a vigorous class of indigenous entrepreneurs. It is a purpose of this book to show, not so much by argument as by depicting Indonesia as it is and has always been, that this is no puzzle at all. The absence of business enterprise obviously has cultural causes related to those of rural stagnation, which has been the subject of inquiry for the greater part of two centuries.

Debate on the huddling of the peasants on small plots, which has been mentioned in the introduction, was stimulated by the Dutch economist, Julius Boeke, Professor of Tropical Economics at the University of Leiden. From 1910, when he wrote his

The cultural barrier

doctoral thesis, until his death in 1956, Boeke argued that Indonesians, like most other Eastern peoples, could not respond to a Western stimulus. It was a mistake, he said, to assume that 'the economic urge is universally human'.[4] The Eastern peoples had arrived at their destination. Their needs were not economic, but social, concerned mainly with religion and prestige. The consequence in the colonies was a dual economy, with the dynamic, Western element leaving the static, indigenous element increasingly far behind. Boeke realized that the native side of the economy was not part of an ethnologically pure culture, but of one that had been disturbed by intrusion. He saw that the West had destroyed the handicrafts economy, stripping the village of its content. But he made the point that whereas capitalism in the West had 'elevated' all classes (including people from deserted villages) so that they became part of an integrated whole, a divergence had developed in the East. 'The basic reason . . . was that there was no force for vigorous development operative in the cultures of such Eastern peoples.'[5] Summarizing his theory Boeke wrote:[6] 'Social dualism is the clashing of an imported social system with an indigenous system of another style. Most frequently the imported social system is high capitalism. But it may be socialism or communism as well, or a blending of them.' Boeke said that economic theories valid for the West had no application in the East whatever. This view, along with his particular version of dualism and his distinction between social and economic needs, was disputed for decades. The debate continued after Boeke's death, and there was sufficient interest in his ideas for some of his works to be published posthumously by a group of Dutch sociologists, who did not necessarily agree with him. We are not concerned here with definitions of needs or dualism; for these concepts are merely the academic dress with which Boeke clothed his more important intuitive judgment that Indonesian economic development was blocked by a culture that retained the pre-capitalist mind.

As an illustration of the pre-capitalist mind, Boeke cited the experience of the Dutch that if Indonesian peasants received higher prices they produced not more but less. If they were granted credit by Dutch banks set up to free them from extortionate money lenders, who were often repaid in rice, they simply increased their indebtedness, because they did not understand

315

money and had not even an elementary conception of accounting. Boeke wrote:[7]

> When the price of rice or coconuts is high, the chances are that less of these commodities will be offered for sale; when wages are raised, the manager of the estate risks that less work will be done; if three acres are enough to supply the needs of the household, the cultivator will not till six; only when rubber prices fall does the owner of a grove begin to tap more intensively ... This inverse elasticity of supply should be noted as one of the essential differences between Western and Eastern economics.

The pre-capitalist mentality, with its various manifestations, still predominates in Indonesia. The fact that the peasant, when he has the choice, grows the most remunerative crop, as before, does not invalidate Boeke's description of his attitude; the tendency is still to seek the satisfaction of minimal needs by the easiest means. Not long before his death Ali Sastroamidjojo, former Prime Minister and leader of the PNI, told me with considerable emphasis that the party's greatest difficulty in building a mass basis was to convince the peasants that they were poor; to this might be added that the Communist Party derived much of its support not from the merely poverty-stricken, but the utterly deprived.

Among the factual arguments against Boeke's conception of a dual economy was that the significant divergence was not between East and West, but between town and country. In an article entitled 'Brown and White Economy: Unity in Diversity', published in 1941,[8] G. H. van der Kolff, Professor of Tropical Economics at the University of Amsterdam, gave convincing examples of peasant conservatism and stagnation in modern Europe: Dutch peasants in one district, for instance, refused to use fertilizer because they thought that the rye it produced would be unfit for bread; a few spread it on their fields after dark, fearing that if they were seen other farmers would molest them. Van der Kolff quoted Lasalle, who in 1863 described German workers in terms similar to those that Boeke had applied to Javanese: 'As long as you have a piece of bad sausage and a glass of beer, you do not observe that you want anything. That is the result of your accursed absence of needs.' The question was not one of race, but of situation, van der Kolff said. What Boeke had observed in Indonesia would be found in any place where the after-effects of difficult, unsafe and expensive communications were still felt. The smallness of communities living in restricted and isolated areas curbed their production in kind and quantity, and consequently limited their demands. After communications had been established it would take time to overcome the psychological effects of isolation.

This statement seems satisfactory as far as it goes. Yet it still has to be explained why the developed countries developed and the others did not. Parallels drawn between Asia today and pre-capitalist Europe are of little significance in this discussion, for if Europe had not possessed unique, latent qualities in addition to those for which parallels may be found, it would have remained static, as Asia did. External cultural influences were neither necessary nor possible in the development of European science and capitalism; on the other hand it is doubtful if Japan, the West's only successful Eastern competitor, would ever have broken from tradition without a Western model to adapt.

The American development economist, Professor Benjamin Higgins, who rejects Boeke's dualism, came to the startling conclusion before the 1965 *putsch* that Java's only hope of producing successful entrepreneurs was to turn Communist. This, it seems, was the penalty of having missed previous opportunities. In his preface to Geertz's *Agricultural Involution* he says:[9] 'There seems to be in the history of each country an "optimal moment" for launching development, a short period of time when sociological, political and economic factors coalesce to provide a climate unusually favourable for a take-off into economic growth.' The advantage of this kind of proposition from the proponent's point of view is that it can never be disproved; either the bus must have been missed, in which case, Higgins says, it may take several generations to turn up again, or it has not yet arrived. There is a curious echo of Marxism here, a kind of historical necessity that has somehow miscarried; to history's innumerable might-have-beens Higgins has added an ought-to-have-been.

The use of the word 'take-off' is melodramatic; there is no reason to believe that any development meriting so spectacular a description will ever take place in most of the countries of the world. Higgins said: 'The story of Java seems to be one of repeated nipping off of a budding entrepreneurial upsurge by a political élite essentially hostile to it.' This statement is unsupported by historical evidence. And even if there were Javanese buds, which is highly questionable, they may never have flowered. Rudimentary commerce and manufacture remained mere buds in most of Asia, whether inhibited by imperialism or not. The Dutch generally considered that the Chinese and Indians were more skilful in the peddling trade than they were; but there is no reason to suppose that this ancient traffic contained any element corresponding to the germ of the European economic mentality. The West alone achieved the great leap to dynamic, modern capitalism, which was qualitatively different from early capitalism. Small beginnings do not necessarily lead to an upsurge; it does not follow that the Red Indians, because they were good at barter and made fine tomahawks, would have built the New York Stock Exchange and established a store of guided missiles if they had been left to themselves. 'The only way in which Java could now provide the coalescence of entrepreneurs and élite would be through the growth of the Communist Party and the establishment of a Communist regime', Higgins says. Whether or not this is so, virtual liquidation of the Communist Party since Higgins wrote has reduced the prospects. As it is, the junta that overthrew Sukarno, like the princes of former times, is in league with Chinese business men; it only throws sops to the inexperienced, indigenous entrepreneur, who shows no sign of becoming the driving force in an economy dominated by foreign capital.

In Geertz's view the ultimate nip in the bud was delivered by the Dutch, whose 'coming crushed the lively trade which had sprung up in the North coast ports – Surabaya, Gresik, Tuban and others'.[10] The fact is that the trade was wiped out in the first place not by the Dutch but by the Javanese Mataram kingdom, whose forces destroyed the coastal towns. Gresik fell in 1613, but recovered after the withdrawal of Mataram troops until it was finally laid waste along with Surabaya between 1623 and 1625. Surabaya capitulated when its inhabitants were dying of starvation caused by Mataram's destruction of crops; 40,000 Madurese were marched off as prisoners to Central Java. Mataram had asked the Dutch to support its attack on Surabaya but they were not interested.[11] Tuban, a walled *kampong* of 1,000 inhabitants, became a Mataram vassal in 1619. It had no wharves; nor did Gresik. It appears that the only wharves and shipwrights on that strip of coast were at Rembang. Most of the ships based on Java were imported from Burma, according to Portuguese records.

The trade had not 'sprung up'; nor was it 'lively'. It had been going on in a static form for a long time in slow junks, which, if they were owned by Javanese, were confined to the archipelago when the Dutch arrived. The trade is described in detail by van Leur,[12] who says that with a few exceptions, it consisted in small peddling, like the bulk of the centuries-old Asian trade at that time; in Gibbon's words, it was 'splendid and trifling'. Generally the pedlars travelled with their bags of pepper, spices, cloths, Chinese porcelain and other exotic products. Even the Chinese, powerful though they were in pre-modern capitalist enterprise, would send sums of 'from four to eight pounds . . . three thousand miles away for making profit in overseas trade'. Dutch records of trade within the archipelago show that as many as 1600 pedlars and crew sailed in as few as thirty-three small junks in one area. In Bantam, the busiest Javanese trading centre, a Netherlands East Indies Company commissioner wrote in a typical report: 'The same day we had a merchant who offered 2 bags of pepper per ell for a piece of madder-red cloth, which cost seven shillings, and it was left to him at $2\frac{1}{2}$; would have let him have it if he had offered $\frac{1}{4}$ more, as the interpreter approved of the sale.'

Geertz has identified in the Javanese mind what he calls vagueness. This quality (as I see it) is not a defect, but arises from a positive rejection of the precise. Statistics, for example, are regarded with disdain, but are tolerated because some semblance of them is necessary in a Western-dominated world. A letter from a colleague, written after the earthquake that occurred in the wilds of Irian Jaya[13] in June 1976, will illustrate this point:

> Their latest masterpiece of statistics [from the Governor of Irian Jaya] is that 5001 people are missing after the earthquake last month. Mintaredja [social Affairs Minister] had earlier announced a death-toll of '9011', but this figure was later denied by General Sutran (the Governor), who replaced it with that equally ludicrous figure. Mintaredja's figure might well have been divined by this *dukun* – but I don't know whether the figure 9011 has some mystic significance or is simply explained by the fact that someone estimated that about 9,000 people had died

overall, then someone added 11 people known to be dead in a specific village, probably outside the area where the 9,000 dead were estimated.

An Indonesian friend whom I asked for some statistics wrote: 'Indonesia is not famous for keeping records nor for its exactness in figures. We are as my [European] boss says a country of *"kira kira"* (approximately). On the same day you will find about the same news items all different kinds of figures in the various newspapers and nobody cares which one is right.' The general attitude to statistics is like that of many Javanese to Islam; as the Surakarta poet prince, Mangkunegara IV (1857–81), put it in the *Serat Wédatama*:[14]

> When you persistently imitate the example of our Lord the
> Prophet, oh, son, you will have gone too far; that quality
> is not able to be sustained, my boy; because you are
> Javanese just a little is enough.

Javanese imprecision is sometimes derided by Sundanese, Sumatrans and Moluccans, whose thinking is generally more direct. One would think it was a long-standing characteristic of the culture; but Geertz is convinced that its origin is comparatively recent. The Javanese were beginning to reach out into new economic and cultural dimensions, he says; but the Dutch intervention put a stop to this development; the Javanese then reverted to what had been a dying tradition and became vague.

Schrieke takes a different view:[15] 'the static society . . . cherished no other ideal than to remain as it was, shunning all change.' There was certainly no sign of departing from ancient custom in Mataram, the most powerful and feared kingdom in the archipelago. Mataram was entirely agricultural. Its ruler, Sultan Agung, derived most of his wealth from the export in small junks of rice grown by his craven peasants. 'I am not a merchant, as those [rulers] of Bantam and Surabaya', he said. The question arises to what extent those on the coast could, in fact, be considered merchants. To the mystical Mataram aristocracy anyone who dabbled even remotely in peddling would have appeared to be a trader. But, despite their trade, rulers on the Javanese coast were largely dependent on agriculture for their income. Wertheim has noted in one phrase that the modern Javanese dislike professional commerce;[16] but, preoccupied by his search for socially dynamic forces à la Weber, he makes no further reference to this determining factor; Geertz, when investigating not economics but religion, found that the upper class used the lowest degree of their hierarchic language when discussing trade, as in a conversation with servants; Raffles said the Javanese had 'contempt for trade' and that 'those of higher rank' thought it 'disgraceful to be engaged in it'. This takes us back to the beginning of the nineteenth century, at the latest.

My view is that there is no evidence that the Javanese have changed this attitude to trade during their recorded history. The ruling junta of today, like the usurpers of yesterday, have adopted traditional aristocratic values. They use selected Chinese – and the Chinese use them – to accumulate wealth. They have no head for business, but collect tribute in return for privilege. If they depart from this ancient practice, as the head of the state oil monopoly, Lieutenant-General Ibnu Sutowo did, the outcome is bankruptcy. Looking at the virility of Chinese commerce throughout South East Asia today, and comparing it with the half-hearted efforts of the Malay stock wherever they are, one finds it hard to believe that the initiative was ever in Javanese hands. Attracted by spices and pepper, the Chinese began trading with Indonesia and migrating to it, usually with no more than a few belongings, many centuries ago. Those who stayed married Indonesian women, but most of their descendants retained the Chinese culture. Princes obviously recognized their commercial superiority by farming out the collection of tolls and taxes to them; Chinese names keep appearing when details of business are recorded; the only coins used when barter did not take place were from China; the Dutch used Chinese artisans and Chinese construction methods to build Batavia, their first town.

Van Leur says:[17] 'Commercial domination [by the princes before the Dutch arrived] was expressed in a number of forms: levies and tolls, enforced stapling, monopolization, occasional trade, shipowning and *commenda* investments, and the practising of salvage rights and piracy as well.' Levies and tolls were thus obviously the princes' main commercial revenue sources, for while the individual parcels and bottomry investments were small, the total value of trade was relatively high. To ensure their income the aristocrats needed not commercial ability but military power;

and for their occasional trading as such and shipping investment, they would have needed Chinese or other foreign advisers, with experience and connexions throughout Asia. The Javanese princes ruled like gods, put on magnificent elephant parades, received envoys, dispensed favours and collected their dues from their agents; the Chinese, Indians or Arabs conducted the business. While there may have been exceptions, no other significant picture is imaginable from a sampling of history and from observations in South East Asia today; even in Bantam, the ruler expressed scorn for merchants, while the Chinese did the work. Edmund Scott, who went to Bantam when the English East India Company followed the Dutch there in the first decade of the seventeenth century, wrote that the Chinese worked day and night while the Javanese 'lay lazily around'. The Javanese were all poor, 'for they have as many slaves who are still lazier than the masters and which eat faster than their pepper or rice growth'. Subsequently the Bantam ruler resisted Dutch attempts to persuade Chinese merchants to move to Batavia, because he knew that their departure would ruin his port.

The paradox of Javanese disdain for trade, on the one hand, and the cupidity of past and present rulers, on the other, is perhaps explained by Benedict Anderson:[18]

... the overt pursuit of wealth that is characteristic of the merchant or businessman shows a lack of Power and therefore a lack of status. This judgment should not be taken to suggest that the typical high-status Javanese is not a man of wealth or that the Javanese tradition does not conceive of riches as an important attribute of the ruler and his closest associates. But money in itself should never be the object of active pursuit. Wealth should flow to the holder of Power, as a consequence of that Power, in the same way that *pusaka*, large populations, wives, neighbouring kingdoms or states flow toward the ruler, as it were, magnetically attracted to the center. The vast wealth that the greatest rulers of the Javanese past are described as possessing is always an attribute of Power, not the means for acquiring it.

Aristocratic dislike of commerce, like peasant stagnation, is not an exclusively Eastern, but a widely found, rural, phenomenon.

Artur Rubinstein gives a good example of its European manifestation in his autobiography. Towards the middle of the nineteenth century Tsar Nicholas I invited German master weavers to establish an industry in Lódz, which was then little more than a village. Attracted by the growing prosperity, Polish Jews poured into the town, learned from the Germans, and set up businesses. With the whole of Russia and a great part of Asia for a market, Lódz became the biggest industrial centre in the empire, after Moscow. Yet the 'native Poles showed little interest in this great opportunity. Business did not attract them; their favourite occupations were agriculture, science, and art. But thousands of peasants came to work in the plants. And so, paradoxically, Lódz appeared to be a foreign town right in the heart of Poland.'

But we are still left with the fact that Asia was virtually static during the period when Europe was being transformed. It may be significant that after all the parallels have been drawn, three unmatched oriental characteristics remain: phenomenal preoccupation with the occult, proverbial despotism and paralysing submissiveness. None of these characteristics is necessarily a precondition of the other, but each could have inhibited thought of the kind that produced modern Western society. In Indonesia they may all be linked. During the Hindu period, which has left an indelible mark on Java, the kings were regarded as manifestations of Vishnu, particularly in his capacity of demon slayer. Thus the people looked to the king not only in fear, but as protector against supernatural powers that were even more dreaded. As late as the second half of the nineteenth century, Pakubuwana IX (1861–93), ruler of Surakarta, was at pains to establish his relation to Ratu Kidul, the awe-inspiring goddess of the South Sea, and to Sunan Lawu, the spirit of Mount Lawu. This was done to preserve the cosmic order; but it also consolidated the prince's power over his spirit-ridden subjects. If spiritual preoccupation, despotism and submissiveness are considered to be likely causes of Indonesian inertia, the solution of the problem must be sought in psychology, where one would expect to find it, not in the mechanical application of the concepts of social dynamics.

In his quest for socially dynamic forces, Wertheim discovers, not one of Higgin's missed buses, but one that failed to arrive on time.[19] He believes that 'bourgeois Islam', which he associates with nineteenth-century Islamic reform, did in fact produce a class of small Indonesian entrepreneurs, but that they came too late in history to compete against big companies that had already evolved before the First World War. The feebleness of these traders, of whom Wertheim gives no details, is exposed by the evident success of Chinese in building up fortunes from nothing throughout Indonesian history up to the present. Bruce Glassburner, Professor of Economics at the University of California, says[20] that the Dutch 'fostered the special economic and social position of the Chinese'. It is important to add that the Dutch had no choice but to use Chinese commercial aptitude; like the princes who farmed out tolls and taxes, they found there was nobody else capable of doing business. Chinese trade was so vital that for a long period the Dutch intervention had no effect on it at all. Van Leur says:[21] 'Economically the Chinese retained their position alongside and under the Company.' Early in the eighteenth century the Chinese were building a 'multitude of ships' in Java. Even after the ghastly muddle of 1740, when the Dutch massacred several thousand who revolted, the Chinese went about their business until today they control almost the entire domestic capital. There is no reason to believe that the Javanese were ever motived by the same economic spirit or ever will be. Some Javanese, the so-called frustrated *pribumi* (indigenous entrepreneurs), covet the profits of commerce; but very few are suited by taste or temperament to the precise calculation and day-to-day grind of trade competition.

The Javanese regents were given an opportunity to become entrepreneurs early in the Dutch occupation, when they were paid for collecting coffee tribute from the peasants. Here, indeed, a bus was missed. The regents mercilessly drove their own people, often with the enlisted aid of Chinese, to extort the utmost from them. If Chinese had been given this privilege of making money by doing nothing they would have saved and established profitable enterprises. But the elegant regents saved nothing; instead, they made a habit of asking for advances, which they squandered on maintaining worthless, traditional façades, which had never shown the slightest sign of disappearing. At the end of the eighteenth century their debt to the Netherlands East Indies Company amounted to the annual value of the entire coffee crop, and had to be written off. Yet not long afterwards, early in the nineteenth century, a Chinese bought the whole of Probolinggo regency,

East Java, for 1 million rix-dollars, when the Governor-General, Herman Willem Daendels, made a brief departure from Dutch land policy. Subsequently Chinese owned sugar mills, in addition to continuing their traditional work as middle men.

If indigenous economic development had begun to take place, which it did not, the Dutch might well have restricted it to certain sectors. But from what has been described it would seem clear that Dutch economic intervention was not responsible, for the persistence of utter stagnation. Yet Indonesia, like other former colonies, is being misled by what amounts to propaganda from the West, which is now happy to blame its forbears for the present miseries of Afro-Asia. Neo-colonialism could hardly have chosen a more diabolical weapon; for by keeping the poor countries ignorant of their real disease, it ensures that they will remain in economic subjection, dependent on the hypocritical wealth-sharing chimeras of the West. With much of the Third World on the brink of starvation, the fashionable whitewashing of realities by academics is more insidious than the old colonial prejudices. If the problems of these countries are to be mitigated, let alone solved, it is of great importance that the cultural factors be better understood.

The need for fresh thinking on Indonesia's deeply rooted problems is apparent in the kind of reasoning that has been recently applied. Geertz, for instance, peremptorily dismisses Boeke, who worked in Java for twenty years, as having 'fanciful' ideas about the Indonesian mind.[22] But his own ideas are by no means down to earth. One learns, in passing, that land reform is not just land reform, but 'minimization of social contrasts based on differential control of agricultural resources'. The sugar farmer does not merely sell to the mill, nor does the mill merely buy from the farmer: the two are engaged in a 'symbiotic' relationship. At one point Geertz says[23] that the 'existence of the colonial government was *decisive* [my italics] because it meant that the growth potential in the traditional Javanese economy . . . was harnessed not to Javanese (or Indonesian) development but to Dutch'; in the previous paragraph he says it was *decisive* 'on the ecological, and *to an extent* [my italics] the economic, level'; elsewhere he qualifies his whole argument by saying that 'whatever value' his thesis may have 'does not lie in any assumption that had Java been "left alone", she would . . . now be in an economically more viable state'; on the other hand, referring to Boeke and ignoring Du Bus, he says categorically: 'The Javanese did not become impoverished because they were "static"; they became "static" because they were impoverished' – by the Dutch. Geertz represents the peasant as 'treading water': higher food production was cancelled out by population rises in an inexorable 'ecosystem' that included the increasingly exploited rice field and the sugar plot, which the peasant was forced to cultivate. The picture is rigidly deterministic, but Geertz anticipates critics by asserting that it is not. Yet the process that he elaborates is valueless as an explanation of peasant stagnation, which is what it is meant to be, unless its determinism is accepted. Geertz finally apologizes for this jumble by saying: 'It is the predicament of all science that it lives by simplification and withers from simplicisticism' – a proposition that must be left for examination by those interested in scientific method.

Higgins, when supporting his missed bus theory, says: 'Certainly any hopes that the Mataram Empire may have had of reuniting Indonesia – to the degree, say, that the country was united by the Majapahit Empire two centuries earlier – were destroyed through the use of main force by the Netherlands East India Company.' The use of the subjunctive does not make this statement less misleading to those easily gulled into the belief that imperialism caused the present Indonesian condition; for it is implied that there was at least a reasonable chance that Mataram would have unified Indonesia if the Dutch had not arrived. In fact there was none, as might be suspected from the introduction to this book. Schrieke[24] has pointed out that the Javanese realm was in a state of chronic dismemberment. He made a study of Java's sparse roads, which had not improved in technology since about the eighth century, to show that communications across the mountainous landscape were too primitive to enable a central kingdom to keep others in permanent subjugation. Bad roads, it will be recalled, defeated Mataram's campaign to dislodge the small Dutch garrison in Batavia. The Dutch did not impede Sultan Agung's doomed attempt to extend his influence, although it could be held against them that they refused to help him destroy Surabaya. They had no interest in territorial control at that time; nor did Agung's successor. Eventually the Dutch were obliged to forbid the futile wars that had been creating famine for centuries on a scale that helped, like disease, to limit the population. As for Majapahit, the tenuous hold of this kingdom over those from which it exacted tribute has been mentioned in the introduction. Indonesia was never united in any sense of the word until the Dutch finally decided to rule it.

The only documented example given by Geertz of a socially dynamic change in Indonesia occurred during the Dutch period. This was the much cited, rudimentary spurt of money-mindedness that began in the Minangkabau society, in Western Sumatra, in the first quarter of this century; it was analysed by Schrieke in a confidential report to his government on the conditions that led to the abortive Communist revolt of 1927. Geertz attaches much importance to Schrieke's remark: 'Here we have to do with a revolution in spirit similar to that of the early capitalist period in Europe as indicated by Max Weber and Sombart. The "economic mentality" has made its entry on the scene.' Schrieke said that the new vitality was accompanied by important social changes: the slackening of family ties, the promotion of individualism and the substitution of individual houses for the traditional one-family house, in which the husband lived with his parents-in-law. To those developments Geertz, with a supplementary invocation of Weber, has added 'the growth of "Protestant ethic" religious ideologies'.

In Schrieke's view this apparent transformation was caused by the abolition of compulsory coffee cultivation in 1908 and the subsequent introduction of money. He wrote:[25] 'A period of declining production, during which the people, glad, as it were, to be freed of a compulsion they loathed, discontinued cultivations, was followed by a period of unprecedented revival.' Peasants staked their claims in abandoned government plantations and cleared jungle to make coffee gardens; some began to process coconuts into copra, to cut out the middle man; new houses were built in at least one previously poverty-stricken district. 'It is clear that we have to do here with the beginning of an agrarian revolution under the influence of the gradual penetration of a money economy', Schrieke reported.

All this reads like the start of one of Higgins' take-offs. But if we are to consider West Sumatra's bucolic flutter as an instance of Indonesian potentiality, reservations have to be made; among them are that the Javanese, not the Minangkabaus, determine Indonesia's fate and that, in any case, the new movement, which was confined to certain areas, ran into a dead end.

The unique Minangkabau culture differs vastly from the Javanese. In the first place Minangkabau society is matrilineal. Then, in a sense, it has always been relatively dynamic. While peasants in Java have clung to their tiny plots, Minangkabau men have migrated to other parts of the archipelago, Malaysia, and beyond, sometimes returning only for the annual Ramadan fast. This custom, known as going *merantu* (abroad) still puzzles anthropologists, who in recent years undertook field work to get to the bottom of it; Schrieke appears to have noticed only the emigration of the land-hungry, but subsequent research has shown the phenomenon to be more complex than that. When abroad, Minangkabaus take jobs; some establish plantations and businesses. Schrieke pointed out that Minangkabau families profited from the overseas earnings of their men; family property, which was owned and exploited in accordance with the *adat* (customary law), was a source of capital for the emigrants and provided money to educate the young; small traders who had been financed with family funds had to render a detailed account of their affairs when they returned home at Ramadan. Possibly the prevalence of these customs among the better-off families indicated a cultural predisposition that enabled the poorer peasants to seize the opportunity when the Dutch introduced money in the region. But Schrieke does not go into that question; nor does he reconcile the long established, West Sumatran, elementary business practices with his statement that the 'economic mentality' was born in the twentieth century. The 'Protestant ethic' was not new, as Geertz implies; it was rooted in the *adat*, which, contrasting with a virtual craving for borrowing among Javanese, rich or poor, imposed severe restrictions on the pledging of family property. The introduction of money did not inspire these principles, but aggravated an existing erosion of them, with a consequent disturbing of consciences, as Schrieke made clear.

Whether or not the Minangkabaus were predisposed to economic innovation, the spreading of money among them did not take place spontaneously, as it had obviously done in dynamic societies. The need for money, Schrieke said, was 'forced on the agrarian village communities of Minangkabau, which were still for the most part economic units, from the outside' – when the Dutch insisted on collecting taxes in cash instead of in kind. At the same time one notices signs of an ephemeral quality in the 'agrarian revolution'. High coffee and rubber prices lured school teachers into abandoning their pupils and working in the fields. It was like the gold rush in nineteenth-century Australia, where men left good jobs for the diggings. Peasants neglected rice to earn relatively good pay in small coffee gardens. 'In Kajai the standard of wages was a shilling three pence a day plus a free meal, the day's work being finished as early as 10 o'clock in the morning', Shrieke recorded. One is reminded of Boeke. To what extent were peasants motived by a desire to work less to supply the same minimal social needs? Further information is required before this question can be satisfactorily answered.

Promising though he thought this purely rural development was, Schrieke emphasized that it had not gone beyond a transitional stage, which he described by quoting Matthew Arnold's lines:

> Between two worlds – one dead,
> The other powerless to be born.

The 'creative leap', for which the 'great change' was seen as preparation fifty years ago, has yet to come. Schrieke said that despite the stirring events that he had observed, the *adat* continued to dominate. It still does, overwhelmingly; in 1971, after replacing several hundred local heads, the junta still found it necessary to send university graduates into Minangkabau villages in an attempt to break it up.

Having examined events in Minangkabau as interpreted by Schrieke and seized upon by Geertz, we shall now look at them again, as a journalist might have seen them at the time. A foreign correspondent, hurriedly flipping over the pages of Schrieke's confidential report, which he would surely have got hold of, would have found several clues to an excellent human interest story. He would have read:[26]

> The demand for money gives rise to an often improvident
> selling and pledging of land, which in its turn creates
> feelings of dissatisfaction among a people for which money
> is still an article of consumption . . . [The correspondent
> would probably not have noticed that this sentence
> might have been written by Boeke; but he would almost
> certainly have spotted that peasants for whom money was

merely an 'article of consumption' could hardly be said
to have an 'economic mentality' or to have undergone a
'revolution in spirit'.] At regular intervals they have to
have money ready for taxes and for payment in lieu of
compulsory services, and thus they often find themselves
compelled to sell their rice at the most unfavourable
moment, when the abundance after the harvest or the
general supply reduce the price to a minimum. The *adat*
or religion brings it about that oxen or buffaloes are
slaughtered on various occasions – a social requirement
there is no escaping – but the Government which is not
prepared to make any discrimination, still demands money in
payment of the slaughter tax. The native administration
makes a point of reminding taxpayers of their liabilities
when it can assume the presence of a certain abundance of
money, and consequently demands taxes from market-goers or
from those organizing a wedding feast – it is a social duty to
provide festivities on the occasion of a woman's first
marriage. In this last case the administration can use as a
sanction the refusal of a permit for the feast if the taxes due
from those concerned and the members of their family
have not been paid.

Permission is often refused those wishing to sell a cow
unless at the same time they pay the income tax due from
them or the sum they owe in lieu of performing statute
labour.

Sitting at his desk and using nothing but the material contained
in Schrieke's report, the correspondent could have written a
harrowing story of isolated communities, primitive in their
agrarian methods, being mercilessly bullied and plundered by a
colonial government; of people who had been mostly content
with subsistence being forced to earn money for tribute to the
foreigner. The peasant had to pay a head tax on the cattle he kept
and a slaughter tax on what he killed; he had to pay to enter the
cattle market and again to have his ox certified healthy by the
food inspector; his beautiful *adat* house, with its buffalo-horn
roof, was taxed; and he had to pay the government for not working
in its service. The correspondent, still relying only on Schrieke,
could have described peasants desperately borrowing on their

family property, to the extent that in some areas all family land had been sold. Had he made an on-the-spot report himself, he could have written heart-breaking accounts of poor people being hounded by tax gatherers when going to weddings or at the markets, where they hoped to satisfy their frugal needs; he could have unearthed tales of elders whose consciences were wounded by their having secretly mortgaged the family land.

Looking at Schrieke's report again, the correspondent would have read: 'money is required to meet all those other needs rice itself cannot fill. Such needs, for instance, as the payment of taxes in lieu of compulsory labour in the first place.' Then, going through his notes on the coffee rush, he might have concluded that the peasants were not motived by anything that could be called an 'economic mentality', but by fear of the government's unrelenting pressure. Looking just at the facts, his view unimpeded by pre-conceptions of social dynamics, the correspondent might have seen not the penetration of a money economy, such as had taken place in Europe, but the imposition of money on a rural people who were bludgeoned into seeking it; not the vague beginnings of dynamic capitalism, but the sterile disturbing of a largely static *adat*.

It does not matter whether or not Boeke's reasoning was valid – Newton and Leibnitz each established a theoretical foundation of the calculus that is considered laughable today, but their intuition was right and the calculus works, resting on a logical basis that may be disputed tomorrow. What matters is that the failure of *homo oeconomicus* to make a substantial appearance in Indonesia is consistent with Boeke's writings. And what matters no less is that something should be done to avert the consequent dangers. The Dutch government's costly 'welfare policy' failed to induce an 'economic mentality' in the Javanese, as Boeke pointed out. The present development policy is also failing for the same cultural reasons.

The most illuminating comments on Indonesia's development problem have been made, as one might hope, by an Indonesian, Soedjatmoko, the former Ambassador to Washington, who is able to look at the culture from both the inside and the outside. I came away from Indonesia convinced that the motivation of almost all Javanese in all classes was utterly unsuited to Western-style development. It seemed that in politics, economics and technology Indonesians were only going through the motions, that they were merely imitating the West, or even just playing an irresponsible game; in general they were concerned with status rather than achievement. I noticed a quality which, I found later, had been described by an anthropologist in colonial days as the 'playful energy' of backward peoples, as against the 'organized energy' of the more advanced. Their politics had been dominated by infantile, suicidal intrigue. They wanted to know about technology, but only saw it as a trick, a kind of magic, rather than as an instrument through which they could express themselves; they had no desire to understand for the sake of understanding, no scientific curiosity; their culture was devoid of the spirit expressed by Michael Faraday when he said he was trying to 'divine God's pattern', since their mysticism had already solved the riddles of the universe. Unaccustomed to induction, people learning new skills simply copied example after example; they found no principle that would guide them when they had no model to follow. This was probably the most significant observation. Raffles appears to be referring to the same characteristic when he says the Javanese are 'disposed to imitate their [the Europeans'] arts and obey their instructions'; he adds that they 'not inaptly compare themselves to a piece of white cloth, on which any dye or shade of colour may be laid'. The Siliwangi Division in West Java provided a good example of empty imitation in 1970, when it tried to copy Communist tactics by planting cells in villages, not realizing that what was essentially a spontaneous organ of resentment and rebellion could not be adapted to win over hostile peasants. Convinced though I was that these and similar observations were valid, I felt unqualified to make out a strong case for their importance, in the face of fashionable thinking that seeks to superimpose an economy on a culture that cannot accept it. Fortunately, I stumbled on a paper written by Soedjatmoko in 1954,[27] and found that what a foreigner had simply noted an Indonesian had at least begun to explain. Those who say there is nothing new in Soedjatmoko's thesis may perhaps care to show why it has been ignored.

Soedjatmoko's views, which are consistent with Boeke's fundamental conception, apply in principle to many poor countries. He wrote that Indonesia was 'faced with problems reaching into the roots of our culture', and warned against the futility of attempting to build an economy without 'systematic stock-taking of the various obstacles that are rooted in our pattern of culture'; ethnological studies should be undertaken to clarify development aims, he said. In various parts of Asia, particularly where the culture bore the stamp of Hindu philosophy, an attitude of *Weltverneinung* still prevailed. In feudal agrarian society man sought to adjust himself to the universe through ritual, fixed numerical formulae, and, on a higher spiritual plane, release from the ego. There was no persistent inquiry, as in the West, where 'the crux of the scientific attitude is the spirit of continual renewal' and 'it is realized that what is today acclaimed as an advance may well become an obstacle.' At the same time Soedjat-moko saw the uselessness of imitating Western political, economic and technological methods. This implicit rejection of hackneyed ideas of acculturation is possibly his most penetrating contribution to the discussion. He wrote:[28]

> we cannot claim that mechanization has been absorbed into our way of life until we can evidence not only the ability to handle and maintain machinery, but also the ability to construct mechanical equipment ourselves and continually evolve new models more suitable to our own requirements. Obviously the machine is both an expression of the level of development and an instrument employed by a society to achieve its aims, and we cannot disassociate machinery and technology in general from the values and the aspirations of any given society. In other words, the machinery and technology used by any people are an embodiment of, and are inseparable from, the culture of that people . . .
>
> . . . we must evoke from within our cultural pattern appropriate stimuli which will serve as a catalytic factor in our social structure, providing an impetus towards a modernization specifically Indonesian in character. Failing this, the adjustment we make will be purely passive: we will not go beyond the level of mere imitation; we will have done no more than shift from one static position to another static position, and we will always be behind . . .
>
> As a prerequisite condition for our mastering of machinery and of modern technology we must first

333

understand the culture and the mental orientation that brought them into being. An understanding of occidental culture, the fountainhead of the modern world, could help us to discover within ourselves dynamic principles of our very own.

While Soedjatmoko was advocating a cultural revolution, he did not believe that it could be achieved by bureaucratic edicts. He said:[29]

The process of change must encompass the entire political-administrative apparatus, from the village level to the national level, and must extend also to juridical institutions and precepts, to consumer habits, and to the standards and the nature of the requirements of every member of the population. We must resolve the various questions as regards the motivation to work, work incentive and the ethics of work involved.

After identifying the root of the development problem, Soedjatmoko outlined the principles of a practical solution and discussed the important question of the extent to which freedom would be possible in a period of transition. A proposal of startling far-sightedness was that bookkeepers and accountants, by means of a government subsidy, should be paid the same salaries as people with academic qualifications. This raising of the income and status of a profession that is catastrophically undermanned would do much to transform the pre-capitalist mentality that dominates the towns not much less than the country; and it might divert some youths from their meaningless studies of law, sociology and economics in universities that are unfit to teach these subjects.

Soedjatmoko's career is one of the many tragedies within the tragedy of Indonesia. Suharto appointed him Ambassador to the United States in 1968. Marshall Green, when he was US Assistant Secretary of State for East Asian and Pacific Affairs, told me that Soedjatmoko was the most capable ambassador in Washington; and President Nixon was reported to have said: 'When Soedjatmoko speaks, we all listen.' Soedjatmoko's reward for his services to his country was a long, ruthless interrogation after the 1974 riots and the disgraceful confiscation of his passport. I had the honour of meeting him only once, during the interval of a concert in 1972, when he had returned from Washington. He then declined an invitation to address the Jakarta Foreign Correspondents' Club, protesting that he had nothing new to say; it occurred to me at the time that the junta had already cast its shadow over him. More than twenty years have passed since Soedjatmoko wrote his paper, at the age of thirty-two; but his warning remains unheeded, and the Indonesian economy staggers from disaster to disaster, dragging the people with it.

CHAPTER TWELVE

The development myth

The Western solution

By 1965, when the junta began to seize power, it should have been obvious from Indonesia's history and culture that a drastic social transformation was needed to set the people on the road to a less miserable existence. But the Western arrogance of the time, inflated by over-confidence arising from the deceptive boom of the sixties, reduced the problem to simple terms. Blame for the economic decline, with its manifold and debatable roots, which by any account are centuries old, was fathered upon Sukarno. This having been done, it was assumed that a fresh start could be made by a handful of Indonesian technocrats, tactfully guided by a corps of wise men from the West. This is not to say that anyone expected a miracle; but it was thought that what was imagined to be sound economic policy would eventually bring about an increase in living standards sufficient to keep the people out of Communist clutches and to secure Indonesia as a strategic base, a source of raw materials and a potential market. Meanwhile in the painful, early stages of development the junta was seen as a police force that would stop the people from rebelling.

The Western attitude was later expressed with bland hypocrisy by a British civil servant, whom I asked why the British Council was spending so much money in Jakarta. 'We are a bit fed up with the Commonwealth countries', he said. 'We are looking for other countries, a bit authoritarian, to share their development with them.' A senior Dutch diplomat was more honest when he justified Holland's support for the junta on the ground that Indonesia was one of the countries that the Dutch economy required as an investment outlet. The British Commonwealth Development Corporation, which was originally established to share in the growth of Britain's former possessions, sent out a shrewd prospector, who had been trained by Marks and Spencer. After having established that the junta was certain to win the 1971 elections, he was ready to spring as soon as the poll was over, when he set up a temporary office in the Hotel Indonesia, and got straight down to business that was beneficial to all social classes at home. Queen Elizabeth followed with a useful visit in March 1974.

But Indonesians had less reason to be pleased. People in Javanese rural areas, who became no better off, and possibly worse, continued to spill into Jakarta, despite regulations intended to stop them; and rather than starve in their overcrowded villages, skeletal-looking poor camped beside foetid canals, which served as both baths and sewers. Initial price stabilization was followed by avoidable inflation and by Pertamina's reckless over-borrowing and irresponsible investment. Instead of a stimulation of Indonesian enterprise came protests that the indigenous businessman was being crushed by favours granted to foreigners and Chinese; and instead of social stability came the riots of January 1974. The impecunious, indigenous businessmen had reason to be disappointed. On 12 March 1966 Suharto had accompanied his banning of the Communist Party with an appeal to the business community to help revive the economy. Just as the Papuans had hoped for a windfall from the Almighty's cargoes, so Javanese businessmen expected that imminent, lavish foreign aid and new government policies would solve what were essentially the problems of inexperience and lack of aptitude.

Suharto's first move to lay the foundations of a new economic approach was to ensure the appointment of the Sultan of Yogyakarta, Hamengkubuwono IX, as Deputy Premier for Economy, Finance and Development in the tentative cabinet over which he and Sukarno wrangled in March 1966. Hamengkubuwono formed an advisory team of five university economists, who took over the technical handling of the economy, with foreign advisers at their side. The team was later joined by Sumitro Djojohadikusumo,

337

who had studied at the Sorbonne, received a PhD from the Rotterdam School of Economics, and had founded the Faculty of Economics at the University of Indonesia. Sumitro, a former PSI member, was allowed to return to Indonesia after having lived in exile since his involvement in the Sumatra rebellion. He was made Trade Minister, and Ali Wardhana Finance Minister, in the Development Cabinet formed by Suharto in June 1968. Wardhana was one of Hamengkubuwono's original five; the four others were given cabinet rank in September 1971. They were Widjojo Nitisastro, Chairman of the National Planning Board (Bapenas); Emil Salim, Vice-Chairman; Subroto, Trade Department Director-General of Research and Expansion, and Mohammad Sadli, Chairman of the Foreign Investment Board.

Nitisastro, Salim and Wardhana all had PhD degrees from the University of California, where they studied with the support of the Ford Foundation, while Sadli had been a fellow at Harvard. This inspired the American New Leftist, David Ransom, writing in *Ramparts*, to brand the team as the Berkeley Mafia and to link them with a Washington conspiracy to infiltrate Indonesia both economically and politically. There is no doubt that Washington was delighted at the appointment of the team and did all in its power to ensure that the Indonesian economy was run in a way that it approved; but no evidence has been produced to justify the pejorative term, Mafia, which unfortunately has found its way into at least one learned work.[1] It is true that some have prospered materially from their alliance with the army and foreign capitalism; Wardhana, for instance, does well out of chicken farming, which, like Suharto, he modestly calls his hobby. But it was not surprising that trained economists were outraged at the appalling state of Indonesia's economy; and it needed no involvement in conspiracy to prompt them to try and lead the nation out of its morass. While they became increasingly disenchanted with the junta, they obviously believed in what they were doing. Broad outlines of their policy were not some speciality of the US State Department or the CIA, but were part of the orthodox economics of the time.

An impressive picture was presented in which the Indonesians listened to Western advice but made the decisions. This eventually became true, but at the outset the whole package of Western technical and financial help was tied to strict fiscal and political conditions. As early as September 1966, when Suharto's victory

was less certain than it appeared to some, the International
Monetary Fund presented a survey of what it considered to be
Indonesia's economic problems to a meeting of Western-bloc
creditors in Tokyo. The IMF exerted a powerful influence on
fiscal measures carried out in the same month and on exchange
and trade changes that immediately followed. It established an
office in Jarkarta early in 1967.

While the junta and its supporting politicians and technocrats
were far from being consciously puppets of the Americans, the
entire Western economic operation was politically motived and
should be seen as part of the struggle between the Communist and
capitalist nations to influence the Third World. The early probings
of the IMF and the first trickle of loans from the Western bloc
resemble a pilot operation, which served the double pupose of
helping Suharto in his battle against Sukarno, by giving the
people hope of economic recovery, and of testing his power to
enforce harsh fiscal measures. The World Bank, whose presence
was vital in any large-scale Western development programme,
watched cautiously before committing itself; it had already
experienced the uncertainty of Indonesian politics when Sukarno
walked out of the bank and other international agencies in August
1965. Late in 1967 a bank team made a survey in Indonesia and
reported that the nation's new policy was intended to strengthen
economic links 'with the non-Communist world'.[2] But the bank
waited until June 1968, when its President, Robert McNamara,
went to Jakarta, three months after Suharto had become President;
with Sukarno finally defeated, McNamara announced that the
bank would establish a resident team of development specialists.
From that time his men played what two of its staff described as
'a major role in Indonesia's economic rehabilitation and subsequently in its economic and social development'.[3]

The bank's staff in Indonesia is by far its largest outside
Washington, and the scope of its involvement is wider and deeper
than in any other country. By December 1968 twelve resident
members were working alongside Indonesians in the National
Planning Board and other bodies; in addition to the Director and
his deputy were three agriculturalists, one man for transport, one
for power and telecommunications, one for economic administration, a general economist and three secretaries. The team was
steadily increased until at times there were as many as thirty men,

including visiting missions, in Indonesia. The West was also represented by several members of the Harvard Development Advisory Service and specialists from the Netherlands and Japan, who were installed in the Planning Board before the bank team arrived. The resident staff had a mandate 'to assist and advise the government . . . in the formation of its economic policies'. In particular, it was instructed to help in preparing a five-year development plan and in formulating the annual national budget. It also helped to draft laws drawn up by the Foreign Investment Board.

The presence of the World Bank and the IMF and the influence of the powerful interests that they represented were sufficient to ensure that expenditure was ruthlessly cut until the budget was balanced, irrespective of the short term effect on industry and on the daily lives of the people. Army and civil service salaries were allowed to rise sharply and repeatedly, but the cost was born by the people, who suffered large increases in the prices of Pertamina's kerosene, from which the government drew revenue. At the beginning, the Indonesian economists became so dedicated to the new counter-inflationary policy that the resident IMF representative, Kemal Siber, a Turkish citizen, had difficulty in persuading them to run the note-printing presses just once to pay for a rice reserve. Siber believed that a reserve was a key to price stability. His measure absorbed about one third of the year's increase in the money supply; but he justified the inflation on the ground that it would not be repeated. Unfortunately his idea did not work, because large amounts of the funds provided were misappropriated by heads of the rice authority, Bulog.

A senior member of the IMF staff at one stage was a Belgian, who had been awarded a PhD by some American university for a thesis on the contributions of NATO countries to NATO. Doubtless this prudently chosen study merited the degree, but it did not seem to indicate that a predilection for the complex socio-economic problems of the Third World was an essential qualification for those sent to help.

If hard work in a planning room could overcome the inertia of centuries, Indonesia would have soon been rolling towards the 'just and prosperous society' that the government promised. The Indonesian technocrats and their foreign colleagues worked into the early hours to get the first Five Year Plan, Repelita 1, ready for announcement on 31 December 1968 and launching on 1 April 1969. Emil Salim, a lively minded South Sumatran, could spare me only a brief interview at his office at the end of the normal working day, but took me to his house to look at documents on which he was working at home in order to spend some time with his family in the evenings. His enthusiasm was irresistible as he incisively explained the origin and evolution of the new policy, while his wife extricated one of their two children from a tangle of long charts, which he kept unrolling to illustrate his points. He recalled that the MPRS had ordered in 1966 that the economy should be first stabilized and then developed. Stabilization was now virtually complete, he said, but to achieve it the government had been compelled to embark on a painful scrapping of the Sukarno government's 'artificial' economy. Projects, even some useful ones, had to be stopped to arrest inflation, he said. Output in some industries, which had depended on an unreal exchange rate applied to the importing of raw materials, was lower in 1966 than in 1964. 'It hurt, but it had to be done', he said.

Repelita was almost wholly financed by the IGGI, but Western supervision did not avert all pitfalls. Two months after the plan was announced the Indonesian Animals and Animal Products Trade Association said there was no hope of fulfilling the export target of 500,000 head of cows and water buffaloes, because there were not enough suitable ships; at least fifteen new vessels were needed, each capable of carrying 500 head at speeds enabling them to make round trips to Hong Kong in thirty days. When I referred the problem to Emil Salim he was dismayed. 'I thought there were enough ships', was all he could say. Someone, given this detail to handle, had obviously not gone into the question thoroughly.

It was impossible to tell how many similar mistakes were made; perhaps not many. But four months after the plan began Suharto said that 'obstructions' were impeding its operation, and a conference of district officials were called to deal with the problem. The South Sumatra Governor complained subsequently that his officials were either incapable of carrying out their part of the plan or were blocking it. At the end of October the government announced that little more than a third of funds allocated for the period ended 17 October had been spent; it blamed bad communications with the provinces. This prompted the editor of the newspaper, *Harian Kami*, Nono Anwar Makarim, to ask why the government was requesting the IGGI to increase its annual aid from the current $500 million to $600 million in the following year. 'Would not the IGGI consider that Indonesia's appetite was greater than its energy?', he asked. Apparently the IGGI did not, for it granted the request.

There is no reliable information about the extent to which Repelita 1 was realized; perhaps it is significant that the Australian National University's *Bulletin of Indonesian Economic Studies*, which gives a detailed survey of the economy every four months, did not broach the subject, although some of its contributors worked in the National Planning Board. However, useful work was undoubtedly done, particularly on larger scale infrastructure. But local development was minimal, partly because local heads frequently spent the piffling village allocation of 100,000 rupiahs (about $250) on luxuries, including motor cycles bought to speed the execution of projects that were never begun.

Incredibly defective co-ordination between the IGGI and the National Planning Board also hampered the smooth running of the plan. IGGI aid was in two forms: project, which is self-explanatory, and programme, consisting of credits for food and other selected commodities. The credits were sold on the open market in Jakarta for rupiahs, which provided the government with counterpart funds needed to buy labour and local materials for foreign projects. At first, because there were few projects, programme aid dominated: in 1969–70 the commitment was for $320 million, compared with $180 million for projects. But in 1972–73 programme commitments totalled $320 million and project $350 million. The IGGI operation is usually represented as a model of co-operation between the West and the Third World, with the West acting as the wise counsellor of its inexperienced beneficiary. But a conscientious Dutch Foreign Ministry official, G. A. Posthumus, broke the usual bureaucrats' defensive silence to show that this was not so.[4] Thinking in the IGGI was confused from the beginning. It was thought that programme aid could be progressively diminished once Indonesia's economy had become stable. It took a prolonged debate to convince the donors, as they called themselves, that the export credit system was the only satisfactory means of providing the counterpart rupiah project funds and of helping the private sector to equip itself.

But this point having been accepted, the necessary co-ordination was not effected. Each IGGI country had its own projects, programmes, and experts, and decided on its own loans and grants. While there was consultation between the members, there was no direct connexion between what they were deciding at their two annual meetings in Holland and what the National Planning Board was doing in Jakarta. The Planning Board's development budget was for one year only. But IGGI project aid, though granted each year, was inevitably spent over a number of years. The Indonesians thus had to provide rupiah counterpart funds each year for foreign projects that had been approved in previous years. This meant they had to adapt their own planning to that of the IGGI members (one of whose aims was merely to increase their exports).

Posthumus said that plans should be made for periods of several years at a time in order to guarantee that foreign projects could be adapted to those that were rupiah-financed, 'rather than the other way round'. This, he said, was crucial for useful functioning of the IGGI. Failure to adopt some system of better co-ordination could account for the fact that while Indonesia usually asked the IGGI for more than it needed, it sometimes received more than it asked for. It also reflects the underlying flaws in the whole operation. The Western countries are more interested in bolstering up an anti-Communist government, and getting what they can out of it in the process, than in genuinely developing the country; the ruling junta is obsessed with a craving for loans; and the technocrats, when it comes to a point, are only going through the motions of economic planning.

While new debts were piling up in the form of the soft loans that were called aid, foreign countries deferred repayment of those that had accumulated before Sukarno fell. The old debts amounted to about $2,100 million; the United States, Great Britain, France, West Germany, Japan, the Netherlands and Italy were owed about $800 million and the Soviet bloc about $1,300 million, mostly for warships, planes and weapons amassed in the West Irian campaign. The Western debtors, known as the Paris Club, commissioned J. H. Abs, a German banker, to work out a plan for deferred payment or, as it was euphemistically called, re-scheduling.[5] Abs proposed that Indonesia repay the West over thirty years and that no further interest be charged. Some Western countries considered the terms too generous: France feared a flood of requests for similar treatment from its former African colonies; Britain had similar misgivings; and Germany objected, probably on principle. Indonesia, on the other hand, considered the proposal too harsh: the Jakarta newspaper, *Chas Minggu*, an American-backed organ of certain generals, wrote nastily of the possibility that friction would arise if the debtors were 'not really sincere' in their desire to help Indonesia. After prolonged haggling the Paris Club agreed in April 1970 that principal should be repaid over the next thirty years and interest over fifteen years beginning in 1985; there was to be no moratorium interest. Each country then negotiated a separate agreement with Indonesia. The Soviet Union made a similar concession in August. For a time it had refused to accept anything less than prompt and full repayment. But in its anxiety to make friends anywhere in the Indian Ocean, it did not want to appear harsher than the West; in fact, its terms were said to be a little more generous than those of the Paris Club. The other Eastern bloc creditors rapidly followed Moscow's example.

While Indonesia received lenient treatment from the West, it showed neither principle nor sympathy in its dealings with unfortunate Yugoslavia, to whom it owed $112.6 million. Most of the debt was for a power plant built at Makasar, road rollers and arms. In 1968 Indonesia promised to repay the debt within ten years, but subsequently asked that the issue be shelved pending Abs's recommendation. A Yugoslav delegation visited Jakarta in October 1970 to try to persuade Indonesia to keep its word. The Yugoslavs pointed out that theirs was also a developing country; the power plant, which was running at a profit, and other equipment had been supplied not by the state but by impecunious socialist enterprises, which had acted on their own initiative. The delegation's pleas were rejected and it went home as much disgusted as aggrieved.

In April 1970 the government fixed the exchange rate by launching the rupiah in the open market and declaring its willingness to buy at 378 to the dollar. On the face of it the decision looked sound, because the rupiah had been stable at 377 for some months. But it soon became obvious that Indonesian technocrats, and probably the IMF, had underestimated the effect of an artificial inflow of dollars, which was not matched by productive effort, in bolstering the rupiah; and Indonesia found that some of its exports could not compete at the fixed rate. The technocrats wanted to devalue, but feared that to do so would undermine confidence at home and abroad. Their chance to extricate themselves came when President Nixon made his first devaluation on 15 August 1971; Indonesia kept the rupiah tied to the dollar, and thus devalued in terms of most currencies. But the Trade Minister, Sumitro Djojohadikusumo, disgraced himself in the eyes of some Indonesian economists when he claimed that the rupiah had not been devalued, since it had remained with the dollar. This double-talk was accompanied by bizarre action at the Bank of Indonesia, which on 15 August strengthened the rate to 376 and refused to accept more than ten dollars, later increased to 100, across the counter, thus giving the impression that the rupiah was about to be revalued. Some people rushed to change their dollars at private exchanges, which paid them only 360; they lost heavily when on 23 August the government surprised the business world by devaluing the rupiah by 10 per cent to 415.

This time Widjojo Nitisastro admitted that devaluation was necessary to safeguard exports, but blamed the world monetary crisis. Among those who expressed approval of the measure was Abs, who not long previously had assured Indonesians that their currency was strong. But there was criticism in the press. The newspaper, *Merdeka*, said claims that the rupiah was stable had proved to be propaganda; the former Vice-President, Mohammad Hatta, said he was 'shocked'; and the economist, Kaptin Adisumarta, pointed out that the rate had been unreal and that Indonesia could help to protect the rupiah by controlling luxury imports.

While the technocrats were criticized and even scorned by some Indonesian academics, they were compensated by the adulation of a band of Australian and American economists, whose careers included specialization in Indonesia. Perhaps the most admired was Sumitro Djojohadikusumo, the Trade Minister; in 1971 Bruce Glassburner, Professor of Economics at the University of California, Davis, described him as 'bold, imaginative, energetic and articulate', and said that he had 'earned a reputation as an economic and financial wizard' when a minister in the 1950s.[6] Sumitro was seen as a sound man, one of those tough-minded economists who, if anyone could, would lift Indonesia from the depths to which politicians and ideological dreamers were supposed to have dragged it. In fact, Sumitro was, above all, political; and his administration of the trade Ministry was wizard-like only in a sense that Glassburner did not intend.

Sumitro's quiet return from exile in 1967 was warmly encouraged by the American Embassy, but the junta approved it with misgiving. Suharto felt that bringing back a notorious Sumatra rebellion leader was risky, but Ali Murtopo, for his own reasons, favoured it. The Americans, with whom Murtopo had links, thought that Sumitro would help to prevent a waste of aid. They knew Sumitro well. In the first place, Washington had encouraged the Sumatra rebellion; then in the late 1950s US naval intelligence recruited him to obtain information about Sukarno and other matters.

Sumitro shrewdly formed a close partnership with Murtopo, and was subsequently said to have diverted profitable business to Murtopo's organization, Opsus, which needed substantial funds of its own to supplement its limited routine budget. With Mochtar Lubis he founded the firm, Indo-Consult, one of whose functions was to steer foreign businessmen through the labyrinth of the Indonesian bureaucracy, a journey that would rarely be undertaken without a lavish distribution of bribes. After his appointment as Trade Minister Sumitro said he had severed connexion with the company; but Lubis continued to spend most of his working days there, handling feasibility studies and other matters.

When Sumitro turned his hand to reorganizing copra exports an IMF man told me that producers' living standards would rise within a year. But Sumitro's copra export syndicate and bodies that were formed for other commodities turned out to be a disaster; and their corrupt management provides one of the shabbiest episodes in Indonesia's post-colonial economic history.[7] The ostensible aim of the arrangement was to arrest a decline in smallholders' incomes. Speculators were to be eliminated and all exports channelled through the syndicates, which were expected to make a united stand against foreign buyers. This was the theory. But the practice was that the syndicates, consisting partly of inexperienced figureheads, farmed out some of their functions to the old middlemen, who continued buying commodities and supplying credit in the villages.

The fees paid by one person for trading rights that have been officially allotted to another are known as *ali baba* money; the system is widely used in Malaysia, where Malays, benefiting from laws that are intended to give them commercial equality with the more enterprising Chinese, are frequently content to sit down and collect their money while the Chinese do the work. In Sumitro's marketing scheme *ali baba* money inevitably came out of returns to the grower, who made a bare living from his usually tiny holding. At the same time the basically rigid marketing system reduced competition among the middlemen, and the producer had less scope for bargaining. In short, a subtle traditional arrangement, in which credit terms, price and personal factors were balanced, was thrown out of gear.

A syndicate of six firms was licensed in 1971 to handle all copra exports, with the Copra Management Board fixing quotas for each and minimum prices paid to the grower. For reasons that have never been explained, a London dealer was appointed sole buying agent for all exports. When some exporters protested that he was not offering the highest prices available, the firms were allowed to sell to other traders. But there was a curious condition, which remained a close secret: the dealer received a commission of $\frac{1}{2}$ per cent on all sales not made through him.

The firm appointed as sole buyer of Indonesian pepper in the United States was Manhattan Commodities, in which certain members of the export syndicate had a 60 per cent interest; it was undercapitalized, suggesting its Javanese origin, and had no experience in the trade. The arrangement was obviously a racket, by which favoured exporters derived profit from both buying and selling. More serious for the pepper growers was failure of the theory that eliminating competition among Indonesian sellers in foreign markets would force prices up; when the entire crop was offered by one dealer at one time, a buyers' market was created and the price dropped. The syndicate was then replaced by three which sold at different times, with the right to by-pass Manhattan Commodities. But the original syndicate could not lose; it received monthly fees from the other exporters, who, apart from this extortion, carried on as in the past.

Six firms were nominally licensed to export hides and skins, but eighteen others, which were designated as approved traders, exported through the six on payment of fees, as in the pepper trade. The eighteen did the work, while the six merely collected their rake-off. But it was the twelve coffee exporting companies, formed in 1972 to replace syndicates that had failed after their establishment in 1969, which provided the richest source of *ali baba* money. The elaborate marketing system of which the companies were part put Sumitro in a powerful position to dispense favours. The company chairmen were not appointed by the shareholders, who were themselves selected exporters, but by Sumitro's Trade Department; in the words of my informant they were not experienced traders but 'colonel so-and-so and brother-in-law so-and-so'. Further, the Trade Department decided who was to receive export quota stamps issued by the International Coffee Organization; these became a valuable source of totally unearned income, and in 1972 were changing hands at the rate of 80 rupiahs (20 US cents) a kilogram. Having obtained the stamps either by grant or purchase, exporters, except large growers and government estates, were obliged to sell through one of the twelve companies. Old hands in the trade said the cost of this system reduced prices paid to growers by 20 per cent, compared with what they would have received by selling through the traditional network.

The grower also suffered through the elimination of exporters, well-known in foreign markets, who specialized in certain types of coffee. But this was not the end of his deprivation. Merchants had to use specified army lorries, at a price, and to pay for signatures to clear their shipments through the ports; there was also a 10 per cent export tax. In all it was estimated that tax and extortion amounted to more than 30 per cent of the f.o.b. price of copra and from 20 to 30 per cent of other commodity prices. The syndicates collapsed and were replaced by other systems, which, though relatively efficient, did nothing for the growers; Sumitro, a past master of euphemism, said the syndicates had outlived their usefulness. The coffee companies, with their government chairmen, continued to satisfy those who benefited from them.

Sumitro's control of opportunities to make fortunes was not limited to primary products; he gave a monopoly, for instance, to each of certain firms in the import of a specified make of motor car. It was hardly to be expected that the junta would leave such lucrative domains in the hands of a singularly independent-minded, civilian Trade Minister, whose enemies went so far as to say that his trade policies were devised to enable him to build up a new power centre, with the support of young PSI remnants.

General Sumitro, who considered his namesake to be politically incorrigible, and the Suharto circle, which wanted a greater share of trade licences and perquisites, decided to get rid of him. They prepared Western diplomats for his downfall with whispers that his technocrat colleagues found him hard to work with, which meant no more than that Sumitro was less 'tamed', to use the word of an army officer, than the others; and Bakin and Kopkamtib sent intelligence men into remote areas to investigate the failure of crumb rubber plants, which had been bought at Sumitro's instigation. While he was on trips abroad, the junta snatched control of wheat imports and sugar from him. Sumitro realized he was in a perilous position and, in my view, tried to build himself into a world figure, in order to make it more difficult to oust him. He went to Brussels for useless talk about tariffs with the EEC; but when he returned he found he no longer controlled motor part imports.

Sumitro's bitterest adversary in the Suharto circle was Humardani (the man known among journalists as Rasputin). The two had operated together for a time, but broke apart in a squalid row over such matters as the cloves trade, in which the Suhartos had a special interest, and the distribution of coffee export coupons and clothing import licenses. Sumitro had put clothing imports in the hands of a Singapore firm, Bian Bee, and, according to a member of Suharto's entourage, 'made a fortune out of it'. Suharto intervened in the name of Indonesian development and ordered that no Singaporeans should be given the monopoly; the business was then divided between two Indonesian firms, one of which was headed by the Suhartos' associate, Lim Siu Liong.

By the middle of 1972 Sumitro could see that he had overreached himself: he had even attempted to wrest control of Pertamina's revenues from Ibnu Sutowo. He tried through an intermediary to make peace with Humardani, who snubbed him and went round referring to him as 'that crook'; Murtopo found it convenient simply to drop him. General Sumitro told Sumitro that he would not remain Trade Minister in the cabinet reshuffle that was to take place after the March 1973 MPR meeting, and offered him an ECAFE post, which the Foreign Ministry had been asked to find, in Bangkok. But Sumitro declined exile and said he wanted to serve Indonesia at home. He was allowed to do so – as State Minister in charge of research, in a country in which research is almost non-existent. His successor was Radius Prawiro, Governor of the Bank of Indonesia, who had never insisted on applying normal banking criteria to credit applications made by Lim Siu Liong and others associated with the inner circle.

Despite the failure of the syndicates, Sumitro's downfall was certainly not the result of relative incompetence; he was at least as able as his colleagues and far more energetic than most, if not all, of them. His fate was that of anyone who, for whatever motive, offered more than token resistance to the junta. It is remarkable that he did not foresee this, that he failed to realize that in an essentially feudal society subservience is more valued than talent and that the rulers will allow only crumbs, not shares, to fall into the laps of their subjects. For a time Sumitro seemed to believe that the technocrats were the junta's equal, or more than equal, partners. Just before the elections, when people were being terrorized throughout the archipelago, I met him at the dinner held to raise funds for Golkar in an extremely luxurious night club (mentioned in chapter 8) owned by Murtopo's organization, Opsus. I asked Sumitro if it would be better for Indonesia if the political parties were allowed a free hand, with the army maintaining a reserve power to be used if wrangling held up legislation and development. 'No', he replied firmly. 'We [the technocrats] cannot work with the politicians.' I put it to him that, in any case, Indonesia could not accumulate nor acquire the capital needed for substantial growth per head of a rapidly rising population. 'Yes, but with the politicians it would be like that', he said, making a gesture to indicate instability. 'With the army we can keep things on an even keel.'

After the 1971 elections Murtopo, who was guest speaker at a Jakarta Foreign Correspondents' Club luncheon, dragged Sumitro along to help him answer questions. Sumitro had already addressed the club and was to do so again, but had not been invited on this occasion; the appearance of a senior minister as an economic valet to a general seemed to symbolize the power structure. Some months before his fall, musing on the army-technocrat alliance, Sumitro showed his usual sense of humour when he said wryly (in a conversation with the author): 'Some are more equal than others.' But he should not have been surprised. At the luncheon following that at which he and Murtopo had performed their duet, Subchan had warned: 'The technocrats think they are using the

army. They will find out who is being used.' Whether or not
Sumitro was an economic wizard, he had high academic qualifications and was a good organizer. The misuse of his talent examplifies
part of the tragedy of Indonesia, where urban cultural chaos
perverts both the thought and the action of men who could do
useful work in countries where, ironically, it is less needed. Those
precious few, rare in any country, whose high integrity keeps their
vision clear, are sidetracked like Soedjatmoko, or land in prison,
like Sarbini.

The voiceless peasants who were providing fortunes for both
merchants and parasites were about 7 million smallholders,
several million labourers who were partly or wholly dependent
on working for them, and their large, ever-increasing families.
In October 1972 Sumitro pointed out that these people totalled
63 per cent of the population. Speaking at a foreign correspondents'
luncheon, he shattered the optimism of some Western observers
when he disclosed that a Trade Department team had forecast
that the meagre per capita income of this vast mass, about 76
million people, would fall during the next ten to fifteen years, if
present economic patterns continued; this conclusion was drawn
from trends in population growth and export prices. It would be
necessary to find new markets, Sumitro said, without explaining
how, and to reinvest the increment in products that had received
little attention in the past. The products included sorghum, for
which there was a good demand in Japan and Western Europe,
cashew nuts and oil and mangrove roots, which made 'good char-
coal for the barbecues of affluent societies'. Thus the most
optimistic hopes for millions of undernourished Indonesians
rested partly on providing fuel to cook the steaks of those who, in
the final account, were benefiting from their exploitation.

In a sally aimed at the inner circle, Sumitro said: 'We shall
have resistance from pressure groups to some of these changes.
If we did not have the support of patriotic elements in the armed
forces – and there are such elements – it would be difficult for us.'
This political statement, with its scathing implication that responsible men could be found in the armed forces if you looked
hard enough for them, showed that Sumitro knew he was finished;
he appeared to be flying a new standard, as a possible rallying
point in the next inevitable Indonesian upheaval. But Sumitro
did not dare to say that oil revenues, which could have been used

to help smallholders, were being squandered on enterprises that
were capital-intensive and nearly always unjustifiable at that stage;
he said nothing of his unfulfilled promise to repeal the 10 per
cent export tax or of the scandalous inflating of f.o.b. prices by
unearned fees and extortion. Yet by the standards of the time his
statement appeared bold. That it should have seemed so, that a
man of Sumitro's potential calibre could only go so far, is also
part of the tragedy of Indonesia, which will only make ripples in
the pervading stagnation as long as such servility remains. To
attempt to launch a Western-style economy with minds inhibited
by feudal restraints is like trying to fly to the moon on *Garuda*.

Static expansion

Despite a substantial increase in rice production brought about
by greater use of fertilizer, extension of irrigation, and the introduction of high yielding seed, the per capita incomes of farmers
had scarcely increased, if at all, by 1974. C. P. Timmer argued that
during 1968–71 a rise in prices of other goods caused a 'fairly
serious decline in real incomes'.[8] He said the conclusion was
inescapable that while a minority of urban consumers were
considerably better-off than they were in the mid-1960s, a good
part of the improvement had been at the expense of the lower two
thirds of the people – those in the rural areas. H. W. Arndt then
pointed out that while it was true that terms of trade had gone
against rice farmers during 1968–71, they had 'moved slightly in
favour' of them in 1966–73.[9] Having thus disposed of what he
called Timmer's key point, he said it became difficult to accept
that the farm population had lost real income in the longer period.

Arndt admitted, however, that while rice production had
increased, that of other staple foods had fallen, largely because
fertilizer and irrigation had been used to produce a second rice
crop on land that in the dry season had been used for cassava,
maize, sweet potatoes, soybeans and groundnuts: an FAO team
estimated that during 1969–73, when rice production per capita
rose from 98.2 kg to 107.8 kg, total staple food production
declined from 167.4 kg to 162.1 kg. It is clear that the government has only succeeded in enabling farmers to resume Boeke's
'static expansion'; for the average rice production per capita
from 1850 to 1900, despite an extraordinary rise in population

and a vast increase in other staple crops, was 106 kg, almost as high as in 1974. There is no reason to believe that the Suharto government, with all its foreign help, will be able to free Indonesia from the bondage of this constant.

While Arndt appeared to demonstrate that in general real farm incomes had not fallen, he was not able to point to any significant improvement per capita. 'At the very least, a lot of Indonesian farmers who, during the years of economic decline, had to switch from eating rice to eating cassava, have been able to switch back again', he wrote. All he could add to this benefit was that 'opportunities' for about half the rural population, who lived on small plots and derived most of their income from day labour and pretty trading, had 'almost certainly increased substantially. . ., though not necessarily for all rural people'.

Whether one sees Arndt's picture as gloomy or as relatively cheerful, there are flaws in it. Arndt compared rice prices with the 62-commodities cost of living index, which is based on Jakarta prices, not those in the country. As Peter McCawley had pointed out in the November 1973 issue of the *Bulletin of Indonesian Economic Studies*, which Arndt edits, indexes in the rural areas differ widely from those in Jakarta (there are two) and from one another. When the 62-commodities index rose 30 per cent from July 1972 to May 1973 increases in the other cities ranged from 12 to 63 per cent. McCawley said the broad impression was that prices tended to increase less in Jarkarta than in other areas and that generally inflation in Indonesia was more serious than some government officials admitted. As McCawley said, the differences 'probably largely reflect local rice prices'; but these are not the prices paid to farmers. A further, more important qualification of Arndt's argument has been made by Ingrid Palmer (in a note on this chapter). She points out: 'his terms of trade could not accommodate the distribution of benefits in the rural areas. For that you would have to study changes (over time) in tenurial arrangements, sharecropping, rents, *de facto* hired labourers, etc. These agrarian relations would be more income-polarizing now than in the past.'

The issue of whether farmers' real incomes had gone up or down or remained static is marginal and is confused by the fact that producers are often buyers, just as small, or tiny, landowners are often tenants. Further, Indonesian statistics are too unreliable

to provide answers to marginal problems. Once, when I asked
Bernard Bell, Resident Director of the World Bank, if he had any
figures to help with a point we were discussing, he said: 'Have I
figures for that? Have I any figures at all?' Arndt conceded that
there might well have been a decline in the real incomes of 'the
bottom 10–20 per cent among the smallest farmers and landless
labourers in Java'. But he was only guessing. In the absence of
better statistics and more precise work, such nice points as whether
or not people are a little better or worse off in a given period will
have to be shelved. In the meantime it may be assumed that the
greater part of the population would have received at best only
a minute share of the claimed 38 per cent increase in the Gross
Domestic Product in the four years from 1969 to 1973 (*BPS
Indikator Ekonomi*).

The stream of peasants to the towns was an obvious sign that at
least the poorer were worse off. Landless wanderers deepened the
poverty of Semarang; in Jakarta they squatted listlessly on the
banks of canals, belying the false prosperity of the towering office
blocks, built largely with Japanese and other foreign money.
Many thousands of young men, with bulging calf muscles that
contrasted grotesquely with protruding ribs, pedalled *becaks*, in
which they often slept for lack of other accommodation. As the
Governor of Greater Jakarta, Lieutenant-General Ali Sadikin
said (in an interview with the author): 'It follows that conditions
elsewhere are worse than the worst here.' The population of
Jakarta rose 60 per cent from 2,906,533 in 1961 to 4,755,279 in
1972, compared with a 21 per cent rise in the total Indonesian
population. Beginning in 1969 Sadikin, a Sundanese, made
several attempts to close the capital to tramps, as the jobless
newcomers were called. By the end of 1972 the flow of new
residents was officially stated to have been reduced from 20,000
to 3,000 a month, but Sadikin said that many more were arriving
illegally, in spite of vigorous police action.

With the dual aim of making Jakarta a modern city and shatter-
ing the illusion that it was a source of limitless employment,
Sadikin drove stall-holders and *becak* drivers into the older
quarters. While he improved conditions in what were considered
to be legitimate *kampongs*, he pulled down squatters' shanties as
fast as they were put up. 'Sometimes it is very hard, and in my
heart I am a bit moved', Sadikin said. 'But if I do not act the

situation will become worse, and more will suffer from it. People would flood in. The 300,000 – 500,000 [living at less than minimal standards] would become 1,000,000.' Sadikin said that migrants were arriving in Jakarta not only from the Javanese rural areas, but from the Outer Islands, particularly from West and North Sumatra where, he said, rice fields needed rehabilitation, plantations were run down and commerce was at a low level. Migration to overcrowded Jakarta from Sumatra, which is sparsely populated and largely covered with jungle, exceeded the trickle in the opposite direction, which was subsidized to relieve pressure in Java.

This contradiction between policy and practice reflects both traditional haphazardness and the estrangement of the junta from the people. While Javanese were being brought into one part of Sumatra, Sumatrans were hungry elsewhere. In September 1970, for example, forty peasants in Labuhan Deli, North Sumatra, were arrested when about to sow rice seed on a state plantation, run for public and private profit by the army. Earlier scores of North Sumatrans saw their desperately needed crops mown down by the army at Tanjung Jati estate. Despair occasionally drove peasants to violence, despite the certainty of punishment. In April 1972 hundreds of farmers killed a civil defence man in Lampung, South Sumatra, when being forced to give up land required for a protective forest; several were arrested.

The hopeless blend of callousness and incompetence, which permeates the rural administration, was exemplified at Klaten, Central Java, in the middle of 1972. Applying the Dutch principle of forced cultivation, state tobacco plantation authorities ordered that certain fields be reserved for tobacco. But peasants went ahead and planted rice as usual. When the time came to put in tobacco, the authorities ordered that all fields be cleared, although many of them would have been ready for harvesting two weeks later. An average crop, on an area of 20 × 150 metres, was worth about 30,000 rupiahs (about $75), but the peasant received only 3,000 rupiahs and sometimes nothing. The authorities said they had given warning in good time through village heads. *Sinar Harapan*, which investigated the matter, could not establish whether the heads had been loath to pass on the instruction or whether the peasants had ignored it, through sheer necessity. But it is clear that there was no sympathy whatever between those administering the land and those trying to subsist on it.

While economists continue their debates, valuable field work has exposed the accelerating misery of the people. Surveys that have been published in the *Bulletin of Indonesian Economic Studies* reveal a pitiful and potentially catastrophic situation. Java, which contains about two thirds of the Indonesian population, produces only about half the nation's rice. In Klaten and elsewhere desperate attempts are being made to coax the *sawah* (wet rice-field) into producing more and more.[10] Small plots are set aside as beds to provide seedlings that can be transplanted almost as soon as a crop has been harvested; in this way, with the use of fertilizer, five crops instead of four are obtained in two years.

Farming in Indonesia is part of a complex cultural pattern, which varies from region to region. In Java it has well-defined links with village structure, social obligation, morals and spiritual life; there are various, long-established, precisely named systems of tenancy, share-cropping and selling. For centuries the harvest in Indonesia, as in many other lands, has been a rite as much as a labour. The harvesters, mostly women, have cut the rice with a small knife, the *ani-ani*, believing that if they use any other tool the rice goddess will punish them. It is a custom that all who wish to take part in the harvest, even those from other villages, are allowed to do so, and receive a share of the crop for their work. At the end of 1972 a survey of four villages that were representative of the main Central Java rice areas showed a rapid and alarming change in harvesting and marketing methods.[11] The invasion of larger and larger bands of unemployed women, who were travelling farther and farther in search of work, was more than the land could support. But landowners could not deny them the right to take part in the harvest; one said 'there would be war' if he refused, and another was beaten when he told women he could not find room for them.

To avoid such clashes many farmers were adopting a modified form of another traditional arrangement, *tebasan*, under which they sold almost mature crops to dealers, who made their own harvesting arrangements. Harvest gangs accepted a smaller share from the dealer than they would have received from the farmer. But they were relatively privileged and if they behaved themselves were reasonably sure of work; sometimes they wore specially coloured hats, or letters on their hats, to show that they belonged to an authorized team; the ancient custom of mutual help thus gave place to patronage and envy. Under another arrangement, *pajegan*, a group of women, as many as ten for a plot of 0.15 hectare, weeded and transplanted in return for meals and the sole right to harvest. This system, which appears to be relatively rare, creates a *fait accompli* that itinerant harvesters accept.

The increasing numbers of harvesters working on diminished plots reduced the size of the shares. Some farmers said they were ashamed to give so little to neighbours, and allowed them to keep one-sixth, instead of the customary one-ninth, of what they had cut; they were less sympathetic to itinerant workers, but were powerless to resist them. It was found that just under half of farmers in a representative sample sold under the *tebasan* system, but, apparently to maintain social prestige, they usually kept one third of their crops to be harvested by neighbours or anyone else who turned up at the right time. Generally, it was the poorer farmers whose consciences were troubled by the greater poverty of their neighbours and disintegration of tradition; those who could least afford it gave most. Farmers who were better off showed little concern for the others; farmer-dealers evaded the harvesters by selling their crops to other dealers just before harvesting.

The prospect of increasingly numerous bands of hungry men and women, armed with knives and roaming the overcrowded land in search of work and food, is ugly enough. But to this Malthusian nightmare the technocrats have added a vast increase in rural unemployment. In an attempt to restore and maintain what may be termed Boeke's constant, they have encouraged drastic production changes without regard to the social consequences. The changes are simple in themselves – the use of the sickle instead of the *ani-ani* and mechanical hulling instead of hand-pounding. Both have caused unemployment. It is estimated that the mechanical huller in Java has already destroyed 125 million woman-days of labour annually among those who are poorest and have the least chance of finding other work.[12] I have seen no global estimate for the ravage of the sickle; but while it takes 200 or more woman-days to harvest one hectare with the *ani-ani*, only seventy-five are needed if the sickle is used. The sickle was introduced in 1968 with the revolutionary HYV (high yielding varieties), for which it is more suitable than the *ani-ani*. Its arrival created a spiritual problem: would the goddess be angry if the *ani-ani* were cast aside? But necessity dictated a convenient rationalization: since the HYV came from a foreign land, some harvesters said, the goddess would not object when an alien tool was used to cut it.

There is, of course, another side to the improved production methods. The package of HYV, fertilizer and pesticides has undoubtedly increased yields to an extent that justifies the term 'green revolution' in Indonesia, as elsewhere. Various technical factors in the marketing system have increased the sum paid to farmers using *tebasan* by 63 per cent. Workers with sickles earn about three times as much in a day as those with the *ani-ani*; on the other hand, 60 per cent fewer women are needed when a crop is harvested with a sickle and sold under *tebasan* than when it is cut with the *ani-ani* and shared among the harvesters on the farm. As with unemployment caused by the sickle, I have seen no global estimate of the economic gain, but it must be considerable.

While hand-pounding in Indonesia in 1972 was costing the farmer $1.45 per 100 kg, mechanical hulling cost only $0.54. The saving to the buyer was 5 rupiahs per kilogram; but at that time prices were rising so fast that it was impossible to tell whether it was passed on to the consumer. Timmer estimated that while the hand-pounders had lost $50 million a year, mechanical milling had yielded a net gain to society of $400 million; he admitted that in a previous paper on the effects of milling he had made various errors, including one of between 100 and 400 per cent, but there seems no reason to believe that he was wrong the second time.[13]

The extent to which the use of HYV and associated techniques in under-developed countries has led to increased poverty among subsistence farmers, while benefiting those with small or large capital, will not be discussed here; this question, which has been the subject of numerous studies in recent years, is still being examined. It is enough to say that the introduction of HYV, the sickle and mechanical hulling in Indonesia exemplifies one of the main difficulties of development, namely, how to raise production without increasing unemployment. Those who undertake the responsibility of dealing with this problem should remember that the raw material of their operations, so often only dimly seen, is human beings, not statistics, and that careless work in the planning room can worsen the sufferings of millions. It should not be forgotten that economists not only differ among themselves on these as on most issues, but that they can make extraordinary slips.

While Timmer, for instance, estimated that mechanical hulling had cost only about 100,000 full time jobs, other economists, inserting their own field data in Timmer's model, arrived at 1.2. million[14] – a figure to which Timmer raised no objection in a subsequent paper.

Timmer's answer to the rice-hulling problem typifies that of many economists, who give a humanitarian nod towards the sufferings revealed by field workers, then carry on as before: after having admitted his errors, he insisted that hand-pounding was economically indefensible, which it is, and supported a proposal that the government should launch a vast public works programme to redistribute part of the net gain among those whose loss of work had made it possible. In a country governed as Indonesia is, such proposals are no more than 'talk from the top', to use Sarbini's phrase. Compared with 125 million woman-days lost in Java in 1972 through mechanical hulling, to say nothing of losses caused by the sickle and industrialization, the regional public works programme for 1972–73 aimed to create only 43.6 million man-days for the whole of Indonesia. As the landless unemployed increase, a disastrous ratio of this order is almost certain to worsen. For the junta and the technocrats, although they are aware of the problem and its political dangers, have their hearts in other affairs; and while they talk of the need to 'improve the rural sector', and make gestures towards doing so, they are unlikely to modify the policy of pouring an often inflated currency into capital intensive industries.

Further, no programme of the kind devised by urban-minded planners working in a city far from the scene could restore the broken cultural fabric of those driven prematurely from their bulging villages by technically fostered unemployment; no building of remote roads and dams would overcome the social instability caused by cutting off millions from their families, friends, customs and the traditional spirit world. What needs to be understood is that no economic plan should be conceived which does not contain as an integral part of it the means of absorbing socially and economically those whom it throws out of work; nothing should be done in the name of the GDP which accelerates the degradation of the inhabitants of Java's rural slum. The alternative view may be seen for what it is if it is expressed in the naive words of a well-meaning Counsellor for Economic Affairs at the United States embassy in Jakarta, who said: 'Sure it's tough. It's a cold shower, like the British going into the Common Market. But they've got to go through it.'

In September 1973 Mohammad Sadli, Minister for Mining and former Labour Minister, said of the effects of mechanical hulling: 'These shifts in employment and income distribution will probably never be registered in a census on account of definitions of employment, but they can shake the foundations of village life.' It was the duty of Sadli and his fellow technocrats to ensure that this did not happen; their failure to prevent the evil reveals a mentality that is unlikely to produce a remedy. In any case, the key to Indonesia's development, if it exists, lies not in economic plans as such, but in a reconstruction of society.

The detachment of urban-minded planners in Jakarta from the mass of farmers was illustrated in field work by Garry Hansen, who investigated Bimas, the scheme under which farmers were sold fertilizer and pesticide on credit.[15] Hansen presented a grotesque picture of bureaucrats forcing the entire package on farmers, who knew from years of experience that parts of it would be harmful. It is perhaps not going too far to say that most of the technocrats retain sufficient of the indigenous mentality to venerate all Western technology as if it were magic: the potions of the *dukuns* are replaced with the formulae of men clever enough to land on the moon. Because of this the technocrats gave little thought to whether chemicals from Germany and Switzerland were useful in specific conditions in Indonesia, while the companies that sold the stuff were, of course, largely concerned with their profits. The farmer, with his feudal mentality, usually deferred to the persuasion or yielded to the force of officials; generally only a tone of voice was needed in the post-*putsch* atmosphere to insinuate that those who rejected the package must surely be working for the PKI.

Apart from its inflexibility, the scheme was impracticable. As Hansen wrote, while the 'bureaucracy was able to cow most of the peasants' into accepting the Bimas package, it lacked the means of instructing them in its use. At meetings, where officials delivered long exhortations, farmers were frequently promised pumps to convert dry fields into the necessary *sawah*; but often the pumps did not arrive and the farmers were left with debts for the package and no crops; sometimes the fertilizer and pesticide were delivered too late for the season.

Occasionally the farmers spoke up. At one meeting an old man complained: 'The yields are not enough to pay back the credit and leave me with a satisfactory surplus. I only want a portion of the Bimas package. I do not want the pesticide. The last time I used the pesticide it killed the fish [cultivated] in the neighbouring pond.' A touching scene ensued. The old man apologized for having spoken so bluntly to his betters. Then for a moment the enforcement of inapplicable modernity gave way to tradition: the official took the old man by the hand, put his arm round his shoulder and the two exchanged warm words.

Other objections were raised: farmers could not afford to collect the fertilizer from the ends of roads at which it was unloaded; pesticide was not needed at all in certain areas; some farmers had already tried using more fertilizer than the package contained, without satisfactory results. The more daring complained that the package price included a technical assistance fee to pay foreign experts and the expenses of students, who were sent to teach new methods to farmers after receiving a smattering of instruction. Two courageous school teachers, who may well have been imprisoned during the subsequent 1971 election campaign, sat with the farmers at one meeting. After pleading that force should not be used, one of them read a local soil analysis showing a deficiency in phosphate, which was not included in the package.

Resentment increased when army-nominated village heads usurped the leadership of committees formed to negotiate with Bimas men. The issue became political, and the farmers fell back on passive resistance. Unused fertilizer piled up until the scheme was temporarily abandoned in the middle of 1970, with most of the credits unpaid. The hostility that it provoked has been described to show not so much the inefficiency of the bureaucracy, which is to be expected in a new country, but the gulf between those who govern Indonesia and those who do most of the work; this is obviously bound to impede such development as is possible.

The rice debacle

Towards the end of 1972 a sudden rice shortage caused suffering throughout the country and alarm in the government. The crisis illustrates the emptiness of political talk about bridging the gap between the poverty-stricken nations and those better off, as if this were largely a matter of shifting wealth from one part of the world to another; for it was brought about by a complex of factors that obstruct significant development – the feudalistic mentality of rulers and ruled, lack of communication at and between all levels, incomprehensible mismanagement and immense corruption.

The famine became acute from November 1972 to January 1973, with people in the towns queuing for rations, while some in rural areas subsisted on leaves, roots, and berries. Prices more than doubled in a few months, sending the nine basic commodities cost of living index up 66 per cent for 1972 and the 62-item index up 25.8 per cent. The shortage and the rocketing prices were finally brought under control by a feverish importing campaign, during which the junta was obliged to break its boycott of trade with Communist China and buy Chinese rice through Hong Kong. The effects on the economy were severe. As Stephen Grenville wrote:[16] 'The breakdown of the hard-won price stability of the past four years and the apparent drop in production which precipitated it ... demonstrate – if demonstration were needed – just how fragile the Indonesian economy remains.' The government expressed hope of restoring its previous consumer price ceiling of fifty rupiahs a kilogram, which was fixed when the price rose 100 per cent from twenty-five rupiahs within several months in 1969; but although some improvement was made for a time people were paying 120 rupiahs for medium grade in the middle of 1973 and 127 rupiahs in September 1976.

The government's blaming of a drought for the shortage cannot be accepted. It is true that there was a drought in Java, but its relative unimportance may be easily established. The dry season crop, which was the one affected, provides only 25 per cent of total production. Foreign experts said that the shortage, for all its serious consequences, was only of the order of 400,000 tons, compared with the year's production of 13.3 million tons. The shortage could have been easily offset by a timely increase in imports, which were as high as 764,000 tons in 1970–71, and by drawing on the reserve, which was supposed to have been established by Bulog, the rice authority.

Bulog, headed by Lieutenant-General Achmad Tirtosudiro, was a strangely autonomous, notoriously corrupt body, which conducted its own bank. Its main responsibility was to keep prices stable by means of a buffer stock; it also supplied the army, civil servants, who received rice as part of their salaries, and charity. These requirements totalled 900,000 tons a year. According to Widjojo Nitisastro, Bulog had a buffer stock 'early in the fiscal year', which begins in April, of 387,000 tons; this, he said, was normally enough to meet shortages for more than three months.

Why this reserve was frittered away even before the shortage became apparent to Indonesian officials in August has never been adequately explained. Corruption certainly played its part. After prices had shot up in 1969 Mochtar Lubis's *Indonesia Raya* pointed out acidly that Bulog had failed to account for stock losses, as they were euphemistically called, in the previous two years. During the 1972 shortage the head of Bulog's marketing department said on 13 November that 30 to 40 per cent of rice that Bulog had injected into the market – he did not say when – had simply disappeared. In a developed country, or one with a social structure that offered some hope of development, there would have been an immediate public inquiry into such a statement. But in Indonesia a few oblique press comments were made, an occasional politician asked a mealy-mouthed question, and the matter ended there.

The Bulog man vaguely blamed Chinese merchants for the disappearance. But members of the Bulog administration were themselves known to be in league with Chinese, who had been manipulating the market for years. In December 1972 students who formed Group Five Action sent parliament a memorandum listing firms owned by Bulog staff, which were buying rice and selling it to Bulog. A knowledgeable member of Suharto's entourage said (in a conversation with the author) that but for Bulog's corruption support prices paid to farmers could have been 36 per cent higher than the floor price that was established in September 1969 to encourage production. 'The rice problem is a blessing in disguise', he said. 'Now everyone is awake. Corruption cannot go on, or we are finished in five years.' On 17 January 1973 Suharto said pointedly that Bulog needed the 'will, ability and honesty' to fulfil its task; but he did not seem to share his subordinate's anxiety, and for some reason waited until the end of May before removing Tirtosudiro honourably from the post he had disgraced.

Meanwhile the flour mills, in which, according to army officers, the Suhartos have an interest, were doing well out of the rice shortage. At that time the United States was supplying about 400,000 tons of wheat to Indonesia annually on extremely soft credit terms under its PL4 credit scheme; the government sold the wheat to flour mills and devoted the proceeds to development projects. In 1971 the price from mills to flour distributors was fixed, approximately on the basis of the American wheat-flour ratio, at 35 rupiahs per kg; but in October 1972, when millions were beginning to clamour for food and millions more could not afford enough at the higher prices, the mills were allowed to charge 42.5 rupiahs, although the price of wheat was unchanged. This profiteering 'shocked the IGGI', in the words of a Western official. But the scandal did not leak out into the Indonesian press. As the *Jakarta Times* columnist, Billy, wrote when Tirtosudiro finally agreed to meet a parliamentary committee to discuss the rice crisis, behind closed doors: 'You folks must not know what was being discussed! Big men's business, you know! You just rest assured that you can continue to buy rice (at high prices, certainly!).' The *Jakarta Times* was one of the newspapers that the junta closed after the January 1974 riots; Billy and his colleagues were among the dozens of journalists forbidden to practise their profession again.

More important than the corruption was the administrative muddle, or lack of administration, which would prevail whether Bulog was honest or not. Harvesting is continuous in Indonesia, but the peaks are in April–May–June, when the big *sawah* crop is gathered, and September–October, for the less important dry crop. In April 1972 an FAO team forecast that because farmers were using less fertilizer than planned, the total crop would be 800,000 tons below the target (which was higher than the previous year's); but the Agriculture Department rejected this survey and insisted that the new target would be achieved.

About the same time a Golkar-led parliamentary committee warned against a rice shortage. This earnest and capable young team had gone into the field to find out whether rice farmers would lose income if the government persisted in forcing more of them to lease their land to sugar estates, which the army had seized from the Dutch in 1957. During its inquiries it discovered that rice would be scarce even if extra sugar were not planted, but officials ignored its warning. While the team did not say so, it appears to have stumbled on the fact that farmers were planting less rice, partly because the floor price fixed in 1969 had not kept pace with their costs and partly in protest against military and bureaucratic oppression. Another danger sign appeared in July, when prices began to rise slowly. The Department of Agriculture remained unruffled, and insisted there was 'plenty of rice'. Apparently the department was run on the principle of what Indonesians call *ABS*, or *Asal Bapak Senang* (as a long as the boss is happy); in other words, if a subordinate thought that the man above him would like to feel that the target was being fulfilled, he would tell him that it was, come drought or flood. The department suggested that speculation was putting up the market; but whether or not this was correct, Bulog, which only a month or two earlier was supposed to have had a reserve of 387,000 tons, failed to make the necessary stabilizing injection.

By this time a drought in Central Java and lower than normal rainfall in Sumatra had killed a good deal of such rice as had been planted. A foreign expert said that it was subsequently shown that the drought had been confirmed in reports from 100 weather stations; but the Meteorological Department either did not receive or read them, and insisted that while rainfall was lower, there was certainly no drought. Suharto, with the backing of the Planning Board, told parliament on 16 August that Indonesia had so much rice that the target for the following year would be reduced. But a week later provincial governors warned Tirtosudiro at a conference in Jakarta that a shortage was imminent. Tirtosudiro did nothing. Suharto sent his special operations man, Ali Murtopo, into the country to find out if there was a drought and if a serious shortage was likely. Murtopo came back with all the essential facts; yet it was not until October, when the market was already in chaos, that the government made a serious attempt to rush imports into the country.

A key factor in the market shortage was that Bulog did not begin buying for its reserve and other purposes until the end of May, instead of in April, and did not make its first big contracts until June. Bulog's excuse was that it had not received the necessary bank credit; the Bank of Indonesia's reply was that Bulog did not ask for it. This was obviously more than just a muddle. It has been established that when Bulog failed to buy, farmers began selling at lower than the guaranteed price. The first assumption made by anyone familiar with market manipulation in Indonesia would be that Bulog men held off to depress prices so that they could then buy cheaply on their own account and sell to themselves, as Bulog, at the support price. Although it seemed extremely likely that this happened, I confess I could not prove it because I did not receive information about the buying delay until the day before leaving Indonesia at the end of January 1973. But that is certainly the way things are done; on 17 April 1975 *Kompas* reported accusations that some petty heads of village marketing units (Badan Unit Usaha Desa – BUUD) were buying rice cheaply and selling it to their units at a profit.

Village heads and other minor officials had been making good money by stealing and selling the Bimas package, before the formation of the BUUD gave them easier opportunities in rice; unlike their betters in Bulog they were sometimes arrested when caught. The most spectacular of the exposed regional frauds were in West Java, where the Siliwangi Division rounded up scores of Bimas men in March and April 1970. One batch of thirty-four were accused in court of having stolen fertilizer valued at $600,000 and thousands of dollars worth of pesticide and seed; sixty others in another district were said by the prosecutor to have stolen 'vast quantities' of fertilizer.

Fertilizer corruption and muddle on a higher level had such a serious effect on rice production that Widjojo Nitisastro made a series of raids, incognito, in January 1973 to uncover hidden hoards. While people were starving because they could not afford the higher rice prices, he found 148,500 tons of fertilizer piled up at six ports. At Cirebon, West Java, thousands of tons were lying in warehouses, while farmers in the region were paying up to forty-five rupiahs per kg instead of the fixed price of twenty-six rupiahs; some of the stock had been imported in September 1971. In passing, he discovered 2,500 tons of urgently needed rice imported from Pakistan, which authorities for some reason had failed to transport to famine areas of Central Java.

It was regrettable that Widjojo, already overworked, had to leave his Planning Board desk at such a time. In the Sukarno period he had found it necessary to enter a sterile debate and write a paper to prove that private enterprise was permissible under a vague article of the Indonesian constitution, which reads: 'The economy shall be organized as a common endeavour based on the principle of the family system.' Now he was obliged to become inspector of fertilizer rackets and bungles. Such contradictions are inevitable when a bridgehead of Western culture is established in an overwhelmingly alien environment. But Widjojo did more than get the stocks moving. His action forced Suharto to take the fertilizer importing business from Pertamina; this was a gain, though small, in the Planning Board's battle to get Ibnu Sutowo's corrupt, blundering giant under control.

But the main problem remained in the rural areas, where peasants were increasingly resistant, and in the end the junta used force to resolve a crisis that had arisen from its own mis-management. Early in 1973 it decided to expedite the restoration of Bulog's stocks through village marketing and processing. Having wiped out spontaneously formed co-operatives on the ground that they were politically motived, it set up BUUD, a network of village units, with the task of buying half of Bulog's requirements from farmers and selling it to Bulog after milling in the village. This rushed attempt to build co-operatives from the top was doomed. Key unit staff (manager, administrator and mill mechanic) were given only two weeks' training. More important, peasants resented the units, which were tyrannically run by often corrupt officials, as a further blow to the already shattered village democracy. The government tried to peg prices unrealistically low, in order to protect consumers in the towns; prices that the units were authorized to pay, while higher than the increased support level, were lower than in the market. Because of this and the obvious profiteering of unit heads, who acted both as buyers and as sellers to the units, peasants sold increasingly to private traders. Officials were faced with failure to reach their Bulog targets, and called in the army to force peasants to sell to them. Peasants who had already sold, or whose crops had failed, were terrified by memories of the army's ruthlessness after the *putsch* and during the 1971 elections. Sometimes in panic they bought rice in other villages, occasionally selling cattle to raise the money; sometimes they paid cash to officials who, when they did not pocket it, tried to fulfil their targets by seeking rice elsewhere, often in vain. Despite warnings in the press that BUUD was breaking down, the junta, ever-confident in the use of force, expanded it. But the system finally collapsed in July, when the government abolished BUUD's quotas.

The story of the 1972–3 rice crisis has been told in some detail because it raises a question vital to the understanding of Indonesia's economic problem, which, like all major economic problems, is largely social. Rice is Indonesia's staple product; its production and marketing have been going on for centuries. If Indonesia is still in a state in which such a muddle occurs, how can it make any substantial progress in modern commerce and industry, which require skill and experience that are practically non-existent in the archipelago?

The pre-capitalist mentality

That such a relatively small rice shortage should have led to a permanent doubling of the price was at first sight puzzling, but two factors were probably sufficient to explain it. The first was that usually only about 25 per cent of production is marketed, the rest being consumed in the villages. But the second, a sharp increase in the money supply, to which Stephen Grenville directed attention[17], was ominous: it suggested that Indonesia was returning to its old habit of printing press finance, not, as in the Sukarno period, to support the budget, but to create credit for junta-backed *cukongs*.

The money supply (currency and demand deposits) had risen by 58 per cent (estimated) in 1969 and 36.4 per cent in 1970, but the effect was not inflationary because renewed confidence caused a rise in public savings. After having established their nest eggs, the moneyed minority began to spend more of their incomes, and the supply was prudently curbed to 28.2 per cent in 1971. Early in 1972, before the rice crisis began, an Indonesian economist, Dr Sumarlin, warned that the money supply increase must be kept to 27 per cent in that year if price rises were to be below 5 per cent. But in 1972 the supply shot up by 47.9 per cent. Grenville pointed out that one of the causes of the increase was large rises in credit advanced to enterprises and individuals. To this observation should be added that a great part of this credit was accorded to *cukongs* associated with the Suharto circle; thus the ruling

elements in the junta, while bullying the peasants, were themselves
a cause of the rice calamity. Grenville wrote: 'It seems that bank
credit control contains as many loose joints as ever and that the
Central Bank has little control over credit creation.' In effect the
cukongs and their military partners determined the money supply;
for the technocrats failed to resist them.

The rise continued with further ill consequences. Money was
increased 41 per cent in 1973, mostly as bank credit, and 40.5 per
cent in 1974, during which year an even more accelerated rate
was arrested by fiscal and monetary controls. These measures
were imposed in April, when the prices of goods except rice were
soaring at an annual rate of 100 per cent and the 62-commodities
index had risen 80 per cent since June 1972, just before the rice
shortage. Among the controls was the requirement of a 30 per
cent deposit against overseas borrowing. This regulation was
repealed with others in November.

By this time events outside the junta's reach had transformed
the situation to its benefit. The Arab-Israeli conflict had led to the
Arab initiative in drastically raising the world oil price. Oil
exports had been the mainspring of Indonesia's economic growth
since the *putsch*. Revenues from oil, more than 70 per cent of
which was produced by Caltex and Stanvac, provided nearly half
of Indonesia's exports and 38 per cent of domestic budget receipts
in 1972-3. The oil was sold at a premium, because of its low
sulphur content, mostly to Japan. Successive price rises from
$2.93 per barrel in April 1972 to $11.70 in April 1974 were a
tremendous windfall. The extra income created a problem by
increasing the scope for credit creation; but it stopped the adverse
trend in the balance of payments resulting from increased rice
purchases and enabled the government to slow down inflation by
means of very large imports of essential commodities. The annual
inflation rate in the first four months of 1975 was relatively low
at 17.5 per cent, perhaps mainly because of a rice subsidy, as
Arndt suggested.[18]

The uncertainties of the Indonesian economy did not dis-
courage foreign economists from debating the issue of when
Indonesia would be able to support a specified GDP growth
without foreign capital.[19] Each disputant trotted out recondite
graphs, equations and identities to prove his point. Yet the
economists neglected a variable so static that it might be called a

constant and a constant so large that it makes all variables meaning-less – the scarcely diminishing shortage of experienced business-men, without whom continued growth must be haphazard, and the ever-present junta, whose plundering causes chronic mis-management and waste.

Despite the predominance of Chinese in commerce, the number of competent businessmen in Indonesia remains very small in proportion to the requirement. The Chinese themselves, apart from those with strong overseas links, are capable only in relation to the others; they make no comparison with the magnates of Singapore, Hong Kong and Taiwan. Reflecting the poor standards of business in general, accountants are extremely scarce. In 1973 the Indonesian Accountants' Association put the number in Jakarta at the low figure of 700; but foreigners believed there were only between 70 and 150, depending on the standard applied.[20] An appeal by Suharto for men to train as accountants met with a poor response; there is no doubt that Javanese, although they are increasingly attracted by the feel of money, continue to find this precise kind of work tedious and distasteful.

The inability of firms to keep proper books, or any books at all, has serious effects on trading, bank credit and income tax. Without accountancy, a firm can make no adequate provision for depreciation, which is usually disregarded in such calculations as are made; nor can it establish the relative profitability of its various operations. Since there is no clearly ascertainable profit figure, income tax payments are generally negotiable, with the result that tax collectors, who in the regions are given quotas to fulfil, are among the most eligible men in the marriage market. The absence of accountants makes it impossible to establish whether a business is credit-worthy; overdrafts are consequently obtained not so much on merit as by bribing the bank manager. A European businessman told me he struck a typical example of this practice when making a sale. After agreeing to the terms, his Indonesian customer patted a brief case packed with bank notes and said: 'Now I am going off to get an overdraft.' Such arrange-ments often lead to bankruptcy, disguised by book entries, with the debtor borrowing increasingly from the bank to pay his overdraft interest.

Abuse of credit was a factor in the crumb rubber bungle, which illustrates in various ways the need for care in thinking about how to help under-developed countries. In 1968 Sumitro Djojohadi-kusumo decided it was time that Indonesian rubber was processed at home, instead of in Singapore. Three Chinese firms with Indonesian names were given credit by Bapindo (Indonesian Development Bank), to buy ten crumb rubber machines from the British firm, Guthrie, and ten from the French firm, Promosi. The decision to use the relatively new crumb process, which had been successfully adopted in Malaysia, was a disaster. The British machines were unsuited to the rubber supplied by small-holders and the French were adapted with difficulty. The main problem was that Indonesian growers customarily left stones and other rubbish in the raw material to make it weigh more; Chinese buyers did not mind this, because it enabled them to bargain over the price. British and French engineers had not expected the quality to be so low; it took the French two costly years, instead of the expected six months, to get the machines working properly.

The Chinese firms, of which at least one had direct ties with the Suharto circle, had been given five year credits at 12 per cent. But, even if the plants had worked properly from the outset, production could not have supported such a high interest rate on the heavy borrowings. The Chinese, with their great experience in rubber, knew this from the beginning, but were unconcerned. In addition to having official support, they were confident that the bank would not foreclose, since it would be unable either to retrieve the machines from remote areas or to find buyers for them. The fashion of setting up crumb factories with lavish credit spread until the Bank of Indonesia ended it by ordering Bapindo to tighten credit terms in September 1972. But by this time Chinese close to the junta, and other merchants, had sufficient plant for their purposes. Altogether there were eighty-five machines, including ten belonging to a state-owned plantation.

While the junta and its technocrats could boast that they had established a new industry, the smallholder suffered. Sumitro prohibited exports of remilled rubber from October 1971. The price of crumb at the end of 1972 was only two thirds of the lowest price of remilled and smoked rubber. At the same time it was more costly to produce: the smoked process cost 1–2 per cent of the export price, remilling 3 per cent (not allowing for depreciation) and crumbing 8 per cent. It was also found, too late, that the crumb machines should have been installed near production sources, such as plantations, since they required fresh latex. Many growers were thus unable to sell their raw material; in West Kalimantan, at least, some smallholders, already living in poverty, took to subsistence fishing.[21]

Reckless and corrupt granting of credit, such as happened in the crumb rubber muddle, produced runs on several banks in 1969–70, when at least eight were suspended from clearing operations for failing to maintain reserves equal to 30 per cent of their deposits. In the confusion the Jakarta Clearing Bank Institute mixed up the name of a bank it had suspended with one it had not, and had to announce a correction. IMF men saved the Bank of Indonesia from collapse by putting its affairs reasonably in order. They began their overhaul of accounts from a certain date, disregarding a room full of earlier records because the task would have been too great. The IMF accountants hoped that when all was sorted out the books would more or less balance. But they found that the four government commercial banks, which were underwritten by the Bank of Indonesia, were technically bankrupt; if the loans granted by two of them, the Bank Negara 46 and the Bank Bumi Daya, had been called in at the end of 1972, those wholly or partly written off would have been several times as great as the banks' capital.[22]

The banks were trying to extricate themselves by lending the debtors money to pay their interest, but this produced no more than an exponential series of book debts. Reforms were introduced, and presumably the banks were kept afloat with some of the created credit. But the same men with the same minds still managed the banks; and businessmen who did not have irresistible claims or military backing were often obliged to pay commissions of 10–20 per cent to obtain overdrafts, sometimes through corrupt and incompetent brokers, who were supposed to assess their credit-worthiness.

Indonesians have always been notorious borrowers, whether in need or not. This attracted the attention of Boeke, who, as Sadli has noted,[23] said that the farmer had not developed a spirit of 'accounting-mindedness' when the use of money spread during colonization. The farmer had never learned to think of profit and loss in terms of money. If he incurred a debt, he forgot about the principal and only worried about his interest obligations; he failed to understand that money was a means of exchange, not a

commodity to be harvested and consumed like rice. It is clear that
the mentality that Boeke observed among peasants still prevails
in high places in Jakarta. I am inclined to think that the attitudes
of the pre-capitalist culture – those of both the peasant and the
bazaar – even colour the emotional responses of many with
Western education, and that the Indonesian technocrats, while
understanding the dangers, do not experience the same outrage
at the violation of credit principles as, say, that of a banker
brought up in Amsterdam. One frequently has the impression
that the technocrats, though not without technical skill, have their
hearts less than their heads in what they are doing; in a sense
they are only going through the motions of conducting an economy
along Western lines.

Despite the pre-capitalist mentality, economic growth remains
possible as long as it is supported by increasing sales of oil produced
by foreigners. But when this source of wealth diminishes, the bizarre
and feeble business world will be unable to achieve the diversifica-
tion and expansion needed to maintain the present growth rate;
nor is it imaginable that it could compete against Japan, Singapore
and Hong Kong, particularly if Indonesian Chinese were excluded,
which is what most indigenous Indonesians want. A delegation of
twenty-eight German business leaders, described as the largest
ever to have left Germany, rejected Indonesia as a source of
serious long-term investment after a visit in April 1972. At a press
conference before leaving Jakarta, the Germans were frank about
the main difficulties: a shortage of skilled management and workers,
the absence of industrial standards and, since most people were
living on subsistence, an insufficiently large domestic market for
industrial goods. Apparently the Germans did not agree with
those who thought it wise to get in early to take advantage of
possible expansion; nor did they relish participation in joint
ventures, which was compulsory under the investment laws.
'Corporation tax makes it impossible for us to form partnerships
with people who have little experience and no capital', one of them
explained. German companies, including Siemens and Kabel und
Metallwerke, have factories in Indonesia, as the Dutch company,
Philips, has; but their operations are small.

The Germans' visit gave rise to one of those Indonesian mysteries
that perplex the most seasoned observer. One hour before the
delegation landed, the German Embassy received a message that

Suharto would be unable to keep his appointment to meet it; later a small paragraph in a newspaper indicated that he had gone to Central Java to meditate. It was astonishing that a man styled as the Development President, who had found time to receive all kinds of business Toms, Dicks and Harrys, should evade such a powerful group of industrialists. Diplomats who more or less knew the country looked for a mystical explanation. An old Indonesia hand at the German Embassy said resignedly: 'It was the *dukuns.*' This remark was certainly on the right track. At that time Humardani was engaged in secret dealings with the Japanese; and it is possible that he thought the presence of Germans in the palace would create a discord in the Indonesian-Japanese duet that he imagined he was conducting in conjunction with the stars.

Soon after the Germans left it was announced that Suharto would visit Japan the following month. This caused great surprise, because Suharto's 1968 state visit to Japan had yet to be returned. His earlier overseas travels had been preceded by months of preparation; now he was to go abroad at short notice, without even the precise date having been fixed when the announcement was made. After a nonsensical official explanation that it had to be kept secret for security reasons, the date was finally determined by *dukuns*, I was told. It was officially stated that Suharto's purpose was to discuss 'important international and bilateral matters'. But before the date was fixed I embarrassed the inner circle by reporting that the real aim was to obtain a huge loan, the proposed details of which were given in my despatch, by mortgaging part of the nation's oil. This report proved to be correct. I mention this not to claim special merit as a correspondent, for my record as a news-gatherer was no better than that of my rivals, but to make the rest of the story, which came from the same sources, more credible.

About a year previously, when Japan had an inconveniently large balance of payments surplus, certain Japanese had the idea of making a special loan to Indonesia; a condition was that means should be found to feed back a percentage through Japanese oil companies to swell the funds of the faction supporting the Prime Minister, Eisaku Sato, in the Liberal-Democratic Party. While Humardani was shuttling between Jakarta and Tokyo to discuss the proposal, it became clear early in 1972 that Sato was to fall from the Prime Ministership. Suharto, who, according to one of my informants, was as obsessed with money as Sukarno had been with women, feared that the opportunity would be lost. He tried to arrange a meeting with Sato, even suggesting a weekend in Bali, failing a more formal arrangement. But in the changed political circumstances the Japanese had lost interest in their proposal, and Sato declined the invitation. Suharto then resolved to go to Tokyo.

Some of Suharto's advisers, including Adam Malik, tried to dissuade him, because they thought that an obviously improvised begging expedition would damage Indonesia's prestige. Malik tried to create a *fait accompli* on 25 April by denying a Tokyo report that Suharto was to meet Sato in Japan. But two days later the Palace, not the Foreign Ministry, announced that the visit would take place in May. Sato found it hard to fit the visit in. He had to handle a parliamentary session, to receive the American Vice-President, Spiro Agnew, on 12 May, and arrange his own impending resignation. But he agreed to a visit beginning on 9 May, when Suharto arrived by commercial airline, instead of in the presidential plane. The Japanese Embassy in Jakarta had said earlier that the trip was informal. The truth of this description was demonstrated in Tokyo when Sato broke away from a luncheon with Suharto to attend to urgent business in parliament. Nevertheless the outcome, as forecast, was a loan, or rather an agreement to lend when projects had been found. The communiqué on the negotiations, which was delayed until after Suharto's departure because of 'unresolved issues', was a parody of diplomatic humbug. The President 'noted Japan's need for low-sulphur oil in mitigating the growing problem of pollution in her efforts to harmonize the various factors of economic and social development'. Indonesia would therefore supply 58 million kilolitres over ten years in excess of normal commercial sales. The Prime Minister 'expressed his appreciation of the President's thoughtfulness' about Japan's pollution problem and undertook to lend Indonesia 62,000 million yen (about $200 million) 'on concessional terms'.

In an attempt to quell protests in Jakarta that Suharto was adopting the bankrupt peasants' practice of *ijon*, selling the crop green, the considerate President and the grateful Prime Minister emphasized that the deal was not an advance payment for future deliveries. But the Japanese Ministry of Trade and Industry revealed on 10 May that an additional $100 million was to be granted 'on a private basis' as an advance payment for oil; subsequently the Sumitomo Bank, representing fifteen financial institutions, said that $40 million had been lent to Pertamina at the interest rate of Asian dollars for six months, then about six per cent. Several side issues of the visit remain to be explored; these include why Suharto insisted on going to Tokyo himself, instead of leaving it to Nitisastro and Malik or Ibnu Sutowo. The affair was odd throughout. An international oil company executive disclosed: 'They went to Tokyo with pipe dreams. Now they have asked us to suggest viable projects to spend the money on.'

Just before Suharto's borrowing spree, IGGI countries had met to consider aid for the following year. They now found themselves in the embarrassing position of having to justify to their taxpayers loans for periods of twenty-five years, during which the principal would be devoured by inflation, at less than half the rates at which Indonesia was borrowing commercially. By this time, despite its indulgence of the junta, the IGGI was tactfully trying to curb Pertamina's over-borrowing on terms that were often expensive. Pertamina kept many of its commercial loans secret, but some international bankers could see they were getting dangerously high. Bernard Bell, World Bank Resident Director, was greatly disturbed that Western and Japanese banks were encouraging Pertamina's vice; he harshly rebuked a representative of a leading New York bank who said Indonesia's substantial oil resources made it unnecessary to study its profit and loss account before lending.

But the borrowing accelerated. Not satisfied with government-approved loans totalling well over $500 million from Japanese and American banks in 1973, Pertamina turned more to short term finance. Loan was repaid with loan until even the more imprudent Japanese and American bankers felt that their gamble had gone on long enough. Funds dried up. During critical months in 1974 Pertamina kept going by withholding quarterly instalments of its own tax and a share of revenue from foreign oil companies payable to the government. But early in 1975 not even this desperate sapping of the nation's finances was enough to meet Pertamina's obligations. In February and March the company defaulted in the repayment of short term American and Canadian bank loans said to total $100 million. Pertamina had crashed at

last and the government had to intervene and borrow about
$1,500 million in the following twelve months to pay its short
term debts. In one of his increasingly frequent departures from a
Pangloss view of the junta and its technocrats, Arndt was to
comment that Pertamina's 'recklessness in financial management
finally threatened the whole development strategy of the regime'[24]
– such as it was, one might add. The planned surplus of 230,000
million rupiahs ($554 million) in the 1974–5 budget was wiped
out; and in a revised estimate of foreign exchange reserves the
expected increase for the year was reduced by $559 million, in
spite of a $200 million reduction in forecast imports.

Great though the damage appeared in the government's books,
the lot of the masses was scarcely worsened, just as it had scarcely
been improved, if at all, in the preceding years. Pertamina's period
of contributing substantially to the exchequer had been brief. The
Corruption Commission found in 1970 that it had failed to pay
the government's full share of foreign companies' profits, except
in 1964–5. This appears to have been rectified, but Pertamina
evaded large amounts of income tax by forcing the Finance
Ministry to accept extraordinary depreciation claims: a tanker
with a twenty-year life, for instance, was written off over five
years, instead of the fifteen normally allowed for tax purposes.

In November 1973, after the oil price rise, Suharto had ordered
the rushed construction of 6,000 fragile, three-roomed elementary
schools, most of which appear to have been completed within a
few months. The January 1974 riots had led to much talk about
further small social measures to be carried out under the second
Five Year Plan, but it was obvious that after Pertamina's failure
there would be little or no money for them.

Suharto, with Sutowo in a temporarily weak position, ordered
the Bank of Indonesia to examine Pertamina's finances. This was
an even more formidable task than that undertaken by the IMF
when it had tried to create order in the bank itself. Pertamina's
accounts were chaotic where they existed, and had never been
audited; an American accountancy firm, which the company
had engaged in 1973 for a limited task, was asked to extend its
work. Pertamina had grown into an unwieldy industrial and
commercial complex said to be among the world's 200 largest.
Sutowo, possibly to increase patronage no less than to satisfy his
megalomania, had sprawled into large and small enterprises that

377

had nothing to do with oil. Lumped with his refineries, tankers, petro-chemical factories and marketing companies were a steel complex (PT Krakatau), insurance business, an extensive rice plantation in Sumatra, real estate, an airline, promotion of tourism in the United States and a restaurant in New York. Pertamina's ramifications have never been fully revealed, but a list published in 1974 contained thirty enterprises.[25] In addition, Sutowo had his personal interests, although it would take more than accountancy to determine where they overlapped with the nation's.

Pertamina and, nominally, the Indonesian government, formed PT Krakatau to build a huge steel complex on and near the site of an almost completed Russian mill at Cilegon, West Java, which was abandoned after the *putsch*. Indonesia is paying the Russians $36,628,349 for the mill on rescheduled debt terms. It declined a Russian offer to activate the plant; and Western companies rejected Indonesian proposals on the ground that the site and design of the project made it unprofitable. After a feasibility study by Eisenbau (Essen), German firms including Ferrostal, Siemens and Kloeckner signed contracts with PT Krakatau to build a new complex. Construction was to include a smelter, large power station, port and railway; a German colony of 3,000 was to live on a luxurious estate with schools, supermarket, concert hall, golf course and bowling alley.

The Germans, while shrewdly avoiding large investments in Indonesia's agriculturally dominated economy, had grasped enormous oil-financed contracts that were described in a German financial journal as 'The Biggest Order of All Time', which one estimate put at $2,400 million. It seemed to be good business, but the Germans were soon lost in the pre-capitalist environment and infected with some of its endemic maladies. After the Pertamina crash, the Minister for Reform of the State Administration, Dr Sumarlin, established that the capital cost of the Siemens installations was three times the current average per kilowatt produced. Ferrostal's prices were so high that investigators suspected that some of the money was handed back to men in PT Krakatau and Pertamina, under the kind of arrangement that the Japanese had developed on a staggering scale. The Germans, knowing Sutowo's power, also appear to have at least connived when PT Krakatau decided to increase its planned steel capacity from 500,000 tons to 2 million tons, without consulting the government or the

378

Planning Board. Mismanagement and manipulation of funds
were so obvious that PT Krakatau's Managing Director was
dismissed in April 1975.

German contractors were kept waiting for substantial arrears
of payments, which in previous months had been made from some
of the short term loans that had brought Pertamina down. The
government, with the technocrats now more in command for the
time being, appointed a commission of foreign consultants to
investigate the entire project. The supermarket, country club
golf course and other amenities were already built; but the future
of the German colony, which at that stage was only embryonic,
remained uncertain. The project would certainly be curtailed;
and there was some talk of writing off the relatively small amount
of work that had been done and integrating the German complex
with an aluminium smelter that the Japanese had agreed in
principle to construct at Asahan, in Sumatra. The Germans,
though clever up to a point, were no match for the Japanese in
Indonesia. They had rushed into Cilegon in 1972 to get big orders,
without sensing the dangers of pre-capitalism; but the experienced
Japanese, in spite of repeated pleas from Indonesia and even
public insults from Adam Malik, had delayed agreeing to the
Asahan project for about three years until in 1975 they brought
off the basis of a deal that was practicable.

Siemens defended the high cost of their plant by saying that
the Indonesians had demanded the highest standards of safety
and other equipment. In other words, they took the view, like the
Russians before them, that if the Indonesians wanted it let them
have it; the difference was only that while the Russians were
politically motived, the Germans were inspired by profit. Their
operation typified those of all foreign investors who are exploiting
Indonesia under the guise of aiding it. In the first years of the
junta's rule foreigners would not invest unless they could be
reasonably sure of getting their entire capital back in about three
years. As the junta increased its hold on the people, this precaution
was relaxed. But the underlying attitude remained the same;
foreigners encouraged the Indonesians to buy more than they
could afford and to pour into capital intensive industries thousands
of millions of dollars that could have been better used to renovate
the rural slum and transfer millions of its inhabitants to other
regions.

While the IGGI countries and World Bank had been worried about Pertamina's borrowing for some time, the default was a shock. The oil price rise had made it appear that soft loans could be progressively diminished. The World Bank had moved in that direction by stopping its soft IDA[26] credits and starting to lend to Indonesia at commercial rates; Holland had sharply reversed its policy of giving more than it lent. In general there was a tendency in the West to suggest that the Arabs should take over some of the expense of helping the needy. The Pertamina crash confused the issue; the question arose whether Indonesia was capable of making proper use of any aid at all. The annual IGGI meeting arranged for April 1975 was deferred until May while experts made a rushed investigation of Indonesia's financial position. All doubts were then resolved. The meeting 'readily accepted'[27] World Bank and IMF recommendations that large-scale aid be continued. Partly on the basis of a World Bank growth projection, which, according to Arndt, 'strains credulity', the IGGI agreed to aid totalling $920 million for 1975–6, compared with $850 million in the previous year and $875 million, the previous maximum, the year before. It also approved in principle Indonesia's proposal to negotiate loans on commercial or concessional terms for a separate one thousand million dollar project scheme.

Nevertheless, the IGGI did not relax its policy of reducing programme aid – import credits originally determined by the balance of payments deficit – as oil exports rose. This form of aid vanished, and Indonesia was obliged to replenish its foreign exchange reserves by borrowing 1,000 million dollars on medium terms from Japanese and American banks. Subsequently the IGGI agreed to aid totalling $1,120 million for 1976–7. The new commitments brought total IGGI aid to $6,837 million since the first grant in 1967. A small amount of the aid is not repayable; but even after allowing for inflation, the junta's overseas debts, including those of Pertamina, exceed the $2,100 million borrowed by all preceding governments since independence. The West is obviously concerned to protect its oil and mineral interests and its capital goods exports, and to bolster up the junta as an anti-Communist bastion in South East Asia. The decision to increase IGGI projects, in spite of the junta's lamentable economic management, was part of the thinking that led the United States to raise military aid in October 1975, from $20 million to $42 million a year, following the Communist victory in Vietnam.

Doubtless the World Bank, IMF, and IGGI countries made it clear that Ibnu Sutowo would have to go. But to have done this brutally would not only have offended the junta; it would have weakened the bastion by upsetting the army's delicate *tugas* patronage system, of which Ibnu Sutowo, with his Pertamina revenues, was the fountain-head. *Tugas* means task or duty. A sergeant will say to an officer that his men want to perform *tugas*. The request is then passed up to higher officers. If it is granted the men are paid for some nominal work, such as repairing a bridge. An officer's power to obtain *tugas* is regarded as a sign of his influence. To put Pertamina's finances on a thoroughly sound footing would interfere with this supplementary income, without which the loyalty of officers and men could not be relied upon. It was possibly considerations such as these that made it difficult to oust Sutowo with the speed that would have been expected; his private financial relationships with the Suharto circle would also have taken time to adjust. Ibnu Sutowo was not dismissed until 3 March 1976, a year after the crash, when another general replaced him. Pertamina's total debts were then estimated at $10,500 million, which was greater than the total 1976–7 national budget and two thirds of the gross domestic product.

Japan, which had gone well to the front as main IGGI contributor since sharing the lead with the United States in the earlier stages, committed itself to $140 million of project aid for 1975–6. The United States, under continual domestic pressure to reduce aid, slipped further back to $50 million; but the World Bank with $400 million and the Asian Development Bank with $120 million continued to make good the US reductions. Other commitments were (millions of dollars); Netherlands 52, Western Germany 42.5, Canada 40, Australia 34, United Kingdom 25.3, Belgium 9, New Zealand 7.2. Total $920 million. France's figure was not announced, but was $33 million for 1976–7, when the US almost doubled its aid and agreed to $99 million; the World Bank lent $550 million.

Even before the Pertamina affair, foreign investment applications were falling, although approvals of those already submitted increased. The Americans, particularly, seemed to be making an increasingly sharp distinction between Indonesia's political and business functions in their strategy. While military and World Bank aid increased, American investments dropped and Japan took the lead in this field as in aid. The following figures for non-oil investment applications approved by the Indonesian government show the shift (millions of dollars): US–Canada 959.6 in 1967–73 and 14.4 in 1974; Japan 633.4 and 450; Hong Kong 267.4 and 178.8, Europe 230.6 and 319.7. The totals for all countries were 2,828.3 and 1,050.5 million dollars. Approval of applications, however, did not necessarily mean that they would be implemented immediately or at all; at the end of September 1973, for example, the cumulative total of actual investments other than oil was about 1,000 million dollars out of about 3,000 million dollars approved. Implemented domestic investment approved by the Suharto administration totalled 1,900 million dollars at the end of March 1973.

Disenchantment had gradually set in at the US Embassy since the late 1960s, when some diplomats and economic attachés sincerely, but naively, believed that the alliance of the junta and the technocrats would bring prosperity to Indonesians and reasonably sound business for all. In February 1975 the US Embassy published a booklet called *Changes in Indonesia's Investment Climate, 1974-75*, in which it complained of 'high and rising costs, increased bureaucratic hazards, and continuing uncertainties about investment groundrules and taxation policies', and pointed to 'the emergence of economic nationalism as perhaps the dominant force shaping investment policies'.

There was, in fact, nothing basically new in this situation. Administrative inexperience, xenophobia and the frustration felt by moneyless entrepreneurs had always been present; and it was inevitable that these tendencies would predominate when the oil price rose and the junta imagined that it had got the economy on its feet. Increased discrimination against foreign capital took the form of reduced tax exemptions, the limiting of more sectors to Indonesians, and rules that businesses should be 51 per cent owned by non-Chinese Indonesians within ten years of their establishment, with the stay of all alien staff except top men limited to three to five years. There were two reasons for this policy. First, the closing of certain sectors was to the advantage of junta-backed Chinese, who held virtually all domestic capital; secondly, the requirement that foreigners should hand over more than half of their businesses to indigenous entrepreneurs was a sop to those whose bitterness at the Chinese monopolization of credit had led to an incessant press campaign. Thus the junta allowed political expediency and the financial interests of a few to jeopardize the flow of capital on which its development policy was supposed to have been based.

It is my view, however, that the 51 per cent rule is merely an unworkable piece of demagogy. No business normally conducted could achieve a return that would enable half of it to be given away to partners who would certainly be sleeping in a financial sense and probably in most others. What is likely to happen is that serious Western investors will diminish and the Japanese, who know how to handle such problems, will adapt the *ali baba* system. The indigenous entrepreneur may get his 51 per cent on paper, but will accept much less in practice, for fear of getting nothing at all. Faces could be easily saved: the foreign firm could explain that, much though it would like to divest itself of more than half of its assets, this was not yet possible because profits had been less than expected; the indigenous partners would accept this situation, to keep the enterprise going in the interests of national development. Meanwhile, in the uncertain political and economic climate, foreigners will understandably try to get their capital back as fast as possible; this, in itself, will keep prices high. It is inconceivable that anyone who knew South East Asia would fail to foresee the *ali baba* outcome of the 51 per cent requirement. That the technocrats introduced the measure was another sign of their powerlessness.

Foreign and domestic capital brought about the establishment of new industries, and rises of several hundred per cent in the production of some that were already existing in 1966. In 1973–4 about 1,000 million metres of textiles, 13.5 million electric bulbs, 29.5 million tubes of toothpaste, 758,000 tons of cement and 230,000 tons of fertilizer were produced; in 1974 car tyres totalled 1,567,000, cars assembled 45,000 and motor-cycles 200,000. Anne Booth and Bruce Glassburner[28] commented that the benefit in some of these industries in terms of domestic value added, measured in world prices, was questionable. Impressive though the statistics are in isolation, they meant little to the masses, who for the most part could not buy any of the goods and were not employed in producing them. According to the 1971 census, only 7.5 per cent of the labour force was engaged in manufacturing; subsequent production increases in industries that were often capital intensive would not have added significantly to this figure. At the same time prices of protected goods soared in some places to an extent scarcely reflected in the cost of living indexes.

At the IGGI meeting in May 1975 the World Bank urged that Indonesia, in spite of higher oil revenue, would need increased aid if the poverty suffered by most of the people were to be substantially alleviated in the next decade. It was thus clear that nine years of military rule and billions of dollars of foreign aid and capital had done virtually nothing to help the great majority of Indonesians. The limit to what can be achieved by present methods is seen in Arndt's plea: 'The objective should be to accelerate growth to a rate which would make it possible, provided income distribution does not worsen, to double the consumption of all Indonesians by 1985.'

There is little hope of Arndt's wish being fulfilled. But if it were, the benefit that most people could hope to expect may be seen from surveys made in the field. J. Ahrens[29] found in 1971–2 that average annual per capita expenditure on all items in Padang, West Sumatra, was about $60; for 46.4 per cent of families it was less than $50 and for 25.3 per cent less than $40. The average annual food expenditure was about $37 a head. Families spending more than $240 a head on all items, the top 1.1 per cent, devoted $168 to food; the food bills of families spending less than $50 ranged from only $15 a head in the lowest category to $30 dollars in the highest. Throughout the survey food spending rose with total spending. Yet the food was at best only basic, and all these people had the same need of nourishment.

Padang, with its port and overlooking mountain, is a relatively prosperous, pleasant, little town, although it has deteriorated since the Dutch left. Crammed Central Java is far worse off; and its inhabitants would scarcely notice the doubling of their minute consumption, spread over ten years. D. H. Penny and M. Singarim-bun[30] found that two thirds of the people in an area chosen for research did 'not earn enough to reach the very modest level' known as *cukupan* (having enough for family needs). They said that poverty in Sriharjo was so great that the poorest were worse fed than Pakistani refugees in India in 1971. Labourers, when they could get work, were paid 30 rupiahs (less than eight US cents) a day. This situation appeared to prevail throughout the Yogyakarta Special Region. Singarimbun published the following note from his field book:

> An itinerant seller slipped crossing a small creek, and broke the entire stock of pots she had been carrying. She wept, and said 'I am bankrupt, ruined.' The total value of her load had been Rp 160 ($0.40).

That is the scene lying behind the new office towers and hotels in Jakarta, the gigantic blunders of Pertamina, the fortunes being amassed by the junta and its *cukongs*, and the graphs and equations of economists.

CHAPTER THIRTEEN

The price of harmony

When the next upheaval takes place in Indonesia, the West may wonder why it spent thousands of millions of dollars in buttressing such a feeble, socio-economic structure as a bastion against Communism. It should be clear by now that it is better to live with the various forms of Asian Communism than to try to contain them. Not that Communism is necessarily a serious possibility in Indonesia; but if it were, nothing that is being done at present would stop it. The junta talks much of the increased danger following the American collapse in Vietnam, but it knows that the greatest threat is from the poverty-stricken masses of Central Java, where most of its forces are deployed. In 1973, when the generals were saying that Peking was behind the youthful Malaysian Chinese guerrillas in Sarawak, one battalion was considered enough to control the entire West Kalimantan frontier. The Indonesian commander of Sinkiang, a Chinese town in West Kalimantan, had to maintain order among a hostile population with a force of Chinese volunteers. Admittedly, the officer could not sleep for fear that a revolt would break out; but what he and the frontier command needed was that a few hundred men should be transferred from their security vigil in Java, not more guns from the United States. Indonesia has only two land frontiers: in Kalimantan and Irian Jaya. Asian Communists have not the ships to launch a successful invasion of the coast. The supplying of $40 million of American military aid each year can have little object other than to help suppress internal rebellion when it comes; if the bullets, shells and missiles are let loose it will not be against Chinese or Vietnamese but Indonesians.

The Russians are playing a quiet, shrewd game in Indonesia. As part of their policy of spreading their influence in the Indian Ocean, they would support in a crisis any government, right, left or centre that helped to secure their passage through the Strait of Malacca. They have only forty-six diplomats, consuls and attachés in Indonesia, compared with 106 American (1976; the Russians increased by two from 1972 and the Americans by twenty-seven). But they are not without friends in the army and civil service, and are prepared to go a long way to win the good graces of the generals. Before the 1971 election results were officially declared, while the Moslems and PNI were still protesting that the poll was unfair, the Russian Ambassador hastened to be the first to call on the Golkar leader, Lieutenant-General Sokowati, and congratulate him on his victory; the Polish Ambassador dutifully followed, and was second. In 1975 the Soviet Union agreed to supply two power plants to Indonesia on soft terms; it followed this in 1976 with a $300 million credit for an aluminium smelter on Bintan Island, in the Riau archipelago, south of Singapore. These were obviously, at least in part, political investments for the future; it would appear that the Russians, who rarely waste money, do not think that many years will pass before events in Indonesia will turn to their advantage. When the Russians first showed interest in the Indian Ocean, they claimed that it was to protect their southern flank from submarine attack; since then they have sent in tank-landing ships. The Angola incident provides a warning of what could happen in the chaos of a Malthusian catastrophe. If Moscow threw its weight behind an armed, separatist faction in Sumatra, as the CIA did in the fifties, it could control the oil installations overnight; the Kremlin could hardly have overlooked this possibility when contemplating the 1980s, during which the USSR will have to begin importing oil in an increasingly competitive world market. The junta can only spare a light defence force for Sumatra, as for Kalimantan, because it does not trust many Sumatrans with guns and requires its Javanese troops to keep order in their home territory. Thus Western economic development policies, which create far more poverty than they alleviate, may have a consequence ironically different from the one intended; the attempt to avert Asian Communism by pouring in unsuitable aid could in fact help to break up the ground for Russian imperialism.

The Russians are in a comfortable position. All they have to do is to sit and watch while the West blunders on with the same mentality as that which produced the Vietnam débâcle and led to the volte face in Africa. When the attempt to plant the nucleus of a Western-style economy in Indonesia has finally broken down, Indonesians will blame capitalism, not their own cultural barrier, for their misery. Vast unemployment and land hunger, while provoking revolutionary ferment in general, will increase the nation's ethnic strains. Regional discontent poses no serious threat to the centre at present; but in the bleak future one revolt could set off a chain. Fighting has continued intermittently in West Irian since the Act of Free Choice; convincing accounts of Papuan attacks and murderous Indonesian reprisals continue to reach exiles in Holland and the government in Papua-New Guinea. Moluccan separatism, though only flickering, is kept alive by expatriates in Holland. Sumatra is quiet, but it cannot be assumed that there would be no rebellion if a chance came. To these potential dangers the junta has added Portuguese Timor, which it bloodily annexed in July 1976, thus taxing further its thinly spread forces in the Outer Islands.

The Suharto junta is a favourite in the West, because it is supposed to have achieved political stability – by means that were condemned when Mrs Gandhi, too friendly to the Soviet Union for Western taste, used them on a relatively miniature scale. But the postponement of Indonesia's 1976 elections, which were ordered by the puppet MPR in March 1973, showed that the army still feared the people. Held on 2 May 1977, the elections gave Golkar 232 of the 360 DPR elective seats (64.4 per cent), while the Development Union Party won 99 and the Indonesian Democratic Party 29. There was an echo of Subchan when Chalid Mawardi, Deputy Secretary-General of the Development Union Party, protested that more than 2,400,000 votes in East Java, where the Moslems are strong, had not been accounted for.

The illusion of stability has been socially costly. The price of Suharto's harmony is the further paralysis of a traditionally submissive people and the consequent congealing of their stagnation. Every new force that bubbled in the primeval, socio-economic mud has been suppressed. The moderate Communist Party, which was as syncretic as Javanese religion itself, was exterminated; Nasakom, the inspired formula with which Sukarno tried to weld the three articulate streams of revolution into a socially dynamic movement, died with it. Western liberalism was crushed in turn. Subchan's attempt to achieve a balance between the parties and the army, which he recognized as a political force, led to his being ousted from office by the junta and (*cui bono?*) could have been linked with his death in what was reported to be a road accident in Saudi Arabia. Sarbini's despair at the impotence of economic policy caused him to form associations that eventually landed him in gaol on the absurd charge of having tried to overthrow the heavily armed junta by unconstitutional means. Soedjatmoko's penetrating essay has remained on the shelf, and his voice on all subjects has been silenced. Trade unions, like political parties, have been virtually abolished; their members are left to the mercy of rapacious Chinese and Western bloc investors, who sweat labour and charge high prices to retrieve their risk capital as fast as possible. The leaders of unions that are still allowed to exist in name have been bullied into obedience, which a report of the World Confederation of Free Trade Unions described as pathetic; the International Labour Organization called off an inquiry into Indonesia's breach of its ILO commitments at the request of frightened union officials. A scorched earth policy has been applied not only to political but to co-operative and other social organizations. Lieutenant-General Amir Machmud publicly warned the wife of an anti-left politician that her patriotic exhibitions of Indonesian products might be considered subversive; she abandoned them in fear, probably groundless, that she or her husband might be arrested. And all this destructive repression of any activity that could be called spontaneous has been carried out by a military gang, which, though crippled by ignorance and rotted by corruption, has assumed the authority and pretended to the virtues of Plato's Guardians.

It is impossible to estimate the social damage that has been done by massacre and political detention. Thousands of those who joined the PKI obviously represented a dynamic force that could have at least contributed to cultural change. Even more valuable, perhaps, were those who joined organizations which, though supported or sponsored by the party, were not Communist. These were often people of character and discernment, who, while sceptical of Marxist dogma and critical of Communist methods, saw promise in the leftist movement as a whole. It is of no account whether their views were right or wrong; what is important is that they thought and acted – and thought and action are what stagnant Indonesia needs. Whatever the merits and demerits of these people, it is my indelible impression that, sample for sample, I saw better faces on Buru Island than outside it. This is not to say there was nothing to admire among those who were free. Exceptional strength, agility and stamina were shown by the lean gangs who worked on the roads. And proletarians who smiled and waved from lorries as one overtook them in a car had an élan which inspired a hope that Indonesia would take a better turn when new leaders emerged from them. Among the élite, too, were men of the zeal and integrity necessary to help bring about some improvement in society. A few have already been mentioned, but to name others would expose them to risk of persecution. One, however, may be added to the short list of those who have already suffered; he is Dr Singgih, son of Ali Sastroamidjojo. Singgih was arrested with three other civilians in September 1976 for allegedly having conspired to overthrow the government. The charge was clearly as false as the one that had been preferred against Sarbini; it would be impossible to dislodge the junta unconstitutionally without military force, and Suharto said that nobody in the army was involved. Doubtless the three other civilians were also men of a calibre to be admired. I mention Singgih only because I happened to meet him once when interviewing his father. He struck me as a man seriously concerned about his country's problems; his integrity was such that rather than work closely with an administration whose conduct he disapproved, he took a post as teacher. His imprisonment was another loss to Indonesia. The lot of other political prisoners appears to have worsened. In June 1976 the ILO rejected an Indonesian government letter answering charges that political prisoners were being used for forced labour.[1] It has been said that many of the prisoners on Buru Island are fed on cassava, while the rice they produce is exported for the profit of army officers.

In a country in which Western democracy has never existed the question of whether Suharto or Sukarno was the more or the less democratic is hardly relevant. It may be said, however, that whereas Sukarno only suppressed those forces which, he believed, threatened directly or indirectly to risk Indonesia's enslavement by neo-colonialism, Suharto has stamped out all others; and while Sukarno acted with the minimum of rigour, Suharto has applied the maximum of ruthlessness. After the 1965 *putsch* Sukarno had only 33 political prisoners that I know of, although there could have been a few others. They had spent much, if not most, of their detention under house arrest. One example may be cited to show how this situation has been misrepresented, largely by journalists who obtained their information from Western embassies. Mochtar Lubis is said by John Hughes[2] to have been 'jailed for nine years for his opposition to the government'. This is what General Nasution says (in an interview with the author):

> Mochtar Lubis's newspaper supported Zulkifli Lubis [who tried to kill Sukarno]. We could not act against him until we found a press card of Mochtar in the possession of one of Lubis's officers, who had been arrested. I told the garrison commander to arrest Mochtar. After his release he went to Israel . . . Sukarno had him arrested again.

Sutan Sjahrir was arrested in January 1962 after Subandrio's dubious intelligence men (BPI) had accused him of being involved in a plot to kill Sukarno. Nasution comments:

> Sukarno was given so-called intelligence reports on an 'American defence group' at secret meetings. I told Sukarno, Yani and others that the reports should be checked. I arrested some of those who made the reports, but the reports continued. After the attempt to kill the President in Makassar we could not resist him. I think Sukarno believed the reports. When an Auri (air force) Mig fired bullets at the palace Sukarno asked at once if there were British, Australian, Dutch or US warships in our waters.

The detention in such circumstances of Lubis, Sjahrir, and others vulnerable to American influence may be debated; I find all detention without trial to be indefensible. But whatever the verdict, Sukarno's violations of human rights are peccadilloes compared with those of Suharto.

Figures can be produced to show that the enclave economy
has fared better under Suharto than under Sukarno. Nevertheless,
the economy during guided democracy was not as chaotic as it is
usually said to have been. Between 1960 and 1965 there were
marked increases in smallholder production, which provides most
of Indonesia's rural exports. Rubber rose from 404,000 to 504,000
metric tons, coffee from 77,900 to 120,700 and tobacco from
49,500 to 55,500; there were small falls in tea and dry copra.
While the returns have to be set against inflation and other
factors, the picture is not one of total disintegration. There were
also small rises in estate production of rubber, coffee and tea in
the same period. The previous chapter has shown, however,
that there is little point in judging economic endeavour in Indonesia by orthodox criteria; for of greater importance than any
statistics is that the fundamental maladies persist. Attempts to
build a class of indigenous entrepreneurs by granting bank credits
for that purpose are certain to fail, as they did under the Old
Order. Sukarno philosophically observed that the cost of credits
that were not repaid could be charged against experience gained
by the nation. But bankrupts rarely learn. The junta began
granting the credits after the riots of January 1974, when it also
introduced the measure to enforce Indonesian participation in
foreign companies, which has been described in the previous
chapter. Most of the inexperienced men who receive the credits
have no chance of competing in trade: all other considerations
apart, the Chinese can easily undercut them because, being more
credit-worthy, they obtain finance at highly advantageous rates
from Singapore and Hong Kong. The fact that the government
is prepared to lend money to men whom financiers consider to
be too risky emphasizes that its gesture is political, not economic;
it is another useless attempt to ensure harmony. Many laments
have been published in the Indonesian press about the plight of
the indigenous, or non-Chinese, entrepreneurs, who are known as
pribumi. Their main organ, the daily newspaper *Nusantara*, which
was among those closed after the riots, claimed that 90 per cent
of domestic capital was in Chinese hands. If this is correct, and
it is probably not far wrong, the question arises as to just what the
pribumi are. If they have no capital, they can have little function,
although they may have imitative aspirations. The prospects of
entrepreneurs who lack capital may be guessed from the conduct

of those who have it. A survey made in 1972 by Lewis T. Wells Jr., consultant to the Harvard Development Advisory Service,[3] shows that most Indonesian businessmen, except when under competition, use machines even when labour, which is cheap, would yield them considerably greater profit; the managers do not want the worry of handling workers and the engineers like to feel they have the latest equipment. This shows that even going concerns, which are heavily protected by tariffs, are run without either business sense or social responsibility.

After the *putsch* the junta gladly accepted foreign guidance, which was aimed at reviving the corpse of the Dutch economy. But before long it matched its increasing appeals for aid with increasing rejection of what it called interference in Indonesia's affairs; this reached the point of arrogance when David Gordon, Bernard Bell's successor as World Bank Resident Director, was only accepted after what amounted to a period of probation. If Western advisers had been able to control the entire economy, including the Pertamina operations and credit, the growing disparity between the few rich and the multitudinous poor would not have been less; indeed, greater efficiency would have increased the polarization. But at least a section of the economy would have been coherent. As it is, what Boeke wrote of one part of society now applies to the whole: 'A precapitalist society is driven further and further away into an exchange economy for which it is not fitted and which it cannot master.' The polarization continues in the sense that a few are getting richer while the majority are, at best, left in poverty. But the situation described by Boeke, in which a dynamic pole contrasted with a static pole, no longer exists. For sound dynamism vanished with the Dutch; and if foreign aid and the small measure of influence that accompanies it were withdrawn, the economy would not merely cease its limited expansion; it would collapse.

It is difficult to imagine an end to Indonesia's socio-economic débacle. Boeke did not rule out that a miracle could occur in the remote future, but if he was fundamentally right about the present, very little can be done within foreseeable time. On the other hand, if Soedjatmoko was correct in assuming that useful cultural change was possible, and it may not be, only a well-led mass revolution could bring it about. Any government that slipped into power by means of intrigue or another coup would lack the essential zeal; nothing short of widespread, rational, revolutionary fervour, of a kind not yet seen in Indonesia, or perhaps anywhere, could induce and promote the necessary psychical metamorphosis. In a situation that demanded intense mental reorientation and discipline of the young, the new leaders would have inherited a feeble educational instrument. The former French Prime Minister, Edgar Faure, who examined Indonesian education for Unesco in 1970, said that if its problems were not solved immediately the result would be disaster. Soon afterwards Soedjatmoko warned of declining intellectual standards; and Professor Slamet Santoso, Acting Rector of the University of Indonesia, said (in an interview with the author) that if his students had any spirit of inquiry, they did not acquire it at the university.

Faure was not thinking of ambitious cultural reform, but merely of orthodox requirements. In 1964 Sukarno announced that all adults under forty-five and all children of school age were literate, compared with 6 per cent in the Dutch period; this was an exaggeration, but Sukarno certainly spent enough of the nation's dwindling income on schools to make his claim reasonably tenable. The junta, with rapidly increasing oil revenue at its disposal, did not even maintain the low standards set by its predecessor. As the population continued to rise, illiteracy increased; in March 1974, the Education Department reported that 36 million people over ten years old (40 per cent of the age group) were illiterate. The department said in 1972 there were no schools for nearly two-thirds of children of school age (seven to nineteen years). The numbers of children attending school, compared with the totals eligible, were: elementary schools, 15.1 million out of 22.9 million; junior high, 1.8 million out of 8.4 million; senior high, 700,000 out of 7.7 million. A survey in one area showed that most failures to complete the elementary course resulted from the inability of parents, whose incomes averaged only 22.65 rupiahs (five US cents) a day, to pay the fees; there is no free education in Indonesia. The Education Department said that to counterbalance its rising population Indonesia needed 135 new teachers every day for a daily influx of 6,800 new pupils. This calculation appears to be based on the net population increase, rather than the net increase in children of school age, but it illustrates the magnitude of the problem, which worsens each year; in 1975, with the population soaring at an estimated rate of 2.1 per cent per annum, births were of the order of 8,000 a day. A shortage of trained teachers and equipment keeps school standards extremely low; in 1973 only 30 per cent of teachers in elementary schools, 36 per cent in lower secondary schools, and 54 per cent in the sparse upper secondary schools were listed as fully qualified. Apart from a few, teachers are not drawn from those most capable of going beyond the three r's; Professor Santoso complained that salaries were so small that even unemployed graduates found it not worth their while to enter the profession. Neglect of education in favour of reckless industrial adventure and gigantic corruption provides perhaps the most damning criterion by which the junta can be judged. But education alone would only worsen Indonesia's difficulties. Most of those who graduate from higher schools and what are called universities have little chance of being re-warded for whatever effort they put into their studies; a Dutch youth affairs consultant found in Surabaya, for instance, that 70 per cent of those leaving secondary schools in 1971 could not find jobs.

In the 1971 census, Indonesia's population was put at 119,182,542; in 1976 it was estimated at more than 130 million; by the year 2000 it will be 280 million, unless the masses end their resistance to birth control or, what is more likely, famine intervenes. If it were possible to isolate Indonesia's main problems from one another, this would be the most serious, but all are inseparable. At present it appears that nothing will stop the population from rising until it is halted by starvation that will make the suffering of Bangla Desh in the early 1970s look like a mere curtain raiser to a Malthusian tragedy. Famine or not, there will be no permanent reduction in Java's inordinate fecundity until the people are led by rulers they trust. It is only by winning the confidence of the villagers, by making them feel secure, that they can be persuaded to abandon their traditional form of old age insurance – large families, of whom the parents hope a few will survive to look after them. While Indonesians are living longer because of measures taken by the World Health Organiza-tion and other factors, the improvement is not enough to over-come peasants' fears of being stranded without support when they are too old to earn or scrounge a living in Java's increasingly overcrowded rural slums. The infant mortality rate remains high; the average life span, though longer than it was, is still estimated at only 48.5 years for men and 49 years for women (1971). A young married couple may well wonder who will look after them if they live longer than most; many will have seen the suffering of the unprotected old in times of acute food shortage. Some authorities have tried to enforce birth control, but there is no conclusive evidence about the result; widespread punishment of those who produced too many children would fan hatred of the army, and, if other social circumstances were critical, might lead to bloodshed. Family planning officials in one Javanese town provided an example of the imitativeness that is sometimes called acculturation when it takes a less ludicrous form: to arouse enthusiasm for their cause they organized a 'Mr and Mrs Condom Quest'.

Whether one has in mind the drastic cultural change that Soedjatmoko deems necessary, or mere economic palliatives, there can be no improvement in the condition of the masses unless the village is made the nucleus of a fresh policy directed by conscientious men. This fact is well recognized by Indonesians who have thought about the subject; development from the village up, rather than from the town down, is a widely repeated slogan, and was one of the Nahdatal Ulama's campaign points in the 1971 elections. Even if the urban economy were less inadequate, it could not be expected to spread with sufficient rapidity to offset the population rise of an increasingly illiterate, tyrannized people, who are almost totally devoid of the necessary skills. The issue is more contentious than it might seem to students of official statements and newspaper clippings. The army and the technocrats frequently refer to the need for rural development, which was supposed to have been the main object of the first five year plan. But, as Sarbini said, all this is 'talk from the top'. What is needed is a vast diversion of resources and creative effort to the villages; the re-establishment of cottage industries and the patient development of light industries, linked with steadily growing social programmes; the coaxing of local initiative until the first, faint sparks become a flicker of rational business activity fed by the rural economy. This inevitably slow process, with its many failures and disappointments, would have to be accompanied by large-scale migration, imaginatively and attractively conceived, to other islands; enough money to finance a substantial increase in the trickle of government-sponsored migration is at present being squandered on useless ventures. But the problem of persuasion and organization would remain formidable, even if funds were provided.

In addition to the partly exploited opportunities in Sumatra, large areas of West Kalimantan remain uninhabited. Chinese, who formerly opened up and cultivated the land, are now forced to huddle in poverty along the coast, since the junta fears that they will harbour guerrillas from Sarawak if they are allowed to return to the interior. Chinese themselves have proposed to the junta that their former lands be handed over to retired servicemen, but their suggestion has been ignored. Meanwhile many Chinese, deprived of their inland farms, have tried to begin life again by tapping disused rubber trees along the coast; they need no foreign aid, nor even Javanese encouragement. This contrast between Chinese initiative and Javanese lack of it raises again the question of whether, in fact, any significant village development is possible at all; and it takes us back to Boeke.

Although Boeke was aware of evidence that might be considered to disprove his views, he maintained until the end that the culture limited the needs of most of the people. He saw, for instance, that some Javanese peasants made sacrifices to educate their children, but he concluded that this was for prestige purposes. In 1955 he wrote in italics: 'The basis for the divergence between Western and Eastern economic theory must be sought in the restrictedness of needs.' Education is regarded by most Javanese as a symbol of status rather than as achievement or illumination; and efforts to acquire it are not inconsistent with Boeke's opinion that the people's needs were purely social. Boeke proposed two means of arresting the decline of peasant living standards: extricating the villages from the bonds of a money economy by strengthening their self-sufficiency, and stopping the depradations of the European sector. The first proposal, which amounted to Ghandiism, will still be disputed by some. But the second has already been proved necessary by events; and Boeke's words apply just as well to junta-backed foreign and Chinese investment today as they did to Dutch enterprise when he wrote in 1927:[4]

And every concession of this kind [to non-native enterprise] –
even if it represents itself under the promising, attractive,
progressive motto of vigorous development, of opening up
the Outer Islands, of industrialization, indeed of the

expansion of public enterprise within or outside the
commercial crop sector – means a step backwards on the
difficult path towards the development of a genuine,
autochthonous Native community, in that, for all its
urgency, such a development is put aside until a more
distant future.

Boeke was not urging a return to the idea of the noble savage,
but was motived by practical considerations. The static, traditional character of Eastern pre-capitalistic society would have to be
consolidated; the 'illusion' that the masses could be 'developed
in a Western way to become a limitless market for Western
industrial products' would have to be abandoned. In a statement
that contrasts with Marx's scorn (see the introduction), Boeke
wrote:[5]

Now it is not at all my intention in village reconstruction
to develop a sort of pure-culture *adat*, keeping the village
free from the taint of the Western spirit. For me it is
merely a question of approach, of educational theory if you
will. This approach begins with the recognition that there
is still such a thing as an Eastern heritage, a legacy which
has just as much right to continue in existence as any other,
and which, if it is revitalized, can form the natural basis for
the entire social structure. It is an approach which
consciously accepts the traditional, archaic sense of village
solidarity in all of its (for us Westerners) oppressive
narrow-mindedness, attempting to reinforce it in the hope
that, once it has grown strong, it will enable the village to
tackle the problems posed by developments and to solve
them in its own way.

Assuming Boeke and Soedjatmoko to be right in their view that
the problem is cultural, although they may differ in estimating the
possibilities of change, how is a social transformation to take place?
Significant acculturation must be ruled out. Any social vitality
capable of development in Indonesia is purely Indonesian; at its
strongest it is highly resistant to alien influence, which provokes a
distaste that is far deeper than chauvinism and may be compared
to the contempt shown by Chinese when they branded foreigners
as barbarians. One may see this in the revulsion of a servant girl,
who asked to be taken home from a carnival when wounded by

the sight of corrupted compatriots writhing and groaning, like Western pop singers, to the din of electric guitars; she preferred the *wayang* music on her transistor set. In addition to cultural resistance, there is a rational doubt whether Western thinking can produce solutions to Indonesian problems. Dr Azhari Zahri wrote in an Indonesian newspaper in August 1972: 'Excessive admiration of the theories of social sciences, particularly those developed by Western scholars, can poison the scholars and intellectuals in our own country and impede the growth of original, scientific creativity.' The question of change induced from the outside was discussed by Mohammed Sadli in an excellent commentary on Boeke, written in the Sukarno period.[6] 'If a bunch of shrewd traders were the representatives of the West, it is not likely that these people and their culture would find appeal', he says. Sadli points out that the cultural contact provided by the Dutch was neither welcome, because it was colonialist, nor of high quality. Most, if not all, Indonesians would say the same of the neo-colonialist presence today. Their feelings were reflected, in part, by Emil Salim, who had the courage to speak up when he was Vice-Chairman of the National Planning Board. The aim of foreign aid, he said, was to increase Western exports.

Sadli's article is in itself an example of cultural difference. Although he could not have written it unless he had studied economics in the United States, is has more nuance than equivalent British or American articles. Sadli is not handicapped by a compulsion either to reject or to accept Boeke's views; yet he does not descend to sterile inconclusiveness. He realizes that the issues in question are not to be resolved by glib rhetoric or brash dismissal of a serious scholar, such as we have observed earlier. He lays out the fabric of Boeke's thinking with delicacy and respect, before subjecting it to examination. When he decides it is time for him to comment, he cautiously makes a tentative statement here and suspends a judgment there, until finally he expresses certain definite reservations. It would be misleading to summarize this intricate model of refined discourse; but it would probably not be wrong to say that Sadli is sympathetic to Boeke's picture, while disagreeing that it is virtually permanent.

Boeke knows a lot about the Javanese village life in the colonial period. His desire to establish a special economic

theory in explanation of these dual societies is perhaps
valid, although many economists will deny this. It all
depends on how one understands economic theory . . . One
last word about Boeke's theory. In a descriptive sense it
certainly contains a lot of truth. It is of crucial importance
to take account of cultural and other human factors in
dealing with development problems. For this he has made
a great contribution.

Sadli became the junta's Minister for Mining. He serves the
New Order no less loyally than he served the Old. These days
he has nothing to say on the fundamental problem that occupied
his sensitive mind in former times. In Indonesia one has to
submit, accept oblivion, or go underground.

It is sometimes overlooked that Indonesians who are said to
be Westernized are in fact part of the mestizo culture[7] formed by
their contact with the Dutch and modified to some extent by
American influence. Some Indonesians make a convincing
impression of being completely Westernized when conversing
with foreign academics. But the Indonesians, as Sukarno was
proud to point out, are an *artiestenvolk*; and what the visiting
scholar often misses is that he is being given an artistic, not an
intellectual, performance. The Indonesian is a talented actor who
easily speaks the lines that politeness or status demand of him on
any given occasion; to a Western scientist he may be a scientist,
but to an Indonesian he will seem to have retained the essentials
of his heritage. Academics who roam the world in search of
confirmation of their theories are exceptionally vulnerable to this
deception, in which the Indonesian often deceives himself,
momentarily, as much as his unintended victim. It is true that
some break the cultural shackles on the free functioning of their
minds sufficiently to excel in examinations or in writing theses.
But when it comes to thought that leads to decision and action,
they are subjected to a cultural drag from which few escape;
consciously or unconsciously they submit to the strongest element
of the mestizo culture in which they are immersed. They are like
swimmers being pulled back by the tide in the opposite direction
to that in which, perhaps wrongly, they wish to travel. In the
end they give in, and some find peace only in the villages, which
they visit for spiritual refreshment.

A tendency for thought to be dissolved in subterfuge is a marked characteristic of the culture. Some examples of this will have been apparent in earlier chapters, but none is more revealing than the frequent, often cynical invocation of *Pancasila*, which is venerated as the nation's political philosophy. The original five points of this *credo* were expounded by Sukarno in a speech on 1 June 1945.[8] They were modified and incorporated in the preamble of the 1945 constitution and were subsequently expressed in the following form: (1) belief in one God; (2) just and civilized humanity; (3) Indonesian unity (nationalism); (4) democracy – conceived by Sukarno as including the principle of deliberation (*permusyawaratan*) among representatives to achieve consensus (*mufakat*); (5) social justice. These five pillars are not as banal as they may look at first sight. In his speech Sukarno elaborated ideas then needed to unite the élite and to bring diverse ethnic groups together. His nationalism, in fact, reached out towards internationalism, when he said that it should not be chauvinist but must aim at integration in the family of nations. His attempt to satisfy all religious groups by affirming an unspecified belief in one God was not wholly successful, since some Moslems were to insist that the only valid religion was Islam; but it served the purpose of the time.

What was meant to provide a broad philosophic base for a nation threatened with disintegration at its birth has now been reduced from a set of principles that had some meaning to a shibboleth that has none. Almost any political action that a group may wish to take is justified by appeal to *Pancasila*, which Sukarno endowed with a mystical sanctity that has been exploited no less by his successors. The present junta calls its rule *Pancasila* democracy; the PNI, it will be recalled, tried to save itself from extinction by declaring that it had found principles consistent with *Pancasila*; when I asked a Moslem student what he thought was the answer to Indonesia's socio-economic problems, he said *Pancasila* was the only solution. An army major told me that just before the *putsch* an air force officer said he was worried about where his loyalties should lie if the generals launched their expected coup against Sukarno. 'I just told him to do whatever *Pancasila* dictated', the major said. The major was amused by his skilful piece of evasion; and the student was also probably being merely careful not to make any remark that would get him into trouble. But where what is said to be a national philosophy has degenerated into a refuge for those afraid of their own ideas, there can be little chance of rational thought superseding the prevailing mysticism. Indonesians will make no progress until they can openly discuss what needs to be done without reference to a formula which is so vague that it is devoid of practical meaning.

Education as commonly conceived will not break down the mystical barriers; for those trapped behind them include many who are educated far above the average. Mysticism is deeply ingrained. Geertz[9] found a good example of it at a school, where students were asked to complete the sentence: 'A man who does not eat much . . .' Some pupils (Geertz does not say how many) said the man would become thin, sick or lack vitamin B. But 150 saw the fast as a source of virtue and power. They said the man would do good actions, get rich quickly or become strong etc. That such answers would be extremely rare among children in the West illustrates the great gap between the two cultures and the unlikelihood that the values of either will be wholeheartedly emulated by the other.

While some Indonesians fear that Western sociologists and economists are putting them on the wrong track, few realize that other Western writers have given them an exaggerated impression of past Javanese achievement; if lessons are to be learned from history, Indonesian scholars will need to make their own estimate from original sources. Careless use by some authors of words such as 'empire', 'greatest' (Palmier), and 'glorious' (Geertz) have created a false picture of the fourteenth century Majapahit kingdom, the main source of national pride. A reader without information other than what is contained in such epithets would imagine a mighty imperial centre, ruled by an aristocracy that was politically and culturally the equal of any in Asia. Possibly the perpetrators of this error have been influenced directly or indirectly by H. Kern, whose interpretation, which was published in the first quarter of this century, is out of date.

An attempt was made in the introduction of this book to tone down the image of the Majapahit empire. The internal picture also needs to be put into focus. Most of what we know about Majapahit society is contained in the *Nagara-Kertagama*, written by the court poet, Rakawi Prapañca. The Dutch scholar, Theodore G. Th. Pigeaud, who translated the work into English and wrote a detailed commentary on it, believes that the kingdom itself occupied almost half of Java.[10] Majapahit did not have its own currency, but imported small, holed, alloy coins, which could be threaded on string, in bulk from China. It seems very probable, Pigeaud says, that Majapahit ports were mainly entrepôts and virtually stations for Chinese, Indian and inter-island commerce. The Javanese share in the sea trade was founded on rice, which the court controlled; rice was exchanged in the Moluccas for spices, which were further bartered for Indian and Chinese goods. The court was Shivaite-Buddhist, with Shivaism predominating and integrated with primeval Javanese belief in a cosmic religious and social order. The king's glory was felt to be enhanced by the presence of two Brahmāns, who were given the predicate *shri*, which was usually reserved for the royal and divine. A third scholar, the holy Bhāmana, applied himself to religious observance. Pigeaud says that the poet was a 'refined Buddhist scholar', but comments:[11]

> Penetrating studies of the four systems of Indian
> philosophy on the part of the Majapahit Court scholars
> seems improbable ... It is impossible to assess the three
> brahmins' real scholarly merits according to Indian
> standards of the time. Perhaps they were considered
> nonentities and charlatans by their learned Indian colleagues.
> On the other hand it is quite possible they possessed real
> knowledge of Indian literature and science. In both cases
> the lucrative position of an honoured guest at a Royal
> Court may have prevailed over the brahmin's disinclination
> for leaving his native country to throw in his lot with a
> foreign, semi-barbarian people in a distant island over
> the sea.

Pigeaud says the people appear to have been barefooted and to have spent most of their time naked from the waist up. The bodies of both sexes, sometimes yellowed with paste, were heavily ornamented with finely wrought objects. The kings may have dressed on very great occasions; religious men and women wore robes of office. Helmets and coats of mail appear to have been used in war. Iron was scarce, and most implements were probably made of wood. It is clear from the poet's detailed description and Pigeaud's notes that the kingdom was firmly ruled and socially coherent. But it is as well to remember, when reading certain works, that it was not Rome, Athens or Peking.

One of the cultural obstacles to radical social change in Java is that the majority are impervious to politico-moral appeal. Such a slogan as 'liberty, equality and fraternity', empty though it may have proved, could never have been born among Java's bucolic egoists, as Marx would have called them. The peasants will rally behind any leader who keeps them in adequate subsistence and gives them a feeling of security. As Multatuli (Eduard Douwes Dekker), author of the Dutch classic novel, *Max Havelaar*, wrote: 'Serving his master is the *religion* of the Javanese.' Spiritual power itself is to most Javanese little more than a weapon, which may be acquired and used for either good or evil, which are seen to be co-existent. A Jesuit with long experience of the country said: 'They cannot take a transcendental view. If I were to say, "Christ is God", they would say, "Quite right, and so is that tree." That is why they cannot be converted to Christianity or Islam.'

While *Gotong royong*, the traditional village co-operation, is supposed to be a moral value,[12] systems of bald reciprocity, which are devoid of comradeship, are more in evidence. Peasant charity exists, but its absence in critical times was apparent during a famine in Indramayu, West Java, in 1970, which, with the inevitable addition of corruption, provided a gloomy illustration of moral bankruptcy. With improbable statistical precision, it was officially stated that 17,622 people were hungry and that 100 tons of rice had been sent to feed them. Some days later, when I went to investigate, people along the main road pointed to villages hidden among trees on distant tracks, where, they said, families were still starving. I drove on to see the acting regency head, who admitted that only seventeen tons of rice had been distributed; sixty-three tons were in a godown and twenty tons had failed to arrive. Asked to explain the delay in getting the rice to the people, he said: 'These things take time.' He merely smiled when I pointed out the urgency. I then drove back and made a tour of villages at the end of dirt roads. People were lying in their small, bamboo houses, pitifully weak and emaciated; they were keeping alive on roots and any vegetable matter that could be digested. One woman, whom I photographed, looked like an inmate of Belsen. I asked a well-nourished woman what had happened to *gotong royong*; why those who had rice did not share it with the others. 'There are too many', she replied. At Kedokanbunder, only fifteen kilometres from Indramayu town, the village head said 3,000 of the 12,000 inhabitants living in scattered communities amid the trees had eaten no rice for several weeks; the only relief from the regency administration was seventy kilograms of an inferior substitute made from maize.

At the end of the tour I went to Indramayu, where I was received by a smooth, uniformed official, who took me to an operations room, where a flagged map showed amounts of rice that were supposed to have been delivered to villages. 'How much went to Kedokanbunder?', I asked, not telling him I had been there. 'About two tons', he replied. – 'No, it didn't', I said pulling a handful of small, mean-looking grains of the substitute from my pocket. 'All they have received is seventy kilograms of this'. He giggled; and I left. It was clear what had happened: rice had been misappropriated all down the line. Twenty tons disappeared between Bandung, the provincial capital, and Indramayu. Most of the rest was put in store to be sold for the benefit of officials. It was the same with the vitamin B that was supposed to be administered to 5,000 beriberi sufferers. I was told that mass injections were taking place in an area that nobody dreamed I would visit; I went there and found it was fiction. Eventually an official admitted that only thirty-five injections had been given. The rest could easily have been sold in Singapore.

During my visit to Kedokanbunder the usual soldier, posted to keep watch on the villagers, sat in a torpor on a bench; the well-fed village officials, wearing their *picis*, were at ease on the high verandah of a large depot of some kind; thousands of people were starving in the woods around them; six were admitted to have died already. A few kilometres away soldiers were tarring a road, as part of the Siliwangi Division's mechanically conceived civic action. If there had been any rapport between the people and the army, this sordid tragedy could never have happened. The soldiers would have been ordered to stop work on the road, open the godown, and distribute the rice. The picture was one of misery, helplessness, indifference and turpitude. It was at that stage that I began to fear that Indonesia was beyond hope.

Corruption is so widespread in Indonesia that a newspaper raised the question of whether it was an inseparable part of the culture. Often bribery is regulated by tradition, and an official is considered to transgress only if he oversteps accepted limits under what is known in one area as the TST (*tahu-sama-tahu*, 'let's keep it to ourselves') system.[13] In Jakarta commission of 10 per cent, or even 20 per cent, from a foreign salesman is considered legitimate. But an official who bought an unsuitable dredger from a Japanese firm, on condition that he received 50 per cent of an inflated price – which happened, I am informed by a European business man – might get into trouble if he were in the wrong circle and were caught. Many religious leaders are contemptibly corrupt. According to the Secretary-General of the Department of Religion, Colonel H. Bahrum Rangkuti, some of them steal part of the *zakat*. Rangkuti, who was a navy chaplain, is a serious Moslem of intellect and integrity; he has studied in Paris, the United States, London, Germany and Pakistan. The army appointed him after the 1971 elections to clear up the vast administrative mess that had accumulated during eighteen years of control by the NU. The Department, with a full-time staff of 160,000, including teachers, had offered tremendous scope for mixing muddle and corruption, and it became impossible to determine where one ended and the other began. Huge debts to builders of mosques, offices and schools were left unpaid. Until Rangkuti took over, 60,000 teachers, of whom possibly only 10,000 or 15,000 were capable of teaching anything, were being paid on the basis of false certificates. The army has dealt with the Moslems, because they are its political enemy; it has yet to deal with itself.

It is obvious that such inertia and corruption can only be overcome, if at all, from the village up. New instructions issued by some supposedly clean government would be easily circumvented by TST and other devices, which the victims – the majority of the people – could never defeat while they remained without initiative. Appeals by Robert McNamara, Chairman of the World Bank, for a redistribution of wealth in the Third World have no application in Indonesia; in the first place, there is very little per head to distribute; secondly, those who needed it most would never receive it. What is required is not redistribution but total social reconstruction; if this is not possible nothing worth while can be done. Without a new society there can be neither fair sharing nor economic growth. Boeke realized that villages could not be transformed from above:[14]

This restoration [of the village] will not take place through the revival of the rural gentry, but must follow more democratic ways. New leaders must spring from the small folks themselves, and must be accompanied by a strong feeling of social responsibility in the people themselves.

The PKI made a start with stimulating village initiative. During the 1955 election campaign, which began early in 1953, it adopted the slogan of 'small but effective actions in the villages'. Its programme included sharing of farm tools, taking advantage of feasts to organize mutual assistance and digging irrigation ditches. Doubtless these activities contributed to the party's tremendous influence among the poorest. Their continuation would have done much more for the peasants than such grandiose waste as the launching in July 1976 of the first of two communications satellites, which were to be linked with fifty ground stations.

While the exploitation of oil and minerals must obviously be fostered, it should be regarded as no more than a bonus from nature, rather than the core of the economy; the attention of the administration should be focused almost entirely on the immediate, practical possibilities of each village, which, when added together, would represent a durable economic foundation that could be built upon, if the peasants could be motived. With a simple people, beginnings must be made with simple opportunities, trivial though these may seem to technocrats, who have found a means of personal expression in the complexities of Western economics. D. H. Penny gives numerous examples of what can be done.[15] A farmer, for instance, wondered why his fifteen-year-old durian tree had not fruited; all that was necessary was to cut down two unproductive trees that were blocking the sun. Similar opportunities were discovered by the Golkar team that stumbled on the impending rice shortage in 1972 (see chapter 12). The team also found an example of what not to do: in one district it had been the practice of women to get up at dawn and walk miles to collect fresh leaves, which they sold in the market as the traditional prepared food wrapping; but they lost even this hard-earned, meagre living when, in the name of modern development, a factory was built to make plastic sheets for the same purpose.

A project initiated by a Catholic lay worker, Brother Korby, puts the fundamental problem in a nutshell. He needs a pump and a few kilometres of pipes to convey water from a river to a village near Jakarta. Irrigation would produce a second crop of rice, which could be sold to provide money for a school and other social development. He has two obstacles: a lack of funds for the equipment and the reluctance of the men to contemplate producing a second crop, which is not necessary for their subsistence. At present his social work is financed by foreign charity. Boeke understood all this perfectly; he knew that the villagers were not waiting to welcome a band of eager crusaders who would bring them a better life; and he devised a set of principles by which, with tactful encouragement, they might be actuated. Development that will directly benefit the people obviously cannot take place without the participation of the people. Two former World Bank officials have pointed out:[16] 'Bringing public services such as better roads, clean water, electric power, health facilities and schools to the "poorest 40 per cent" will be possible only if village organizations participate actively in making decisions and carrying plans into effect.' The phrase 'poorest 40 per cent' is, of course, meaningless in a society dominated by extreme poverty, and by putting it in inverted commas the authors seem to show they are aware of it.

Assuming that Javanese villages can be vitalized, improved or merely rescued, who is to initiate the work? The present junta is disqualified, since it is dreaded in the villages. In one way or another the army has antagonized the entire rural population. The *abangan* peasants remain embittered by the massacre that followed the *putsch*; the Moslems and their followers were the greatest sufferers of the 1971 election campaign; and all were victims of the BUUD persecution. So great is the fear that in 1972 peasants in south-west Java fled from Indonesian sociological students, believing they were a Golkar team like the one that had bullied them during the elections. Unfortunately, the army is the only body that is organized from Jakarta down to every village. The Moslems have strong village links in some areas; but none of their old parties had an adequate regional structure, and their remnants are divided into religious, social and sheer opportunist factions.

Possibly rebellious Moslem youth of the kind I met far from Jakarta will eventually contribute to a new ideological basis; they have at least made a beginning with private expression of contempt for their effete and corrupt urban leaders. In Java Islam faces the difficulty that many *abangan* peasants dislike and even ridicule it in its relatively pure form; but if the young Moslems denounced the *hajis*, not as such but as money lenders and exploiters, they might win wide support. Their inevitable infiltration by secular revolutionaries could well produce a syncretic ideology akin to the Islamic Marxism that has emerged in the Middle East; this, with the nationalist element taken for granted, would be the apotheosis of Sukarno's Nasakom. There are good precedents for such a movement. In the 1920s what is described as Islamic communism became at one stage the main security anxiety of the Dutch. Misbach, a *haji* and member of the Sarekat Islam, led the movement, which was particularly strong in the Surakarta area.[17] Its leading exponents were not *abangan* but Moslem. Communists in the SI were embarrassed by this departure from orthodox Marxism, but could not condemn it because of its popularity.[18] If one were looking for clues to the future of Indonesia one might well find them in Misbach. He was one of the few rebels whom the Dutch considered to be an idealist, rather than a seeker of personal power. They arrested him and finally sent him to the Boven Digul settlement, in New Guinea. But Islamic communism persisted and spread to Sumatra.

No clues to radical change will be found in the remnants of the old urban political élite. As has been pointed out in chapter 2, the function of these visitors to Indonesian history has been greatly exaggerated by academics. There were no real links between them (excluding the PKI) and the peasants – who must be motived if the nation is to become more than a semi-modern enclave in a stagnant morass. The nature of the raw material with which new leaders would have to work in attempting to reconstruct society has been well described in a study of agrarian radicalism by Sartono Kartodirdja.[19] Sartono shows how discontent, arising sporadically in the villages, becomes merged with the religious symbols of millenarianism, messianism, nativism and *jihat*. Movements so inspired are often manipulated by power groups for their own ends (thus making nonsense of theories that leaders represent so-called *alirans* (streams) in society; witness the earlier mentioned hotchpotch of a dancing *ulama* leading a Moslem party with a substantially *abangan* following). Sartono says that studies of the agrarian social base have been neglected 'in the work of political scientists concerned with Indonesia, which has largely been focused on constitutional forms, governmental institutions, organizational conflict, and policy making on the national level' – in short, activities of groups described in chapter 2 as being devoid of socio-economic substance.

A leader who set out to achieve more than a fairer sharing of poverty would have to deliberately exploit the superstitions discussed by Sartono to win the support of the people, then begin to channel their energies into constructive activity. But he could only make a beginning; for the task would require generations of conscientious guidance. The leader would be confronted with formidable problems: the cultural barrier, including the bazaar mentality of the Javanese trader and values which, in general, are unsuited to the rationality needed for economic development; education, with minimal funds and inadequately trained teachers; population growth that will rapidly outbalance the means of either producing or importing sufficient food; a shortage of capital needed to set a widespread, indigenous economy in motion; and village inertia.

The unity and influence of whatever revolutionary group emerges at the next significant stage in Indonesia's history would depend almost entirely on the leader, who would need to combine Sukarno's insight and charisma with Suharto's firm grip. His surest means of rallying the nation would be to claim inheritance of the messages of the nation's founder, for whom the people's nostalgia increases as their hatred of the junta rises. He would probably have to be a soldier, since without control of a strong military force, he would be unable to maintain order. This would be a good thing, provided he genuinely applied Nasution's doctrine of the armed forces' dual function – civilian and military – and worked in partnership with civilians; for only the army has the experience to administer Indonesia.

Meanwhile Suharto has done a service by putting an end to the hysterical vaingloriousness that Sukarno was obliged to arouse to hold the nation together without force; he has cooled the infantile frenzy generated by independence. Political and social life that emerges from his deep freeze could be more vital in the end than what was born in the heat of young nationalism.

An Indonesian writer, when asked by a Western academic whether he thought communism would provide a solution, said:

'No, we are a sensuous people.' This remark has important implications. If Weber was correct in asserting that early Protestant asceticism was essential to the genesis of modern capitalism, it may be inferred that Indonesians have not the moral discipline to create either communism or capitalism. As Soedjatmoko said in his 1954 article, whatever the solution is, only Indonesians can find it; but not until they have done the cultural stock-taking that he recommends.

Postscript

Developments occurred in the first quarter of 1978 that illustrate Indonesia's capacity for demonstrating the maxim, *plus ça change, plus c'est la même chose*. Lieutenant-General Ali Murtopo, deputy head of Bakin, appeared to commit a *volte-face*. He announced at an Indonesian Democratic Party rally on 24 January that a marble headstone was at last to be placed on Sukarno's unmarked grave; the inscription was to be: 'Bung Karno, the mouthpiece of the Indonesian people, proclamator of the republic and founder of *pancasila*'. But this gesture did not indicate a change of heart among the generals; it reflected the continuing troublesomeness of Moslem politicians, the exploitability of Sukarnoist sentiment, and Murtopo's unfailing astuteness at political manipulation.

Moslems are greedy for posts in the cabinet. They still condition and control the emotions of a third of the population, whose fear of hell, as has been said in this book, is even greater than their fear of the army. Murtopo would not have gone near the rally, had it not been that Moslem politicians were becoming more audacious. Partly, but not wholly, because of Catholic influence in his entourage, he has always seen the Moslems as enemies not less formidable than the Communists were; his skilful manoeuvre was clearly a renewal of the junta's early tactics of balancing the secular nationalists against them.

Further developments along this path are possible. Murtopo is acutely aware of social trends, suppressing this and exploiting that as he thinks the occasion demands. His proposed inscription on the headstone has put him within one step of embracing Nasakom, if he should choose to do so, though it would be under some other name, such as Nasasoc (socialism instead of communism) which Sukarno came to accept for a time after the *putsch*. By this means he could hope to weld all three political tendencies – Moslem, secular nationalist, and leftist – into a unified group under army control. Murtopo's Sukarnoism would not be what Sukarno intended; but it would at least be consistent with the social components that Sukarno identified.

Meanwhile Moslem politicians were prodding students into further demonstrations, particularly in Bandung and at the University of Indonesia. The press also dared to raise its voice again, but was quickly silenced by the temporary banning of eight newspapers towards the end of January. Dozens of student leaders and, it was reported, several retired military officers were arrested after demonstrations against corruption and *cukongs* had occurred almost daily. Dr Ismail Suny, Professor of Constitutional Law at the University of Indonesia, said at a student panel discussion that a general possessed deposits of $330 million in the Bank of Central Asia. He was also arrested; the government said he could not substantiate his charge.

There were increasing public demands for Suharto to step down from the presidency, largely because of his family's connexions with *cukongs*; but it was clear that the generals were solidly behind their leader, and the MPR re-elected him on 23 March. Suharto then reinforced the army's rule by eliminating the only two politicians from his cabinet and increasing the number of ministerial generals from five to eleven. This gave the army about half the portfolios, the remainder being occupied by technocrats and other non-party civilians. Whether Suharto retired or not would make no basic difference to the power structure and none at all to the psycho-cultural factors that will determine the fate of Indonesians throughout the foreseeable future.

Glossary

abangan	Depreciatory name given by purer Moslems to those whose beliefs and practices are less purely Islamic (see ch. 8, n. 8)
adat	customary law
alang	a kind of sedge
Bakin (Badan Koordinasi Intelijens)	Intelligence Co-ordinating Body
bapak	father, respected elder
becak	three-wheeled pedi-cab
Bhārata Yuddha	the decisive battle in the *Mahābhārata*
bung	brother, comrade
BPI (Badan Pusat Intilijens)	Central Intelligence Body
BTI (Barisan Tani Indonesia)	Indonesian Peasant League
Conefo	Conference of New Emerging Forces
cukong	Chinese financier
DPR (Dewan Perwakilan Rakyat)	parliament
dukun	adviser on personal problems, healer, sorcerer
Fundwi	Fund of the United Nations for the Development of West Irian
gamelan	Javanese orchestra
Garuda	eagle (bird of Hindu mythology)

414

Glossary

Gerwani (Gerakan Wanita Indonesia)	Indonesian Woman's Movement
haji	one who has made the pilgrimage to Mecca
IGGI	Inter-Governmental Group on Indonesia
IPKI (Ikatan Pendukung Kemerdekaan Indonesia)	League for the Defence of Indonesian Independence
jihat	holy war
kafir	unbeliever (in Islam)
Kami (Kesatuan Aksi Mahasiswa Indonesia)	Indonesian Students' Action Front
kampong	1 village, hamlet; 2 town quarter (often occupied by the less well-to-do)
Kappi (Kesatuan Aksi Pelajar Pelajar Indonesia)	Indonesian Pupils' Action Front
kebaya	woman's blouse
kyahi	reverend or honourable (applied as adjective or noun to Islamic scholars and teachers or to others considered to be spiritual elders)
Kopkamtib (Komando Pemulihan Keamanan dan Ketertiban)	Command for Restoration of Security and Order
Korpri (Korps Pegawai Negeri)	Civil Servants' Corps
Kostrad (Komando Strateji Angatan Darat)	Strategic Reserve Command
kraton	royal residence
Mahābhārata	Indian epic adapted in the *wayang*
Minangkabau	a West Sumatran ethnic group
MPR (Majelis Permusyawaratan Rakyat)	People's Consultative Assembly; MPRS – provisional (sementara) assembly
musyawarah	consultation, deliberation
mufakat	consensus
Nasakom	name given by Sukarno to what he saw as the combined forces of nationalism, religion (*agama*) and communism
Nekolim	neo-colonialism and imperialism
NU (Nahdatul Ulama)	Moslem Theologians' Council

415

Glossary

OPM (Organisasi Papua Merdeka)	Free Papua Movement
Pancasila	Indonesia's five-point national philosophy: belief in one God, just and civilized humanity, national unity, democracy by consensus of representatives, and social justice
Parkindo (Partai Kristen Indonesia)	Indonesian Protestant Party
Parmusi (Partai Muslimin Indonesia)	Indonesian Moslem Party
pasar	market (bazaar)
Pemuda Rakjat	Popular Youth
Permesta (Perjuangan Semesta)	Common Struggle
pesantren	religious seminary
pici	a hat resembling a fez
PKI (Partai Komunis Indonesia)	Indonesian Communist Party
PNI	Indonesian National Party
priyayi	formerly a feudal official; currently a gentleman (see ch. 8 n. 8)
PRRI (Pemerintah Revolusioner Republik Indonesia)	Revolutionary Government of the Indonesian Republic
PSI	Indonesian Socialist Party
PSII (Partai Sarekat Islam Indonesia)	Indonesian Islamic Union Party
pusaka	heirloom
sate	small pieces of meat on a skewer
sawah	wet rice-field
SI (Sarekat Islam)	Islamic Union
Sobsi (Sentral Organisasi Buruh Seluruh Indonesia)	All-Indonesia Labour Unions' Federation
Tritura (Tri Tuntutan Rakyat)	People's Three Demands
ulama	Moslem theologians (Arabic plural, used also as singular in Indonesia)
wayang kulit	puppet shadow play mostly based on the Hindu epics, *Mahābhārata* and *Rāmayāṇa*
zakat	obligatory Moslem alms

Notes

Preface

1 *Listener*, vol. 2, no. 2384, 5 December 1974, p. 726.

Introduction: Roots

1 Unofficial estimate made early in 1976; see chapter 1.
2 *Bulletin of Indonesian Economic Studies*, Canberra, vol. XI, no. 2, July 1975, p. 9.
3 *A Handbook of Marxism*, London, Victor Gollancz, 1935, p. 186.
4 *Indonesian Economics: The Concept of Dualism in Theory and Practice*, by Dutch Scholars, The Hague, W. van Hoeve Publishers, 1961, p. 391, n. 15.
5 J. C. van Leur, *Indonesian Trade and Society*, The Hague, W. van Hoeve Publishers, 1967, p. 261.
6 *A Handbook of Marxism*, p. 181.
7 Thomas Stamford Raffles, *The History of Java*, London, Black, Parbury & Allen; and John Murray, 1817, pp. 272–3.
8 European astronomy was unknown. Raffles records (ibid., p. 473): 'The Javanese of today have no pretensions to astronomy as a science. The seasons are determined by reference to a system no longer perfectly understood, either in its principle or application.'
9 *Indonesian Economics: The Concept of Dualism in Theory and Pratice*, p. 275.
10 Van Leur, op. cit., p. 257; see also p. 98.
11 Bernard H. M. Vlekke, *Nusantara*, Brussels, Les Editions A. Manteau, 1961, p. 24.
12 *Indonesian Sociological Studies: Selected Writings of B. Schrieke*, Pt 2, The Hague and Bandung, W. van Hoeve, 1957, p. 273.

13 O. W. Wolters, *Early Indonesian Commerce*, Ithaca, Cornell University Press, 1967.
14 Schrieke, op. cit., pp. 299–301.
15 Van Leur, op. cit., p. 177.
16 Vlekke, op. cit., p. 162.
17 Ibid., p. 243.

Chapter 1: The prisoners

1 Pramoedya Ananta Toer, *A Heap of Ashes*, Edited and Translated by Harry Aveling, University of Queensland Press, 1975, p. XXI.
2 Soekarno, *Nationalism, Islam and Marxism*, introduction by Ruth T. McVey, Ithaca, Cornell University, Modern Indonesia Project no. 48, 1970, p. 25.

Chapter 2: Sukarno's burden

1 Two of Sukarno's wives, Hartini and Ratna Sari Dewi, have valuable collections of letters.
2 *Sukarno, an Autobiography as told to Cindy Adams*, Hong Kong, Gunung Agung, 1965, p. 39.
3 Sartono Kartodirdjo in *Culture and Politics in Indonesia*, edited by Claire Holt, Ithaca and London, Cornell University Press, 1972, pp. 71–125.
4 Bernhard Dahm, *Sukarno*, Ithaca and London, Cornell University Press, 1969, p. 14.
5 Ruth T. McVey, *The Rise of Indonesian Communism*, Ithaca, Cornell University Press, 1965, p. 390, n. 58.
6 Bernard H. M. Vlekke, *Nusantara*, Brussels, Les Editions A. Manteau, 1943, pp. 147–8.
7 Ruth T. McVey in her introduction to Soekarno, *Nationalism, Islam and Marxism*, Ithaca, Cornell University, Modern Indonesia Project no. 48, 1970, p. 1.
8 *Indonesia Accuses*, edited by Roger K. Paget, Kuala Lumpur, Oxford University Press, 1975.
9 Ibid., p. 108.
10 Legge says of Partindo that there was 'opposition to what was felt to be a change in the very character of the PNI'. He adds that the PNI's 'more cautious leadership found a home in Partindo, which sought mass membership but which looked to action within the law rather than outside it. Radical opinion was turning in the direction of the New PNI.' (J. D. Legge, *Sukarno, A Political Biography*, Harmondsworth, Penguin Books, 1973, pp. 121–2). On the other hand, Dahm says: 'Essentially there was no difference between the Partindo and the old PNI. It was obvious that only the name had been changed to avoid harassment based on the judgement against the old PNI.' (Dahm, op. cit., p. 131). Since Indonesian political wrangles are equivocal at the best of times, it would probably be pointless to

investigate this contradiction, but Legge's view has the air of having been constructed.

11 The precise date of Sjahrir's return does not appear to be clear; Legge (op. cit. p. 122) says 'in late 1931 or early 1932', while Dahm (*History of Indonesia in the Twentieth Century*, London, Pall Mall Press, 1971, p. 67) says '1931'.
12 Ibid., p. 68.
13 Legge, op. cit., p. 134.
14 Dahm, *Sukarno*, op. cit., p. 220.
15 Ibid., p. 116.
16 Ibid., p. 234.
17 Ibid., p. 236.
18 Ibid., pp. 272–3.
19 Ibid., p. 278.
20 Excluding gratuitous comments on Brigadier Mallaby, J. G. A. Parrott has given a useful account of the critical stage of this operation in *Indonesia*, Cornell, no. 20, October 1975, p. 87.
21 Legge, op. cit., p. 215.
22 Dahm, *Sukarno*, op. cit., p. 323–5.
23 Dahm and Legge both describe Sukarno as a figure-head, which is the only term applicable during the period mentioned.
24 Sukarno, *Autobiography*, p. 62.
25 Dahm, *Sukarno*, op. cit., p. 172.
26 Ibid., p. XIV.
27 Ibid., p. VIII.
28 Ibid., p. 349.
29 *Nationalism, Islam and Marxism*, p. 50.
30 Dahm, *Sukarno*, op. cit., p. 39.
31 McVey, *Rise*, op. cit., pp. 96–8, 104.
32 Herbert Feith, *The Decline of Constitutional Democracy in Indonesia*, Ithaca and London, Cornell University Press, 1962, p. 23.
33 Some writers have tried to interpret even the 1971 election results in terms of so-called *alirans* (streams) in society. Ruth McVey gets closer to reality when she says: 'the ideological labels attached to them [the *alirans*] are generally used rather loosely to refer to several different and not entirely overlapping types of cleavage. We thus observe them rather as images in a bad mirror – clearly present, but with perversely altering forms.' The question is how clearly; certainly not enough for classification. A good sample of the material available is given in the fifth last paragraph of this book. Among the leading classifiers is Feith. After beginning with the solidarity makers and administrators he went on to identify five streams of thought, ingeniously illustrated by what looks like a weather chart (*Indonesian Political Thinking, 1945–1965*, edited by Herbert Feith and Lance Castles, Ithaca and London, Cornell University Press, 1970, p. 14.) This prompted the Indonesian political analyst, Alfian, to ask drily whether Feith's framework was 'better than the others or worse'. (*Indonesia*, Cornell, no. 11, April 1971, p. 195). Subsequently Feith

classified writers on Indonesia as a 'radical' school, which had itself criticized the 'technocratic liberalism' and 'humanitarian liberalism' of two other academics. (*Bulletin of Indonesian Economic Studies*, vol. X, no. 2, July 1974, p. 114.)

34 Dahm, *Sukarno*, op. cit., p. 35.

35 Clifford Geertz, *Peddlers and Princes*, Chicago and London, The University of Chicago Press, 1963.

36 Feith, op. cit., p. 112. The estimate is based on newspaper circulations.

37 Ibid., p. 433.

38 Ibid., p. 603.

39 Ibid., p. 88.

40 Dahm, *History*, op. cit., p. 183.

41 *Sukarno, An Autobiography*, p. 291; Sukarno mentioned Boeke at his trial in 1930.

42 Bruce Grant, *Indonesia*, London and New York, Melbourne University Press, 1964, pp. 74–5.

43 Legge, op. cit., p. 306.

44 Geertz sees the traditional Javanese kingdom as a 'theatre state'. (*Islam Observed*, New Haven and London, Yale University Press, 1968, pp. 36–8, 74, 82–7.) For Feith on the use of symbols see Ruth T. McVey (ed.), *Indonesia*, Yale University, 1967, p. 385. Geertz says: 'Spectacle was what the state was for; its central task was less to govern – a job that villagers largely accomplished for and among themselves – than to display in liturgical form the dominant themes of Javanese culture. The capital was a stage upon which priests and nobles, headed by the king, presented an endless pageant.' It is at least questionable whether 'theatre' is an appropriate word to denote a state in which religion and religious pageantry were an instrument of a very practical power. But to declare that Sukarno was trying to recreate such a state and to imply that this was his only aim is certainly going too far. Geertz bases his assertion on a few quotations from Sukarno, a misleading, potted biography, and a list of projects. One of the projects is the national monument, which Sukarno claimed was erected to give pride to a people whom, he said, colonialism had reduced to what the Dutch regarded as 'frogs and worms'; another was the 'circus ceremonialism of the Asian Games', which obviously had a political purpose, like China's subsequent ping pong diplomacy.

45 Legge's unsubstantiated assertion that Sukarno was mainly concerned with merely balancing the PKI and the army is disposed of in a factual article by Peter Christian Hauswedell in *Indonesia*, Cornell, no. 15, April 1973, p. 109.

46 *Nationalism, Islam and Marxism*, p. 60. Whether or not one agrees with this distinction, it is certainly more defensible than Dahm implies, apart from the fact that it was intended to achieve what was for Sukarno the larger purpose of unity.

47 Letter kindly shown to the author by Hartini Sukarno.

48 Dahm, *Sukarno*, op. cit., p. xii.

49 Ibid., p. viii.

Chapter 3: The enigma of the *putsch*

1 There is a school of thought among academics who are still investigating the *putsch* that the failure of tanks to arrive is not important; the view is taken that the rebels were relying on Sukarno's endorsement rather than military strength and that Colonel Latief, their operational commander, had access to armour in Jakarta, which he could have used. This argument seems to be mistaken. In such an operation Latief could not have counted on officers outside the conspiracy either to obey his orders or keep quiet about them. Further, even Suharto felt obliged to call in tanks from Bandung before moving into occupied buildings. The rebels needed tanks because, like Suharto, they wanted a walkover, not a battle. It is impossible to say what would have happened if the tanks had arrived as planned; but Suharto's task would certainly have been much more difficult. Speculation that the rebels were merely putting on some kind of show for Sukarno to ratify is the result of an attempt to find a rational core in a totally irrational situation. There seems to be nothing to prove that the rebels relied on Sukarno to ensure the success of their military action.

2 O. G. Roeder, *The Smiling General*, Jakarta, Gunung Agung, 1970, p. 11.

3 General Nasution confirmed to the author that Bambang had followed Martadinata to Kostrad.

4 Letters, including one facsimile, from Sukarno to Dewi, published in the *NRC Handelsblad*, Rotterdam, 22 September 1973. Dewi informed the author that she had advised Sukarno to trust Nasution.

5 John Hughes, *The End of Sukarno*, London, Angus & Robertson, 1968, p. 44.

6 *Indonesia*, Cornell, no. 15, April 1973, p. 1.

7 Benedict R. Anderson and Ruth T. McVey, *A Preliminary Analysis of the October 1, 1965, Coup in Indonesia*, Ithaca, Cornell University, Modern Indonesia Project no. 52, 1971.

8 J. D. Legge, *Sukarno, A Political Biography*, Harmondsworth, Penguin Books, 1973, p. 387.

9 Confirmed to the author by Nasution.

10 Bernhard Dahm, *History of Indonesia in the Twentieth Century*, London, Pall Mall Press, 1971, chapter VIII.

11 Ibid., p. 294, n. 2.

12 Anderson and McVey, op. cit.

13 Ruth T. McVey, *The Rise of Indonesian Communism*, Ithaca, Cornell University Press, 1965, pp. 323–46.

14 Nasution appears to have been referring to what was described as a record of the interrogation of Bambang, which was subsequently published as a typewritten book (*The Devious Dalang*, The Hague, Interdoc Publishing House, undated). Kopkamtib appears to have avoided committing itself to the document; the editor of the book, Antonie C. A. Dake, merely says that he 'laid hands' on it. The interrogation appears to be contrived; for the interrogators often show

that they know what Bambang is about to say, and lead him. Evidence that Sukarno received a note (from Untung) on the eve of the coup is vague.
15 Dahm, op. cit., p. 232; Hughes, op. cit., p. 21.
16 *Journal of Contemporary Asia*, vol. 1, no. 2, winter 1970, p. 56.
17 Hughes, op. cit., p. 59.
18 *Indonesia*, pp. 16–17.
19 Hughes, op. cit., p. 149.
20 Legge, op. cit., pp. 398–9.
21 *International Herald Tribune*, 28 April 1976.
22 In referring to the PKI factor, Sukarno used the word *keblingeran*, which is derived from Javanese. Dr J. J. Ras is of the opinion that Sukarno chose this word deliberately because it can be given two meanings. Any Javanese, he informs me, would read it as 'being tricked'. But it can also mean 'mistaken', a meaning that Sukarno could have given it when faced by people hostile to the PKI. At a press conference attended by foreign correspondents Sukarno, in fact, translated *keblingeran* as 'mistakes' (made by the PKI leadership); he also translated '*tidak benar*' ('not right' – the inverted commas are his) as 'nuts'.

Chapter 4: The rise of Suharto

1 John Hughes, *The End of Sukarno*, London, Angus & Robertson, 1967, p. 220.
2 O. G. Roeder, *The Smiling General*, Jakarta, Gunung Agung, 1970, p. 42.
3 Bernhard Dahm, *History of Indonesia in the Twentieth Century*, London, Pall Mall Press, 1971, p. 240; my account of the demonstration
3 is from the Algemeen Nederlands Persbureau-Agence France-Presse correspondent's file.
4 This comment is based on observation of subsequent demonstrations. See also Roger Kent Paget, 'Youth and the wane of Sukarno's government,' Cornell University Ph.D. thesis, 1970, p. 22. Paget also refers to the link between the army and the student movement and the obscure origin of Kami.
5 Letters from Sukarno to Dewi, published in the *NRC Handelsblad*, Rotterdam, 22 September 1973.
6 Dahm, op. cit., p. 243.
7 J. D. Legge, *Sukarno, A Political Biography*, Harmondsworth, Penguin Books, 1973, p. 403. Legge is vague about the meaning of the 11 March Order, but he says that Sukarno, in spite of his denial, had given his 'authority' to Suharto.
8 It should be emphasized that the correspondent (a Dutchman) was expressing his own views, not those of the agencies. Nevertheless, his reports clearly reflect the outlook of Western diplomats in Jakarta at that time.
9 J. D. Legge, op. cit., p. 404.

Chapter 5: The United Nations fiasco

1 The Indonesian government renamed West Irian, Irian Jaya in February 1973.
2 F. C. Kamma, *Koreri, Messianic Movements in the Biak-Numfor Cultural Area*, The Hague, Martinus Nijhof, 1972; for the cargo cult in Madang see Peter Lawrence, *Road Belong Cargo, A Study of the Cargo in the Southern Madang District, New Guinea*, Manchester, Manchester University Press, 1964. (My account was taken from a presumably accurate review of this book in *Le Monde*.)

Chapter 7: Corruption and beyond

1 *International Herald Tribune*, 17 September 1975.

Chapter 8: Split and rule

1 Information from one of Suharto's political organizers. However, it is apparent that Suharto found Sarwo Edhie excessively prone to taking political initiative in general.
2 This account of events leading to Suharto's choice of Golkar comes from one of those who carried out his orders.
3 For an account of the army's prolonged wrangle with the political parties see Harold Crouch, *Indonesia*, Cornell, No. 11, April 1971, p. 177. Time, however, has invalidated some of his comments, such as 'the army sees a need to permit the civilian parties to function as natural means of political expression and as links between the government and the people.'
4 Three parties bore the name PNI at different times: the party founded by Sukarno in 1927, which dissolved itself when he was in prison; a party that he formed immediately after independence, but which collapsed when his idea of a single party state was abandoned; the well-known PNI of independence days, which was formed by the élite at the outset of the parliamentary interregnum in November 1945.
5 Sukarno's wives: He married Tjokroaminoto's daughter, Sitti Utara, to please Tjokroaminoto, when he was about twenty and she about sixteen; Sukarno said it was a 'hanging marriage', which was not consummated. After a divorce he married Garnasih Sanusi Inggit, his landlady in Surabaya, who was a dozen years older than himself. While in exile in Bengkulu he fell in love with Fatmawati, when she was seventeen, he forty, and Inggit more than fifty; he married her by proxy from Batavia in June 1943; she bore him five children. On 7 July 1954 he married Hartini, then twenty-eight, who already had five children by a husband whom she divorced; she bore Sukarno two children. In 1963 he secretly married Ratna Sari Dewi, whom he had met in Tokyo; she bore him a daughter. He married Haryati in 1964 and divorced her at her own request. It is questionable whether he married Yurike Sanger, who is often said to be his seventh wife.

423

6 *Weekend, The Sunday Mail Magazine*, Singapore, 1 August 1971, p. 10.
7 J. D. Legge, *Sukarno, A Political Biography*, Harmondsworth, Penguin Books, 1972, p. 408.
8 Clifford Geertz, *The Religion of Java*, Chicago, Free Press, 1960, p. 6. Geertz's classification is: '*Abangan*, representing a stress on the animistic aspects of the over-all Javanese syncretism and broadly related to the peasant element in the population; *santri*, representing a stress on the Islamic aspects of the syncretism and generally related to the trading element (and to certain elements in the peasantry as well); and *prijaji*, stressing the Hinduist aspects and related to the bureaucratic element . . . They are not constructed types, but terms and divisions the Javanese themselves apply.' Theodore G. Th. Pigeaud says that Geertz's choice of terms is 'not wholly satisfactory' (*Java in the 14th Century*, The Hague, Martinus Nijhoff, 1962, vol. IV, p. 468.) Koentjaraningrat points out that *priyayi* are a social, not a religious, class. (See Heather Sutherland, 'The Priyayi', in *Indonesia*, Cornell, no. 19, April 1975, p. 57; Sutherland herself finds important regional differences in the '*priyayi* culture' and function.) There is also disagreement with Geertz's use of the term *santri*, which has been widely adopted by academics working in other fields. J. Gonda, explaining the etymology of the word, which is Sanskrit, says it means 'a pupil of a Muslim religious school, a Muslim seminarist or divinity student', sometimes also 'a pupil or scholar'. (*Sanskrit in Indonesia*, International Academy of Indian Culture, Nagpur, 1952.) W. F. Wertheim prefers the word *putihan*, which, he says, was used by Dutch scholars until Geertz popularized *santri*. In general scholars at Amsterdam and Leiden find Geertz's classification wrong in terminology and artificial in conception. In my analogy of the spectrum no sharp division exists at any point; and when antipathy exists it is only at the extremes. I am indebted to Dr J. J. Ras, senior lecturer in Indonesian language and literature at the University of Leiden, for the following clarification: *Priyayi:* In feudal times *priyayis* were aristocrats, not always financially well off, who were frequently employed in government service. Nowadays the word is often taken to mean no more than gentleman, conceived as one of superior manner and station who neither works with his hands nor is engaged in commerce. This is the sense in which it is most used in both speech and modern literature. The term *priyayi putri*, meaning lady, is also used. *Putihan* (white ones) and *abangan* (red ones): These words are both pre-Islamic. White was associated with the heavens, hence with the religious élite; the *abangan* were those on the ground. In early Islamic days the political and religious élite merged and were called *putihan;* the term is associated with the white Moslem robes only by coincidence. Today the *putihan*, a very small minority, consist of the *santri* and pious men living in the precincts of the mosque. *Santri:* The term is as defined by Gonda; it means those who live and study in the *pesantren*. Generally the purer Moslems outside the

pesantren do not call themselves *santri;* for they are not *santri*. But other Javanese often brand them pejoratively as *santri*, particularly in moments of irritation; the phrase *santri buki* (rotten *santri*) is current. It is conceivable, however, that some Javanese who are not *santri* have adopted the extended meaning of the word to denote themselves. (I know a Javanese, not a good Moslem, who decided after reading Geertz that he was a *santri:* he knew he was not a *priyayi* and probably preferred not to be thought of as *abangan*.)

9 Bernhard Dahm, *History of Indonesia in the Twentieth Century*, London, Pall Mall Press, 1971, p. 264. Suharto's real motive was disclosed by one of his entourage.

10 Some Indonesians thought that *sukuism* (ethnic rivalry) might have been a factor in the Indramayu murders. They pointed out that the Sundanese, who inhabit West Java, resent Javanese domination; Sundanese officers might have vented their feelings on the Moslems, not as Moslems but as Javanese. I have no confirmation of this theory, but ethnic grievances and cultural antipathy often account for the heat in what seem, on the surface, to be purely political conflicts.

11 K. E. Ward, 'A preliminary analysis of the 1971 elections in East Java,' unpublished essay, Centre for South East Asian Studies, Melbourne, November 1971.

Chapter 9: The end of politics

1 It is not stated in the law when the DPR approved it; DPR proceedings are not always clear cut.

2 Bernhard Dahm, *History of Indonesia in the Twentieth Century*, London, Pall Mall Press, 1971, p. 263.

3 This was the final distribution. The original plan provided for 131 from the provinces, 112 selected in proportion to party election results (including Golkar's), and 10 for the less successful parties.

Chapter 11: The cultural barrier

1 Clifford Geertz, *The Religion of Java*, Chicago, Free Press, 1960, p. 16.

2 Ibid., p. 22.

3 Ruth T. McVey, *The Rise of Indonesian Communism*, Ithaca, Cornell University Press, 1965, p. 303.

4 *Indonesian Economics: The Concept of Dualism in Theory and Practice*, by Dutch Scholars, The Hague, W. van Hoeve Publishers, 1961, p. 11.

5 Ibid., p. 172–3.

6 J. H. Boeke, *Economics and Economic Policy of Dual Societies*, Haarlem, Tjeenk Willink & Zoon, 1953, p. 4.

7 *Indonesian Economics*, p. 19. Response to higher prices, which has been observed, could be accompanied by lower output of other crops, the total effort remaining static.

8 Ibid., p. 217.

9 Clifford Geertz, *Agricultural Involution*, Berkeley, Los Angeles and London, University of California Press, 1963, p. ix.
10 Geertz, *The Religion of Java*, op. cit., p. 5.
11 Bernard H. M. Vlekke, *Nusantara*, Brussels, Les Editions A. Manteau, 1961, p. 415, n. 12.
12 J. C. van Leur, *Indonesian Trade and Society*, The Hague, W. van Hoeve Publishers, 1967, pp. 135-7, 197-200; see also 'peddling' in the index.
13 The Indonesian government renamed West Irian as Irian Jaya in February 1973.
14 *Indonesia*, Cornell, no. 14, October 1972, p. 169.
15 *Indonesian Sociological Studies*, Selected Writings of B. Schrieke, part two, The Hague and Bandung, W. van Hoeve, 1957, p. 99.
16 W. F. Wertheim, *Indonesian Society in Transition*, The Hague and Bandung, W. van Hoeve, 1959, p. 141-2: 'In many parts of the Outer Islands the indigenous population's dislike of professional trading was less marked than in Java, so that the status system based on ethnic groups, which left trade to the Foreign Oriental, did not exert anything like the same influence on the social pattern as it did in Java.'
17 Van Leur, op. cit., p. 92.
18 Claire Holt (ed.), *Culture and Politics in Indonesia*, Ithaca and London, Cornell University Press, 1972, p. 41. Anderson emphasizes the difficulty of expressing the Javanese concept of power in Western terms and the Western concept in Javanese terms (pp. 4-8). In the West, for instance, power is an abstraction that implies a relationship; for the Javanese it is a constant, concrete quantum of 'mysterious and divine energy', which may be concentrated in one place only at the expense of another.
19 Wertheim, op. cit., pp. 98-9, 218-21.
20 Bruce Glassburner (ed.), *The Economy of Indonesia*, Ithaca and London, Cornell University Press, 1971, p. 9.
21 Van Leur, op. cit., p. 237.
22 Geertz, *Agricultural Involution*, op. cit., p. 48 n.
23 Ibid., p. 141.
24 Schrieke, op. cit., pp. 100, 217-18, passim.
25 Ibid., part one, 1955, p. 99.
26 Ibid., pp. 108-9.
27 Soedjatmoko, *Economic Development as a Cultural Problem*, Ithaca, Cornell University, Modern Indonesia Project no. 17, 1958.
28 Ibid., pp. 6-9.
29 Ibid., pp. 16-17.

Chapter 12: The development myth

1 Rex Mortimer (ed.), *The Showcase State*, Sydney, Angus & Robertson, 1973, p. 60.
2 *Bulletin of Indonesian Economic Studies*, Canberra, vol. X, no. 2, July 1974, p. 59.

3 Ibid., p. 56.
4 *BIES*, vol. VIII, no. 2, July 1972, p. 55.
5 Abs told journalists in Jakarta that it was impossible to give a precise figure for the debts, but this is the total usually published.
6 Bruce Glassburner (ed.), *The Economy of Indonesia*, Ithaca and London, Cornell University Press, 1971, p. 433.
7 This account of the operation of the syndicates comes from a foreign expert who made a report on them.
8 *BIES*, vol. XI, no. 1, March 1975, p. 86.
9 Ibid., p. 86-7.
10 Widya Utami, John Ihalauw, 'Some consequences of small farm size,' *BIES*, vol. IX, no. 2, July 1973, pp. 49-50.
11 William L. Collier, Gunawan Wiradi, Soentoro, 'Recent changes in rice harvesting methods,' *BIES*, vol. IX, no. 2, July 1973, p. 36.
12 William L. Collier, 'Choice of technique in rice milling,' *BIES*, vol. X, no. 1, March 1974, p. 120.
13 Ibid., pp. 122, 125.
14 Ibid., p. 116.
15 Garry Hansen, 'Episodes in rural modernization,' *Indonesia*, Cornell, no. 11, April 1971, p. 63.
16 *BIES*, vol. IX, no. 1, March 1973, p. 1.
17 Ibid., p. 18.
18 *BIES*, vol. XI, no. 2, July 1975, p. 18.
19 Alan M. Strout, H. W. Arndt, R. M. Sundrum, *BIES*, vol. IX, no. 2, July 1973, pp. 77-99.
20 *BIES*, vol. IX, no. 2, July 1973, p. 24.
21 I stumbled on this information when in West Kalimantan; doubtless similar distress occurred elsewhere.
22 Information from an international banker.
23 *The Economy of Indonesia*, p. 106.
24 *BIES*, vol. XI, no. 2, July 1975, p. 8.
25 *BIES*, vol. X, no. 2, July 1974, pp. 26-8.
26 The International Development Association (IDA) is an affiliate of the World Bank (International Bank for Reconstruction and Development), which was formed in 1960 to provide soft loans. Its credits are interest-free, repayable in fifty years with a grace period of ten years before the first instalment. Criteria of eligibility for the loans are national poverty, economic reliability and inability to repay on commercial terms.
27 *BIES*, vol. XI, no. 2, July 1975, p. 2.
28 *BIES*, vol. XI, no. 1, March 1975, p. 25, n. 30.
29 *BIES*, vol. X, no. 3, November 1974, p. 123; my figures have been deduced from Ahrens's.
30 D. H. Penny and M. Singarimbun, *Population and Poverty in Rural Java: Some Economic Arithmetic from Sriharjo*, Ithaca, Department of Agricultural Economics, Cornell University, 1973, pp. 5, 44.

Chapter 13: The price of harmony

1 *International Herald Tribune*, Paris, 22 June, 1976.
2 John Hughes, *The End of Sukarno*, London, Angus & Robertson, 1967, p. 261.
3 *Bulletin of Indonesian Economic Studies*, Canberra, vol. IX, no. 3, November 1973, p. 62.
4 *Indonesian Economics: The Concept of Dualism in Theory and Practice* by Dutch Scholars, The Hague, W. van Hoeve Publishers, 1961, p. 277.
5 Ibid., p. 45.
6 Bruce Glassburner (ed.), *The Economy of Indonesia*, Ithaca and London, Cornell University Press, 1971, p. 114.
7 Wertheim points out that the Dutch component is itself mestizo, having acquired Indonesian traits during (and since) the nineteenth century. See *Indonesian Society in Transition*, The Hague and Bandung, W. van Hoeve, 1959, pp. 174–5, 309, passim.
8 Herbert Feith and Lance Castles, *Indonesian Political Thinking, 1945–1965*, Ithaca and London, Cornell University Press, 1970, p. 40.
9 Clifford Geertz, *The Religion of Java*, Chicago, Free Press, 1960, p. 323.
10 Theodore G. Th. Pigeaud, *Java in the Fourteenth Century*, The Hague, Martinus Nijhoff, vol. IV, 1962, p. 497.
11 Ibid., p. 270.
12 Sartono Kartodirdjo in *Culture and Politics in Indonesia*, edited by Claire Holt, Ithaca and London, Cornell University Press, 1972, p. 77.
13 D. Mitchell in *BIES*, vol. VI, no. 2, July 1970, p. 82.
14 Quoted by Sadli in Glassburner, op. cit., p. 101.
15 *BIES*, no. 8, October 1967, p. 35.
16 *BIES*, vol. X, no. 2, July 1974, p. 83.
17 Ruth T. McVey, *The Rise of Indonesian Communism*, Ithaca, Cornell University Press, 1965, p. 171.
18 Ibid., p. 186.
19 Sartono., op. cit., p. 71.

Index

Index

Index

Daud Beureueh, M., 265
David, A., 223–5
Democratic Development (group) 282, 284
Despotism, xiii, 3, 323
Development Union: group, 282: Party, 284
Dewi, Ratna Sari, 98, 102–3, 128, 131, 135, 241
Dharsono, Maj.-Gen, 236
Diah, B. M., 151
Diponegoro Division, 143, 148–9, 298
Diponegoro, Prince, 19
Djarnawi Hadikusuma, 252–5
Djuanda cabinet, 79
DPR, 80–1, 282, 301
Drake, Sir Francis, 13
Du Bus de Gisignies, Viscount, 7
Dukuns, 38, 75, 119, 158, 293–4, 311–12, 374
Dulles, J. F., 80
Dutch (see also Netherlands), 4–5, 8, 13; enterprises seized, 79
Dutch East India Company: army, size of, 18; massacres, 15 (Banda), 324 (Chinese); and Mataram, 17–18, 318, 326–7; policy, finances, 14–16, 18; spices destroyed by, 17
Dwi-fonski, 155, 410
Dwikora cabinet, 143
Dyaks, 209–10

East India Company (English), 14, 19
Economy: banking, 365, 370; crumb rubber, 371–2; economic motive (and lack of), 21–3, 314–17, 320–2, 324, 327–31, 334, 370, 397; economic take-off, 4, 71, 317; foreign debts, 343–4, 380; industry, 383–4; inflation, 74; investment, 373, 378–9, 382; money supply, 368–9; oil, 369, 375–6; pre-capitalist attitudes 71–3, 82, 315–16, 329–30, 334, 373–4, 393, 398; prices, 362,

364, 369; rupiah, 211, 344–5; Western enclave, 211–12, 336–52
Elections: *1955*, 74–5, 251; postponed, 147; *1971*, 235, 248–9, 265–71; results, 267; *1977*, 388
Elizabeth II, Queen, 337
Ethnic groups, 74; separatism, 388
Europe, dynamism, 5
European Communities, 349

Famine, 404–5
Fatmawati, 241, 264
Faure, E., 394
Feith, H., 69, 76–7, 419 n. 3, 420 n. 44
Fifth force, 87, 93–5, 105
Fischbeck, F., 32
Floating mass principle, 285
France, 169–70, 194
Fundwi (Fund of the United Nations for the Development of West Irian), 174, 196

Gajah Mada, 11
Geertz, C., 8, 71–3, 250, 312, 318–21, 325–7, 402, 420 n. 44, 424 n. 8
Generals' Council (alleged), 97, 102, 105, 111, 113, 127
Germans, 344, 373, 378–9
Gerwani, 105–7
Ghana, 194
Gilchrist, Sir Andrew, 125
Glassburner, B., 324, 345, 383
Golkar (*see* Sekber Golkar)
Gonda, J., 424 n. 8
Gonggrijp, G. L., 4
Gordon, D., 393
Gotong royong, 404
Grant, B., 83
Greater Southeast Financial & Development Corporation, 225–6
Green, Marshall, 334
Grenville, S., 362, 368–9
Gresik, 318
Guided democracy, 78–9, 81, 84–5

Hadikusumo, K. B., 57

431

Index

Hadisubeno Sosrowerdjojo, 239–40, 262–3
Hafas, Tengku D., 275, 297
Hakim, A. R., 137
Halim air base, 87, 94, 99–100, 105–7, 111
Hamengkubuwono IX, Sultan, 143–4, 288, 337
Hansen, G., 360–1
Hardi, 239
Hardjanto, Ibnu, 226
Harian Rakjat, 105, 109
Hariati, 98
Harjono, Maj.-Gen., 98
Hartini, 89, 101, 240–2, 312
Hartono, Lt.-Gen. (KKO), 152, 154–5
Hartono, Maj-Gen., 220–1
Hartono, M., 260–1
Hasasan, B., 291
Hatta, M., 51–3, 55, 57, 60–5, 77, 81, 156, 265, 345
Hauswedell, P. C., 420 n. 45
Hawkins, F. N., 225–6
Higgins, B. 317–18, 326
Hinduism, 9, 250, 271, 333
Hodge, E., 35
Huda, *Haji*, H., 256
Hughes, J., 103, 106–8, 118, 120–1, 131, 391
Humardani, Maj.-Gen. S., 292–3, 297–8, 304, 307, 349, 374

Ibrahim, M. C., 283
IGGI, 293, 341–3, 364, 376, 380–1
Ihalauw, J. 427 n. 10
Imamura, Lt.-Gen., 56
India, 10–11, 63, 76, 403
Indische Partij, 45
Indische Sociaal-Democratische Vereeniging, 46
Indonesia: Committee for Preparation of Independence, 60; history, 9–23; Republic of, 60, 61–4
Indonesia in Miniature, 277–81
Indonesian Council of Churches, 271

Indonesian Democratic Party, 285
Inggit, Garnasih, 51
International Labour Organization, 389–90
International Monetary Fund, 339, 346, 372, 380
IPKI, 249
Irian Jaya: 64, 77, 163–99; Act of of Free Choice, 163–7, 186–93; Fundwi, 196; rebellion, 167–8, 171–2, 192, 388
Isnaeni, M., 263, 285, 287

Jakarta, 15
Jakarta Charter, 60
Japanese, 51, 53–61, 247, 304–5, 340, 374–6, 379, 381–2
Java, 11
Javanese, 4–6, 8–9; cosmic harmony, religion, 11, 37, 48–9, 250, 323, 404
Jayabaya, 44, 53–4, 60
Jockell, G., 191–2
Joku, J., 179
Jouwe, N., 168, 180, 194, 196

Kamarusaman (*see* Sjam)
Kami, 132–3, 136–7, 229, 422 n. 4
KAP-Gestapu, 132
Kappi, 133, 229–30
Kartakasuma, Lt.-Gen., 290
Kasieppo, F., 175
Katoppo, A., 279–80
Kemal Idris, Brig.-Gen., 124
Kern, H., 402
KKO (marines), 148–9
Koentjaraningrat, 424 n. 8
Kolff, G. H. van der, 316
Kopkamtib (*see also* Sumitro, Gen.) 40, 213, 275, 278–80, 291, 296, 305–6
Korby, Brother, 407
Korpri, 237, 245, 262
Krakatau (PT), 378
Kris, 311
Kruschev, N., 104
Kwee Som Tjok, 296–7

432

Index

Land-holdings, 7–8
Latief, Col., 113, 117–18
Legge, J. D., 84, 110, 139, 150, 152, 244, 418 n. 10, 420 n. 45
Leimena, J., 100, 135, 143, 149–50
Lekra, 30, 32, 38
Leur, J. C. van, 4, 9, 14, 319, 321, 324
Lev, D., 84
Lim Bian Coen, 132
Lim Bian Kie, 132, 236–8, 301
Lim Poo Hien, 225–7
Lim Siu Liong, 221, 225, 349
Linggajati Agreement, 63
Living standards, 337, 351–5, 384–5
Loeis, W., 187
Lubis, M., 215–16, 219, 306, 346, 391
Lubis, N., 257
Lubis, Zulkifli, 391
Lukman, 136
Luns, J. 166–7

McCawley, P., 353
Machmud, Lt.-Gen. Amir, 143, 193, 205, 245, 247, 253, 270, 276, 278, 389
McNamara, R., 339, 406
McVey, R. T., 40, 104, 110, 419 n. 33
Madiun rebellion, 69
Madura, 260–1, 271, 318
Maeda, Admiral, 61
Magic (see also occult), 4, 9, 20, 51, 183, 259–61
Majapahit, 11, 326–7, 402–4
Makarim, N. A., 342
Makasar, 17
Malacca, 12, 16
Malays, 321, 347
Malaysia, 41, 209–10; Confrontation, 87, 92–3, 143, 151, 209
Malik, A., 40, 61, 120, 140, 143, 149, 152–3, 175, 191, 231, 275, 292, 313, 375, 379
Mallaby, Brig. A. W. S., 62
Mandatjan, L., 168, 171–3

Mangkunegara IV, 320
Mangkupradja, Gatot, 57
March 11 Order, 138–9, 147–8, 150, 156
Marhaenism, 66, 245, 262
Martadinata, Admiral E., 101, 155
Martinot, J. W. M., 67
Marx, Karl, 3
Marxism, 45, 66; Islamic, 409
Mashuri, 98, 154, 261
Masjumi, 59, 79, 251–2, 254–5, 306
Massacres: 1965, 120–5, 130; Purwodadi, 205–6
Mataram, 15, 318, 326–7
Material Spiritual (group), 282
Maukar, D., 130
Mawardi, C., 388
Mentality (see also dukuns, economy (economic motive, pre-capitalist attitudes), magic, mysticism, occult, Ratu Adil, superstition), 2–3, 66, 124, 140–1, 285, 319–20, 332, 356, 360, 362, 397–2, 401–2, 404
Migration, 90, 396
Minangkabau, 327–9
Mintaredja, 253–5, 284, 287, 319
Minto, Lord, 19
Misbach, Haji (Islamic communist), 409
Mokogenta, Lt.-Gen., 228
Moluccas, 12–13, 18
Moraes, Dom, 32–5
Moro, I., 257
Moslems (see also traders), 7, 11–12, 16–17, 60, 121–3, 132, 249–57, 260–1, 264, 271, 284, 286, 290, 300, 303–4, 388; corruption, 406; youth (see also Ansor), 408
Mountbatten, Lord, 62
MPR(S), 80–1, 84, 131, 142, 145–8, 153, 248, 252, 286–8; composition, 272–4
Muhammidiyah, 254–5
Muljadi, Admiral, 153, 155
Multatuli (Eduard Douwes Dekker), 404
Murba, 249, 284

433

Index